Fodor's Eleventh Edition

Philadelphia and the Pennsylvania Dutch Country

The complete guide, thoroughly up-to-date

Packed with details that will make your trip

The must-see sights, off and on the beaten path

What to see, what to skip

Vacation itineraries, walking tours, day trips

Smart lodging and dining options

Transportation tips

Key contacts, savvy travel advice

When to go, what to pack

Clear, accurate, easy-to-use maps

Books to read, videos to watch, background essay

Fodor's Travel Publications
www.fodors.com

W9-AZZ-890

Fodor's Philadelphia and the Pennsylvania Dutch Country

EDITOR: Linda Cabasin

Editorial Contributors: Anne Dubuisson Anderson, Robert DiGiacomo, Joyce Eisenberg, Janis Pomerantz, Barbara Ann Rosenberg

Editorial Production: Brian Vitunic

Maps: David Lindroth, *cartographer*; Rebecca Baer, Robert Blake, *map editors*

Design: Fabrizio La Rocca, *creative director*; Guido Caroti, *art director*; Jolie Novak, *photo editor*

Cover Design: Pentagram

Production/Manufacturing: Bob Shields

Cover Photograph: H. Mark Weidman

Copyright

ISBN 0–679–00399–1

ISSN 1098–9358

11th Edition

Special Sales

Fodor's Travel Publications are available at special discounts for bulk purchases for sales promotions or premiums. Special editions, including personalized covers, excerpts of existing guides, and corporate imprints, can be created in large quantities for special needs. For more information, contact your local bookseller or write to Special Markets, Fodor's Travel Publications, 201 East 50th Street, New York, NY 10022. Inquiries from Canada should be directed to your local Canadian bookseller or sent to Random House of Canada, Ltd., Marketing Department, 2775 Matheson Boulevard East, Mississauga, Ontario L4W 4P7. Inquiries from the United Kingdom should be sent to Fodor's Travel Publications, 20 Vauxhall Bridge Road, London SW1V 2SA, England.

PRINTED IN THE UNITED STATES OF AMERICA

10 9 8 7 6 5 4 3 2 1

Important Tip

Although all prices, opening times, and other details in this book are based on information supplied to us at press time, changes occur all the time in the travel world, and Fodor's cannot accept responsibility for facts that become outdated or for inadvertent errors or omissions. So **always confirm information when it matters,** especially if you're making a detour to visit a specific place.

CONTENTS

Maps

ON THE ROAD WITH FODOR'S

THE TRIPS YOU TAKE this year and next are going to be significant trips, if only because they'll be your first in the new millennium. Acutely aware of that fact, we've pulled out all stops in preparing Fodor's *Philadelphia and the Pennsylvania Dutch Country*. To guide you in putting together your travel experience, we've created multiday itineraries and neighborhood walks. And to direct you to the places that are truly worth your time and money in these important years, we've rallied the team of endearingly picky know-it-alls we're pleased to call our writers. Having seen all corners of Philadelphia and the Pennsylvania Dutch Country, they're real experts on the subjects they cover for us. If you knew them, you'd poll them for tips yourself.

Anne Dubuisson Anderson loves her home in Philadelphia but makes frequent trips to its outskirts for a dose of the quieter life. She has served as both writer and editor for books and articles on travel and parenting, including the Compass guide to Alaska. Her son was an eager assistant for her research on the Lancaster County and Side Trips chapters of this book. His favorite discovery, for obvious reasons, was Hershey, while Anne particularly enjoyed feasting on the art in the many Brandywine Valley museums.

Freelance writer **Robert DiGiacomo,** who updated Nightlife and the Arts, Outdoor Activities and Sports, and Bucks County, has lived in Center City for the past decade. He writes for many national and regional publications, including *Travel Holiday* and *MidAtlantic Travel,* and is a contributor to Fodor's *USA* and the Road Guide series. Although his travels frequently take him to far corners of the world, he also enjoys the local scene—and an authentic soft pretzel with mustard.

Philadelphia native **Joyce Eisenberg** happily adventured around her hometown to update Destination: Philadelphia and the Pennsylvania Dutch Country and Exploring Philadelphia. She is the editor of special sections for Philadelphia's *Jewish Exponent* newspaper and former editor of the Philadelphia edition of *TravelHost* magazine. Like Dorothy in *The Wizard of Oz,* she says, "There's no place like home." For her, that home is Philadelphia, which she loves for its unpretentious small-town feel and big-town cultural attractions.

Freelance writer **Janis Pomerantz** put her keen eye for shopping to good use in her update of that chapter. A native Philadelphian, she has traveled to places from Hong Kong to Mexico, but she'd still rather be in Philadelphia.

Barbara Ann Rosenberg, who revised the Dining and Lodging chapters this year, is a Center City–based food and travel writer who keeps on top of the local dining scene. (Her frequent indulgences at Philadelphia restaurants are beginning to show!) The lodging update kept her busy inspecting—sometimes in a hard hat—the host of hotels under construction. Among the national magazines she writes for frequently is the *Robb Report.* She also serves as the Philadelphia correspondent for the James Beard House.

A University of Pennsylvania graduate, New York–based Fodor's editor **Linda Cabasin** never misses the Flower Show or a chance to study the paintings of Thomas Eakins at the Philadelphia Museum of Art. Her travels to the area often take her to favorite spots such as the conservatories at Longwood Gardens.

Don't Forget to Write

Keeping a travel guide fresh and up-to-date is a big job. So we love your feedback—positive and negative—and follow up on all suggestions. Contact the Philadelpia editor at editors@fodors.com or c/o Fodor's, 201 East 50th Street, New York, New York 10022. And have a wonderful trip!

Karen Cure
Editorial Director

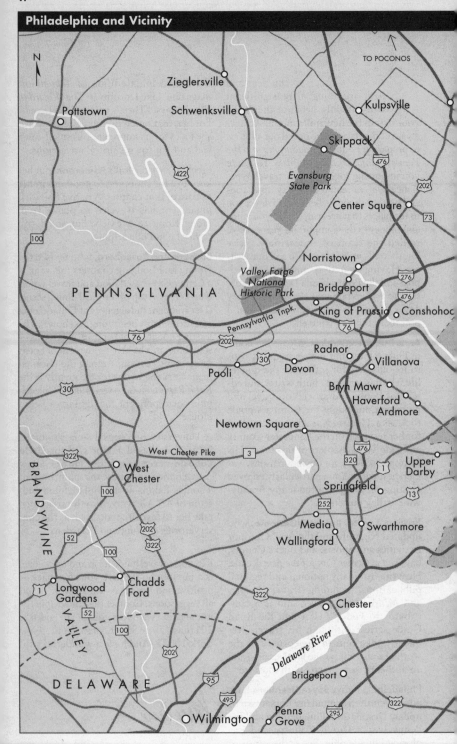

N

TO POCONOS

Zieglersville

Pottstown

Schwenksville

Kulpsville

Skippack

476

422

202

Evansburg
State Park

Center Square

73

100

Norristown

PENNSYLVANIA

Valley Forge
National
Historic Park

Bridgeport

276

476

Pennsylvania Tnpk.

King of Prussia

Conshohoc

76

202

76

Radnor

30

Villanova

Paoli

Devon

Bryn Mawr

30

Haverford
Ardmore

Newtown Square

476

West Chester Pike

3

320

1

Upper
Darby

322

West
Chester

Springfield

13

100

252

202

Media

Swarthmore

52

322

Wallingford

100

BRANDYWINE

Longwood
Gardens

Chadds
Ford

322

Chester

1

52

VALLEY

100

Delaware River

202

DELAWARE

95

Bridgeport

495

Penns
Grove

322

295

Wilmington

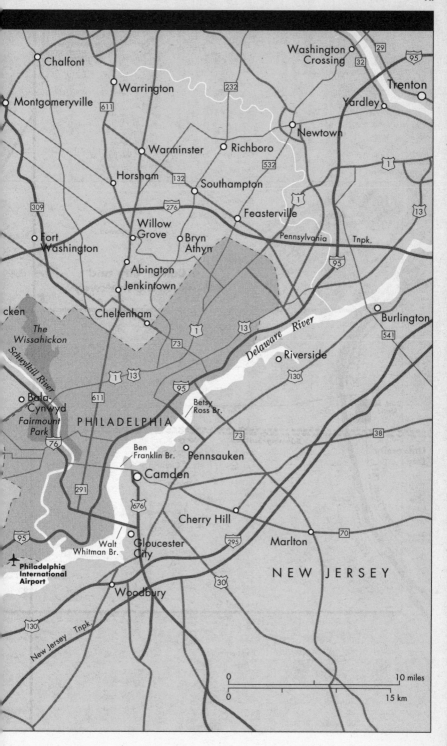

Chalfont

Warrington

232

Washington
Crossing

32

29

95

Montgomeryville

611

Trenton

Yardley

Newtown

1

Warminster

Richboro

532

Horsham

132

Southampton

1

13

309

Willow
Grove

Feasterville

Pennsylvania   Tnpk.

Fort
Washington

Bryn
Athyn

95

Abington

Jenkintown

Burlington

Cheltenham

541

cken

The
Wissahickon

1

13

Delaware River

73

Riverside

Schuylkill River

1 13

130

95

Bala-
Cynwyd

611

Betsy
Ross Br.

38

Fairmount
Park

PHILADELPHIA

76

Ben
Franklin Br.

Pennsauken

73

Camden

291

676

Cherry Hill

70

95

Walt
Whitman Br.

Gloucester
City

295

Marlton

NEW JERSEY

Philadelphia
International
Airport

Woodbury

30

130   New Jersey Tnpk.

0   10 miles

0   15 km

Downtown Philadelphia

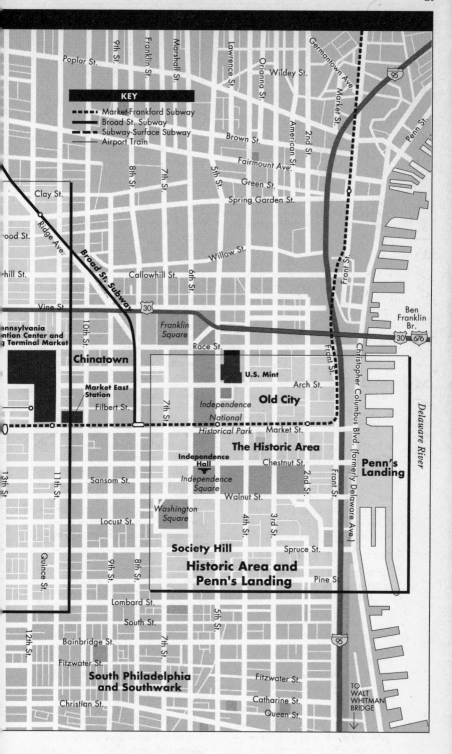

KEY
- - - - Market-Frankford Subway
———— Broad St. Subway
- - - Subway-Surface Subway
———— Airport Train

Poplar St.

9th St.

Franklin St.

Marshall St.

Lawrence St.

Orianna St.

Wildey St.

Germantown Ave.

Market St.

Penn St.

95

Brown St.

American St.

2nd St.

Fairmount Ave.

5th St.

8th St.

7th St.

Green St.

Spring Garden St.

Clay St.

Ridge Ave.

ood St.

Broad St. Subway

hill St.

Callowhill St.

6th St.

Willow St.

Front St.

Ben Franklin Br.

Vine St.

10th St.

30

Franklin Square

ennsylvania ntion Center and g Terminal Market

Chinatown

Race St.

U.S. Mint

30 76

Delaware River

Market East Station

Filbert St.

7th St.

Independence National Historical Park

Old City

Arch St.

Market St.

The Historic Area

Christopher Columbus Blvd. (formerly Delaware Ave.)

Penn's Landing

13th St

11th St.

Independence Hall

Independence Square

Sansom St.

Chestnut St.

2nd St.

Front St.

Washington Square

Walnut St.

4th St.

3rd St.

Locust St.

Society Hill

Spruce St.

Quince St.

9th St.

8th St.

Historic Area and Penn's Landing

Pine St.

Lombard St.

South St.

5th St.

12th St.

Bainbridge St.

Fitzwater St.

7th St.

95

South Philadelphia and Southwark

Fitzwater St.

TO WALT WHITMAN BRIDGE

Christian St.

Catharine St.

Queen St.

SMART TRAVEL TIPS A TO Z

Basic Information on Traveling in Philadelphia and the Pennsylvania Dutch Country, Savvy Tips to Make Your Trip a Breeze, and Companies and Organizations to Contact

AIR TRAVEL

BOOKING YOUR FLIGHT

When you book, **look for nonstop flights** and **remember that "direct" flights stop at least once.** Try to avoid connecting flights, which require a change of plane.

CARRIERS

➤ MAJOR AIRLINES: **American** (☎ 800/433–7300). **Continental** (☎ 800/523–3273). **Delta** (☎ 800/221–1212). **Northwest** (☎ 800/225–2525). **TWA** (☎ 800/221–2000). **United** (☎ 800/241–6522). **US Airways** (☎ 800/428–4322).

➤ SMALLER AIRLINES: **Air Tran** (☎ 800/825–8538). **Midwest Express** (☎ 800/452–2022).

➤ FROM CANADA: **Air Canada** (☎ 800/776–3000).

➤ FROM THE U.K.: Only **British Airways** (☎ 0345/222–111) serves Philadelphia directly. Other carriers include **American** (☎ 0345/789–789), via Boston; **United** (☎ 0800/888–555), via New York; and **Virgin Atlantic** (☎ 01293/747–747), via Washington, D.C. or New York.

CHECK-IN & BOARDING

Assuming that not everyone with a ticket will show up, airlines routinely overbook planes. When that happens, airlines ask for volunteers to give up their seats. In return these volunteers usually get a certificate for a free flight and are rebooked on the next flight out. If there are not enough volunteers, the airline must choose who will be denied boarding. The first to get bumped are passengers who checked in late and those flying on discounted tickets, so **get to the gate and check in as early as possible,** especially during peak periods.

Always **bring a government-issued photo I.D. to the airport.** You may be asked to show it before you are allowed to check in.

CUTTING COSTS

The least-expensive airfares to Philadelphia and the Pennsylvania Dutch Country must usually be purchased in advance and are non-refundable. It's smart to **call a number of airlines, and when you are quoted a good price, book it on the spot**—the same fare may not be available the next day. Always **check different routings** and look into using different airports. Travel agents, especially low-fare specialists (☞ Discounts & Deals, *below*), are helpful.

Consolidators are another good source. They buy tickets for scheduled international flights at reduced rates from the airlines, then sell them at prices that beat the best fare available directly from the airlines, usually without restrictions. Sometimes you can even get your money back if you need to return the ticket. Carefully read the fine print detailing penalties for changes and cancellations, and **confirm your consolidator reservation with the airline.**

When you **fly as a courier** you trade your checked-luggage space for a ticket deeply subsidized by a courier service. There are restrictions on when you can book and how long you can stay.

➤ CONSOLIDATORS: **Cheap Tickets** (☎ 800/377–1000). **Up & Away Travel** (☎ 212/889–2345). **Discount Airline Ticket Service** (☎ 800/576–1600). **Unitravel** (☎ 800/325–2222). **World Travel Network** (☎ 800/409–6753).

ENJOYING THE FLIGHT

For more legroom **request an emergency-aisle seat.** Don't sit in the row in front of the emergency aisle or in front of a bulkhead, where seats may not recline. If you have dietary concerns, **ask for special meals when booking.** These can be vegetarian, low-cholesterol, or kosher, for example. On long flights, try to maintain a normal routine, to help fight jetlag. At night **get some sleep.** By day **eat light meals, drink water** (not alcohol), and **move around the cabin** to stretch your legs.

FLYING TIMES

Flying time from Boston is 1 hour; from Chicago, 2¼ hours; from Miami, 2½ hours; from Los Angeles, 6 hours.

HOW TO COMPLAIN

If your baggage goes astray or your flight goes awry, complain right away. Most carriers require that you **file a claim immediately.**

➤ AIRLINE COMPLAINTS: U.S. Department of Transportation **Aviation Consumer Protection Division** (✉ C-75, Room 4107, Washington, DC 20590, ☎ 202/366–2220). **Federal Aviation Administration Consumer Hotline** (☎ 800/322–7873).

AIRPORTS & TRANSFERS

The major gateway to Philadelphia is Philadelphia International Airport, 8 mi from downtown in the southwest part of the city. Renovations in the past few years have made the terminals more appealing; shops and more eating options are welcome additions.

➤ AIRPORT INFORMATION: **Philadelphia International Airport** (✉ 8900 Essington Ave., off I–95, ☎ 215/937–6800 for operator; 215/937–6937 for general information; 800/745–4283 for arrival and departure times and gate assignments).

TRANSFERS

Allow at least a half hour, more during rush hour, for the 8-mi trip between the airport and Center City. By car the airport is accessible via I–95 south or I–76 east.

Taxis at the airport are plentiful but expensive—a flat fee of $20 plus tip. Follow the signs in the airport and wait in line for a taxi. Shuttle buses are also available. They cost $10 and up per person and will make most requested stops downtown as well as to the suburbs. For shuttles, you show up at the dispatcher's desk, and the appropriate shuttle will be summoned.

SEPTA (Southeastern Pennsylvania Transportation Authority) runs the Airport Rail Line R1, which leaves the airport every 30 minutes from 6:10 AM to 12:10 AM. The trip to Center City takes about 20 minutes and costs $5. Trains serve the 30th Street, Suburban (Center City), and Market East stations.

➤ BY LIMOUSINE: **Carey Limousine Philadelphia** (☎ 215/492–8402). **First Class Luxury Limo** (☎ 215/946–0535).

➤ BY TRAIN: For schedules and other information, call the **Airport Information Desk** (☎ 215/937–6937) or **SEPTA** (☎ 215/580–7800).

BOAT & FERRY TRAVEL

The RiverLink Ferry, a seasonal (April–December) passenger ferry between Philadelphia and Camden, site of the New Jersey Aquarium, has hourly departures from Penn's Landing on the hour, daily 10–5 (weekends only in December), with extended hours for Penn's Landing and Blockbuster-Sony Entertainment Centre concerts. The cost is $5 round-trip.

➤ FERRY SERVICE: **RiverLink Ferry** (✉ Penn's Landing near Walnut St., ☎ 215/925–5465).

BUS TRAVEL TO AND FROM PHILADELPHIA

Greyhound Lines operates long-haul service to Baltimore, Washington, DC, New York, Wilmington, and points beyond out of the terminal at 10th and Filbert streets, just north of the Market East commuter rail station. NJ Transit stops at the Greyhound terminal and offers service between Philadelphia and Atlantic City and other New Jersey destinations.

➤ CONTACTS: **Greyhound Lines** (☎ 215/931–4075 or 800/231–2222). **NJ Transit** (☎ 215/569–3752).

BUS TRAVEL WITHIN PHILADELPHIA

Buses make up the bulk of the SEPTA system, with 110 routes extending throughout the city and into the suburbs. Bus 76, called the "Ben FrankLine," connects the zoo in West Fairmount Park with Penn's Landing at the Delaware River, stopping at major sights along the way including the Pennsylvania Convention Center and the art museum. Route 76 operates daily from around 9 to 6; it runs later on Wednesday evening, when the Philadelphia Museum of Art stays open until 8:45.

The distinctive purple minibuses you'll see around Center City are SEPTA's convenience line for visitors, the PHLASH. The 33 stops in the loop run from the Philadelphia Museum of Art on the Benjamin Franklin Parkway through Center City to Penn's Landing. Since a ride on the PHLASH costs $1.50 for a one-way ticket, **consider the handy all-day, unlimited-ride pass available for $3.** These buses run daily from 10 AM to midnight in the summer, 10 to 6 September 15–May 14. There is service every 10 minutes.

The base fare for subways, trolleys, and buses is $1.60, paid with exact change or a token. Transfers cost 40¢. Senior citizens (with valid ID) ride free during off-peak hours and holidays. Tokens sell for $1.15 and can be purchased in packages of 2, 5, or 10 from cashiers along the Broad Street subway and Market–Frankford lines and in many downtown stores (including some Rite Aid pharmacies).

If you plan to travel extensively within Center City, it's a good idea to **get a SEPTA pass.** The Day Pass costs $5 and is good for 24 hours of unlimited use on all SEPTA vehicles within the city, plus one trip on any regional rail line including the Airport Express train. A weekly transit pass costs $17.25. Tokens and transit passes are good on buses and subways but not on commuter rail lines.

You can purchase tokens and transit passes in the SEPTA sales offices in the concourse below the northwest corner of 15th and Market streets; in the Market East station (✉ 8th and Market Sts.); and in 30th Street Station (✉ 30th and Market Sts.). They are also sold at the Philadelphia Visitors Center (✉ 16th St. and John F. Kennedy Blvd.).

Though SEPTA's automated answering system has cut down on your phone wait, **be prepared for a busy signal and a long time on hold.**

➤ CONTACTS: **SEPTA** (☎ 215/580–7800; 215/580–7777 for a schedule).

BUSINESS HOURS

Banks are open weekdays 9–3; a few are open Saturday 9–noon. The main post office is open 24 hours daily; some branches are open 9 to 5 weekdays, and Saturday 9 to noon. All banks and post offices are closed on national holidays.

MUSEUMS & SIGHTS

Many museums and sights are open 10–5; a few stay open late one or two evenings a week, and a number are closed on Monday. Historic Area sights are open daily, with longer hours in the summer, but it's wise to check ahead, as National Park Service staffing issues can create changes from week to week.

SHOPS

Downtown shopping hours are generally 9:30 or 10 to 5 or 6. Many stores are open until 9 PM on Wednesday. Most downtown stores are closed on Sunday, but the Bourse and the Gallery are open noon–5. Antiques stores and art galleries may be closed some mornings or weekdays; it's wise to call ahead for hours.

CAMERAS & PHOTOGRAPHY

➤ PHOTO HELP: **Kodak Information Center** (☎ 800/242–2424). *Kodak Guide to Shooting Great Travel Pictures,* available in bookstores or from Fodor's Travel Publications (☎ 800/533–6478; $16.50 plus $4 shipping).

EQUIPMENT PRECAUTIONS

Always **keep your film and tape out of the sun.** Carry an extra supply of batteries, and **be prepared to turn on your camera or camcorder** to prove to security personnel that the device is real. Always **ask for hand inspection of film,** which becomes clouded after successive exposures to airport X-ray machines, and **keep videotapes away from metal detectors.**

CAR RENTAL

Rates in Philadelphia begin at $25 a day and $176 a week for an economy car with air-conditioning, an automatic transmission, and unlimited mileage. This does not include airport surcharges and the tax on car rentals, which is 9%.

➤ MAJOR AGENCIES: **Alamo** (☎ 800/327–9633; 020/8759–6200 in the U.K.). **Avis** (☎ 800/331–1212; 800/879–2847 in Canada; 02/9353–9000 in Australia; 09/525–1982 in New Zealand). **Budget** (☎ 800/527–0700; 0144/227–6266 in the U.K.). **Dollar** (☎ 800/800–4000; 020/8897–0811 in the U.K., where it is known as Eurodollar; 02/9223–1444 in Australia). **Hertz** (☎ 800/654–3131; 800/263–0600 in Canada; 0990/90–60–90 in the U.K.; 02/9669–2444 in Australia; 03/358–6777 in New Zealand). **National InterRent** (☎ 800/227–7368; 0345/222525 in the U.K., where it is known as Europcar InterRent).

CUTTING COSTS

To get the best deal, **book through a travel agent who will shop around.** Also **price local car-rental companies,** although the service and maintenance may not be as good as those of a major player. Remember to ask about required deposits, cancellation penalties, and drop-off charges if you're planning to pick up the car in one city and leave it in another. If you're traveling during a holiday period, also make sure that a confirmed reservation guarantees you a car.

Do **look into wholesalers,** companies that do not own fleets but rent in bulk from those that do and often offer better rates than traditional car-rental operations.

➤ LOCAL AGENCIES: **Ace Rent-a-Car** (☎ 215/492–8554 or 888/386–7368). **Enterprise Rent-a-Car** (☎ 800/736–8222).

➤ WHOLESALERS: **Auto Europe** (☎ 207/842–2000 or 800/223–5555, FAX 800–235–6321).

INSURANCE

When driving a rented car you are generally responsible for any damage to or loss of the vehicle as well as for any property damage or personal injury that you may cause. Before you rent see what coverage your personal auto-insurance policy and credit cards already provide.

For about $15 to $20 per day, rental companies sell protection, known as a collision- or loss-damage waiver (CDW or LDW), that eliminates your liability for damage to the car. In most states you don't need a CDW if you have personal auto insurance or other liability insurance. However, **make sure you have enough coverage to pay for the car.** If you do not have auto insurance or an umbrella policy that covers damage to third parties, purchasing liability insurance and a CDW or LDW is highly recommended.

REQUIREMENTS & RESTRICTIONS

In Philadelphia and the Pennsylvania Dutch Country you must be 21 to rent a car, and rates may be higher if you're under 25. You'll pay extra for child seats (about $3 per day), which are compulsory for children under five, and for additional drivers (about $2 per day). Non-U.S. residents will need a reservation voucher, a passport, a driver's license, and a travel policy that covers each driver, in order to pick up a car.

SURCHARGES

Before you pick up a car in one city and leave it in another **ask about drop-off charges or one-way service fees,** which can be substantial. Note, too, that some rental agencies charge extra if you return the car before the time specified in your contract. To avoid a hefty refueling fee **fill the tank just before you turn in the car,** but be aware that gas stations near the rental outlet may overcharge.

CAR TRAVEL

Getting to and around Philadelphia by car can be difficult and at rush hour can be a nightmare. The main east–west freeway through the city, the Schuylkill Expressway (I–76), is often tied up for miles.

The main north–south highway through Philadelphia is the Delaware Expressway (I–95). To reach Center City heading southbound on I–95, take the Vine Street exit.

From the west the Pennsylvania Turnpike begins at the Ohio border and intersects the Schuylkill Expressway (I–76) at Valley Forge. The Schuylkill Expressway has several exits in Center City. The Northeast Extension of the turnpike, renamed I–476, runs from Scranton to Plymouth Meeting, north of Philadelphia. From the east the New Jersey Turnpike and I–295 access U.S. 30, which enters the city via the Benjamin Franklin Bridge, or New Jersey Route 42 and the Walt Whitman Bridge into South Philadelphia.

With the exception of a few wide streets (notably the Benjamin Franklin Parkway, Broad Street, Vine Street, and part of Market Street), streets in Center City are narrow and one-way. Philadelphia's compact 2-square-mi downtown is laid out in a grid. The traditional heart of the city is Broad and Market streets, where City Hall stands. Market Street divides the city north and south; 130 South 15th Street, for example, is in the second block south of Market Street. North–south streets are numbered, starting with Front (1st) Street, at the Delaware River, and increasing to the west. Broad Street is the equivalent of 14th Street. The diagonal Benjamin Franklin Parkway breaks the grid pattern by leading from City Hall out of Center City into Fairmount Park.

GASOLINE

Gasoline costs about $1.23 to $1.47 per gallon in Philadelphia. Most Center City (downtown) gas stations can be found on Broad Street.

PARKING

Parking in Center City can be tough. A spot at a parking meter, if you're lucky enough to find one, costs 25¢ per 15 minutes. Parking garages are plentiful, especially around Independence Park, City Hall, and the Pennsylvania Convention Center, but can charge up to $1.50 per 15 minutes and up to $20 or so for the day. Fortunately the city is compact, and you can easily **get around downtown on foot or by bus after you park your car.**

RULES OF THE ROAD

Rights turns on red are permitted (unless otherwise indicated) in Philadelphia and in Pennsylvania. Speed limits in the city are generally 35–40 mph, 55 mph on the surrounding highways.

CHILDREN IN PHILADELPHIA

Philadelphia is a very child-friendly city, with many attractions and activities for young ones. Pick up copies of the free monthly publications *Parent's Express* and *Metro Kids,* which include up-to-date listings of museum exhibitions, festivals, films, and bookstore readings for children. These are available in bookstores, cafés, and libraries. If you are renting a car don't forget to **arrange for a car seat** when you reserve.

FLYING

If your children are two or older **ask about children's airfares.** As a general rule, infants under two not occupying a seat fly at greatly reduced fares or even for free. Experts agree that it's a good idea to use safety seats aloft for children weighing less than 40 pounds. Airlines set their own policies: U.S. carriers usually require that the child be ticketed, even if he or she is young enough to ride free, since the seats must be strapped into regular seats. Do **check your airline's policy about using safety seats during take-off and landing.** And since safety seats are not allowed just everywhere in the plane, get your seat assignments early.

When reserving, **request children's meals or a freestanding bassinet** if you need them. But note that bulkhead seats, where you must sit to use the bassinet, may lack an overhead bin or storage space on the floor.

LODGING

Most hotels in Philadelphia allow children under a certain age to stay in their parents' room at no extra charge, but others charge for them as extra adults; be sure to **find out the cutoff age for children's discounts.**

SIGHTS & ATTRACTIONS

Places that are especially good for children are indicated by a rubber duckie icon in the margin.

CONCIERGES

Concierges, found in many hotels, can help you with theater tickets and dinner reservations: a good one with connections may be able to get you seats for a hot show or prime-time dinner reservations at the restaurant of the moment. You can also turn to your hotel's concierge for help with travel arrangements, sightseeing plans, services ranging from aromatherapy to zipper repair, and emergencies. Always, **always tip** a concierge who has been of assistance (☞ Tipping, *below*).

CONSUMER PROTECTION

Whenever shopping or buying travel services in Philadelphia, **pay with a major credit card** so you can cancel payment or get reimbursed if there's a problem. If you're doing business with a particular company for the first time, **contact your local Better Business Bureau and the attorney general's offices** in your state and the company's home state, as well. Have any complaints been filed? Finally, if you're buying a package or tour, always **consider travel insurance** that includes default coverage (☞ Insurance, *below*).

➤ LOCAL BBBs: **Council of Better Business Bureaus** (✉ 4200 Wilson Blvd., Suite 800, Arlington, VA 22203, ☎ 703/276–0100, FAX 703/ 525–8277).

CUSTOMS & DUTIES

When shopping, **keep receipts** for all purchases. Upon reentering the country, **be ready to show customs officials what you've bought.** If you feel a duty is incorrect or object to the way your clearance was handled, note the inspector's badge number and ask to see a supervisor. If the problem isn't resolved, write to the appropriate authorities, beginning with the port director at your point of entry.

IN AUSTRALIA

Australia residents who are 18 or older may bring home $A400 worth of souvenirs and gifts (including jewelry), 250 cigarettes or 250 grams of tobacco, and 1,125 ml of alcohol (including wine, beer, and spirits). Residents under 18 may bring back $A200 worth of goods. Prohibited items include meat products. Seeds, plants, and fruits need to be declared upon arrival.

➤ INFORMATION: **Australian Customs Service** (Regional Director, ✉ Box 8, Sydney, NSW 2001, ☎ 02/9213–2000, FAX 02/9213–4000).

IN CANADA

Canadian residents who have been out of Canada for at least 7 days may bring home C$500 worth of goods duty-free. If you've been away less than 7 days but more than 48 hours, the duty-free allowance drops to C$200; if your trip lasts 24–48 hours, the allowance is C$50. You may not pool allowances with family members. Goods claimed under the C$500 exemption may follow you by mail; those claimed under the lesser exemptions must accompany you. Alcohol and tobacco products may be included in the 7-day and 48-hour exemptions but not in the 24-hour exemption. If you meet the age requirements of the province or territory through which you reenter Canada, you may bring in, duty-free, 1.14 liters (40 imperial ounces) of wine or liquor *or* 24 12-ounce cans or bottles of beer or ale. If you are 16 or older you may bring in, duty-free, 200 cigarettes and 50 cigars. Check ahead of time with Revenue Canada or the Department of Agriculture for policies regarding meat products, seeds, plants, and fruits.

You may send an unlimited number of gifts worth up to C$60 each duty-free to Canada. Label the package UNSOLICITED GIFT—VALUE UNDER $60. Alcohol and tobacco are excluded.

➤ INFORMATION: **Revenue Canada** (✉ 2265 St. Laurent Blvd. S, Ottawa, Ontario K1G 4K3, ☎ 613/993–0534; 800/461–9999 in Canada).

IN NEW ZEALAND

Homeward-bound residents 17 or older may bring back $700 worth of souvenirs and gifts. Your duty-free allowance also includes 4.5 liters of wine or beer; one 1,125-ml bottle of spirits; and either 200 cigarettes, 250 grams of tobacco, 50 cigars, or a combination of the three up to 250 grams. Prohibited items include meat products, seeds, plants, and fruits.

➤ INFORMATION: **New Zealand Customs** (Custom House, ✉ 50 Anzac Ave., Box 29, Auckland, New Zealand, ☎ 09/359–6655, FAX 09/359–6732).

IN THE U.K.

From countries outside the EU, including the United States, you may bring home, duty-free, 200 cigarettes or 50 cigars; 1 liter of spirits or 2 liters of fortified or sparkling wine or liqueurs; 2 liters of still table wine; 60 ml of perfume; 250 ml of toilet water; plus £136 worth of other goods, including gifts and souvenirs. If returning from outside the EU, prohibited items include meat products, seeds, plants, and fruits.

➤ INFORMATION: **HM Customs and Excise** (✉ Dorset House, Stamford St., Bromley Kent BR1 1XX, ☎ 020/7202–4227).

IN THE U.S.

Non-U.S. residents ages 21 and older may import into the United States 200 cigarettes or 50 cigars or 2 kilograms of tobacco, 1 liter of alcohol, and gifts worth $100. Meat products, seeds, plants, and fruits are prohibited.

➤ INFORMATION: **U.S. Customs Service** (inquiries, ✉ 1300 Pennsylvania Ave. NW, Washington, DC 20229, ☎ 202/927–6724; complaints, ✉ Office of Regulations and Rulings, 1300 Pennsylvania Ave. NW, Washington, DC 20229; registration of equipment, ✉ Registration Information, 1300 Pennsylvania Ave. NW, Washington, DC 20229, ☎ 202/927–0540).

DINING

Philadelphia has simple sandwich shops as well as elegant eateries serving the trendiest food. The restaurants we list are the cream of the crop in each price category. Properties indicated by an ✕☎ are lodging establishments whose restaurant warrants a special trip.

CATEGORY	COST*
$$$$	over $45
$$$	$35–$45
$$	$20–$35
$	under $20

per person for a three-course meal, excluding drinks, service, and 7% sales tax

RESERVATIONS & DRESS

Reservations are always a good idea: we mention them only when they're essential or are not accepted. Book as far ahead as you can, and reconfirm as soon as you arrive. We mention dress only when men are required to wear a jacket or a jacket and tie. Use your judgment when dining out; for more expensive places, you'll probably feel more comfortable being more smartly dressed.

WINE, BEER & SPIRITS

The legal drinking age in Pennsylvania is 21. Many restaurants are licensed to served liquor, and state-run package stores, called state stores, sell wine and other spirits. Beer is also sold from certain distribution centers.

DISABILITIES & ACCESSIBILITY

LODGING

When discussing accessibility with an operator or reservations agent **ask hard questions.** Are there any stairs, inside *or* out? Are there grab bars next to the toilet *and* in the shower/tub? How wide is the doorway to the room? To the bathroom? For the most extensive facilities meeting the latest legal specifications **opt for newer accommodations.**

TRANSPORTATION

➤ COMPLAINTS: **Disability Rights Section** (✉ U.S. Department of Justice, Civil Rights Division, Box 66738, Washington, DC 20035-6738, ☎ 202/514–0301; 800/514–0301; 202/514–0301 TTY; 800/514–0301 TTY, FAX 202/307–1198) for general complaints. **Aviation Consumer Protection Division** (☞ Air Travel, *above*) for airline-related problems. **Civil Rights Office** (✉ U.S. Department of Transportation, Departmental Office of Civil Rights, S-30, 400 7th St. SW, Room 10215, Washington, DC 20590, ☎ 202/366–4648, FAX

202/366–9371) for problems with surface transportation.

➤ INFORMATION: **SEPTA Paratransit** (☎ 215/580–7365; TTY 215/580–7853).

TRAVEL AGENCIES

In the United States, although the Americans with Disabilities Act requires that travel firms serve the needs of all travelers, some agencies specialize in working with people with disabilities.

➤ TRAVELERS WITH MOBILITY PROBLEMS: **Access Adventures** (✉ 206 Chestnut Ridge Rd., Rochester, NY 14624, ☎ 716/889–9096), run by a former physical-rehabilitation counselor. **Accessible Journeys** (✉ 35 W. Sellers Ave., Ridley Park, PA 19078, ☎ 610/521–0339 or 800/846–4537, FAX 610/521–6959). **CareVacations** (✉ 5-5110 50th Ave., Leduc, Alberta, Canada T9E 6V4, ☎ 780/986–6404 or 877/478–7827, FAX 780/986–8332) has group tours and is especially helpful with cruise vacations. **Flying Wheels Travel** (✉ 143 W. Bridge St., Box 382, Owatonna, MN 55060, ☎ 507/451–5005 or 800/535–6790, FAX 507/451–1685). **Hinsdale Travel Service** (✉ 201 E. Ogden Ave., Suite 100, Hinsdale, IL 60521, ☎ 630/325–1335, FAX 630/325–1342).

➤ TRAVELERS WITH DEVELOPMENTAL DISABILITIES: **New Directions** (✉ 5276 Hollister Ave., Suite 207, Santa Barbara, CA 93111, ☎ 805/967–2841 or 888/967–2841, FAX 805/964–7344). **Sprout** (✉ 893 Amsterdam Ave., New York, NY 10025, ☎ 212/222–9575 or 888/222–9575, FAX 212/222–9768).

DISCOUNTS & DEALS

Be a smart shopper and **compare all your options** before making decisions. A plane ticket bought with a promotional coupon from travel clubs, coupon books, and direct-mail offers may not be cheaper than the least expensive fare from a discount ticket agency. And always keep in mind that what you get is just as important as what you save.

DISCOUNT PASS

If you're planning to visit some of the city's top museums, **look into City-Pass,** which offers 50% savings on admission to six attractions and is valid for nine days. The pass costs $27.50 (less for senior citizens and children) and covers the Academy of Natural Sciences, the Franklin Institute, Independence Seaport Museum, the New Jersey State Aquarium and Camden Children's Garden, the Philadelphia Museum of Art, and the Philadelphia Zoo. You can buy the pass at any of the attractions or at the gift shop of the Philadelphia Visitors Center; because the passes are tickets, you also avoid any ticket lines.

➤ CONTACT: **CityPass** (☎ 707/256–0490).

DISCOUNT RESERVATIONS

To save money, **look into discount-reservations services** with toll-free numbers, which use their buying power to get a better price on hotels, airline tickets, even car rentals. When booking a room, always **call the hotel's local toll-free number** (if one is available) rather than the central reservations number—you'll often get a better price. Always ask about special packages or corporate rates.

➤ AIRLINE TICKETS: ☎ **800/FLY–4–LESS.** ☎ **800/FLY–ASAP.**

➤ HOTEL ROOMS: **Accommodations Express** (☎ 800/444–7666). **Central Reservation Service (CRS)** (☎ 800/548–3311). **Hotel Reservations Network** (☎ 800/964–6835). **Players Express Vacations** (☎ 800/458–6161). **Quickbook** (☎ 800/789–9887). **Room Finders USA** (☎ 800/473–7829). **RMC Travel** (☎ 800/245–5738). **Steigenberger Reservation Service** (☎ 800/223–5652).

PACKAGE DEALS

Don't confuse packages and guided tours. When you buy a package, you travel on your own, just as though you had planned the trip yourself. Fly/drive packages, which combine airfare and car rental, are often a good deal. In cities, ask the local visitor center about hotel packages that include tickets to major museum exhibits or other special events.

EMERGENCIES

Philadelphia police patrol frequently in tourist areas, particularly during the peak summer season. Hotel staff or shopkeepers can also assist in getting help for an emergency situation.

➤ EMERGENCY SERVICES: **Ambulance, fire, police** (☎ 911).

➤ HOSPITALS: Near the historic area: **Pennsylvania Hospital** (✉ 8th and Spruce Sts., ☎ 215/829–3000 for information; 215/829–3350 for emergency room). Near City Hall: **Hahnemann** (✉ Broad and Vine Sts., ☎ 215/762–7000 for general information; 215/762–7963 for emergency room). Near Rittenhouse Square: **Graduate Hospital** (✉ 1800 Lombard St., ☎ 215/893–2000 for general information; 215/893–2350 for emergency room).

➤ 24-HOUR PHARMACIES: **CVS Pharmacy** (✉ 1826–30 Chestnut St., ☎ 215/972–1401). **Rite Aid** (✉ 2017–2023 S. Broad St., ☎ 215/467–0850).

ETIQUETTE & BEHAVIOR

When you are visiting among the Amish in Lancaster County, **remember to respect their values.** They believe that photographs and videos with recognizable reproductions of them violate the biblical commandment against making graven images. You will be asked to refrain from photographing or making videos of the Amish, and you should comply.

GAY & LESBIAN TRAVEL

➤ GAY- AND LESBIAN-FRIENDLY TRAVEL AGENCIES: **Different Roads Travel** (✉ 8383 Wilshire Blvd., Suite 902, Beverly Hills, CA 90211, ☎ 323/651–5557 or 800/429–8747, ℻ 323/651–3678). **Kennedy Travel** (✉ 314 Jericho Turnpike, Floral Park, NY 11001, ☎ 516/352–4888 or 800/237–7433, ℻ 516/354–8849). **Now Voyager** (✉ 4406 18th St., San Francisco, CA 94114, ☎ 415/626–1169 or 800/255–6951, ℻ 415/626–8626). **Skylink Travel and Tour** (✉ 1006 Mendocino Ave., Santa Rosa, CA 95401, ☎ 707/546–9888 or 800/225–5759, ℻ 707/546–9891), serving lesbian travelers.

HOLIDAYS

Major national holidays include New Year's Day (Jan. 1); Martin Luther King, Jr., Day (3rd Mon. in Jan.); President's Day (3rd Mon. in Feb.); Memorial Day (last Mon. in May); Independence Day (July 4); Labor Day (1st Mon. in Sept.); Thanksgiving Day (4th Thurs. in Nov.); Christmas Eve and Christmas Day (Dec. 24 and 25); and New Year's Eve (Dec. 31).

INSURANCE

The most useful travel insurance plan is a comprehensive policy that includes coverage for trip cancellation and interruption, default, trip delay, and medical expenses (with a waiver for preexisting conditions).

Without insurance you will lose all or most of your money if you cancel your trip, regardless of the reason. Default insurance covers you if your tour operator, airline, or cruise line goes out of business. Trip-delay covers expenses that arise because of bad weather or mechanical delays. Study the fine print when comparing policies.

British and Australian citizens need extra medical coverage when traveling overseas.

Always **buy travel policies directly from the insurance company;** if you buy it from a cruise line, airline, or tour operator that goes out of business you probably will not be covered for the agency or operator's default, a major risk. Before you make any purchase **review your existing health and home-owner's policies** to find what they cover away from home.

➤ TRAVEL INSURERS: In the U.S., **Access America** (✉ 6600 W. Broad St., Richmond, VA 23230, ☎ 804/285–3300 or 800/284–8300), **Travel Guard International** (✉ 1145 Clark St., Stevens Point, WI 54481, ☎ 715/345–0505 or 800/826–1300). In Canada, **Voyager Insurance** (✉ 44 Peel Center Dr., Brampton, Ontario L6T 4M8, ☎ 905/791–8700; 800/668–4342 in Canada).

➤ INSURANCE INFORMATION: In the U.K. the **Association of British Insurers** (✉ 51–55 Gresham St., London EC2V 7HQ, ☎ 020/7600–3333, ℻ 020/7696–8999). In Australia the **Insurance Council of Australia** (☎ 03/9614–1077, ℻ 03/9614–7924).

LODGING

Philadelphia is undergoing a lodging boom, and you'll have a choice of everything from homey Victorian bed-and-breakfasts to luxurious modern hotels. The lodgings we list are the cream of the crop in each price category. We always list the facilities that are available—but we don't specify whether they cost extra: When pricing accommodations, always ask what's included and what costs extra. Properties indicated by an ✕⌑ are lodging establishments whose restaurant warrants a special trip.

Assume that hotels operate on the European Plan (EP, with no meals) unless we specify that they use the Continental Plan (CP, with a Continental breakfast daily), Breakfast Plan (BP, with a full breakfast daily), Modified American Plan (MAP, with breakfast and dinner daily), or the Full American Plan (FAP, with all meals).

CATEGORY	PHILADELPHIA*	OTHER AREAS*
$$$$	over $230	over $200
$$$	$160–$230	$145–$200
$$	$100–$160	$85–$145
$	under $100	under $85

All prices are for a standard double room, excluding tax (14% in Philadelphia, 8% in Bucks County, and 6% in Lancaster County).

APARTMENT RENTALS

If you want a home base that's roomy enough for a family and comes with cooking facilities **consider a furnished rental.** These can save you money, especially if you're traveling with a group. Home-exchange directories sometimes list rentals as well as exchanges.

➤ INTERNATIONAL AGENTS: **Hometours International** (⌧ Box 11503, Knoxville, TN 37939, ☎ 423/690–8484 or 800/367–4668). **Interhome** (⌧ 1990 N.E. 163rd St., Suite 110, N. Miami Beach, FL 33162, ☎ 305/940–2299 or 800/882–6864, FAX 305/940–2911). **Rent-a-Home International** (⌧ 7200 34th Ave. NW, Seattle, WA 98117, ☎ 206/789–9377 or 800/964–1891, FAX 206/789–9379). **Vacation Home Rentals Worldwide**

(⌧ 235 Kensington Ave., Norwood, NJ 07648, ☎ 201/767–9393 or 800/633–3284, FAX 201/767–5510). **Hideaways International** (⌧ 767 Islington St., Portsmouth, NH 03801, ☎ 603/430–4433 or 800/843–4433, FAX 603/430–4444; membership $99).

B & B S

For information about bed-and-breakfasts and reservation services in Philadelphia, Bucks County, and Lancaster County, *see* Chapter 4, Chapter 9, and Chapter 10.

HOME EXCHANGES

If you would like to exchange your home for someone else's **join a home-exchange organization,** which will send you its updated listings of available exchanges for a year and will include your own listing in at least one of them. It's up to you to make specific arrangements.

➤ EXCHANGE CLUBS: **HomeLink International** (⌧ Box 650, Key West, FL 33041, ☎ 305/294–7766 or 800/638–3841, FAX 305/294–1448; $93 per year). **Intervac U.S.** (⌧ Box 590504, San Francisco, CA 94159, ☎ 800/756–4663, FAX 415/435–7440; $83 for catalogues).

HOSTELS

No matter what your age you can **save on lodging costs by staying at hostels.** In some 5,000 locations in more than 70 countries around the world, Hostelling International (HI), the umbrella group for a number of national youth-hostel associations, offers single-sex, dorm-style beds and, at many hostels, couples rooms and family accommodations. Membership in any HI national hostel association, open to travelers of all ages, allows you to stay in HI-affiliated hostels at member rates (one-year membership is about $25 for adults; hostels run about $10–$25 per night). Members also have priority if the hostel is full; they're eligible for discounts around the world, even on rail and bus travel in some countries. Membership in the U.S. is $25, in Canada C$26.75, in the U.K. £9.30, in Australia $44, in New Zealand $24.

➤ ORGANIZATIONS: **Australian Youth Hostel Association** (⌧ 10 Mallett St.,

SMART TRAVEL TIPS A TO Z

Camperdown, NSW 2050, ☎ 02/
9565–1699, FAX 02/9565–1325).
**Hostelling International—American
Youth Hostels** (✉ 733 15th St. NW,
Suite 840, Washington, DC 20005, ☎
202/783–6161, FAX 202/783–6171).
Hostelling International—Canada (✉
400–205 Catherine St., Ottawa,
Ontario K2P 1C3, ☎ 613/237–7884,
FAX 613/237–7868). **Youth Hostel
Association of England and Wales** (✉
Trevelyan House, 8 St. Stephen's Hill,
St. Albans, Hertfordshire AL1 2DY,
☎ 01727/855215 or 01727/845047,
FAX 01727/844126). **Youth Hostels
Association of New Zealand** (✉ Box
436, Christchurch, New Zealand, ☎
03/379–9970, FAX 03/365–4476).

HOTELS

All hotels listed have rooms with a
private bath unless otherwise noted.

➤ TOLL-FREE NUMBERS: **Adam's Mark**
(☎ 800/444–2326). **Best Western** (☎
800/528–1234). **Choice** (☎ 800/221–
2222). **Clarion** (☎ 800/252–7466).
Colony (☎ 800/777–1700). **Comfort**
(☎ 800/228–5150). **Days Inn** (☎
800/325–2525). **Doubletree and Red
Lion Hotels** (☎ 800/222–8733).
Embassy Suites (☎ 800/362–2779).
Fairfield Inn (☎ 800/228–2800).
Four Seasons (☎ 800/332–3442).
Hilton (☎ 800/445–8667). **Holiday
Inn** (☎ 800/465–4329). **Howard
Johnson** (☎ 800/654–4656). **Hyatt
Hotels & Resorts** (☎ 800/233–1234).
La Quinta (☎ 800/531–5900). **Mar-
riott** (☎ 800/228–9290). **Le Meridien**
(☎ 800/543–4300). **Omni** (☎ 800/
843–6664). **Quality Inn** (☎ 800/228–
5151). **Radisson** (☎ 800/333–3333).
Ramada (☎ 800/228–2828). **Renais-
sance Hotels & Resorts** (☎ 800/468–
3571). **Ritz-Carlton** (☎ 800/241–
3333). **Sheraton** (☎ 800/325–3535).
Sleep Inn (☎ 800/753–3746). **Westin
Hotels & Resorts** (☎ 800/228–3000).
Wyndham Hotels & Resorts (☎ 800/
822–4200).

MAIL & SHIPPING

➤ POST OFFICES: **Main Post Office** (✉
2970 Market St., ☎ 215/895–8000).

MEDIA

NEWSPAPERS & MAGAZINES

The Philadelphia *Inquirer* and the
Philadelphia *Daily News* are the city's
main daily newspapers. The monthly
Philadelphia magazine contains
listings and advertisements of interest
to visitors as well as residents.

RADIO & TELEVISION

AM radio: KYW 1060, news and
weather. FM radio: WXPN 88.5,
University of Pennsylvania, news and
music, including jazz; WHYY 90.1,
National Public Radio; WMMR 93.3,
album rock; WYTU 92, country.

Channel 3 is CBS; channel 6, ABC;
channel 10, NBC; channel 12, PBS.

MONEY MATTERS

Philadelphia is a major city and can
be expensive, although it is less so
than New York. A cup of coffee will
cost $1 at a diner but $2–$3 at an
upscale restaurant; a sandwich will
set you back $4–$6. Taxi rides begin
at $1.80 and can quickly add up to $6
or more for a ride across Center City.
Most sites in Independence National
Historical Park are free; museums in
the city cost $3–$9. Prices throughout
this guide are given for adults. Substantially reduced fees are almost
always available for children, students, and senior citizens. For information on taxes, *see* Taxes, *below*.

ATMS

Cirrus (☎ 800/424–7787). **Plus** (☎
800/843–7587).

CREDIT CARDS

Throughout this guide, the following
abbreviations are used: **AE**, American
Express; **D**, Discover; **DC**, Diner's
Club; **MC**, MasterCard; and **V**, Visa.

➤ REPORTING LOST CARDS: **American
Express** (☎ 800/300–8765). **Diner's
Club** (☎ 800/234–6377). **Discover**
(☎ 800/347–2683). **MasterCard** (☎
800/826–2181). **Visa** (☎ 800/336–
8472).

PACKING

Portage and luggage trolleys are hard
to find, so **pack light.** Philadelphia is a
fairly casual city, although men will
need a jacket and tie in some of the
better restaurants. Jeans and sneakers
or other casual clothing are fine for
sightseeing. You'll need a heavy coat
for winter, which can be cold and
snowy. Summers are hot and humid,

but you'll need a shawl or jacket for air-conditioned restaurants. Many areas are best explored on foot, so **bring good walking shoes.**

In your carry-on luggage **bring an extra pair of eyeglasses or contact lenses** and **enough of any medication you take** to last the entire trip. You may also want your doctor to write a spare prescription using the drug's generic name, since brand names may vary from country to country. In luggage to be checked, **never pack prescription drugs or valuables.** To avoid customs delays, carry medications in their original packaging. And don't forget to copy down and carry addresses of offices that handle refunds of lost traveler's checks.

CHECKING LUGGAGE

How many carry-on bags you can bring with you is up to the airline. Most allow two, but not always, so make sure that everything you carry aboard will fit under your seat, and get to the gate early. Note that if you have a seat at the back of the plane, you'll probably board first, while the overhead bins are still empty.

If you are flying internationally, note that baggage allowances may be determined not by piece but by weight—generally 88 pounds (40 kilograms) in first class, 66 pounds (30 kilograms) in business class, and 44 pounds (20 kilograms) in economy.

Airline liability for baggage is limited to $1,250 per person on flights within the United States. On international flights it amounts to $9.07 per pound or $20 per kilogram for checked baggage (roughly $640 per 70-pound bag) and $400 per passenger for unchecked baggage. You can buy additional coverage at check-in for about $10 per $1,000 of coverage, but it excludes a rather extensive list of items, shown on your airline ticket.

Before departure **itemize your bags' contents** and their worth, and label the bags with your name, address, and phone number. (If you use your home address, cover it so that potential thieves can't see it readily.) Inside each bag **pack a copy of your itinerary.** At check-in **make sure that each bag is correctly tagged** with the destination airport's three-letter code. If your bags arrive damaged or fail to arrive at all, file a written report with the airline before leaving the airport.

PASSPORTS & VISAS

When traveling internationally **carry a passport even if you don't need one** (it's always the best form of ID), and **make two photocopies of the data page** (one for someone at home and another for you, carried separately from your passport). If you lose your passport promptly call the nearest embassy or consulate and the local police.

CANADIANS

A passport is not required to enter the United States, but it is a good idea to carry one, as proof of citizenship (a birth certificate or valid passport) and photo identification may be requested.

U.K. CITIZENS

British citizens need a valid passport to enter the United States. If you are staying for fewer than 90 days on vacation, with a return or onward ticket, you probably will not need a visa. However, you will need to fill out the Visa Waiver Form, 1-94W, supplied by the airline.

➤ U.K. Citizens: **U.S. Embassy Visa Information Line** (☎ 01891/200–290; calls cost 49p per minute, 39p per minute cheap rate) for U.S. visa information. **U.S. Embassy Visa Branch** (✉ 5 Upper Grosvenor Sq., London W1A 1AE) for U.S. visa information; send a self-addressed, stamped envelope. Write the **U.S. Consulate General** (✉ Queen's House, Queen St., Belfast BTI 6EO) if you live in Northern Ireland. Write the **Office of Australia Affairs** (✉ 59th fl., MLC Centre, 19-29 Martin Pl., Sydney NSW 2000) if you live in Australia. Write the **Office of New Zealand Affairs** (✉ 29 Fitzherbert Terr., Thorndon, Wellington) if you live in New Zealand.

PASSPORT OFFICES

The best time to apply for a passport or to renew is during the fall and winter. Before any trip, check your passport's expiration date, and, if necessary, renew it as soon as possible.

➤ AUSTRALIAN CITIZENS: **Australian Passport Office** (☎ 131–232).

➤ CANADIAN CITIZENS: **Passport Office** (☎ 819/994–3500 or 800/567–6868).

➤ NEW ZEALAND CITIZENS: **New Zealand Passport Office** (☎ 04/494–0700 for information on how to apply; 04/474–8000 or 0800/225–050 in New Zealand for information on applications already submitted).

➤ U.K. CITIZENS: **London Passport Office** (☎ 0990/210–410) for fees and documentation requirements and to request an emergency passport.

REST ROOMS

Rest rooms are available in department stores, visitor centers, hotels, restaurants, and tourist attractions. In fancier restaurants, ask before you enter.

SAFETY

As in many other major cities, sections of Philadelphia range from posh old-money enclaves to inner-city slums. Center City and the major tourist destinations are safe during the day. After dark, exercise caution in the neighborhoods ringing downtown. You can **ask hotel personnel or the Philadelphia Visitors Center about the safety of places** you're interested in visiting. As you would in any city, **keep your car locked and watch your possessions carefully.** Remember to **remove items from your car.**

Subway crime has diminished in recent years. During the day cars are crowded and safe. However, platforms and cars can be relatively empty in the late evening hours. SEPTA train travelers should **avoid North Philadelphia Station,** which is in an economically depressed neighborhood. Instead of waiting for a subway or train in off hours, **take a cab late at night.**

SENIOR-CITIZEN TRAVEL

To qualify for age-related discounts **mention your senior-citizen status up front** when booking hotel reservations (not when checking out) and before you're seated in restaurants (not when

paying the bill). When renting a car ask about promotional car-rental discounts, which can be cheaper than senior-citizen rates.

Seniors should avail themselves of an enormous array of discounts. From cut-rate Amtrak tickets to free rides on SEPTA buses, from numerous hotel discount rates to free admissions at attractions, from 10% senior discounts at various restaurants to flat-rate programs at leading car-rental companies, Philly promises its senior-citizen visitors will leave the city richer in more ways than one. For a complete list on all the discount options, **ask for the "Seniors on the Go" booklet,** available from the Philadelphia Convention and Visitors Bureau (☞ Visitor Information, *below*).

➤ EDUCATIONAL PROGRAMS: **Elderhostel** (✉ 75 Federal St., 3rd fl., Boston, MA 02110, ☎ 877/426–8056, ℻ 877/426–2166).

SIGHTSEEING TOURS

Following are some sightseeing options for Philadelphia. For information about special tours in the Brandywine Valley, Bucks County, and Lancaster County, *see* the A to Z sections at the end of Chapters 8, 9, and 10.

CARRIAGE RIDES

Numerous horse-drawn carriages wend their way through the narrow streets of the historic area. Tours last anywhere from 15 minutes to an hour and cost from $15 to $60. Carriages line up on Chestnut and 6th Streets near Independence Hall between 10 AM and 6 PM and at South Street and 2nd Street between 7 PM and 12 AM. You can reserve a carriage and be picked up anywhere downtown. Carriages operate year-round, except when the temperature is below 20°F or above 94°F.

➤ CARRIAGE OPERATORS: **'76 Carriage Company** (☎ 215/923–8516). **Society Hill Carriage Company** (☎ 215/627–6128).

MULTILINGUAL TOURS

Centipede Tours can supply German-, French-, Spanish-, or Italian-speaking guides for all parts of Philadelphia.

➤ TOUR COMPANY: **Centipede Tours** (☎ 215/735–3123).

ORIENTATION TOURS

Two companies offer narrated tours in buses designed to resemble Victorian-style trolleys. With both companies, the fare is an all-day pass, allowing unlimited on/offs. Board at any stop including the Philadelphia Visitors Center, the Pennsylvania Convention Center, and the Liberty Bell.

The Philadelphia Trolley Works tour takes about 90 minutes and costs $14. The tour makes 20 stops on a route covering the historic area, the Benjamin Franklin Parkway, the Avenue of the Arts (South Broad St.), Fairmount Park, the Philadelphia Zoo, Eastern State Penitentiary, and Penn's Landing.

American Trolley Tours offers free pickup at major hotels as well as historic sites, the Pennsylvania Convention Center and the Visitors Centers. Tours run every 45 minutes between 9 and 3:45 and take approximately two hours; the cost is $14.

➤ TOUR COMPANIES: **American Trolley Tours** (☎ 215/333–2119). **Philadelphia Trolley Works** (☎ 215/923–8522).

RIVER CRUISES

Liberty Belle Cruises, aboard a new 600-passenger Mississippi paddle-wheel riverboat, offer lunch, dinner, and Sunday brunch cruises with a banjo player, sing-alongs, and a buffet. Board at Penn's Landing (✉ Columbus Blvd. at Lombard Circle).

The *Spirit of Philadelphia* runs lunch and dinner cruises along the Delaware River. This three-deck ship leaves Penn's Landing at Lombard Circle and Columbus Boulevard for lunch, dinner, and moonlight cruises. Dinner cruises include a band and singing waitstaff, while both moonlight and Saturday afternoon "Philly Jam" cruises have a bar, band, and dancing.

➤ CRUISE BOATS: *Liberty Belle* **Cruises** (☎ 215/629–1131). *Spirit of Philadelphia* (☎ 215/923–1419).

SPECIAL-INTEREST TOURS

➤ AFRICAN-AMERICAN HISTORY: **Tour of Possibilities** (☎ 215/877–7004) will custom design a tour of Philadelphia's African-American history.

➤ JEWISH HISTORY: **Jewish Walking Tours of Philadelphia** (☎ 215/934–7184) offers tours of the historic sites of the city's old immigrant quarter (Society Hill and Queen Village) on Tuesday and Thursday, April through November.

➤ ITALIAN MARKET: **Italian Market Tours** (☎ 215/334–6008) gives an afternoon's introduction to this vibrant area's cultural and historic sites. The tour includes visits to cheese, meat, and pastry shops, a cooking demonstration, and jaunts to the "birthplace" of the Philly steak sandwich, Chubby Checker's work-site, and the street where Sylvester Stallone's character in *Rocky* lived.

WALKING TOURS

➤ TOUR COMPANIES: **Centipede Tours** (☎ 215/735–3123) offers a candlelight stroll through Society Hill led by guides in Colonial dress. Tours begin at Welcome Park (✉ Walnut and 2nd Sts.) Friday and Saturday at 6:30 PM, May–October. **Foundation for Architecture** (☎ 215/569–3187) tours focus on architecture but also touch on history. Area tours include Chestnut Hill, Manayunk, and Spruce Hill. Theme tours include Art Deco, skyscrapers, the University of Pennsylvania campus, and Judaic architecture and influence. Most tours begin weekends at 2 and occasionally on Wednesday at 6.

STUDENTS IN PHILADELPHIA

➤ STUDENT IDS & SERVICES: **Council on International Educational Exchange** (CIEE, ✉ 205 E. 42nd St., 14th fl., New York, NY 10017, ☎ 212/822–2600 or 888/268–6245, FAX 212/822–2699) for mail orders only, in the U.S. **Travel Cuts** (✉ 187 College St., Toronto, Ontario M5T 1P7, ☎ 416/979–2406 or 800/667–2887) in Canada.

SUBWAY TRAVEL

The Broad Street Subway runs from Fern Rock station in the northern part of the city to Pattison Avenue and the sports complex (First Union Center and Veterans Stadium) in South Philadelphia. The Market–

SMART TRAVEL TIPS A TO Z

Frankford line runs across the city from the western suburb of Upper Darby to Frankford in the northeast. Both lines shut down from midnight to 5 AM, during which time "Night Owl" buses operate along the same routes.

FARES & SCHEDULES

For fare information, *see* Bus Travel within Philadelphia, *above*.

➤ SUBWAY INFORMATION: **SEPTA** (☎ 215/580–7800; ☞ Bus Travel within Philadelphia, *above*).

TAXES

SALES TAX

The main sales tax in Philadelphia and the surrounding areas is 7%. This tax also applies to restaurant meals. Various other taxes—including a liquor tax—may apply. There is no sales tax on clothing.

HOTEL

Besides the room rate, you pay a 14% hotel tax (7% state, 7% city, in Philadelphia; hotel tax is 8% in Bucks County and 6% in Lancaster County).

TAXIS

Cabs cost $1.80 at the flag throw and then $1.80–$2.30 per mile. They are plentiful during the day downtown—especially along Broad Street and near hotels and train stations. At night and outside Center City, taxis are scarce. You can call for a cab, but they frequently show up late and occasionally never arrive. Be persistent: Calling back if the cab is late will often yield results.

➤ TAXI COMPANIES: **Olde City Taxi** (☎ 215/338–0838). **Quaker City Cab** (☎ 215/728–8000). **Yellow Cab** (☎ 215/922–8400).

TIME

Philadelphia and the Pennsylvania Dutch Country are in the eastern time zone. Daylight savings time is in effect from early April through late October; eastern standard time, the rest of the year. Clocks are set ahead one hour when daylight savings time begins, back one hour when it ends. Philadelphia is 3 hours ahead of Los Angeles, 1 hour ahead of Chicago, 6 hours behind London, and 15 hours behind Sydney.

TIPPING

At restaurants, a 15% tip is standard for servers; up to 20% may be expected at more expensive establishments. The same goes for taxi drivers, bartenders, and hairdressers. Coat checkers usually expect $1–$2; bellhops and hotel and airport porters should get $1 per bag. Hotel maids in upscale hotels should get about $1 per day of your stay. For local sightseeing tours, you may individually tip the driver-guide $1–$5, depending on the length of the tour and the number of people in your party, if he or she has been helpful or informative. Ushers in theaters do not expect tips.

A concierge typically receives a tip of $5–$10, with an additional gratuity for special services or favors.

TELEPHONES

Philadelphia has two area codes: 215 and the new 267, which is being assigned to new numbers. Because of this, the city now requires that you dial all ten digits of a telephone number even for local calls.

TOURS & PACKAGES

On a prepackaged tour or independent vacation everything is prearranged so you'll spend less time planning—and often get it all at a good price.

BOOKING WITH AN AGENT

Travel agents are excellent resources. But it's a good idea to collect brochures from several agencies because some agents' suggestions may be influenced by relationships with tour and package firms that reward them for volume sales. If you have a special interest **find an agent with expertise in that area;** ASTA (☞ Travel Agencies, *below*) has a database of specialists worldwide.

Make sure your travel agent knows the accommodations and other services of the place they're recommending. Ask about the hotel's location, room size, beds, and whether it has a pool, room service, or programs for children, if you care about these. Has your agent been there in person or sent others whom you can contact?

Do some homework on your own, too: Local tourism boards can provide information about lesser-known and small-niche operators, some of which may sell only direct.

BUYER BEWARE

Each year consumers are stranded or lose their money when tour operators—even large ones with excellent reputations—go out of business. So **check out the operator.** Ask several travel agents about its reputation, and try to **book with a company that has a consumer-protection program.** (Look for information in the company's brochure.) In the United States, members of the National Tour Association and United States Tour Operators Association are required to set aside funds to cover your payments and travel arrangements in case the company defaults. It's also a good idea to choose a company that participates in the American Society of Travel Agent's Tour Operator Program (TOP); ASTA will act as mediator in any disputes between you and your tour operator.

Remember that the more your package or tour includes the better you can predict the ultimate cost of your vacation. Make sure you know exactly what is covered, and **beware of hidden costs.** Are taxes, tips, and transfers included? Entertainment and excursions? These can add up.

➤ TOUR-OPERATOR RECOMMENDATIONS: **American Society of Travel Agents** (☞ Travel Agencies, *below*). **National Tour Association** (NTA, ✉ 546 E. Main St., Lexington, KY 40508, ☎ 606/226–4444 or 800/682–8886). **United States Tour Operators Association** (USTOA, ✉ 342 Madison Ave., Suite 1522, New York, NY 10173, ☎ 212/599–6599 or 800/468–7862, ℻ 212/599–6744).

TRAIN TRAVEL

Philadelphia's 30th Street Station (✉ 30th and Market Sts.) is a major stop on Amtrak's Northeast Corridor line. You can **travel by train between Philadelphia and New York City on the cheap** by taking the SEPTA commuter line R7 to Trenton, New Jersey, and transferring to a NJ Transit

commuter line to Manhattan. Ask for the excursion rate. The trip takes an extra 30 minutes, but costs about $12, versus Amtrak's $42. Amtrak also serves Philadelphia from points west, including Harrisburg, Pittsburgh, and Chicago.

At press time, 150 mph high-speed Acela service was scheduled to replace Metroliner service in the Northeast Corridor (Boston to Washington, D.C.) in spring 2000, cutting travel times between key cities substantially. For example, it will take four hours to travel from Boston to Philadelphia on Acela, less than the time it now takes to travel from Boston to New York on regular Amtrak service.

At the 30th Street Station you can connect with SEPTA commuter trains to two downtown stations—Suburban Station, at 16th Street and John F. Kennedy Boulevard (near major hotels), and Market East Station, at 10th and Market streets (near the historic district)—and to outlying areas.

Philadelphia's fine network of commuter trains, operated by SEPTA (☞ Bus Travel within Philadelphia, *above*), serves both the city and the suburbs. The famous Main Line, a cluster of affluent suburbs, got its start—and its name—from the Pennsylvania Railroad route that ran westward from Center City.

All trains serve 30th Street Station (✉ 30th and Market Sts.), where they connect to Amtrak trains, Suburban Station (✉ 16th St. and John F. Kennedy Blvd., across from the Visitors Center), and Market East Station (✉ 10th and Market Sts.), beneath the Gallery at Market East shopping complex. Fares, which vary according to route and time of travel, range from $2.50 to $5 one-way. These trains are your best bet for reaching Germantown, Chestnut Hill, Merion (site of the Barnes Foundation), and other suburbs.

PATCO (Port Authority Transit Corporation) High Speed Line trains run underground from 16th and Locust streets to Lindenwold, New Jersey. Trains stop at 13th and Locust, 9th and Locust, and 8th and Market streets, then continue across the Benjamin Franklin Bridge to Camden. It's one way to get to the New Jersey State Aquarium or the Blockbuster-Sony Entertainment Centre; NJ Transit has a shuttle bus from the Broadway stop to the aquarium on weekends and to the center during performances. Fares run 75¢ to $1.60. Sit in the very front seat for a great view going across the bridge.

For information on train service for the Brandywine Valley, Bucks County, and the Pennsylvania Dutch Country, *see* Arriving and Departing *in* the A to Z sections at the end of Chapters 8, 9, and 10.

➤ TRAIN INFORMATION: **Amtrak** (☎ 215/824–1600 or 800/872–7245). **New Jersey Transit** (☎ 215/569–3752). **PATCO** (☎ 215/922–4600). **SEPTA** (☎ 215/580–7800).

TRAVEL AGENCIES

A good travel agent puts your needs first. Look for an agency that has been in business at least five years, emphasizes customer service, and has someone on staff who specializes in your destination. In addition **make sure the agency belongs to a professional trade organization.** The American Society of Travel Agents (ASTA), with 27,000 agents in some 170 countries, is the largest and most influential in the field. Operating under the motto "Integrity in Travel," it maintains and enforces a strict code of ethics and will step in to help mediate any agent-client disputes if necessary. ASTA also maintains a Web site that includes a directory of agents. Note that if a travel agency is also acting as your tour operator, *see* Buyer Beware *in* Tours & Packages, *above*.

➤ LOCAL AGENT REFERRALS: **American Society of Travel Agents** (ASTA, ☎ 800/965–2782 24-hr hot line, FAX 703/684–8319, www.astanet.com). **Association of British Travel Agents** (✉ 68–271 Newman St., London W1P 4AH, ☎ 020/7637–2444, FAX 020/7637–0713). **Association of Canadian Travel Agents** (✉ 1729 Bank St., Suite 201, Ottawa, Ontario

K1V 7Z5, ☎ 613/521–0474, FAX 613/521–0805). **Australian Federation of Travel Agents** (✉ Level 3, 309 Pitt St., Sydney 2000, ☎ 02/9264–3299, FAX 02/9264–1085). **Travel Agents' Association of New Zealand** (✉ Box 1888, Wellington 10033, ☎ 04/499–0104, FAX 04/499–0786).

TROLLEYS

Philadelphia once had an extensive trolley network, and in the summer and during certain holidays, you can still ride on a SEPTA (☞ Bus Travel within Philadelphia, *above*) line in some of the few remaining Presidential Conference Committee cars, popular in the 1940s. The "Welcome Line" runs a short downtown loop, with some cars continuing out to the zoo in West Fairmount Park. For privately run trolleys, *see* Orientation Tours *in* Sightseeing Tours, *above*.

VISITOR INFORMATION

For general information before you go, call the Convention and Visitors Bureau, Independence National Historical Park, and state tourism office. When you get there, stop by the Philadelphia Visitors Center, just one block from City Hall, and the Independence National Historical Park visitor center. If you are planning to make side trips from Philadelphia or are traveling on to Bucks County or Lancaster County, you should also *see* Visitor Information *in* the A to Z sections of Chapters 8, 9, and 10.

Visitors should note that by late 2000 or early 2001, the Philadelphia Visitors Center and the Independence National Historical Park Visitor Center will close. The Gateway Visitor Center, a new facility with expanded services, will open on 6th Street between Market and Arch streets.

TOURIST INFORMATION

➤ CITY: **Philadelphia Convention and Visitors Bureau** (✉ 1515 Market St., Suite 2020, 19102, ☎ 215/636–3300 or 800/537–7676, FAX 215/636–3327). **Philadelphia Visitors Center** (✉ 16th Street and John F. Kennedy Blvd., ☎ 215/636–1666).

➤ NATIONAL PARK: **Independence National Historical Park** (⊠ Visitor Center, 3rd and Chestnut Sts., ☎ 215/597–1785 or 215/597–8974, for a recorded message; mailing address is ⊠ 313 Walnut St., 19106).

➤ REGIONAL: **Greater Philadelphia Tourism Marketing Corporation** (☎ 888/467–4452).

➤ STATE: **Pennsylvania Office of Travel and Tourism** (☎ 717/787–5453; 800/847–4872 for brochures).

➤ IN THE U.K.: **Pennsylvania Tourism Office** (⊠ Suite 302, 11–15 Betterton St. Covent Garden, London WC2H 9BP, ☎ 020/7470–8801, FAX 020/7470–8810).

WEB SITES

Do **check out the World Wide Web** when youíre planning. Youíll find everything from up-to-date weather forecasts to virtual tours of famous cities. Fodor's Web site www.fodors.com, is a great place to start your online travels. For more information specifically on Philadelphia, side trips, and the Pennsylvania Dutch Country, take a look at the sites listed below. Besides material on sights and lodgings, most have a calendar of events and other special features, some of which are noted.

➤ WEB SITES: **www.gophila.org** presents trip-planning from the Greater Philadelphia Tourism Marketing Corporation, which represents Bucks, Chester, Delaware, Montgomery, and Philadelphia counties. **www.libertynet. org**, the Web site of the Philadelphia Convention and Visitors Bureau, has general information about the city, current events, and links to dozens of tour operators and local attractions. **www.nps.gov/inde** is the National Park Service site for Independence National Historical Park. **www.pavisnet.com**, the site of the Pennsylvania Visitors Network, is a good place to check for current events and activities for children. **www.phillynews.com** con-

tains an electronic version of the Philadelphia *Inquirer.* **www.phl.org**, the site of Philadelphia International Airport, lets you access information on parking, car rentals, and currency exchange. **www.septa.com**, the site for the transportation agency SEPTA, provides schedules, detailed maps and fares for its bus, train, and subway routes, and news about changes on the lines due to construction.

www.brandywinevalley.com is the site of the Chester County Tourist Bureau. **www.buckscountycvb.org** has information from the Bucks County Conference and Visitors Bureau. **www.800PAdutch.com** has information about events and links to accommodations in Lancaster County and the Pennsylvania Dutch Country. **www.hersheypa.com** covers attractions and events in Hershey. **www.nps.gov/gett** is the site of Gettysburg National Military Park. **www.nps.gov/vafo** can help you plan a visit to Valley Forge National Historical Park. **www.valleyforge.com** has information about Valley Forge.

WHEN TO GO

Any time is right to enjoy the area's attractions, and a variety of popular annual events take place throughout the year (☞ Festivals and Seasonal Events *in* Chapter 1). The period around July 4th is particularly festive; there are special activities in the historic area throughout the summer. Concert season runs from October through the beginning of June. You may find some better lodging deals in the winter.

CLIMATE

Like other northern American cities, Philadelphia can be hot and humid in the summer and cold in winter (winter snowfall averages 21 inches).

➤ FORECASTS: **Weather Channel Connection** (☎ 900/932–8437), 95¢ per minute from a Touch-Tone phone.

SMART TRAVEL TIPS A TO Z

The following are average daily maximum and minimum temperatures for Philadelphia.

Climate in Philadelphia

Jan.	40F	4C	May	72F	22C	Sept.	76F	24C
	27	- 3		54	12		61	16
Feb.	41F	5C	June	81F	27C	Oct.	67F	19C
	27	- 3		63	17		50	10
Mar.	49F	9C	July	85F	29C	Nov.	54F	12C
	34	- 1		68	20		40	- 4
Apr.	61F	16C	Aug.	83F	28C	Dec.	43F	6C
	43	6		67	19		31	- 1

1 DESTINATION: PHILADELPHIA AND THE PENNSYLVANIA DUTCH COUNTRY

A CITY OF NEIGHBORHOODS

ONCE UPON A TIME, Philadelphia was the kind of place you would go on your fourth-grade field trip, with required stops at the Liberty Bell and the Betsy Ross House. Or you'd pass through for the day between longer visits to New York and Washington, DC, those attention-grabbing cities to the north and south.

These days, though, Philadelphia has shed its poor stepsister image. It's a hot destination in its own right, thanks to blockbuster art exhibitions, new theaters, extravagant festivals, some of the nation's finest restaurants, fast and furious hotel development, and big plans for transforming the city's waterfront, historic areas, and sports stadiums.

Still, when visitors arrive, they discover that much of Philadelphia's appeal lies not in its hyped-up new attractions but in its more genteel, long-reigning pleasures: attending a Philadelphia Orchestra concert, lingering over the quintessentially American paintings of Benjamin West and Winslow Homer in the ornate Pennsylvania Academy of the Fine Arts, or touring that icon of freedom, Independence Hall.

Some big-name out-of-towners have put Philadelphia on their agenda, including delegates to the Republican National Convention of summer 2000 and the folks at Disney, who chose the City of Brotherly Love as the site of DisneyQuest, their latest entertainment venture. "If we were the same old stodgy city of the 1970s, Disney probably wouldn't be coming here," bragged Ed Rendell, Philadelphia's popular ex-mayor, who is credited with fashioning much of the city's makeover. Rendell, a Democrat, was also instrumental in arranging to bring the Republican National Convention to the city. (Curiously, in its days as the nation's capital, fashionable Philadelphia was called the "Republican Court.")

In spite of this recent attention, the city is defined not by out-of-towners but by its locals. Philadelphia is the nation's fifth-largest city (with a population of 1.6 million, metro area 5.78 million), but unlike numbers one to four—New York, Los Angeles, Chicago, and Houston—where party chitchat might begin with "So where are you from?" and end with "Not from here," in Philadelphia, it's more likely to be "Where did you go to high school?" "Oh! Do you know . . . ?" "Yeah, that's my cousin." More Philadelphians grow up and stay put than do residents of any other city in the country, and it's not uncommon for families to live in the same house from one generation to the next. The roots run deep in William Penn's "greene countrie towne."

Philadelphia is a manageable city: streets are laid out in straight-angle grids, buildings and values are solid, and neighborhoods ethnic. To Manhattanites and others, these qualities may brand Philadelphia provincial, but locals say it's what makes their city livable.

Most of Philadelphia's neighborhoods are just beyond William Penn's original 2-square-mi downtown area (known as Center City), but they could be miles away. Some of the Ukrainian old-timers who live in Fairmount, a mile from City Hall, brag that they haven't been downtown in a decade. In years past, residents of Northeast Philadelphia, which itself contains tens of little neighborhoods, lobbied to secede from the city and form their own government.

The city's Cinderella story has been staged mostly in the downtown area. Like many American cities, Philadelphia still struggles with issues of education, housing, and the loss of industrial jobs. But since 1992, major crimes in the Center City district have decreased by 30%, lighting levels have been doubled, and previously homeless people have been hired to clean the sidewalks, remove graffiti, serve as guides, and work in partnership with the police. These days, the residential real estate market in Center City is sizzling; homeowners who couldn't turn a profit are now involved in bidding wars. Along with low interest rates, one factor driving the homes sales is the city's revitalization in the '90s under Mayor Rendell.

A number of the city's most revered institutions are involved in renovation—or relocation—projects, with the goal of making them more user-friendly. The Philadelphia Orchestra will be moving into the new Regional Performing Arts Center on the Avenue of the Arts, while its old home, the Academy of Music, has been revamped. The Liberty Bell is moving into spacious new quarters with a better view of Independence Hall, and the city's baseball and football teams are in the early stages of new stadium construction.

These days, Philadelphia's oldest neighborhood, aptly named Old City, is its hippest. On the first Friday evening of each month, dozens of galleries lure city dwellers and suburbanites with wine, cheese, and engaging new exhibits of painting and sculpture. In this neighborhood, which stretches from Front to Fifth streets, and Chestnut to Vine streets, the old and new gracefully coexist. The white-steeple Christ Church, former house of worship for 15 signers of the Declaration of Independence, shares Second Street with the Continental, a cool martini bar in a 1950s diner. The gable-roof Colonial home of Betsy Ross keeps company with cast-iron-front warehouses transformed into chic loft apartments.

In fact, Philadelphia contains more historic buildings than similar acreage in any other American city. The Colonial homes in Society Hill, the Georgian and Federal mansions in Fairmount Park, and the Victorian Gothic buildings on Boathouse Row are architectural gems.

There are also big and small pleasures beyond the architectural ones to delight visitors: the Picassos at the Philadelphia Museum of Art and the Pennsylvania Dutch food specialties at the Reading Terminal Market, the world-class Philadelphia Orchestra and the out-of-this-world sequined and feathered Mummers, the nation's biggest Fourth of July celebration and a tiny Colonial street, Elfreth's Alley.

Those straight, tree-lined streets are courtesy of William Penn, the city's Quaker founder, who arranged homes on their plots so that children would have plenty of green space. When the city soared upward, Penn's penchant for space prevailed. "Our Philadelphia streets do not care to be mere tunnels, like the canyon flumes of Manhattan," wrote Christo-

pher Morley, a famous Philadelphia writer of the early 1900s. "We have a lust for sun and air."

Philadelphians also have a lust for soft pretzels smeared with mustard; a rabid devotion to their sports teams, whether they are winning or losing; pride in their historic treasures; and a passion for the small town/big city that they call home.

–Joyce Eisenberg

NEW AND NOTEWORTHY

In the mid-1990s, Philadelphia set out to lure convention and tourism business by investing in new hotels, a new convention center, renovation projects, and a major advertising campaign. Now, at the millennium, the investment has paid off with at least one grand prize—the **Republican National Convention**, which is coming to town July 29–August 4, 2000, with its 20,000 delegates and 15,000 journalists. Traveling to the city around this time will require some careful planning, but at any other time you'll easily reap the benefits of the city's efforts.

Philadelphia scored again when Disney Regional Entertainment chose the city as a site for **DisneyQuest,** a giant indoor, interactive theme park set to open in early 2001; you'll also find DisneyQuests in Chicago and Orlando. The facility will be the anchor of a new development showcasing family-oriented entertainment, **Pavilion at Market East.** Add in a remarkable hotel boom (a 57% increase in the number of rooms in the city since 1995), major revitalization of Independence National Historical Park, a huge development project at Penn's Landing, work in progress on the Regional Performing Arts Center, and the promise of two new sports stadiums, and you could say that the city has hit a grand slam.

Indeed, Philadelphia has a lot to celebrate as it greets the new millennium with the 18-month-long **Millennium Philadelphia** celebration (July 4, 1999–January 1, 2001, the *official* start of the new millennium), which promises something for everyone. The event kicked off with *The Photo of* *the Century,* a picture taken in front of Independence Hall with 100 contest winners from across the nation who were born on the Fourth of July.

Independence National Historical Park is in the midst of a major revitalization, much of it planned for completion by late 2000 or early 2001. The **Liberty Bell** is moving closer to Independence Hall, to a new complex with a bell chamber, an exhibit space with historical displays and memorabilia, and a new covered waiting area. The new **Gateway Visitor Center,** a block from Independence Hall, will provide expanded tourism services and replace the two current visitor centers. On Constitution Day, September 17, 2000, the **National Constitution Center** will break ground; the proposed opening is two years later on the 215th anniversary of the signing of the U.S. Constitution.

Penn's Landing is bustling with the construction projects: a new hotel; an aerial tram that will whisk people between the Philadelphia and Camden riverfronts; and the **Family Entertainment Center,** with a 20–24 screen megaplex, an IMAX theater, an interactive attraction focusing on different periods of American history, and two full-size, year-round ice rinks.

On the **Avenue of the Arts,** folks are singing the praises of the **Prince Music Theater,** a new permanent home for the musical theater company of the same name and a venue for film festivals. The **Academy of Music,** the only surviving European-style opera house in America, is in the midst of extensive renovation and modernization. Down the street, work on the $245 million **Regional Performing Arts Center** is under way; plans include a 2,500-seat concert hall specifically designed for the Philadelphia Orchestra. The orchestra is celebrating a century of excellence with a year of special musical events (September 99–May 2000).

Meanwhile, the University of Pennsylvania is sprucing itself up with the development of **Sansom Common,** encompassing a hotel, restaurants, and shops. **University City,** an area just west of Center City that includes Penn, hosts Go West! Go International! Third Thursdays, with late hours at museums and galleries and special discounts and activities at restaurants.

State funding has been authorized for **two new sports stadiums** for Philadelphia. The Phillies baseball team and the Eagles football team will move from their current shared home, Veterans Stadium, into two new, single-sport stadiums in 2001 or 2002.

Just about all of the city's top museums are offering enticing new permanent exhibitions. The **University Museum of Archaeology and Anthropology** recently unveiled *Canaan and Ancient Israel,* with priceless artifacts that illuminate the politics, family life, commerce, and religious practices of the people of the Holy Land. The **Franklin Institute Science Museum** marked its 175th anniversary in 1999 with a new exhibit honoring its namesake, including Franklin's actual lightning rod, while the **Philadelphia Zoo** celebrated 125 years with the opening of its new Primate Reserve. Across the Delaware River, Camden is in bloom with the opening of the **Camden Children's Garden,** adjacent to the New Jersey State Aquarium. The giganotosaurus, the biggest meat-eating dinosaur ever discovered, is the main attraction at the renovated Dinosaur Hall in the **Academy of Natural Sciences.** The **Atwater Kent Museum** acquired more than 320 covers drawn by Norman Rockwell for the *Saturday Evening Post,* and the **Insectarium** was bequeathed a 63,000-specimen collection of butterflies and moths. The city has packaged some of these attractions with the new **CityPass,** a pay-one-price booklet that contains tickets to six top area sights at 50% off admission prices (☞ Discounts & Deals *in* Smart Travel Tips A to Z).

Trains, boats, and planes: A project to overhaul part of the Reading Terminal Headhouse and give the **Pennsylvania Convention Center** a grand front entrance from Market Street has been completed. **Amtrak** plans to introduce new high-speed Acela service along the Northeast Corridor sometime in 2000, eliminating the Metroliner. The new **Cruise Terminal** at the Philadelphia Naval Business Center, just downriver from Penn's Landing, is now open and hosting cruise ships from the Eastern Seaboard, Bermuda, Canada's Atlantic provinces, and the Caribbean. **Philadelphia International Airport,** the fastest-growing airport among the nation's top 25 airports, has a new international terminal and the Philadelphia Marketplace, with more than 30 shops and eateries. By summer 2001 the airport will open two new US Airways terminals, including one for international flights.

WHAT'S WHERE

Back in the 18th century William Penn laid out his new city of Philadelphia as though it were a huge chessboard. Charles Dickens lamented in 1842 that "it is a handsome city but distractingly regular: After walking about it for an hour or two, I felt that I would have given the world for a crooked street." Still, today many people readily give thanks to ol' Billy Penn. Two main thoroughfares intersect the center of the city: Broad Street (the city's spinal column, which runs north to south), and Market Street (which runs east to west). Where Broad and Market meet, neatly dividing the city center into four segments, you'll find City Hall, Philadelphia's center of gravity.

What makes Philadelphia different from other urban centers around the world? Simply stated, this sprawling cosmopolis has the feel of a friendly small town. Actually, several small towns, as Philly is a city of distinct neighborhoods, each with its own personality, rhythm, and lore. Here's a quick overview of the city's main districts plus some of the other destinations in this guide.

Benjamin Franklin Parkway

From City Hall the Benjamin Franklin Parkway stretches northwest to a Greco-Roman temple on a hill—the Philadelphia Museum of Art. The parkway is the city's Champs-Elysées, a grand boulevard designed by French architects and alive with flowers, trees, and fountains. Along the way are many of the city's grandest buildings and finest cultural institutions: the Academy of Natural Sciences, the Franklin Institute, and the Rodin Museum. Don't forget to check out the great paintings of Thomas Eakins at the Philadelphia Museum of Art. If Philadelphia's soul could be said to have been captured in a single image, it would likely be Eakins's *Concert Singer,* a portrait of Weda Cook, a friend of Walt Whitman.

Center City

As a cultural palimpsest, Philadelphia has many pasts, but if you're interested in its present and future, head for Center City. This is Philly's business district, anchored by Oz-like skyscrapers and solidly Victorian City Hall, crowned by the enormous statue of William Penn. From Chinatown to Rittenhouse Square, Center City is crammed with sights. A sample? How about the Academy of Music; that leviathan horn of plenty, the Reading Terminal Market; the bustling Pennsylvania Convention Center; Thomas Jefferson University (home to Philly's greatest painting, Thomas Eakins's *Gross Clinic*); and for those with itchy credit cards, the Shops at Liberty Place. In broad local usage, Center City refers to the entire area between the Delaware and Schuylkill rivers (east and west boundaries) and Vine and South streets (north and south)—an area that would be synonymous with downtown in another city—but here it refers specifically to the business district around City Hall and Market Street.

Fairmount Park

When in need of elbow room, Philadelphians head for Fairmount Park, whose 8,500 acres make it the largest landscaped city park in the world. Deemed by many Philly dwellers to be their own backyard, Fairmount beckons with a wide range of pleasures. Joggers, walkers, and bicyclists consider it prime territory. Along Kelly Drive stand the Victorian houses of Boathouse Row, headquarters of the rowing clubs that make up what's called the "Schuylkill Navy." The Mann Center for the Performing Arts hosts open-air concerts in the summer. Children flock to the comfortably scaled Philadelphia Zoo. Many people are also drawn to the centuries-old houses that dot the park, including Mt. Pleasant, Strawberry Mansion, and Lemon Hill. Here you can also find the noted Greek Revival Fairmount Waterworks. The Wissahickon, in the northern section of the park, beckons the adventurous with miles of paths through the gorge carved by Wissahickon Creek.

Germantown and Chestnut Hill

When Germantown, an area north of Center City, was settled by Germans fleeing economic and religious turmoil, it was way out in the country, linked to the city 6 mi away by a dirt road. Before long, the Germans' modest homes and farms were interspersed with the grand homes of affluent Philadelphians who hoped to escape the city's summer heat. They escaped the heat but not the British, who occupied the town and deployed troops from here during the Battle of Germantown. Today Germantown is an integrated neighborhood prized for its large old homes; several of the historic houses that line Germantown Avenue are open for tours. Over the years, development continued along the avenue, farther from the city, culminating in Chestnut Hill, today one of Philadelphia's prettiest neighborhoods.

The Historic District

No matter how you first approach Philadelphia, all things start at Independence National Historical Park. As the birthplace of the country, "America's most historic square mile" was the arena across which the nation strode to its national identity and independence. It's impossible to list the historical highlights because *everything* is a highlight. Independence Hall—where the Declaration of Independence was approved and the U.S. Constitution adopted—Congress Hall, Old City Hall, Carpenters' Hall, Franklin Court, Declaration House, and, of course, the Liberty Bell are just some of the attractions. If seeing these sights doesn't bring out your gee-whiz patriotism, nothing will.

Manayunk

This old mill town, wedged between the Schuylkill River and some very steep hills 7 mi northwest of Center City, was once crucial to Philadelphia's industrial fortune; it became part of the city in 1854. Today it's bringing in dollars with its restaurants and boutiques. In the 12 years since Manayunk was designated a historic district, it has become the city's hottest neighborhood. More than a half mile of stores stretch along Main Street, while behind it are remnants of the Schuylkill Navigational Canal that originally brought life to this area.

Old City

Long considered one of Society Hill's poorer neighbors and known as a melting pot for immigrants, Old City is associated with three historic monuments: Christ Church, Elfreth's Alley, and the Betsy Ross House. Landmarked by its gleaming white spire, Christ Church is a gem of English Palladian architecture (its central window was the model for the one in Independence Hall). A few blocks north you'll find Elfreth's Alley, the most beautifully preserved street in the city—by some magical flick of a Wellsian time machine, you feel transported back to the 18th century here. To find the Betsy Ross House, look for the 13 stars and the 13 stripes flying from a second-story window of 239 Arch Street, a splendid example of a Colonial Philadelphia house. Today the area is also known for its chic art galleries, cafés, and restaurants, and its rehabbed houses and residential lofts. The presence of theater and dance companies, art workshops, and design firms adds to the neighborhood's renewed vitality as a cultural, shopping, and dining district.

Penn's Landing

Ever since William Penn sailed up the Delaware into Dock Creek, Philadelphia's waterfront has been a vibrant part of the city's life. Once home to sailing ships and counting houses and still one of the world's largest freshwater ports, Penn's Landing today has become a 37-acre-long riverside park, the site of concerts and festivals all summer long. It's also home to the Independence Seaport Museum and a flotilla of ship museums: the USS *Becuna,* the USS *Olympia,* and the *Gazela of Philadelphia.* A ferry link to the New Jersey State Aquarium and Camden Children's Garden and the Blockbuster-Sony Music Entertainment Centre has helped revitalize part of Camden's waterfront.

Rittenhouse Square

Like a grande dame, Rittenhouse Square is never in a hurry. The prettiest of Philadelphia's public squares, it beckons frazzled city dwellers to slow down and find balm among its blades. Today the park is the heart of upper-crust Philly. Christopher Morley, the humorist and author of *Kitty Foyle,* was alluding to a district like Rittenhouse Square when he described Philadelphia as being "at the confluence of the Drexel and Biddle families." Swank hotels and modern office buildings now intrude, but the trappings of onetime grandeur remain on view in its Victorian town houses. Many treasures are tucked away here, including the Curtis Institute of Music and the Rosenbach Museum and Library, home to 130,000 manuscripts, including James Joyce's *Ulysses.*

Society Hill

Society Hill is Philadelphia as it has been for more than 200 years. Old chimney pots, hidden courtyards, ornate door knockers, and cobblestone streets: Untouched by neon lights, Society Hill basks in its own patina. Although many houses are "trinity" abodes (one room to a floor), others are numbered among America's Federal-style showplaces, including the Physick House and the Powel House. Sit outside them for a while and watch the people go by, and not just those of the 20th century: Guides in Colonial dress sometimes lead candlelight strolls through the district.

South Philadelphia

Yes, this is the neighborhood that gave the world Rocky Balboa, as well as Bobby Rydell, Frankie Avalon, and Fabian. The city's "Little Italy" can sometimes seem more Naples than Philly—just take in the five-block outdoor Italian Market, where piles of peppers and mountains of mozzarella make your taste buds sit up and beg. You can satisfy your cravings in any number of eateries here, many of them simple neighborhood spots.

Southwark

Chiseled in stone on the facade of an old Southwark building are the words: ON THIS SITE IN 1879, NOTHING HAPPENED! Today a great deal is happening in this district, which stretches from Front to 6th streets and from South to Washington avenues. The renovation generation has helped make the Queen Village area a winner in the revival-of-the-fittest contest among Philly's neighborhoods. As a result, rents here are catching up to nearby Society Hill. Although Southwark has never been as renowned as its neighbor, it contains some of the most charming streets in the city, such as Hancock and Queen. For real Philly flash, check out the Mummers Museum, on Washington Avenue.

University City

Once known as the "Athens of America," Philadelphia claims an astonishing concentration of colleges and universities, nearly unrivaled in the country. Two of the larger institutions, the University of Pennsylvania and Drexel University, are in an area dubbed University City in West Philadelphia. Here, too, is the University Museum, containing one of the world's finest archaeology and anthropology collections. City buses travel along Walnut Street from Society Hill to University City; 34th and Walnut streets is the stop for Penn. One block north is the Institute of Contemporary Art, with its innovative exhibitions. Take Locust Walk to explore this Ivy League campus; ivy really does cling to the buildings.

Side Trips: Brandywine Valley and Valley Forge

Think of the Brandywine Valley, and the paintings of Andrew Wyeth come to mind: stone or clapboard farmhouses, forests that could tell a story or two, and meadows with getaway space and privacy. The valley's palette is quintessentially Wyeth, too—russet, fieldstone gray, shades of amber. A journey through this valley can make for a restful experience. Chadds Ford, the heart of Wyeth Country, is near the splendid homes and estates of the du Ponts: Winterthur, Nemours, and Longwood Gardens. Nearby, Valley Forge, the site of George Washington's heroic 1777–78 encampment, awaits.

Bucks County

Long a vacation spot for New Yorkers as well as for Philadelphians, Bucks County is a day-tripper's delight, filled with historic sites, artists' colonies, nature preserves, old fieldstone inns, and country-chic restaurants. Once hailed as the "Genius Belt" and home to such luminaries as Dorothy Parker, James Michener, and Oscar Hammerstein II, the region is packed with attractions: New Hope and Lahaska offer delightful shopping and antiquing; Doylestown has Fonthill, a millionaire's do-it-yourself castle right out of the Brothers Grimm; and the Delaware Canal towpath runs through countryside that conjures up England's Cotswolds.

Lancaster County, Hershey, and Gettysburg

An hour's drive from Philadelphia are Lancaster County and the Pennsylvania Dutch Country, known for delicious foods and tranquil farmlands. The folks responsible are the "Plain" people, who still use horse-drawn buggies and dress simply and unfussily, as their families have dressed for centuries. Around the hub of Lancaster you can tour farmers' markets (shoofly pie should be at the top of your take-home goody list) or replicas of Amish villages, or you can stop in at the oldest pretzel bakery in the country and twist your own pretzel. Shoppers will find antiques, crafts, and abundant outlet stores in the area, too. For dessert head west to Hershey, the only town in the world that has streetlights shaped like foil-wrapped Hershey Kisses. About 55 mi from Lancaster is Gettysburg, where the greatest artillery battle on this continent was fought in July 1863—and later immortalized through the words of Lincoln's Gettysburg Address.

PLEASURES AND PASTIMES

The Spirit of 1776

Many Americans think they know something about the birthplace of the nation: Benjamin Franklin, Thomas Jefferson's drafting of the Declaration of Independence, the sayings of Poor Richard, the signing of the Constitution. Still, these grade school facts and figures do little to prepare you for the actual Philadelphia experience. To walk through "America's most historic square mile"—Independence National Historical Park—is a tour that exercises not only the feet but the spirit. Who can fail to be moved by the words PROCLAIM LIBERTY THRO' ALL THE LAND," inscribed on America's best-loved relic, the Liberty Bell?

The story begins in 1753, when the Provincial Assembly, meeting at Independence Hall, notified the British Parliament of its refusal to "make laws by direction." The meeting of the Second Continental Congress in 1775 then lighted the fuse for the American Revolution. The spirit of 1776 found its fullest expression as Congress acted on Richard Henry Lee's famous Resolution for Independence. Today Independence National Historical Park continues to embody America's noblest ideals.

Oh, Dem Golden Slippers

Buttoned-up Philadelphia explodes in a tidal wave of sequins, feathers, riotous sound, and pageantry every New Year's Day: the Mummers Parade. For this day of sudden liberation, the City of Brotherly Love dons "dem Golden Slippers" and cakewalks up Broad Street in a parade that outglit-ters Las Vegas. This little shindig, initially brought from England, had its American beginnings early in the 19th century, when gaily costumed groups rang doorbells, seeking donations after reciting rhymes intended to explain their strange garb. Add in Philly's heritage of minstrel shows and vaudeville, and you wind up with today's 12 nonstop hours of song, dance, and costumed splendor. If you're not in town for this phenomenon, you can still catch its flavor at the Mummers Museum; the Mummers also stage a summer parade around July 4, during the city's Sunoco Welcome America Festival.

Philly Flavors

Philadelphia has finally managed to beat those cordon bleus. For decades gourmet groupies wrote the city off as a lackluster dining center. How things have changed! In 1994 Philly was named the best restaurant city in the nation, according to the *Condé Nast Traveler*'s readers' poll. The soufflé continued to rise with the opening of the Striped Bass in 1994, hailed by *Esquire* as Restaurant of the Year. And the béarnaise never curdles at Le Bec-Fin, which some epicureans cite as the greatest temple of French gastronomy in America. Today the city holds stellar Italian and Chinese restaurants as well as notable seafood and steak houses, not to mention a wide variety of ethnic eateries from Mexican to Vietnamese. Quintessential Philly dining spots include the City Tavern (called by John Adams "the most genteel tavern in America"), Reading Terminal Market, and Jim's Steaks.

The Emerald City

Envisioned by William Penn as a "greene countrie towne," Philadelphia is famous as a city with a green thumb. It counts its trees as avidly as a miser counts gold and now claims more than 2 million—maples, elms, oaks, beeches, and poplars—scattered among city squares, parks, streets, and innumerable backyards. The city's main "garden" is Fairmount Park, the largest municipal park in the world. For Philly at its flower-spangled best, check out some of the great Society Hill house gardens. Continuing evidence that Philly is "the city with the country heart" is the annual Philadelphia Flower Show—the largest indoor horticultural event in the world—

held every March at the Pennsylvania Convention Center. Around the area other gardens beckon, whether it's the Morris Arboretum, in the city's northwest corner; Bartram's Garden, America's oldest surviving botanical garden, in southwest Philly; manicured Longwood Gardens, in Kennett Square; or the springtime splendors of Winterthur, near Wilmington, Delaware.

Artistically Speaking

Artistically, Philadelphia has always been fertile aesthetic territory. From the innovative, probing realism of such 19th-century masters as Thomas Eakins and Robert Henri to famous collectors such as the McIlhennys and the Arensbergs—among the first Americans to collect works by Monet, Matisse, and Duchamp—Philadelphia has always played off the contrast between its traditionally staid origins and a lively interest in the new. Nowhere is this more evident than at the Barnes Foundation, with a collection of 175 Renoirs alone in its Merion mansion. Out in the Brandywine Valley, the Brandywine River Museum showcases the art of native son Andrew Wyeth and his famous family. Thanks to the Philadelphia Museum of Art, Philadelphia Art Alliance, the Painted Bride Art Center, the Institute of Contemporary Art, and the Pennsylvania Academy of the Fine Arts, the city's art scene remains as spirited as ever. The performing arts rival the fine arts, with the Avenue of the Arts development on Broad Street serving as a new focus for venues as diverse as the Academy of Music, the Wilma Theater, the Prince Music Theater, and the Philadelphia Arts Bank, among others.

Sportsmania

Philadelphia is one of only three cities on the East Coast with four major professional sports teams—the Phillies (baseball), the Eagles (football), the 76ers (basketball), and the Flyers (hockey)—teams that claim devoted fans. But there's another sport at which Philadelphians are expert: spectating. Forget about just passing the popcorn; be prepared to throw snowballs at Santa Claus! Visiting teams say they've never seen anything like the behavior of Philly's sports fans, whose hijinks make events at the First Union Center and Veterans Stadium shake, rattle, and roll.

GREAT ITINERARIES

You could easily spend two weeks exploring Philadelphia, but if you're here for just a short period, you need to plan carefully so you don't miss the must-see sights. These suggested itineraries will help you structure your visit efficiently. *See* the neighborhood exploring tours in Chapter 2 for more information about individual sights; you may have to revise your itinerary depending on the day of the week. For itineraries that cover Bucks County and Lancaster County, *see* Chapters 9 *and* 10.

If You Have 2 Days

Begin your first day with an exploration of the city's historic district. Sign up at the **Independence National Historical Park Visitor Center** for a walking tour hosted by a National Park Service guide; try a go-at-your-own-pace tour offered by Audio Walk and Tour; or take a walk on your own. For lunch, proceed to the **Reading Terminal Market,** where dozens of ethnic food stands await. (The market is closed Sunday.) After lunch walk about a mile east on Arch Street (or take a bus on Market Street) to Old City; **Christ Church,** the **Betsy Ross House,** and **Elfreth's Alley** are all in close proximity. The galleries and cafés in the area may tempt you to take a short break from your pursuit of history. In the late afternoon head back to Independence Hall for a **horse-drawn carriage ride.** Have dinner at one of the trendy restaurants in Old City; then catch the **Lights of Liberty** walking sound-and-light show (March–December, weather permitting).

Spend the morning of Day 2 exploring the **Philadelphia Museum of Art,** on Benjamin Franklin Parkway, followed by lunch in the museum's lovely dining room. Afterward, depending on your interests and the day of the week, you could head to Merion by bus or car to see the world-renowned collection of Impressionist paintings at the **Barnes Foundation** (open Friday–Sunday). You could also walk to **Eastern State Penitentiary Historic Site** for a hard-hat tour of a former prison or to the **Franklin Institute Science Museum.** While there, be sure to catch the current Omniverse Theater film. Another option is to stop at **DisneyQuest Philadelphia** (opening early in 2001), an indoor virtual-reality amusement park for children and wannabe children. At night, visit a waterfront club or restaurant or pick a place with your favorite kind of food.

If You Have 4 Days

Follow the two-day itinerary described above, with one exception: Instead of having lunch at the Reading Terminal Market on Day 1, dine at the restored **City Tavern** in the historic district, where the costumed waitstaff serves food of the Colonial period (make reservations in advance). If time is limited, grab a sandwich at the **Bourse** before heading to the **Old City** sights. Start Day 3 in Center City with a ride to the top of **City Hall** for a pigeon's-eye view of the city. Next, head across the street to the **Masonic Temple** for a surreal tour through time—and architectural history—led by a Mason. Art lovers may prefer a visit to the **Pennsylvania Academy of the Fine Arts,** two blocks north of City Hall at Broad and Cherry streets. Eat lunch at the **Reading Terminal Market,** where you can sample the real Philadelphia "cuisine"—cheesesteaks, soft pretzels, and Bassett's ice cream—or something else from the dozens of food stalls.

If you're a fan of Disney productions, now may be the time to spend the afternoon at **DisneyQuest Philadelphia,** an indoor amusement park. If you prefer the great outdoors, visit **Penn's Landing,** where you can check out the **Independence Seaport Museum** and/or take the ferry across the river to the **New Jersey State Aquarium and Camden Children's Garden.** At sunset have a drink on the deck of the *Moshulu,* which is docked on the Delaware River.

On Day 4 leave the city behind for a day trip by car to the Brandywine Valley. Your first stop will be the **Brandywine River Museum,** in Chadds Ford, which showcases the art of Andrew Wyeth and his family, as well as works by other area painters and illustrators. Next, head south to **Winterthur** and feast your eyes on Henry Francis du Pont's extraordinary collection of American decorative art in an equally extraordinary mansion. Spend the balance of your day strolling through **Longwood Gardens,** in Kennett Square, which is in bloom even in winter. If it's a Tuesday,

Thursday, or Saturday in summer, stay for dinner and the fountain light show.

If You Have 6 Days

Follow the first three days of the four-day itinerary outlined above. Begin Day 4 by exploring either **Society Hill** or the **Rittenhouse Square** area. Then take a bus west on Walnut Street to the **University Museum of Archaeology and Anthropology,** in University City. You can have lunch at the museum or on campus. In the afternoon return to Center City to the **Philadelphia Visitors Center,** at 16th Street and John F. Kennedy Boulevard, to pick up the Philadelphia Trolley Works' narrated tour of **Fairmount Park;** or if you have children along, visit the **Philadelphia Zoo.** Afterward, drive or catch the SEPTA R6 train to **Manayunk,** where you can have dinner in one of the restaurants lining Main Street; many stores here are open late, too.

On Day 5 head out of the city by car to **Valley Forge National Historical Park,** where you can hike or picnic after you've taken the self-guided auto tour of General Washington's winter encampment. If you like to shop, spend the afternoon at **The Plaza & The Court,** in nearby King of Prussia. Or drive back toward the city to take in the **Barnes Foundation,** the **Eastern State Penitentiary,** or the **Franklin Institute**—whichever ones you didn't see on Day 2.

Another option for Day 5 is to stay in the city and explore **Southwark** and **South Philadelphia.** Follow up a visit to the **Mummers Museum** with a strut along 9th Street, site of the outdoor **Italian Market.** You can pick up the makings for a great picnic or duck into one of the restaurants here for lunch. In the afternoon visit the museums you missed on Day 2. Check the local papers for an evening activity—perhaps a sporting event at the South Philadelphia stadiums, a show in Center City, or live music at a jazz club.

For Day 6, head to the **Brandywine Valley,** described in Day 4 of the four-day itinerary above.

FODOR'S CHOICE

No two people will agree on what makes a perfect vacation, but it's fun and helpful to know what others think. We hope you'll have a chance to experience some of Fodor's Choices yourself while visiting Philadelphia and the Pennsylvania Dutch Country. For detailed information about each, refer to the appropriate chapters.

Quintessential Philadelphia

⭐ **A walk across the Benjamin Franklin Bridge.** From dawn to dusk you can jog, walk, or bicycle the 1¾-mi span. The metal walkway 150 ft over the Delaware River gives you a terrific view of the waterfront.

⭐ **Boathouse Row illuminated at night.** Every night the dozen or so houses lining the Schuylkill River just beyond the Philadelphia Museum of Art are outlined by hundreds of tiny white lights. There's a magical feel to the way they shimmer and reflect in the river. Views are best from the West River Drive.

⭐ **The city's 10-day Fourth of July celebration.** Philadelphia throws itself a spectacular birthday party each year—the Sunoco Welcome America Festival—with several nights of fireworks, an illuminated boat parade, outdoor concerts with superstar talent, and the awarding of the Philadelphia Liberty Medal to world leaders.

⭐ **A walking tour of Independence National Historical Park.** Even if you're not a history buff, you'll probably experience a few quivers. Start at the Visitor Center and follow the redbrick road past a dozen stirring sites, including Independence Hall and the Liberty Bell.

⭐ **A run up the steps of the Philadelphia Museum of Art, followed by a visit.** If you saw Sylvester Stallone do it in the *Rocky* movies, you *will* have the urge to run up the steps. Go ahead, indulge! Then, unlike Rocky, *go inside* and discover one of the world's great collections of art.

⭐ **Lunch on a park bench in Rittenhouse Square.** With majestic elms, Victorian statues, and playing children, Philadelphia's toniest downtown park seems to have sprung from the brush of Mary Cassatt.

⭐ **An afternoon at the Barnes Foundation.** In this Merion mansion is one of the world's finest collections of Impressionist and post-Impressionist art, eccentrically hung floor to ceiling between household tools, antique door latches, and folk art. Sixty-five works by Matisse,

66 by Cézanne, and 175 by Renoir are just part of the bounty.

After Hours

⭐ **Delaware River waterfront.** You can club-hop by river taxi to more than a dozen nightspots along the water near the Ben Franklin Bridge.

⭐ **First Fridays.** On the first Friday of each month from 5 to 9, the chic galleries of Old City open their doors to browsers and buyers alike with receptions and exhibit openings. The area is great for dining and strolling, too.

⭐ **Lights of Liberty.** When the sun goes down, the streets around Independence Hall become the stage set for a dazzling walking sound-and-light show (March through December). The high-tech extravaganza brings to life the history of our nation in its early years.

⭐ **Manayunk.** This old mill neighborhood has been transformed into a mecca for upscale diners and shoppers who want to see and be seen on trendy Main Street.

⭐ **A Philadelphia Orchestra concert at the Academy of Music.** Even if you didn't plan ahead, you can often get last-minute tickets for performances in the nosebleed section, four stories above the pit. (There are afternoon concerts, too.)

⭐ **South Street.** From fine restaurants to tattoo parlors, from art galleries to condom boutiques, South Street—from Front to 7th streets—is, as the song says, "the hippest place in town."

⭐ **Zanzibar Blue.** The hottest *and* the coolest jazz room in town, with the best local and national talent.

Comforts

⭐ **Four Seasons.** Philly's swankiest hotel has the best restaurants, service, and—if you get a room overlooking the fountains in Logan Circle—the most romantic views. *$$$$*

⭐ **The Rittenhouse.** You'll be pampered at this elegant small hotel that makes the best of its setting on tony Rittenhouse Square. *$$$$*

⭐ **St. Regis Philadelphia.** The St. Regis has brought its own impressive standards of luxury to the space that was formerly occupied by the Ritz-Carlton. *$$$$*

★ **Penn's View Inn.** Urban charm and a fine Italian restaurant distinguish this Old City inn. $$–$$$

★ **Rittenhouse Bed and Breakfast.** A Rittenhouse Square location and plenty of amenities make this very comfortable B & B an excellent value. $–$$

Flavors

★ **Fountain Restaurant.** One of the city's top tables keeps drawing locals and visitors because of its elegant setting in the Four Seasons hotel and outstanding contemporary fare such as sautéed venison in homemade pasta. $$$$

★ **Le Bec-Fin.** *Formidable!* The most prestigious restaurant in town, the Bec is internationally renowned for its impeccable service, elegant decor, and the soufflés of owner-chef Georges Perrier. You can also check out the exuberant, less pricey ($$–$$$) Brasserie Perrier up the street. $$$$

★ **Jake's.** Fine contemporary crafts decorate a stellar eatery in Manayunk; try the scallops if you want to taste perfection. $$$–$$$$

★ **Striped Bass Restaurant and Bar.** At this chic see-and-be-seen spot, the food (all seafood) is delicious, and so is the stunning setting in a former brokerage house. Striped Bass continues to serve up surprises. $$$–$$$$

★ **Overtures.** This stylish, creative restaurant serves up good-value French-inspired fare. The lavender-scented rack of lamb is always a winner. $$–$$$

Brandywine Valley

★ **Longwood Gardens.** The number-one attraction in the Brandywine Valley has more than 1,000 acres of flowers, trees, color, and beauty, 365 days a year.

★ **Brandywine River Museum.** A converted 19th-century gristmill on the banks of the Brandywine is the showcase for the art of three generations of the Wyeth family.

★ **Winterthur Museum and Gardens.** The most glamorous attic in the world, Henry Francis du Pont's nine-story mansion is filled with an unrivaled collection of American decorative arts from 1640–1860. The gardens are particularly lovely in spring.

Bucks County

★ **Fonthill.** The astonishing storybook castle-home of Henry Chapman Mercer in Doylestown has an air of magic and fantasy. The walls and ceilings are lined with Arts and Crafts–style tiles from Mercer's Moravian Pottery and Tile Works.

★ **Tubing on the Delaware.** For a summer delight travel down the Delaware River in an inner tube or a canoe rented from Bucks County River Country Canoe and Tube.

★ **Exploring along River Road.** Drive north out of New Hope (Route 32) along the Delaware River towpath, past old stone farmhouses, 18th-century mills, and lush rolling hills.

Lancaster County

★ **Visit a farmers' market.** For the best "sweets and sours" and chowchow, head for the Central Market in downtown Lancaster or the Green Dragon Farmers Market and Auction, in Ephrata.

★ **Exploring Amish Country.** To see the Amish farms and roadside stands, drive along the back-country roads between Routes 23 and 340 or take a leisurely ride to Paradise aboard the old-fashioned steam train of the Strasburg Railroad.

★ **Eat family style.** Try one of the all-you-can-eat restaurants like Good 'N Plenty or Plain & Fancy Farm. There's no menu—they'll bring you all the Pennsylvania Dutch food you can eat.

FESTIVALS AND SEASONAL EVENTS

For exact dates and other information about the following events, contact the **Philadelphia Visitors Center** (☞ Visitor Information *in* Smart Travel Tips A to Z).

WINTER

➤ SECOND FRI. EVENING IN DEC.: During **Elfreth's Alley Christmas Open House** (⊠ Elfreth's Alley, between Front, 2nd, Arch, and Race Sts., ☎ 215/574–0560), the community opens its early 18th century homes to the public for tours.

➤ DEC.: **Christmas House Tours** (☎ 215/235–7469) take you around the Colonial and Federal mansions in Fairmount Park, which are decorated for Christmas.

➤ DEC.: *The Nutcracker* (⊠ Academy of Music, Broad and Locust Sts., ☎ 215/893–1999), the Pennsylvania Ballet's production of the Tchaikovsky classic, is a Philadelphia Yuletide tradition.

➤ DEC. 25: **Washington Crossing the Delaware** (⊠ Washington Crossing Historic Park, Washington Crossing, ☎ 215/493–4076) is reenacted with four 40-ft replicas of Durham boats. On Christmas Day 1776, George Washington and his troops took the Hessian camp at Trenton by surprise.

➤ DEC. 27–JAN. 1: **Neighbors in the New Year** (⊠

Penn's Landing, ☎ 215/636–1666) is six days of entertaining events, including a Mummers Fest at the Pennsylvania Convention Center. The culmination is a New Year's Eve celebration with fireworks over the Delaware River.

➤ JAN. 1: The **Mummers Parade** (☎ 215/636–1666) is an all-day event during which some 30,000 sequined and feathered paraders—members of string bands, "fancies," comics, and fancy brigades—march north on Broad Street to City Hall. The Fancy Brigade Finale is a ticket-only event at the Pennsylvania Convention Center.

➤ FEB.: **Black History Month** is celebrated with exhibits, lectures, and music at the Afro-American Historical and Cultural Museum (⊠ 701 Arch St., ☎ 215/574–0380), plus related events around the city.

➤ EARLY–MID-FEB.: **PECO Energy Jazz Festival** ☎ (215/636–1666) is a jazz-packed weekend of more than 90 events around the city: concerts, club tours, jazz brunches, dance parties, and more. Many events are free.

SPRING

➤ FEB.–MAY: **Chinese New Year** (⊠ Chinese Cultural Center, 125 N. 10th St., ☎ 215/923–6767) celebrations include 10-course banquets from

Tuesday through Sunday nights beginning at 6:30.

➤ LATE FEB.–EARLY MARCH: The **Philadelphia Flower Show** (⊠ Pennsylvania Convention Center, 12th and Arch Sts., ☎ 215/988–8800), the nation's largest and most prestigious indoor flower show, has acres of exhibits and themed displays. Other events are part of Flower Show Week.

➤ MAR.: The **St. Patrick's Day Parade** (☎ 215/636–1666) brings the wearing of the green to Benjamin Franklin Parkway.

➤ MAR.: The **Food Network's The Book and the Cook** (☎ 215/636–1666) teams the city's best chefs and the world's top cookbook authors in a week-long event held in 60 restaurants. Festivities include wine tastings, market tours, and food sampling. It kicks off with the Book and the Cook Fair, at the Pennsylvania Convention Center.

➤ APR.: The **Philadelphia Antiques Show** (⊠ 103rd Engineers Armory, 33rd St. above Market St., ☎ 215/387–3500) showcases museum-quality antiques, lectures, and appraisals.

➤ LATE APR.: **Penn Relays** (⊠ Franklin Field, 33rd and Spruce Sts., ☎ 215/898–6154) is one of the world's oldest and largest amateur track meets.

➤ LATE APR.: **Valborgsmässoafton** (⊠ American-Swedish Historical Museum, 1900 Pattison Ave., ☎ 215/389–1776), the traditional Swedish welcome to spring, has food, song, dance, and bonfires.

➤ LATE APR. OR MAY: **Springtime in the Park** (☎ 215/235–7469) combines the elegance of 18th-century furniture with the beauty and color of spring floral designs when florists decorate seven Fairmount Park houses.

➤ LATE APR.–MAY: **Philadelphia Open House** (☎ 215/928–1188) is a three-week period when selected private homes, gardens, and historic buildings in neighborhoods around the city open their doors to the public.

➤ LATE APR.–MAY: **Pride-Fest Philadelphia** (215/732–3378) is the nation's most comprehensive gay and lesbian symposium and festival, with a street festival and symposiums and parties at locations around the city.

➤ EARLY MAY: International House's **Philadelphia Festival of World Cinema** (☎ 800/969–7392) presents more than 100 features, documentaries, and short films from more than 30 countries at venues throughout the city during the first two weeks of May.

➤ MAY: The Pennsylvania Academy of the Fine Arts annual **Student Art Exhibition** (⊠ Broad and Cherry Sts., ☎ 215/972–7600) presents the work of this talented student body for viewing and purchase.

➤ MOTHER'S DAY WEEKEND: The **Dad Vail Regatta** (☎ 215/248–2600) is the largest collegiate rowing event in the country. Up to 500 shells from more than 100 colleges race on a 2,000-meter course on the Schuylkill River in Fairmount Park.

➤ THIRD WEEK IN MAY: For more than 80 years, the **Rittenhouse Square Flower Market** (⊠ 18th and Walnut Sts., ☎ 215/271–7149) has held this two-day sale of plants, flowers, and food, including the traditional candy lemon stick.

➤ MEMORIAL DAY WEEKEND: **First Union Jam on the River** (⊠ Penn's Landing, ☎ 215/636–1666) is Philadelphia's kickoff to summer, showcasing the best of the bayou with a weekend of music, food, and crafts from New Orleans, in a family-oriented event.

➤ MEMORIAL DAY–SEPT.: At the **Head House Crafts Fair** (⊠ 2nd and Pine Sts., ☎ 215/790–0782), more than 30 artisans exhibit jewelry, stained glass, leather, and quilts on summer weekends, noon–11 Saturday and noon–6 Sunday.

➤ LATE MAY–EARLY JUNE: The **Devon Horse Show and Country Fair** (⊠ Devon Fairgrounds, U.S. 30, Devon, ☎ 610/964–0550), first held in 1896, is a nine-day event in which top riders compete for more than $200,000 in prize money.

SUMMER

➤ LATE MAY–AUG.: Longwood Gardens's **Summer Festival of Fountains** (⊠ U.S. 1, Kennett Square, ☎ 610/388–1000) includes fountain displays during the day and fountain light shows set to music several nights a week.

➤ EARLY JUNE: The **Rittenhouse Square Fine Arts Annual** (⊠ Rittenhouse Sq., 18th and Walnut Sts., ☎ 877/689–4112), America's oldest (1931) and largest outdoor juried art show, exhibits works by more than 100 Delaware Valley artists.

➤ FIRST WEEKEND IN JUNE: **Elfreth's Alley Fete Days** (⊠ Elfreth's Alley, between Front, 2nd, Arch, and Race Sts., ☎ 215/574–0560) is the time for open houses on America's oldest continuously occupied street, along with food and fife-and-drum music.

➤ EARLY JUNE: The **First Union U.S. Pro Cycling Championship** (☎ 877/573–7437), the country's premier bicycle race, attracts the world's top cyclists to its 156-mi course, including the grueling Manayunk Wall. A two-week celebration leads up to the event.

➤ MID-JUNE: The **Mellon Jazz Festival** (☎ 610/667–3559) presents music from local talent to the top names in jazz in a weeklong series of concerts (many free) at locations around town.

➤ LAST WEEKEND IN JUNE: The **Manayunk Annual Arts Fest** (⊠ Main St., ☎ 215/790–0782) lines this neighborhood's main drag with more than 200 artists from all over the country displaying arts and crafts.

➤ JUNE–JULY: The **Philadelphia Orchestra's Summer Season** (⊠ Mann Center for the Performing Arts, 52nd St. and Parkside Ave., ☎ 215/893–1999) showcases noted guest conductors and soloists in six weeks of outdoor concerts.

➤ LATE JUNE–JULY 4: Philadelphia's premier event, the **Sunoco Welcome America Festival** (☎ 215/636–1666 or 800/770–5883) celebrates America's birthday in America's birthplace. Highlights of the more than 50 free happenings are three big-name outdoor concerts; two are at Penn's Landing (one followed by fireworks, the other by a lighted boat parade on the Delaware). The third, the July 4th finale, concludes with fireworks and music in front of the Philadelphia Museum of Art. Among the other events are a patriotic parade on the Parkway, the awarding of the Philadelphia Liberty Medal, a Family Festival, a Summer Mummers Parade, and a costumed reenactment at Ft. Mifflin.

➤ SUNDAY BEFORE JULY 14: The Eastern State Penitentiary (✉ 22nd St. and Fairmount Ave., ☎ 215/236–3300) reenacts the storming of the Bastille at a **Bastille Day Celebration,** which includes an appearance by Marie Antoinette.

➤ AUG.–MID-OCT.: In Lancaster County, the **Pennsylvania Renaissance Faire** (✉ Mount Hope Estate and Winery, Manheim, ☎ 717/665–7021) is a re-creation of Elizabethan England, with 11 stages and a jousting area. There are magicians, storytellers, and performers; craftspeople demonstrating ancient arts; and food of the period. It's open Saturday–Monday until Labor Day, and weekends only after that.

➤ WEEKEND BEFORE LABOR DAY: The **Philadelphia Folk Festival** (✉ Old Pool Farm, Schwenksville, ☎ 215/242–0150 or 800/556–3655), America's oldest (1962) continuous folk festival, lasts three days. Performers range from the relatively new to folk superstars. There's also food, folk dancing, and sing-alongs.

➤ LABOR DAY WEEKEND: **YO! Philadelphia** (✉ Penn's Landing, ☎ 215/636–1666) celebrates Philly style with games, children's activities, ethnic foods, and live music—oldies and contemporary—that originated in the city.

➤ LABOR DAY WEEKEND: The big **Long's Park Art & Craft Festival** (☎ 717/295–7054) in Lancaster offers three days of contemporary fine art and crafts, a food fair, and children's activities.

AUTUMN

➤ SEPT.: The **Philadelphia Distance Run** (☎ 610/293–0786) is the country's premier half-marathon, with more than 7,000 runners completing a 13-mi course through downtown and along the Schuylkill River.

➤ MID-SEPT.: The **Philadelphia Fringe Festival** (☎ 215/413–1318) presents 11 days of avant-garde performances—dance, music, theater, poetry, puppetry, and performance art—at various sites in Old City.

➤ LATE SEPT.: The **Von Steuben Day Parade** (☎ 215/636–1666), along Benjamin Franklin Parkway, honors the Prussian general who trained the Continental soldiers at Valley Forge.

➤ EARLY OCT.: The **Avenue of the Arts Festival** (☎ 215/731–9668) spotlights the city's music and dance groups with performances on outdoor stages on South Broad Street.

➤ OCT.: The **Pulaski Day Parade** (☎ 215/636–1666) marches up Broad Street; the Polish-American Congress honors this Polish general, a hero of the Revolutionary War.

➤ SECOND MON. IN OCT.: The **Columbus Day Parade** (☎ 215/636–1666) includes both a parade on South Broad Street and a festival at Marconi Plaza.

➤ OCT.: **Candlelight Tours of the Edgar Allan Poe National Historic Site** (✉ 532 N. 7th St., ☎ 215/597–8780) celebrate Halloween and Poe with "ghostly" weekend walks through the house.

➤ EARLY NOV.: The **Philadelphia Museum of Art Craft Show** (✉ Pennsylvania Convention Center, 12th and Arch Sts., ☎ 215/684–7930) is four days of exhibits by 100 top national craftspeople.

➤ LATE NOV.: The **Thanksgiving Day Parade** (✉ Benjamin Franklin Pkwy., ☎ 215/636–1666) has thousands of marchers, floats, and local personalities.

➤ NOV. OR DEC.: The **Dog Show** (✉ Pennsylvania Convention Center, 12th and Arch Sts., ☎ 215/947–1677), sponsored by the Kennel Club of Philadelphia, includes 2,500 entries.

2 EXPLORING PHILADELPHIA

As the city that gave us the Declaration of Independence and the Twist, William Penn's principles of peace and purity and the soft pretzel, Philadelphia can be both significant and lighthearted. It delivers all the art and cultural treasures you'd expect from the nation's fifth-largest city (and more), plus more chapters of American history than you'll find anywhere else—packaged in an appealingly quirky town with a friendly feel.

By Joyce
Eisenberg

O N THE WHOLE I'D RATHER BE IN PHILADELPHIA."

W. C. Fields may have been joking when he wrote his epitaph, but if he were here today, he would eat his words. They no longer roll up the sidewalks at night in Philadelphia. A construction boom, a restaurant renaissance, and cultural revival have helped transform the city. For the past decade there has been a new optimistic mood, aggressive civic leadership, and national recognition of what the locals have long known: Philadelphia can be a very pleasant place to live—a city with an impressive past and a fascinating future. For many observers, Philadelphia really *is* the only civilized big city in America.

FROM BENJAMIN FRANKLIN TO GRACE KELLY

Philadelphia is a place of contrasts: Grace Kelly and Rocky Balboa; Le Bec-Fin—perhaps the nation's finest French haute cuisine restaurant—and the fast-food heaven of Jim's Steaks; Independence Hall and the Mario Lanza Museum; 18th-century national icons with 21st-century-style skyscrapers soaring above them. The world-renowned Philadelphia Orchestra performs at the Academy of Music, a dignified, opulent opera house on Broad Street. Along the same street 25,000 Mummers dressed in outrageous sequins and feathers pluck their banjos and strut their stuff to the strains of "Oh, Dem Golden Slippers" on New Year's Day. City residents include descendants of the staid Quaker founding fathers, the self-possessed socialites of the Main Line (remember Katharine Hepburn and Cary Grant in *The Philadelphia Story*?), and the unrestrained sports fans, who are as vocal as they are loyal. Together all these people make for a wonderful mix.

Historically speaking, Philadelphia is a city of superlatives: the world's largest municipal park; the best collection of public art in the United States; the widest variety of urban architecture in America; and according to some experts, the greatest concentration of institutions of higher learning in the country.

A CITY OF NEIGHBORHOODS

In addition, Philadelphia is known as a city of neighborhoods (109 by one count). Shoppers haggle over the price of tomatoes in South Philly's Italian Market; families picnic in the parks of Germantown; street vendors hawk soft pretzels in Logan; and all over town kids play street games such as stickball, stoopball, wireball, and chink. It's a city of neighborhood loyalty: Ask a native where he's from and he'll tell you: Fairmount, Fishtown, or Frankford, rather than Philadelphia. The city's population is less transient than that of other large cities; people who are born here generally remain, and many who leave home to study or work eventually return. Although the population is 1.6 million, residents are intricately connected; on any given day, a Philadelphian is likely to encounter someone with whom he grew up. The "it's-a-small-world" syndrome makes people feel like they belong.

THE PHILADELPHIA STORY

William Penn founded the city in 1682 and chose to name it Philadelphia—Greek for "brotherly love"—after an ancient Syrian city, site of one of the earliest and most venerated Christian churches. Penn's Quakers settled on a tract of land he described as his "greene countrie towne." After the Quakers, the next wave of immigrants to arrive were Anglicans and Presbyterians (who had a running conflict with the "stiff Quakers" and their distaste for music and dancing). The new residents forged traditions that remain strong in parts of Philadelphia today: united families, comfortable houses, handsome furniture, and good education. From these early years came the attitude Mark Twain summed up as: "In Boston, they ask: 'What does he know?' In New York, 'How much does he make?' In Philadelphia, 'Who were his parents?' "

The city became the queen of the English-speaking New World from the late 1600s to the early 1800s. In the latter half of the 1700s Philadelphia was the largest city in the Colonies, a great and glorious place. So, when the delegates from the Colonies wanted to meet in a centrally located, thriving city, they chose Philadelphia. They convened the First Continental Congress in 1774 at Carpenters' Hall. The rest, as they say, is history. It is here that the Declaration of Independence was written and adopted, the Constitution was framed, the capital of the United States was established, the Liberty Bell was rung, the nation's flag was sewn by Betsy Ross (though scholars debate this), and George Washington served most of his presidency.

GETTING YOUR BEARINGS

Today you will find Philadelphia's compact 2-square-mi downtown (William Penn's original city) nestled between the Delaware and the Schuylkill (pronounced *skoo*-kull) rivers. Thanks to Penn's grid system of streets—laid out in 1681—the downtown area is a breeze to navigate. The traditional heart of the city is Broad and Market streets (Penn's Center Square), where City Hall now stands. Market Street divides the city north and south; 130 South 15th Street, for example, is in the second block south of Market Street. North–south streets are numbered, starting with Front (1st) Street, at the Delaware River, and increasing to the west. Broad Street is the equivalent of 14th Street. The diagonal Benjamin Franklin Parkway breaks the rigid grid pattern by leading from City Hall out of Center City into Fairmount Park, which straddles the Schuylkill River and the Wissahickon Creek for 10 mi.

Although Philadelphia is the fifth-largest city in the nation (1.6 million people live in the city, 5.78 million in the metropolitan area), it maintains a small-town feel. It's a cosmopolitan, exciting, but not overwhelming city, a town that's easy to explore on foot yet big enough to keep surprising even those most familiar with it. If you plan to visit the city's major museums, check out CityPass (☞ Discounts & Deals *in* Smart Travel Tips A to Z), a discount pass that admits you to six museums for one price.

AROUND INDEPENDENCE HALL

The Most Historic Square Mile in America

Any visit to Philadelphia, whether you have one day or several, should begin in the city area that comprises Independence National Historical Park. Philadelphia was the birthplace of the United States, the home of the country's first government, and nowhere is the spirit of those miraculous early days—the boldness of conceiving a brand-new nation—more palpable than along the cobbled streets of the city's most historic district.

In the late 1940s, before civic-minded citizens banded together to save the area and before the National Park Service stepped in, the Independence Hall neighborhood was crowded with factories and run-down warehouses. Then the city, state, and federal government took interest. Some buildings were restored, and others were reconstructed on their original sites; several attractions were built for the 1976 Bicentennial celebration. Today the park covers 42 acres and holds close to 40 buildings. Urban renewal in Independence Mall plaza and in Washington Square East (Society Hill) have ensured that Independence Hall will never again keep unsightly company. The city's most historic area is now also one of its loveliest.

The best time to visit Independence National Historic Park is on America's birthday; expect crowds, though. Here, in America's birthplace, the city throws a 10-day party with parades (including the Mummers and an illuminated boat procession), outdoor concerts, elaborate fireworks, and the awarding of the prestigious Philadelphia Liberty Medal to a world leader. If you visit anytime during the summer, there are plays, musicals, parades, and more; town criers dressed in 18th-century garb perform short vignettes about life in Colonial America. The town criers dispense maps and schedules of their performances. For information on the entertainment schedule, call **Historic Philadelphia, Inc.** (☎ 800/764–4786).

The Independence National Historical Park Visitor Center, Independence Hall, and the Liberty Bell Pavilion are open daily year-round from 9 to 5. Other park buildings are also open daily, although their hours may vary from season to season, depending on park staffing and the number of visitors. The 24-hour hot line at the park visitor center (☞ *below*) will give you current hours plus a schedule of park programs. Except as noted, all attractions run by Independence National Historical Park are free.

You can easily explore the park on your own; in each building a knowledgeable park ranger can answer all your questions. On spring weekends and in summer, the rangers lead a variety of walking tours; some are specifically for families. In winter, if there's adequate staffing, the rangers give entertaining talks in various buildings. Inquire about these in the morning at the information desk of the visitor center.

If you are planning a trip in late 2000 or in 2001, take note: A number of construction projects are transforming Independence Mall. These include a new pavilion for the Liberty Bell, just 200 yards away from the old site. This change of scene will allow you to view the bell with Independence Hall in the background and to linger longer by the bell without being shooed on by rangers who are ready to address the next group. The new Gateway Visitor Center, on 6th Street between Market and Arch streets, will replace the current facility at 3rd and Chestnut streets. Both projects are scheduled for completion in late 2000 to early 2001. Groundbreaking for a new museum, the National Constitution Center, at 6th and Arch streets, is set for September 2000. The historic district also has a futuristic new neighbor, DisneyQuest (set to open early in 2001), just one block from where the Declaration of Independence was drafted. If you've got children in tow, you'll want to spend the good part of a day there.

Numbers in the text correspond to numbers in the margin and on the Historic Area and Penn's Landing map.

A Good Walk

This walk back in time will immerse you in Colonial history. The best place to orient yourself is at the **Independence National Historical Park Visitor Center** ① on 3rd and Chestnut streets. Directly across 3rd Street is the **First Bank of the United States** ②, a handsome example of Federal architecture. A redbrick path alongside manicured lawns and ancient oaks and maples leads to the first group of historic buildings, Carpenters' Court; **Carpenters' Hall** ③, with its displays of 18th-century tools, is on your left. On your right is **Pemberton House,** now a bookstore and gift shop. Behind the bookstore is the **New Hall Military Museum** ④; it contains a variety of weapons and uniforms. Leave Carpenters' Court and continue west on the redbrick path across 4th

20

The Historic Area and Penn's Landing

0   220 yards
0   200 meters

N

KEY

- - - - Market-Frankford
Subway

Arch St.

Gateway Visitor Center
(to Open by early 2001) Commerce St.

Market-Frankford Subway

TO DISNEYQUEST
←

Market St.

7th St.

6th St.

5th St.

4th St.

Ranstead St.

Chestnut St.

Sansom St.

*Independence
Square*

Walnut St.

*Washington
Square*

Locust St.

SOCIETY HILL

St. Joseph's Way

Marshalls Ct.

Spruce St.

7th St.

Cypress St.

6th St.

5th St.

Lawrence Ct.

Cypress St.

4th St.

Panama St.

Pine St.

Willings

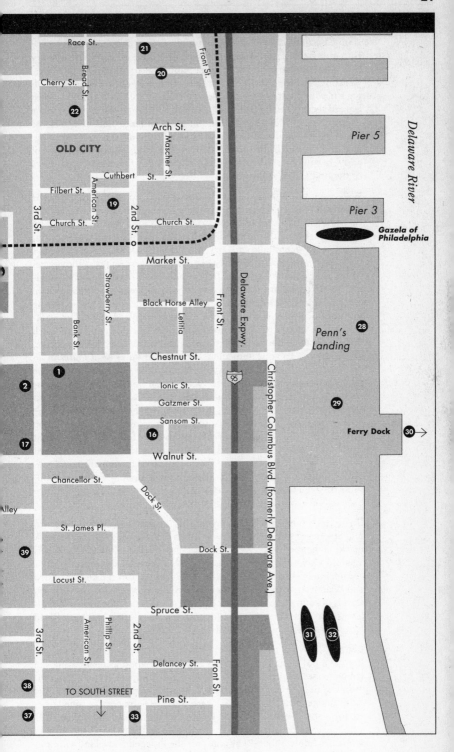

Race St.

Bread St.

Cherry St.

Front St.

OLD CITY

Arch St.

Mascher St.

Cuthbert

Filbert St.

American St.

Church St.

3rd St.

2nd St.

St.

Church St.

Market St.

Strawberry St.

Black Horse Alley

Front St.

Bank St.

Letitia

Chestnut St.

Delaware Expwy.

Penn's Landing

Pier 5

Delaware River

Pier 3

Gazela of Philadelphia

Ionic St.

Gatzmer St.

Sansom St.

95

Christopher Columbus Blvd. (formerly Delaware Ave.)

Ferry Dock

Walnut St.

Chancellor St.

Dock St.

St. James Pl.

Alley

Dock St.

Locust St.

Spruce St.

3rd St.

American St.

Phillip St.

2nd St.

Delancey St.

Front St.

TO SOUTH STREET

Pine St.

Street to the Parthenon look-alike, the **Second Bank of the United States** ⑤, with its portrait gallery of Colonial Americans. Its entrance is on Chestnut Street. As you continue west on that path, which now runs along cobblestone Library Street, you'll see on your right **Library Hall** ⑥, a reconstruction of the first public library in the United States. Crossing 5th Street, you arrive at **Independence Square;** the first building on your right is **Philosophical Hall,** home of the country's oldest learned society. Just behind it is **Old City Hall** ⑦, home of the U.S. Supreme Court from 1791 to 1800. Tours of **Independence Hall** ⑧, where the Declaration of Independence was signed, begin in the courtyard alongside Old City Hall. Just past Independence Hall, on the corner of 6th and Chestnut streets is **Congress Hall** ⑨, with the restored chambers of the first U.S. Congress.

Walk back through the square to 6th and Walnut streets to the **Curtis Center** ⑩; peek into the lobby to see the spectacular glass mosaic mural by Maxfield Parrish and Louis Comfort Tiffany. Then head north on 6th Street (here dubbed Independence Mall West). Just past Chestnut Street, walk diagonally into the mall. One block up is Philadelphia's best-known symbol, the **Liberty Bell** ⑪. Head west on the walkway between Market and Chestnut streets under the Rohm and Haas Building. You'll pass the sculpture-fountain *Milkweed Pod.* Installed in 1959, it was one of the first examples of Philadelphia's law requiring public buildings to spend 1% of construction costs for art. The walkway will lead you to 7th Street. Directly in front of you is the **Balch Institute for Ethnic Studies** ⑫, with its library and exhibits on immigration and ethnicity. To your immediate left is the **Atwater Kent Museum** ⑬, which chronicles the city's history. Next to the Balch Institute is the reconstructed **Declaration House** ⑭, where Thomas Jefferson wrote his rough draft of the Declaration of Independence. One block west, but light-years away in ambience, is the new **DisneyQuest** indoor theme park. If you have time to see just one other site (and particularly if you have children in tow), make it **Franklin Court** ⑮. To get there, turn right (east) on Market to Number 316. After seeing the Colonial-era print shop and post office, head into the courtyard to the underground museum that celebrates the achievements of Benjamin Franklin. Continue through the courtyard to Chestnut, turn left (east), and you'll be back at the visitor center.

If you have more time and energy, continue east on Chestnut Street to 2nd Street and turn right. Halfway down the block is **Welcome Park** ⑯, marking the spot where William Penn once lived. Follow Walnut Street a half block west to see the **Philadelphia Merchant's Exchange,** the city's commercial center for part of the 19th century. On the corner of 3rd and Walnut streets is the lavishly furnished **Bishop White House** ⑰, which stands in contrast to the simply furnished **Todd House** ⑱, home of Dolley Madison, at the corner of 4th and Walnut streets. Alongside Todd House is a lovingly maintained 18th-century garden.

TIMING

If you've put on your walking shoes and are good at negotiating the cobblestones, you can wander through this compact area in about 90 minutes. But the city's atmospheric historic district warrants a slower pace. Budget a full day here. An early start lets you reserve timed tickets for a tour of the Todd and Bishop White houses and adjust your schedule to catch some of the special events on the visitor center's daily schedule. Allow about 40 minutes for the Independence Hall tour and another hour each at Franklin Court and the Todd and Bishop White houses. Allow 30 minutes each at Declaration House and the visitor center, where it's a good idea to see the film *Independence* before you set out. From March through December, you might want to dine in the area and then catch the new Lights of Liberty (☞ *below*) walking sound-and-light show. In summer, when Independence Hall is open until 8, you could visit it last and then head for the show. Another option, if you're a Disney devotee, is to immerse yourself in history in the morning and DisneyQuest in the afternoon, although this is a lot to cram into one day.

Sights to See

⑬ **Atwater Kent Museum.** Philadelphia's official history museum, the Atwater Kent is dedicated to telling the Philadelphia story from the city's founding more than 300 years ago until today. Started in 1938 by Atwater Kent, a wealthy inventor, radio magnate, and manufacturer, the museum houses over 100,000 objects—everything from textiles to toys—that illustrate what everyday life was like for generations of Philadelphians. It occupies an elegant 1826 Greek Revival building designed by John Haviland, who was also the architect of the Eastern State Penitentiary (☞ The Benjamin Franklin Parkway, *below*). The museum recently acquired a sizable collection of works by Norman Rockwell, the most well-known American illustrator of the 20th century, including the artist's 324 covers for the *Saturday Evening Post.* ⊠ *15 S. 7th St.,* ☎ *215/922–3031.* ☜ *$3, free Sun. until noon.* ⊙ *Sept.-June, Wed.–Mon. 10–5; July–Aug., daily 10–5.*

⑫ **Balch Institute for Ethnic Studies.** More a research center than a museum, the Balch Institute has a 60,000-volume library on immigration history and ethnicity that is open to the public several days a week. *Discovering America: The Peopling of Pennsylvania* is an exhibition tracing the diversity of the ethnic groups in the state, from Native Americans and Europeans to newer arrivals from Asia and other countries. Changing exhibitions examine contemporary issues of ethnic and racial identity. ⊠ *18 S. 7th St.,* ☎ *215/925–8090.* ☜ *$3.* ⊙ *Exhibitions, Mon.–Sat. 10–4; library, Tues., Thurs., and Sat. 10–4.*

⑰ **Bishop White House.** Built in 1786, this restored upper-class house embodies Colonial and Federal elegance. It was the home of Bishop William White (1748–1836), rector of Christ Church, first Episcopal bishop of Pennsylvania, and spiritual leader of Philadelphia for 60 years. White, a founder of the Episcopal church after the break with England, was chaplain to the Continental Congress and entertained many of the country's first families, including Washington and Franklin. The second-floor study contains much of the bishop's own library. Unlike most houses of the period, the bishop's house had an early form of flush toilet. The house tour is not recommended for small children, who may get bored. ⊠ *309 Walnut St.,* ☎ *215/597–8974.* ☜ *$2; purchase tickets at the visitor center for one of the daily 1-hr tours that include the Todd House and the Bishop White House.* ⊙ *Tours daily at 10, noon, and 2; open house (no tickets required) at 2:45.*

③ **Carpenters' Hall.** This handsome, patterned red-and-black brick building dating from 1770 was the headquarters of the Carpenters' Company, a guild founded to support carpenters, who were both builders and architects in this era, and to aid their families. In September 1774 the First Continental Congress convened here and addressed a declaration of rights and grievances to King George III. Today re-creations of Colonial settings include original Windsor chairs and candle sconces and displays of 18th-century carpentry tools. The Carpenters' Company still owns and operates the building. ⊠ *320 Chestnut St.,* ☎ *215/597–8974.* ☜ *Free.* ⊙ *Jan.–Feb., Wed.–Sun. 10–4; Mar.–Dec., Tues.–Sun. 10–4.*

⑨ Congress Hall. Formerly the Philadelphia County Courthouse, Congress Hall was the meeting place of the U.S. Congress from 1790 to 1800—one of the most important decades in our nation's history. Here the Bill of Rights was added to the Constitution; Alexander Hamilton's proposals for a mint and a national bank were enacted; and Vermont, Kentucky, and Tennessee became the first new states after the original Colonies. On the first floor is the House of Representatives, where President John Adams was inaugurated in 1797. On the second floor is the Senate chamber, where in 1793 George Washington was inaugurated for his second term. Both chambers have been authentically restored. ⊠ *6th and Chestnut Sts.,* ☎ *215/597–8974.* ▦ *Free.* ☉ *Sept.–June, daily 9–5; July–Aug., daily 9–6.*

⑩ Curtis Center. The lobby of the Curtis Publishing Company building has a great treasure: a 15- by 50-ft glass mosaic mural, *The Dream Garden,* based on a Maxfield Parrish painting. It was executed by the Louis C. Tiffany Studios in 1916. The work's 260 colors and 100,000 pieces of opalescent hand-fired glass laced with gold leaf make it perhaps the finest Tiffany mural in the world. Privately owned by the estate of a local art patron, the mural was put up for sale for $9 million in 1998, but after public outcry the Philadelphia Historical Commission voted to designate it a "historic object," the first such designation in the city's history, and that stopped the sale. ⊠ *6th and Walnut Sts.,* ☎ *215/238–6450.* ▦ *Free.* ☉ *Weekdays 9–5, Sat. 8–5.*

⑭ Declaration House. In a second-floor room that he had rented from bricklayer Jacob Graff, Thomas Jefferson (1743–1826) drafted the Declaration of Independence in June 1776. The home was reconstructed for the Bicentennial celebration; the bedroom and parlor in which Jefferson lived that summer were re-created with period furnishings. The first floor has a Jefferson exhibition and a seven-minute film, *The Extraordinary Creation.* The display on the Declaration of Independence shows some of the changes Jefferson made while writing it. You can see Jefferson's original version—which would have abolished slavery had the passage not been stricken by the committee that included Benjamin Franklin and John Adams. ⊠ *7th and Market Sts.,* ☎ *215/597–8974.* ▦ *Free.* ☉ *Daily 10–4.*

۞ DisneyQuest Philadelphia. This new five-story, 80,000-square-ft interactive indoor venue, set to open in early 2001, provides a bit of Disney without visiting a theme park, thanks to virtual reality and computer animation. Attractions include a river-raft Virtual Jungle Cruise; a roller-coaster ride on CyberSpace Mountain; a flight through the streets of Agrabah on Aladdin's Magic Carpet Ride; and a battle with the evil Hades in Hercules in the Underworld. You can also learn techniques of animation or create your own toys and stickers. In addition, there are video games galore. DisneyQuest is the anchor of the Pavilion at Market East, a new development featuring family-oriented entertainment, multiplex movie theaters, attractions, retail shops, and restaurants. ⊠ *8th and Market Sts.,* ☎ *not available at press time (call 215/ 636–1666).* ☉ *Opening early 2001.*

❷ First Bank of the United States. A fine example of Federal architecture, the oldest bank building in the country was headquarters of the government's bank from 1797 to 1811. Designed by Samuel Blodget, Jr. and erected in 1795–1797, the bank was an imposing structure in its day, exemplifying strength, dignity, and security. Head first to the right, to the north side of the structure, to find a beautiful wrought-iron gateway topped by an eagle. Pass through it into the courtyard, and you magically step out of modern-day Philadelphia and into Colonial America. Before you do so, check out the bank's beautiful pediment. Executed in 1797 by Clodius F. Legrand and Sons, its cornucopia, oak branch, and American eagle are carved from mahogany—a late-18th-century masterpiece that has withstood acid rain better than the bank's marble pillars. ⊠ *120 S. 3rd St.* ⊘ *Interior closed to public.*

🖐 ⓵⑤ **Franklin Court.** In 1763, at the age of 57, Benjamin Franklin (1706–1790) built his first permanent home in Philadelphia, in a courtyard off Market Street. This underground museum on the site of the house is an imaginative tribute to a Renaissance man: scientist and inventor (of bifocals and the lightning rod), philosopher and writer, savvy politician and successful businessman. Franklin, publisher of *Poor Richard's Almanac,* helped draft the Declaration of Independence and negotiate the peace with Great Britain. He also helped found Pennsylvania Hospital, the University of Pennsylvania, the Philadelphia Contributionship, and the American Philosophical Society.

In the courtyard adjacent to the museum, architect Robert Ventura erected a steel skeleton of Franklin's former home. You can peek through "windows" into cutaways to see wall foundations, outdoor privy wells, and other parts of his home that were uncovered during excavations. Within the museum the accomplishments of the statesman, diplomat, scientist, inventor, printer, and author are brought to life. Dial-a-quote to hear his thoughts or pick up a telephone and listen to what his contemporaries really thought of him. There is also an informative 20-minute film on Franklin's life. At the Market Street side are several houses, now exhibition halls, that Franklin had rented in addition to his main home. In one, you can see how Franklin fireproofed the building: His interest in fireproofing led him to experiment with kite flying and lightning (remember the delightful rendition of those experiments in Disney's animated cartoon *Ben and Me*?). Here, too, you'll find a restoration of a Colonial-era print shop and a post office. Don't forget to get a letter hand-stamped with a "B. FREE FRANKLIN" cancellation. ⊠ *314–322 Market St., or enter from Chestnut St. walkway,* ☎ *215/597–8974.* 🎫 *Free.* ⊘ *Sept.–June, daily 9–5; July–Aug., daily 9–8.*

★ ⑧ **Independence Hall.** The birthplace of the United States, this redbrick building with its clock tower and steeple is one of our nation's greatest icons. America's most historic building was constructed in 1732–1756 as the Pennsylvania State House. What happened here between 1775 and 1787 changed the course of American history—and the name of the building to Independence Hall. The delegates to the Second Continental Congress met in the hall's Assembly Room in May 1776, united in anger over the blood that had been shed when British troops fired on citizens in Concord, Massachusetts. In this same room George Washington was appointed commander in chief of the Continental Army, Thomas Jefferson's eloquent Declaration of Independence was signed, and later the Constitution of the United States was adopted. Here the first foreign minister to visit the United States was welcomed; the news of Cornwallis's defeat was announced, signaling the end of the Revolutionary War; and, later, John Adams and Abraham Lincoln lay in state. The memories this building holds linger in the collection of polished muskets, the silver inkstand used by delegates to sign the Declaration of Independence, and the "Rising Sun" chair in which George Washington sat. (After the Constitution was adopted, Benjamin Franklin said about the sun carving on the chair, "I have the happiness to know that it is a rising and not a setting sun.")

In the **East Wing**—attached to Independence Hall by a short colonnade—you can embark on free tours that start every 15 to 20 minutes and last 35 minutes. Admission is first come, first served; you may have to wait. The **West Wing** of Independence Hall contains an exhibit of the national historical parks's collection of our nation's founding documents: the final draft of the Constitution, a working copy of the Articles of Confederation, and the first printing of the Declaration of Independence.

In front of Independence Hall, next to the statue of George Washington, note the plaques marking the spots where Abraham Lincoln stood on February 22, 1861, and where John F. Kennedy delivered an address on July 4, 1962. Each year on July 4, the Philadelphia Liberty Medal is presented here to a world leader. With Independence Hall in front of you and the Liberty Bell behind you, this is a place to stand for a moment and soak up a sense of history. ⊠ *Chestnut St. between 5th and 6th Sts.,* ☏ *215/597–8974.* ⊡ *Free.* ☉ *Sept.–June, daily 9–5; July–Aug., daily 9–8.*

❶ Independence National Historical Park Visitor Center. The staff of park rangers here answer questions and distribute maps and brochures on Independence National Historical Park and other sites in the historic area. Before you set off on a walking tour, acquaint yourself with this period of American history by watching the founding fathers come to life in the 30-minute movie *Independence.* A city information desk is inside the center, as is an excellent bookstore, where you can stock up on books, videos, brochures, prints, wall hangings, and souvenirs about historic figures and events. The most popular items are the tiny Liberty Bell reproductions. The bell atop the visitor center's tower, cast at the same foundry as the Liberty Bell, was a Bicentennial birthday gift from Queen Elizabeth II. Note: By late 2000 or early 2001, this visitor center will close. The Gateway Visitor Center, a new facility with expanded services, will open on 6th Street between Market and Arch streets.

To see two of the city's famous historic homes—the Bishop White and Todd houses—you'll need to stop at the information desk to purchase a ticket ($2) and reserve a spot on one of the hour-long tours. ⊠ *3rd and Chestnut Sts.,* ☏ *215/597–8974.* ☉ *Sept.–June, daily 9–5; July–Aug., daily 9–6.*

NEED A
BREAK?
The **Custom House Cafe** (⊠ 103 S. 2nd St., ☏ 215/627–0654) serves a great cup of coffee, along with cold drinks, sandwiches, muffins, and bagels. If you want to get an early start sightseeing, you can stop by here first; the café opens weekdays at 7, Saturday at 8, Sunday at 10.

Independence Square. On July 8, 1776, the Declaration of Independence was first read here in public. Although the square is not as imposing today, it still has great dignity. You can imagine the impact the reading had on the Colonists. ⊠ *Bounded by Walnut and Chestnut Sts. and 5th and 6th Sts.*

★ ⓫ Liberty Bell. The bell fulfilled the biblical words of its inscription when it rang to "proclaim liberty throughout all the land unto all the inhabitants thereof," beckoning Philadelphians to the State House yard to hear the first reading of the Declaration of Independence. Ordered in 1751 and originally cast in England, the bell cracked during testing and was recast in Philadelphia by Pass and Stow two years later. To keep it from falling into British hands during the Revolution—they would have melted it down for ammunition—the bell was spirited away by horse and wagon to Allentown, 60 mi to the north. The bell is the subject of much legend; one story says it cracked when tolled at the funeral of Chief Justice John Marshall in 1835. Actually, the bell cracked slowly over a period of years. It was repaired but cracked again in 1846 and was then forever silenced. It was called the State House Bell until the 1830s, when a group of abolitionists adopted it as a symbol of freedom and renamed it the Liberty Bell.

After being housed in Independence Hall for more than 200 years, the bell was moved to a glass-enclosed pavilion for the Bicentennial, in 1976. This modern home is an incongruous setting for such a historic object, but it does display the bell 24 hours a day. While the building is open, rangers and volunteers tell the story. After hours you can press a button on the outside walls to hear a recorded account of the bell's history. By late 2000 or early 2001, the bell will be moving again, 200 yards closer to Independence Hall, just off the corner of 6th and Chestnut streets. The new Liberty Bell complex will house a bell chamber, an interpretive exhibit area with historic displays and memorabilia, and a new covered area for people waiting in line. ⊠ *Market St. between 5th and 6th Sts., ☎ 215/597–8974. ▧ Free. ☉ Sept.–June, daily 9–5; July–Aug., daily 9–8.*

NEED A BREAK?   Enter the **Bourse** (⊠ 5th Street across from the Liberty Bell Pavilion, ☎ 215/625–0300) and you're in another century. The skylighted Great Hall, with its Corinthian columns, marble, wrought-iron stairways, and Victorian gingerbread details, has been magnificently restored. Built in 1895 as a stock exchange, it now houses shops and a food court, where you can grab a cup of cappuccino or a Philly cheese steak.

❻ Library Hall. This 20th-century building is a reconstruction of Franklin's Library Company of Philadelphia (☞ Rittenhouse Square, *below*), the first public library in the Colonies. Home of the library of the American Philosophical Society, one of the country's leading institutions for the study of science, it is basically a research facility for scholars. Its vaults contain such treasures as a copy of the Declaration of Independence handwritten by Thomas Jefferson, William Penn's 1701 Charter of Privileges, and journals from the Lewis and Clark expedition of 1803–06. The library's collection also includes first editions of Newton's *Principia Mathematica,* Franklin's *Experiments and Observations,* and Darwin's *On the Origin of Species.* The lobby has fascinating changing exhibitions that showcase the society's collection. ⊠ *105 S. 5th St., ☎ 215/440–3400. ▧ Free. ☉ Weekdays 9–4:45.*

★ ☾ Lights of Liberty. A nighttime multimedia extravaganza, billed as the "world's first walkable sound-and-light show," takes place in five acts throughout Independence National Historical Park. The one-hour show, which dramatizes the events that led up to the American Revolution, takes you back to British Philadelphia in 1763 at Franklin Court, the site of Ben Franklin's home, and culminates in the grand finale at Independence Hall on July 8, 1776, with the first public reading of the Declaration of Independence. You wear 3-D sound wireless headsets and view high-definition five-story projections on the area's historic buildings. The show features special effects and a stirring musical score recorded by the Philadelphia Orchestra. Narration is available in German, Japanese, Spanish, Italian, and English, and in adult and children's versions. The walking distance is a half mile, and wheelchairs are available. There are six shows per hour; call for reservations and schedule. ⊠ *PECO Energy Liberty Center, 6th and Chestnut Sts., ☎ 215/542–3789. ▧ $18; $50 family package with 2 adult and 2 children's tickets. ☉ Mar.–Dec., daily, from just after dark, weather permitting.*

❹ New Hall Military Museum. The original of this reconstructed 1790 building briefly served as headquarters for the U.S. Department of War.

On display are Revolutionary War uniforms; medals; and authentic weapons, including powder horns, swords, and a 1763 flintlock musket. Dioramas depict highlights of the Revolutionary War. The building also houses a Marine Corps memorial. ⊠ *Chestnut St. east of 4th St.,* ☎ *215/597–8974.* ⊠ *Free.* ⊘ *Daily 10–4.*

❼ Old City Hall. Independence Hall is flanked by Congress Hall to the west and Old City Hall to the east: three distinctive Federal-style buildings erected to house the city's growing government. But when Philadelphia became the nation's capital in 1790, the just-completed city hall was lent to the federal government. It housed the U.S. Supreme Court from 1791 to 1800; John Jay was the Chief Justice. Later, the boxlike building with a peaked roof and cupola was used as the city hall. Today an exhibit presents information about the early days of the federal judiciary. ⊠ *5th and Chestnut Sts.,* ☎ *215/597–8974.* ⊠ *Free.* ⊘ *Daily 9–5.*

Pemberton House. "America's National Parks" store sells books, videos, and souvenirs, plus Civil War, Revolutionary War, and Constitution memorabilia. ⊠ *316 Chestnut St.,* ☎ *215/597–8019.* ⊘ *Daily 9–5.*

Philadelphia Merchant's Exchange. Designed by the well-known Philadelphia architect William Strickland and built in 1832, this impressive Greek Revival structure served as the city's commercial center for 50 years. It was both the stock exchange and a place where merchants met to trade goods. In the tower a watchman scanned the Delaware River and notified merchants of arriving ships. The exchange stands behind Dock Street, a cobblestone thoroughfare closed to traffic. The building is not open to the public. ⊠ *3rd and Walnut Sts.*

Philosophical Hall. This is the headquarters of the American Philosophical Society, founded by Benjamin Franklin in 1743 to promote "useful knowledge." The members of the oldest learned society in America have included Washington, Jefferson, Lafayette, Emerson, Darwin, Edison, Churchill, and Einstein. Erected between 1785 and 1789 in what has been called a "restrained Federal style" (designed, probably, to complement, not outshine, adjacent Independence Hall), Philosophical Hall is brick with marble trim and has a handsome arched entrance. The society's library is across the street in Library Hall (☞ *above*). ⊠ *104 S. 5th St.,* ☎ *215/440–3400.* ⊘ *Closed to the public except by appointment.*

❺ Second Bank of the United States. When Second Bank President Nicholas Biddle held a design competition for a new building, he required all architects to use the Greek style; William Strickland, one of the foremost architects of the 19th century, won. Built in 1824, the bank, with its Doric columns, was based on the design of the Parthenon and helped establish the popularity of Greek Revival architecture in the United States. The interior banking hall, though, was Roman, with a dramatic, barrel-vault ceiling. Housed here are portraits of prominent Colonial Americans by noted artists such as Charles Willson Peale, William Rush, and Gilbert Stuart. Don't miss Peale's portrait of Jefferson: It's the only one that shows him with red hair. The permanent exhibition, *Portraits of the Capital City,* has a life-size wooden statue of George Washington by William Rush; a mural of Philadelphia in the 1830s by John A. Woodside Jr.; and the only known likeness of William Floyd, a lesser-known signer of the Declaration of Independence. ⊠ *420 Chestnut St.,* ☎ *215/ 597–8974.* ⊠ *$2.* ⊘ *Sept.–June, daily 10–4; July–Aug., daily 10–6.*

❶⓼ Todd House. Built in 1775 by John Dilworth, Todd House has been restored to its 1790s appearance, when its best-known resident, Dolley Payne Todd (1768–1849), lived here. She lost her husband, the

Quaker lawyer John Todd, to the yellow fever epidemic of 1793. Dolley later married James Madison, who became the fourth president. Her time as a hostess in the White House was quite a contrast to her years in this simple home. There's an 18th-century garden next to Todd House. ⊠ *4th and Walnut Sts.,* ☎ *215/597–8974.* ⌚ *$2; purchase tickets at the visitor center for one of the daily 1-hr tours that include the Todd House and the Bishop White House.* ☉ *Tours daily at 10, noon, and 2; open house (no tickets required) at 2:45.*

⑯ **Welcome Park.** In the park, on a 60-ft-long map of Penn's Philadelphia carved in the pavement, sits a scale model of the Penn statue that sits atop City Hall. The wall surrounding the park displays a time line of William Penn's life, with information about his philosophy and quotations from his writings. The park was the site of the slate-roof house where Penn lived briefly and where he granted the Charter of Privileges in 1701. (The *Welcome* was the ship that transported Penn to America.) Written by Penn, the Charter of Privileges served as Pennsylvania's constitutional framework until 1776; the Liberty Bell was commissioned to commemorate the charter's 50th anniversary. The City Tavern, across the street, marks the site where George Washington once dined. It is still open for historically correct lunches and dinners (☞ Chapter 3). ⊠ *2nd St. just north of Walnut St.*

OLD CITY
Living "North of Market"

In Colonial days, the rich folks in residential Society Hill spoke in hushed tones of those who lived "north of Market," for this area, between Front and 5th streets and Chestnut and Vine streets, was the city's commercial area for industry and wholesale distributors, filled with wharves and warehouses and taverns. It also held the modest homes of the craftsmen and artisans who resided here. Old City (as it became known some 40 years ago, to distinguish it from the national park area) is aptly named: it is one of the city's oldest and most historic neighborhoods, home to Elfreth's Alley; the Betsy Ross House; and Christ Church, where George Washington and John Adams came (across the tracks!) to worship at services. There's evidence of the Quaker presence here, too, in the Arch Street Meeting House.

Today Old City is Philadelphia's trendiest neighborhood, a local version of New York's SoHo. Many cast-iron building facades remain, though the old warehouses, with telltale names such as the Sugar Refinery and the Hoopskirt Factory, now house well-lighted loft apartments popular with artists and architects. There are small theaters—the Painted Bride, the Arden Theatre Company—and numerous art galleries. In the past few years, more restaurant have opened here than in any other part of the city. The Old City Arts Association hosts a festive, popular event the first Friday of each month—known, appropriately enough, as First Friday—when the galleries throw open their doors during evening hours.

Numbers in the text correspond to numbers in the margin and on the Historic Area and Penn's Landing map.

A Good Walk
A walk through Old City begins at 2nd and Market streets, location of the impressive **Christ Church** ⑲, attended by George and Martha Washington, among other notables. Continuing north on 2nd Street for a block and passing Arch Street, you'll come to a tiny Colonial street on the right, **Elfreth's Alley** ⑳; two houses are open to the public. Head

back to 2nd Street, turn right (north), and a few footsteps will take you to the **Fireman's Hall Museum** ㉑, with exhibits on the history of fire fighting. If you then follow 2nd Street back to Arch and turn right (west), you'll find the most popular residence in Philadelphia, the **Betsy Ross House** ㉒.

A bit farther along, between 321 and 323 Arch Street, you can peer into the gated **Loxley Court** and its 18th-century houses and then cross the street to the Society of Friends' **Arch Street Meeting House** ㉓. Just ahead one block is the **Christ Church Burial Ground,** final resting place for Ben Franklin and other signers of the Declaration of Independence. Across 5th Street is the **Free Quaker Meeting House,** built for Friends who had been disowned by their pacifist meetings for participating in the Revolutionary War. Diagonally across Arch Street stands the **United States Mint** ㉔, where you can watch coins being made. If you're up for an adventure—and a hearty 1¼-mi walk (each way)—you could cross the Benjamin Franklin Bridge. The walkway entrance is about two blocks north of the Mint, on 5th Street. Otherwise, turn left (south) on 5th Street, cross Arch Street, and walk until you find a redbrick courtyard, entrance to the modern building that houses both the **National Museum of American Jewish History** ㉕ and **Mikveh Israel** ㉖, the oldest Jewish congregation in Philadelphia. Walking two blocks west on Arch Street to 7th Street brings you to the **Afro-American Historical and Cultural Museum** ㉗, with displays that illuminate the black experience through the centuries. At this point you might want to follow 7th Street (on foot or by bus) five blocks north to the residence and exhibits at the Edgar Allan Poe National Historic Site.

TIMING

If possible, set aside four–five hours on a Sunday for your visit to Old City. You could attend the 9 AM service at Christ Church, as George and Martha Washington did, and then join the 10:30 Quaker meeting at the Arch Street Friends Meeting House, where William Penn worshiped. Try to avoid scheduling a Monday visit, when two of the top sights—the Betsy Ross House and Elfreth's Alley—are closed. On a weekday it's worth your while to see the coin-making operation at the Mint. If you detour to the Poe House, allow another two hours. You can take this walk in any kind of weather and at any time of year since the neighborhood is a small one.

Sights to See

㉗ **Afro-American Historical and Cultural Museum.** Permanent and changing exhibits are dedicated to the history, fine art, artifacts, crafts, and culture of African-Americans in the United States—with a focus on Philadelphia and Pennsylvania. Past exhibitions have showcased African-American female sculptors, slavery artifacts, and sports in Philadelphia. Every February the museum presents a jazz series. The museum's gift shop stocks the area's widest selection of books on black culture, history, fiction, poetry, and drama, along with African textiles and sculpture and African-American jewelry, prints, and tiles. Opened in the Bicentennial year of 1976, this is the first museum of its kind funded and built by a city. ✉ *701 Arch St.,* ☎ *215/574–0380.* 🎟 *$6.* ☉ *Tues.–Sat. 10–5, Sun. noon–5.*

㉓ **Arch Street Meeting House.** Constructed in 1804 for the Philadelphia Yearly Meeting of the Society of Friends, this building of simple lines is still used for that purpose, as well as for biweekly services. The largest Friends meeting house in the world, it was built to hold 3,000 people. When a contemporary architect measured the space, he determined that each of those folks would have only 18 inches to sit in. Today the meeting house can accommodate about 800 21st-century-size behinds.

WILLIAM PENN AND HIS LEGACY

BORN IN LONDON in 1644 into a nobleman's family, William Penn was truly a rebel with a cause. He attended Oxford University, studied law, and tried a military career (in emulation of his father, an admiral in the British Navy). It was at Oxford that Penn first heard Quaker preachers professing that each life is part of the divine spirit, and that all people should be treated equally, even royalty. At 23, he joined the Quakers (the Religious Society of Friends) and was promptly expelled from Oxford and from his home.

Penn was imprisoned in the Tower of London a few times for his heretical pamphlets, but he was spared worse persecution because of his friendship with King Charles II. He asked the king to grant him land in the New World for a Quaker colony; 10 years later he was given a large tract in payment of a debt Charles owed to his late father.

And so in 1682 Penn began his "Holy Experiment," hoping to prove that a state could be founded on principles of religious and civil freedom. He bought land from the Native Americans and established a peace treaty with them that lasted for 70 years. The Quaker tenets of religious liberty, complete separation of church and state, and the power of the provincial assembly to call and adjourn itself and to originate and amend bills were declared in the 1701 Charter of Privileges, a model for the U.S. Constitution.

As a city planner, Penn mapped out Philadelphia as a "greene countrie towne" with broad, straight streets. He positioned each house in the middle of its plot, so that every child would have green grass and play space; he named its streets—Walnut, Spruce, Chestnut—for trees, not for men. As a reformer, Penn was responsible for humane prisons and asylums; good medical care and education for all; and limiting the application of the death penalty to two offenses rather than 200.

In England, he led early protests for women's rights and against slavery and war. The Quakers in Philadelphia would become leaders in all these causes.

Penn's legacy in Philadelphia and the state is profound: the state was named by King Charles for Penn's father. His original city plan has survived, and his statue looks out over it from atop City Hall. The Arch Street Friends Meeting House, on land Penn set aside as a Quaker burying ground, still holds weekly meetings. William Penn Charter, a private Friends School, has operated continuously since it was founded in 1689. What's most remarkable is that Penn spent only four of his 74 years in Pennsylvania.

During the first visit, from 1682 to 1684, he established his haven for Quakers and its liberal government. He was called back to England in 1684 and remained there until 1699, caring for his ill wife, Gulielma Maria Springett, who would die without ever seeing his beloved Pennsylvania. He was engaged in legal battles with Lord Baltimore over ownership of the neighboring colony of Maryland. Penn was suspected of plotting with the former Catholic King, James II, to overthrow the current Protestant monarchy of William and Mary, who revoked his charter in 1692 for 18 months.

Penn made his second trip to America with his second wife, Hannah Callowhill Penn, in 1699. The couple moved into Pennsbury Manor (☞ Chapter 9) along the upper Delaware River. He had to return to England yet again in 1701; there he was consumed by the political and legal problems of his colony, a term in prison for debt, and then illness. Penn died before he could return to Pennsylvania. After his death, his wife honored him by assuming the governorship for nine years. In Philadelphia today, Welcome Park (☞ Around Independence Hall) and the Arch Street Meeting House (☞ Old City) offer some insight into Penn's accomplishments.

Among the most influential members in the 19th century was Lucretia Mott (1793–1880), a leader in the women's suffrage, anti-war, and anti-slavery movements. A small museum in the meeting house presents a series of dioramas and a 14-minute slide show depicting the life and accomplishments of William Penn (1644–1718), who gave the land on which the meeting house sits to the Society of Friends. Quaker guides give tours year-round. ⊠ *4th and Arch Sts.,* ☎ *215/627–2667.* ☞ *$1 minimum donation requested.* ☉ *Mon.–Sat. 10–4; services Thurs. at 10 and Sun. at 10:30.*

OFF THE
BEATEN PATH

BENJAMIN FRANKLIN BRIDGE – When the bridge opened in 1926, its 1,750-ft main span made it the longest suspension bridge in the world. Paul Cret, architect of the Rodin Museum, was the designer. A blue paint job and a lighting system that shows off its contours have made the bridge more beautiful than ever. You can get an excellent view of riverfront Philadelphia by walking or bicycling across the smooth, resurfaced walkway; the south walkway has the best view. Cars, trucks, and trains zoom past, and brisk winds make your face tingle as you cross the Delaware River, 150 ft below. Start the 1¾-mi walk (one-way) from either the Philadelphia side, two blocks north of the U.S. Mint, or the Camden, New Jersey, side. ⊠ *5th and Vine Sts.,* ☎ *215/218–3750.* ☞ *Free.* ☉ *Daily 6 AM–around 6 PM).*

★ ☾ ㉒   **Betsy Ross House.** It's easy to find this little brick house with the gabled roof: Just look for the 13-star flag displayed from its second-floor window. Whether Betsy Ross, also known as Elizabeth Griscom Ross Ashbourn Claypoole (1752–1836)—who worked in her family's flag making and upholstery business—actually lived here and whether she really made the first Stars and Stripes is debatable. Nonetheless, the house, built about 1760, is a splendid example of a Colonial Philadelphia home and is fun to visit. Owned and maintained by the city, the eight-room house overflows with artifacts such as a family Bible and Betsy Ross's chest of drawers and reading glasses. The small rooms hold period pieces that reflect the life of this hardworking Quaker (who died at the age of 84, outliving three husbands). You may have to wait in line here, as this is one of the city's most popular attractions. The house, with its winding narrow stairs, is not accessible to people with disabilities. Alongside the house is brick-paved Atwater Kent Park, with a fountain, benches, and the graves of Betsy Ross and her third husband, John Claypoole. ⊠ *239 Arch St.,* ☎ *215/627–5343.* ☞ *Free.* ☉ *Tues.–Sun. 10–5.*

NEED A
BREAK?

Mulberry Market (⊠ 236 Arch St., ☎ 215/592–8022) is a great little market stocked floor to ceiling with goodies, from freshly baked breads and steaming coffee to deli sandwiches and cereal. You can pick up anything you might need for a picnic or to stock your hotel room. The small restaurant in the rear is open daily from 7 AM to 10 or 11 PM.

⑲   **Christ Church.** The Anglicans of the Church of England built a wooden church on this site in 1697. When they outgrew it, they erected a new church, the most sumptuous in the Colonies, designed by Dr. John Kearsley and modeled on the work of famed English architect Sir Christopher Wren. The symmetrical, classical facade with arched windows, completed in 1754, is a fine example of Georgian architecture; the church is one of the city's treasures. The congregation included 15 signers of the Declaration of Independence. The bells and the soaring 196-ft steeple, the tallest in the Colonies, were financed by lotteries run by Benjamin Franklin. Brass plaques mark the pews of George and Martha Washington, John and Abigail Adams, Betsy Ross, and others. Two blocks west of the church is **Christ Church Burial Ground** (☞ *below*). ✉ *2nd St. north of Market St.*, ☎ *215/922–1695.* ☉ *Mar.–Dec., Mon.– Sat. 9–5, Sun. 1–5; Jan.–Feb., Wed.–Sat. 9–5, Sun. 1–5; services Sun. 9 and 11, Wed. noon.*

Christ Church Burial Ground. Weathered gravestones fill the resting place of five signers of the Declaration of Independence and other Colonial patriots. The best-known is Benjamin Franklin; he lies alongside his wife, Deborah, and their son, Francis, who died at age four. According to local legend, throwing a penny onto Franklin's grave will bring you good luck. Although visitors can no longer walk through the cemetery, you can toss your penny from outside the iron gate. ✉ *5th and Arch Sts.*, ☎ *215/922–1695.*

OFF THE
BEATEN PATH

EDGAR ALLAN POE NATIONAL HISTORIC SITE – One of America's most original writers, Edgar Allan Poe (1809–1849), lived here from 1843 to 1844; it is the only one of his Philadelphia residences still standing. During that time some of his best-known short stories were published: "The Telltale Heart," "The Black Cat," and "The Gold Bug." You can tour the three-story brick house; to evoke the spirit of Poe, the National Park Service deliberately keeps it empty. An adjoining house has exhibits on Poe and his family, his work habits, and his literary contemporaries; there is also an eight-minute film and a small Poe library and reading room. A statue of a raven helps set the mood. Special programs include Poetry Month tours (usually March or April) and popular "ghostly" tours in October (reservations required). The site, easily reached from the Afro-American Historical and Cultural Museum, is five blocks north of Market Street. SEPTA Bus 47 travels on 7th Street to Spring Garden Street, where you should disembark. ✉ *532 N. 7th St.*, ☎ *215/597–8780.* 🎟 *Free.* ☉ *June–Oct., daily 9–5; Nov.–May, Wed.–Sun. 9–5.*

★ ⑳ **Elfreth's Alley.** The alley, the oldest continuously occupied residential street in America, dates to 1702. Much of Colonial Philadelphia resembled this area, with its cobblestone streets and narrow two- or three-story brick houses. These were modest row homes, most built for rent, lived in by craftsmen, such as cabinetmakers, silversmiths, pewterers, and their families. They also housed captains and others who made their living in the city's busy shipping industry. The earliest houses (two stories) have pent eaves; taller houses, built after the Revolution, show the influence of the Federal style. The Elfreth's Alley Association has restored Numbers 124, home of a Windsor chair maker, and 126, a Colonial dressmaker's home, with authentic furnishings and a Colonial kitchen. On the first weekend in June residents celebrate Fete Days, when about 25 of the 30 homes are open to the public for tours hosted by guides in Colonial garb; a fee is charged. On the second Friday evening in December, homeowners again welcome visitors for a candlelight Christmas tour. The rest of the year only Numbers 124 and 126 are open. ✉ *Front and 2nd Sts. between Arch and Race Sts.*, ☎ *215/574–0560.* 🎟 *$2 for Nos. 124 and 126.* ☉ *Jan.–Feb., Sat. 10–4, Sun. noon–4; Mar.–Dec., Tues.–Sat. 10–4, Sun. noon–4.*

☾ ㉑ **Fireman's Hall Museum.** Housed in an authentic 1876 firehouse, this museum traces the history of fire fighting, from the volunteer company founded in Philadelphia by Benjamin Franklin in 1736 to the professional departments of the 20th century. The collection includes early hand- and horse-drawn fire engines, such as an 1815 hand pumper and a 1907 three-horse Metropolitan steamer; fire marks (18th-century building signs marking them as insured for fire); uniforms; and other memorabilia. ✉ *147 N. 2nd St.*, ☎ *215/923–1438.* 🎟 *Free; donations welcome.* ☉ *Tues.–Sat. 9–4:30.*

Free Quaker Meeting House. This was the house of worship for the Free "Fighting" Quakers, a group that broke away from the Society of Friends to take up arms against the British during the Revolutionary War. The building was designed in 1783 by Samuel Wetherill, one of the original leaders of the group, after they were disowned by their pacifist brothers. Among the 100 members were Betsy Ross (then Elizabeth Griscom) and Thomas Mifflin, a signer of the Constitution. After the Free Quaker group dissolved (many left to become Episcopalian), the building was used as a school, library, and warehouse. The meeting house, built in the Quaker plain style with a brick front and gable roof, has been carefully restored. ⊠ *500 Arch St.,* ☎ *215/597–0060.* ☉ *Closed during Independence Mall construction; will reopen late 2000 or early 2001.*

Loxley Court. One of the restored 18th-century houses in this lovely court was once home to Benjamin Loxley, a carpenter who worked on Independence Hall. The court's claim to fame, according to its residents, is as the spot where Benjamin Franklin flew his kite in his experiment with lightning; the key tied to it was the key to Loxley's front door. ⊠ *321–323 Arch St.*

❷❻ **Mikveh Israel.** Nathan Levy, a Colonial merchant whose ship, the *Myrtilla,* brought the Liberty Bell to America, helped found this Jewish congregation in 1740, making it the oldest in Philadelphia and the second oldest in the United States. The original synagogue was at 3rd and Cherry streets; the congregation's current space (1976) is in the Sephardic style and occupies the same building as the **National Museum of American Jewish History** (☞ *below*). The synagogue's cemetery (about eight blocks away, outside Old City) dates from 1740 and is the oldest surviving Jewish site in Philadelphia. It was the burial ground for the Spanish-Portuguese Jewish community. Among those buried here are Nathan Levy; Haym Salomon, a financier of the American Revolution; and Rebecca Gratz, the inspiration for the character Rebecca in Sir Walter Scott's novel *Ivanhoe.* ⊠ *Synagogue: 44 N. 4th St.,* ☎ *215/922–5446.* ☉ *Mon.–Thurs. 10–5, Fri. 10–3, Sun. noon–5. Services Fri. evening and Sat. 9 AM. To arrange a tour, call the National Museum of American Jewish History (☞ below).* ⊠ *Cemetery: Spruce St. between 8th and 9th Sts.,* ☎ *215/922–5446.* ☉ *Guide present in summer, Mon.–Thurs. 10–4; Sept.–June, visiting arrangements made through synagogue office.*

❷❺ **National Museum of American Jewish History.** Established in 1976, this small museum is the only one in the nation dedicated exclusively to collecting, preserving, and interpreting artifacts pertaining to the American Jewish experience. It presents exhibits and programs exploring not only Jewish life but also issues of American ethnic identity, history, art, and culture. A powerful permanent exhibition, *Creating American Jews,* tells the history of this community through diaries, letters, and oral histories. The museum shares a building with **Mikveh Israel** (☞ *above*). ⊠ *55 N. 5th St.,* ☎ *215/923–3811.* ☎ *$3.* ☉ *Mon.–Thurs. 10–5, Fri. 10–3, Sun. noon–5.*

❷❹ **United States Mint.** The first U.S. mint was built in Philadelphia at 16th and Spring Garden streets in 1792, when the Bank of North America adopted dollars and cents instead of shillings and pence as standard currency; the current mint was built in 1971. On the self-guided tour, which takes about 45 minutes, you can see blank disks being melted, cast, and pressed into coins, which are then inspected, counted, and bagged. The visitors' gallery has an exhibition of medals from the nation's wars, including the Medal of Honor, the Purple Heart, and the Bronze Star. Seven beautiful Tiffany glass tile mosaics depict coin making in ancient Rome. A shop in the lobby sells special coins and medals—in mint condition. ✉ *5th and Arch Sts.,* ☎ *215/408–0114.* 🎟 *Free.* ☉ *Sept.–Apr., weekdays 9–4:30; May–June, Mon.–Sat. 9–4:30; July–Aug., daily 9–4:30. Coinage machinery operates weekdays only.*

SOCIETY HILL AND PENN'S LANDING
Enduring Grace and the Waterfront City

During the 18th century Society Hill was—as it still is today—Philadelphia's showplace. A beautifully preserved district, it is easily the city's most photogenic neighborhood, filled with hidden courtyards, delightful decorative touches such as chimney pots and brass door knockers, wrought-iron foot scrapers, and other remnants from the days of horse-drawn carriages and muddy, unpaved streets. Here time has not quite stopped but meanders down the cobblestone streets, whiling away the hours.

A trove of Colonial- and Federal-style brick row houses (homes with common sidewalls), churches, and narrow streets, Society Hill stretches from the Delaware River to 6th Street, south of Independence National Historical Park. Those homes built before 1750 in the Colonial style generally have 2½ stories and a dormer window jutting out of a steep roof. The less heavy, more graceful houses built after the Revolution were often in the Federal style, popularized in England during the 1790s.

Here lived the "World's People," wealthier Anglicans who arrived after William Penn and loved music and dancing—pursuits the Quakers shunned when they set up their enclave in Old City, north of Market Street, in a less desirable commercial area. The "Society" in the neighborhood's moniker refers, however, to the Free Society of Traders, a group of business investors who settled here on William Penn's advice.

Today many Colonial homes in this area have been lovingly restored by modern pioneers who began moving into the area 40 years ago and rescued Society Hill from becoming a slum. Inspired urban renewal efforts have transformed vast empty factory spaces into airy lofts; new town houses were carefully designed to blend in with the old. As a result, Society Hill is not just a showcase for historic churches and mansions but a living, breathing neighborhood.

Before setting out to explore Society Hill, you may want to tour Philadelphia's nearby waterfront, with attractions that include a maritime museum, historic marine vessels, and an aquarium. Those who don't wish to enjoy this waterside detour should jump ahead in the following walk to Head House Square.

Numbers in the text correspond to numbers in the margin and on the Historic Area and Penn's Landing map.

A Good Walk

Begin your waterfront visit at **Penn's Landing** ㉘, a riverfront promenade with a maritime museum, historic ships, and restaurants. To get there, cross the Walnut Street Bridge at Front Street, which deposits you at the **Independence Seaport Museum** ㉙, with its engaging interactive exhibits and nautical artifacts. Right in front of the museum, you can catch the "ferry to the fishies": from April through December, the RiverLink Ferry crosses the Delaware River to Camden, New Jersey, in about 10 minutes, leaving you a few steps from the **New Jersey State Aquarium and Camden Children's Garden** ㉚.

On your return you'll see the tall masts of the 1883 fishing ship *Gazela of Philadelphia,* docked next to the museum—when it's in port. A five-minute stroll south along the river brings you to two historic ships well worth a visit. Descend the steep metal ladder into the **USS Becuna** ㉛. Arise from the depths of this submarine and cross the gangplank for a decidedly different shipboard experience on Commodore Dewey's flagship, the **USS Olympia** ㉜. If you have a car, before you head to Society Hill you could take a detour to visit Ft. Mifflin and the John Heinz National Wildlife Refuge at Tinicum, both near the airport.

Your next stop is Society Hill. Backtrack half a block north on Columbus Boulevard to cobblestone Dock Street and turn left—right will land you in the Delaware River. Just ahead are the Society Hill Towers, three high-rise apartment buildings designed in the early '60s by I. M. Pei. These, along with the Society Hill Townhouses at 3rd and Locust streets, were the winning entries in a design competition for housing that would symbolize the renewal of Society Hill. Today the tall buildings seem out of scale with the rest of the neighborhood. At the dead end turn left. You'll be walking along 38th Parallel Street; in the park to your left is Philadelphia's Vietnam Veterans Memorial. Turn right (west) on Spruce Street and left (south) on 2nd Street to Delancey Street. On summer weekends you may want to continue a few blocks farther on 2nd Street to **Head House Square** ㉝, a Colonial marketplace that hosts a crafts and fine arts fair. Just one block ahead is **South Street,** with its funky shops, bookstores, restaurants, and bars. Otherwise, walk west along Delancey Street, lined with some of the city's prized Colonial homes.

On your right at 4th Street is the freestanding **Physick House** ㉞, with its superb Federal and Empire furnishings. In the next few blocks, you'll see three of the city's historic churches. Follow 4th Street half a block south to Pine Street and turn right (west) toward 6th Street. Between Pine and Lombard streets, on what has been renamed Richard Allen Avenue, is **Mother Bethel African Methodist Episcopal Church** ㉟. Head east on Pine Street; on your right, just before 4th Street, is **Old Pine Street Presbyterian Church** ㊱. This, and **St. Peter's Episcopal Church** ㊲, which dominates most of the next block, were designed by Robert Smith. St. Peter's slim belfry tower is six stories high, topped by a wooden steeple. On the northwest corner of 3rd and Pine streets is the **Thaddeus Kosciuszko National Memorial** ㊳, honoring the Polish general who fought in the Revolution.

Turn left (north) on Third Street. Within a few blocks, you'll come across the brownstones of **Bouvier's Row** (Nos. 258–262), once owned by Jacqueline Kennedy Onassis's ancestors. Just a few doors up is the brick Georgian **Powel House** ㊴, filled with fine 18th-century furniture. Continue north on 3rd Street to Willings Alley (just opposite the former Old St. Paul's Church). Turn left and then right into the courtyard of **Old St. Joseph's Church** ㊵, the city's first Catholic church. Walk up the alley to 4th Street and then a half block south to **Old St. Mary's Church** ㊶, another early Catholic church. Following 4th Street back north brings you to the nation's oldest fire-insurance company, the **Philadelphia Contributionship for the Insurance of Houses from Loss by Fire** ㊷. Turn left on Walnut Street to 6th Street, and you'll come upon tree-shaded **Washington Square,** one of the five in Penn's original city plan. On the east side of the square is the **Athenaeum** ㊸ research library and gallery. If you have an interest in medicine, walk two blocks south and two more west to Pennsylvania Hospital, the nation's oldest.

TIMING

You could easily spend a whole day here, with the bulk of your time allotted to Penn's Landing. If your kids are in tow, you'll want to allow an hour and a half for the Independence Seaport Museum and its historic boats and another two–three hours for the ferry ride and visit to the aquarium. You'll need about one hour to walk through Society Hill, more if you tour the Powel and Physick houses. If walking is your main interest, save this excursion for a warm day, because it can be quite windy along the waterfront. In winter you can ice-skate at the River-Rink. The prime time for this walk? A summer Sunday, when Penn's Landing bustles with festivals and Head House Square turns into an open-air fine arts and crafts market.

Sights to See

43 **Athenaeum.** Housed in a national landmark Italianate brownstone dating from the mid-1800s and designed by John Notman, the Athenaeum is a research library specializing in architectural history and design. Its American Architecture Collection has close to a million items. The library, founded in 1814, contains significant materials on the French in America and on early American travel, exploration, and transportation. Besides books, the Athenaeum has notable paintings and period furniture; changing exhibits are presented in the gallery. ⊠ *219 S. 6th St.,* ☎ *215/925–2688.* ☜ *Free.* ☉ *Gallery, weekdays 9–5; tours and research by appointment only.*

Bouvier's Row. Three of the Victorian brownstones on a stretch of 3rd Street near Spruce Street, often called Bouvier's Row, were once owned by the late Jacqueline Kennedy Onassis's ancestors. Michel Bouvier, her great-great-grandfather—the first of the family to come from France—and many of his descendants lie in the family vault at Old St. Mary's Church (☞ *below*), a few blocks away on 4th Street. ⊠ *258–262 S. 3rd St.*

OFF THE BEATEN PATH

FT. MIFFLIN – Within this 49-acre National Historic Landmark, you can see cannons and carriages, officers' quarters, soldiers' barracks (which contain an exhibition called *Defense of the Delaware*), an artillery shed, a blacksmith shop, a bomb shelter, and a museum. Because of its Quaker origins, Philadelphia had no defenses until 1772, when the British began building Ft. Mifflin. It was completed in 1776 by Revolutionary forces under General Washington. In a 40-day battle in 1777, 300 Continental defenders held off British forces long enough for Washington's troops to flee to Valley Forge. The fort was almost totally destroyed but was rebuilt in 1798 from plans by French architect Pierre Charles L'Enfant, who also designed the plan for Washington, DC. In use until 1962, the fort has served as a prisoner-of-war camp, an artillery battalion, and a munitions dump. Special events include Civil War Garrison Days in October and a reenactment of the siege of Ft. Mifflin held in November. From Penn's Landing you can easily hop on I–95 to reach the fort; call for directions. ⊠ *Island and Hog Island Rds., on the Delaware River near Philadelphia International Airport,* ☎ *215/685–4192.* ☜ *$5.* ☉ *Apr.–Nov., Wed.–Sun. 10–4; tours at 11, 1, and 3.*

Gazela of Philadelphia. Built in 1883 and formerly named *Gazela Primeiro,* this 177-ft square-rigger is the last of a Portuguese fleet of cod-fishing ships. Still in use as late as 1969, it is the oldest and largest wooden square-rigger still sailing. As the Port of Philadelphia's ambassador of goodwill, the *Gazela* sails up and down the Atlantic Coast from May to October to participate in harbor festivals and celebrations. It is also a school ship and a museum. An all-volunteer crew of 35 works on ship maintenance from November to April, while it's in port. ⊠ *Penn's Landing at Market St.,* ☎ *215/923–9030.* ⊙ *Call ahead; tours can be arranged when the ship is in port.*

㉝ Head House Square. This open-air Colonial marketplace, extending from Pine Street to Lombard Street, is a reminder of the days when people went to central outdoor markets on designated days to buy food directly from the farmers. It was first established as New Market in 1745. George Washington was among the people who came here to buy butter, eggs, meat, fish, herbs, and vegetables. The Head House, a boxy building with a cupola and weathervane, was built in 1803 as the office and home of the market master, who tested the quality of the goods. Today, on weekends from Memorial Day through September, the square is home to a crafts and fine arts fair with more than 100 Delaware Valley artists. It bustles from noon until 11 on Saturday nights and from noon to 6 on Sunday, with free children's workshops from 1 to 3. ⊠ *2nd and Pine Sts.,* ☎ *215/790–0782.*

NEED A
BREAK?

Ready for milk and cookies? **Koffmeyers** can deliver on the latter. The store is famous for their all-natural old-fashioned cookies. Try the chocolate chip and macadamia nut cookie or a Head House Square—a vanilla brownie filled with chocolate and walnuts. ⊠ *Head House Sq. at 2nd and Lombard Sts.,* ☎ *215/922–0717.*

★ ☙ **㉙ Independence Seaport Museum.** Philadelphia's maritime museum houses many nautical artifacts, figureheads, and ship models as well as interactive exhibits that convey just what the Delaware and Schuylkill Rivers have meant to the city's fortunes over the years. You can climb in the gray, cold wooden bunks used in steerage, unload cargo from giant container ships with a miniature crane, weld and rivet a ship's hull, or even hop in a scull and row along the Schuylkill. Enter the museum by passing under the three-story replica of the Benjamin Franklin Bridge. ⊠ *211 S. Columbus Blvd., at Walnut St.,* ☎ *215/925–5439.* ⊡ *$5 museum only; $7.50 museum and USS Olympia (☞ below) and USS Becuna (☞ below).* ⊙ *Daily 10–5.*

OFF THE
BEATEN PATH

JOHN HEINZ NATIONAL WILDLIFE REFUGE AT TINICUM – More than 280 species of ducks, herons, egrets, geese, gallinules, and other birds have been spotted at this preserve. Among the resident earthbound animals are turtles, foxes, muskrats, deer, raccoons, weasels, and snakes. Facilities in this 1,200-acre freshwater tidal marsh, the largest remaining in Pennsylvania, include 8 mi of foot trails, an observation blind, an observation deck, boardwalks through the wet areas, and a canoe launch into the 4½-mi stretch of Darby Creek that runs through the preserve (the best way to see it). A new environmental education center with a library, classrooms, and exhibits is set to open in summer 2000. Bird-watchers can prepare for their visit by calling 215/567–2473 for recent sightings. The refuge is convenient to I–95, which you can pick up from Penn's Landing. Call for directions. ⊠ *86th St. and Lindbergh Blvd.,* ☎ *215/365–3118.* ⊡ *Free.* ⊙ *Daily 8–sunset; visitor center daily 9–4.*

㉟ Mother Bethel African Methodist Episcopal Church. Society Hill holds a notable landmark in the history of African-Americans in the city. In 1787, Richard Allen led fellow blacks who left St. George's Methodist Church as a protest against the segregated worship. Allen, a lay minister and former slave who had bought his freedom from the Chew family of Germantown, purchased this site in 1791. It is believed to be the country's oldest parcel of land continuously owned by African-Americans. When the African Methodist Episcopal Church was formed in 1816, Allen was its first bishop. The current church, the fourth on the site, is an example of the 19th-century Romanesque Revival style, with broad arches and a square corner tower, opalescent stained-glass windows, and stunning woodwork. The earlier church buildings were the site of a school where Allen taught slaves to read and also a stop on the Underground Railroad. Allen's tomb and a small museum are on the lower level. ⊠ *419 Richard Allen Ave., 6th St. between Pine and Lombard Sts.,* ☎ *215/925–0616.* 🖃 *Free.* ☉ *Museum and guided tours, Tues.–Sat. 10–3.*

★ ℃ ⑳ **New Jersey State Aquarium and Camden Children's Garden.** This marvel across the Delaware River in Camden combines entertainment, science education, and cutting-edge technology with more than 4,000 aquatic animals representing some 500 species. *Ocean Base Atlantic* has a 760,000-gallon open ocean tank (the country's second largest) with sharks, stingrays, sea turtles, 1,400 fish, and a diver who can answer your questions via a "scubaphone." *WOW! Weird? Or Wonderful?* showcases 400 of the world's most unusual fish. Inguza Island features African penguins. There are also daily seal shows, dive demonstrations, live animal talks, and theater presentations. The delightful 4-acre Children's Garden, opened in 1999, is an interactive horticultural playground with theme exhibits. You can smell, hear, touch, and even taste some of the elements in the Dinosaur, Butterfly, Storybook, Picnic, and World's Kitchen gardens. To get here, drive or take the ferry from Penn's Landing. *Aquarium:* ⊠ *S. Riverside Dr., Camden, NJ,* ☎ *609/365–3300.* 🖃 *$10.95 for aquarium only; $11.95 for aquarium and garden.* ☉ *Mid-Mar.–mid-Sept., daily 9:30–5:30; mid-Sept.–mid-Mar., daily 10–5.* ⊠ *RiverLink Ferry: Penn's Landing near Walnut St.,* ☎ *215/925–5465.* 🖃 *$5 round-trip.* ☉ *April–Nov.; departs from Penn's Landing every hour on the hour, daily 10–5; departs from New Jersey every hour on the ½ hour, daily 10:30–5:30; Dec., weekends 10–5. Extended hours for Penn's Landing events and Blockbuster-Sony Entertainment Centre concerts.*

㊱ **Old Pine Street Presbyterian Church.** Designed by Robert Smith in 1768 as a simple brick Georgian-style building, Old Pine is the only remaining Colonial Presbyterian church and churchyard in Philadelphia. Badly damaged by British troops during the Revolution, it served as a hospital and then a stable. In the mid-19th century, its exterior had a Greek Revival face-lift that included Corinthian columns. In the 1980s, the interior walls and ceiling were stenciled with thistle and wave motifs, a reminder of Old Pine's true name—Third, Scots, and Mariners Presbyterian Church, which documented the congregation's mergers. The beautifully restored church is painted in soft shades of periwinkle and yellow. In the churchyard are the graves of 100 Hessian soldiers from the Revolution—and of Eugene Ormandy, former conductor of the Philadelphia Orchestra. ⊠ *412 Pine St.,* ☎ *215/925–8051.* 🖃 *Free.* ☉ *Mon.–Sat. 9–5.*

㊵ **Old St. Joseph's Church.** In 1733, a tiny chapel was established by Jesuits for Philadelphia's 11 Catholic families. It was the first place in the English-speaking world where Catholic mass could be legally celebrated, a right granted under William's Penn 1701 Charter of Privileges, which guaranteed religious freedom. But freedom didn't come easy; on one occasion Quakers had to patrol St. Joseph's to prevent a Protestant mob from disrupting the service. The present church, built in 1839, is the third on this site. The late 19th-century stained-glass windows are notable. ⊠ *321 Willings Alley,* ☎ *215/923–1733.* ☉ *Daily 11–4; from 1:30 to 4, stop at the rectory for admittance.*

㊶ **Old St. Mary's Church.** The city's second-oldest Catholic church, circa 1763, became its first cathedral when the archdiocese was formed in 1808. A Gothic-style facade was added in 1880; the interior was redone in 1979. The stained-glass windows, a ceiling mural of St. Mary, and brass chandeliers that hung in the Founders Room of Independence Hall until 1967 are highlights. Commodore John Barry, a Revolutionary War naval hero, and other famous Philadelphians are buried in the small churchyard. ⊠ *252 S. 4th St.,* ☎ *215/923–7930.* ☉ *Mon.–Sat. 9–4:45; mass Sat. 5 PM, Sun. 9 and 10:30 AM.*

㉘ **Penn's Landing.** The spot where William Penn stepped ashore in 1682 is the hub of a 37-acre riverfront park that stretches from Market Street south to Lombard Street. Walk along the waterfront and you'll see scores of pleasure boats moored at the marina and cargo ships chugging up and down the Delaware. Philadelphia's harbor, which includes docking facilities in New Jersey and Delaware, is one of the world's largest freshwater ports. In warm weather, Penn's Landing is the scene of the annual Jam on the River and YO! Philadelphia festivals, as well as jazz and big band concerts, ethnic festivals, children's events, and more. In winter (from the Friday after Thanksgiving to early March), you can ice-skate outdoors at the **Blue Cross RiverRink.** The **Independence Seaport Museum** (☞ *above*) is here, too, just across the river by ferry from the **New Jersey State Aquarium** (☞ *above*). The development of this area—an ambitious effort to reclaim the Delaware River waterfront—began in 1967 and has started in earnest once again. Works in progress include the Hyatt Regency Hotel, with a late 2000 opening, an aerial tram with accompanying laser light show that will link Camden and Philadelphia's waterfronts, and the $180 million Family Entertainment Center (scheduled to open in late 2001). ⊠ *On the Delaware River from Market St. to Lombard St.,* ☎ *215/923–4992.*

OFF THE
BEATEN PATH

PENNSYLVANIA HOSPITAL – Inside the fine 18th-century original buildings of the oldest hospital in the United States are the nation's first medical library and first surgical amphitheater (an 1804 innovation, with a skylight). The hospital also has a portrait gallery, early medical instruments, art objects, and a rare-book library with items dating from 1762. The artwork includes the Benjamin West painting *Christ Healing the Sick in the Temple.* Dr. Thomas Bond thought of the idea of a community hospital to improve care for the poor and enrolled Benjamin Franklin in his vision. The Pennsylvania Assembly agreed to put up £2,000 if those interested in a hospital could do the same: It took Franklin only a month and a half to raise the money. Today Pennsylvania Hospital is a full-service modern medical center four blocks southwest of the Athenaeum (☞ *above*). Pick up a copy of "Pennsylvania Hospital: A Walking Tour" at the Welcome Desk just off the 8th Street entrance. ⊠ *8th and Spruce Sts.,* ☎ *215/829–7352.* ▣ *Free.* ☉ *Weekdays 8:30–5; call to arrange a guided group tour for 10 or more.*

㊷ **Philadelphia Contributionship for the Insurance of Houses from Loss by Fire.** The Contributionship, the nation's oldest fire insurance company, was founded by Benjamin Franklin in 1752; the present Greek Revival building with fluted marble Corinthian columns dates from 1836 and has some magnificently elegant salons (particularly the boardroom, where a seating plan on the wall lists Benjamin Franklin as the first incumbent of seat Number One). The architect, Thomas U. Walter, was also responsible for the dome and House and Senate wings of the U.S. Capitol in Washington, DC. This is still an active business, but a small museum is open to the public. ⊠ *212 S. 4th St.,* ☎ *215/627–1752.* ▣ *Free.* ☉ *Weekdays 10–3.*

★ **㉞** **Physick House.** Built in 1786, this is one of two remaining freestanding houses from this era in Society Hill (you will see plenty of the famous Philadelphia row houses here). It is also one of the most beautiful homes in America, with elegantly restored interiors and some of the finest Federal and Empire furniture in Philadelphia. Touches of Napoléon's France are everywhere: the golden bee motif woven into upholstery; the magenta-hue Aubusson rug (the emperor's favorite color); and stools in the style of Pompeii, the Roman city rediscovered at the time of the house's construction. Upstairs in the parlor, note the inkstand that still retains Benjamin Franklin's fingerprints. The house's most famous owner was Philip Syng Physick, the "Father of American Surgery" and a leading physician in the days before anesthesia. His most celebrated patient was Chief Justice John Marshall. The garden planted on three sides of the house is filled with plants common during the 19th century: Complete with an Etruscan sarcophagus, a natural grotto, and antique cannon, it is considered by some to be the city's loveliest. ⊠ *321 S. 4th St.,* ☎ *215/925–7866.* 🖾 *$3.* ☉ *Sept.–May, Thurs.– Sat. 11–2; June–Aug., Thurs.–Sun. noon–4; guided tours on the hr.*

★ ③⑨ **Powel House.** The 1765 brick Georgian house purchased by Samuel Powel in 1769 remains one of the most elegant homes in Philadelphia. Powel—the "Patriot Mayor"—was the last mayor of Philadelphia under the Crown and the first in the new republic. The lavish home, a former wreck saved from demolition in 1930, is furnished with important pieces of 18th-century Philadelphia furniture. A mahogany staircase from Santo Domingo embellishes the front hall, and there is a signed Gilbert Stuart portrait in the parlor. In the second-floor ballroom, Mrs. Powel—the city's hostess-with-the-mostest—served floating islands and whipped syllabubs to distinguished guests (including Adams, Franklin, and Lafayette) on Nanking china that was a gift from George and Martha Washington. Today the ballroom can be rented for parties and special events. ⊠ *244 S. 3rd St.,* ☎ *215/627–0364.* 🖾 *$3.* ☉ *Thurs.–Sat. noon–5, Sun. 1–5; other times by appointment.*

★ ③⑦ **St. Peter's Episcopal Church.** One of the city's loveliest churches, founded by members of Christ Church (☞ *Old City, above*) who were living in newly settled Society Hill, St. Peter's has been in continuous use since its first service on September 4, 1761. William White (Bishop White), rector of Christ Church, also served in that role at St. Peter's until his death in 1836. The brick Palladian-style building was designed by Scottish architect Robert Smith, who was responsible for Carpenters' Hall and the steeple on Christ Church. William Strickland's simple steeple, a Philadelphia landmark, was added in 1842. Notable features include the grand Palladian window on the chancel wall, high-back box pews that were raised off the floor to eliminate drafts, and the unusual arrangement of altar and pulpit at either end of the main aisle. The design has been called "restrained," but what is palpable on a visit is the silence and grace of the stark white interior. In the churchyard lie Commodore John Hazelwood, a Revolutionary War hero, painter Charles Willson Peale, and seven Native American chiefs who died of smallpox on a visit to Philadelphia in 1793. ⊠ *313 Pine St.,* ☎ *215/925–5968.* ☉ *Weekdays 9–4, Sat. 11–3, Sun. 1–3. A guide is on hand weekends to answer questions; tours can be arranged by calling ahead on weekdays.*

South Street. Philadelphia's most bohemian neighborhood is crammed with craft shops and condom stores, coffee bars and tattoo parlors, ethnic restaurants and New Age book shops. At night it's crammed with people—those who hang out, and those who come to watch them, giving South Street the offbeat, off-color feel of Greenwich Village mixed with Bourbon Street. To some, it's still "the hippest street in town," as the Orlons called it in their 1963 song, although flower children have been replaced by teens with pierced eyebrows. ⊠ *South St. from Front St. to about 10th St., Lombard St. to Bainbridge St.*

③⑧ Thaddeus Kosciuszko National Memorial. A Polish general who later became a national hero in his homeland, Kosciuszko came to the United States in 1776 to help fight in the Revolution; he distinguished himself as one of the first foreign volunteers in the war. The plain three-story brick house, built around 1776, has a portrait gallery; you can also view a six-minute film (in English and Polish) that portrays the general's activities during the Revolution. ⊠ *301 Pine St.,* ☎ *215/597–8974.* ▣ *Free.* ☾ *June–Oct., daily 9–5; Nov.–May, Wed.–Sun. 9–5.*

⊙ ③① USS *Becuna*. You can tour this 318-ft-long "guppy class" submarine, which was commissioned in 1944 and conducted search-and-destroy missions in the South Pacific. The guides—all World War II submarine vets—tell amazing stories of what life was like for a crew of 88 men, at sea for months at a time, in these claustrophobic quarters. Then you can step through the narrow walkways, climb the ladders, and glimpse the torpedoes in their firing chambers. Children will love it, but it's fascinating for adults, too. ⊠ *Penn's Landing at Spruce St.,* ☎ *215/922–1898.* ▣ *$5 for USS Becuna and USS Olympia (☞ below); $7.50 for boats and the Independence Seaport Museum (☞ above). The ticket booth by the boats is closed seasonally; tickets must be purchased at the museum on weekdays Sept.–May.* ☾ *Daily 10–5.*

⊙ ③② USS *Olympia*. Commodore George Dewey's flagship at the Battle of Manila in the Spanish-American War is the only remaining ship from that war. Dewey entered Manila Harbor after midnight on May 1, 1898. At 5:40 AM, he told his captain, "You may fire when ready, Gridley," and the battle began. By 12:30 the Americans had destroyed the entire Spanish fleet. The *Olympia* was the last ship of the "New Navy" of the 1880s and 1890s, the beginning of the era of steel ships. You can tour the entire restored ship, including the officers' staterooms, engine room, galley, gun batteries, pilothouse, and conning tower. ⊠ *Penn's Landing at Spruce St.,* ☎ *215/922–1898.* ▣ *$5 for USS Olympia and USS Becuna (☞ above); $7.50 for boats and the Independence Seaport Museum (☞ above). The ticket booth by the boats is closed seasonally; tickets must be purchased at the museum on weekdays Sept.–May.* ☾ *Daily 10–5.*

Washington Square. This leafy area resembling a London square has been through numerous incarnations since it was set aside by William Penn. From 1705 until after the Revolution, the square was lined on three sides by houses and on the fourth by the Walnut Street Prison. The latter was home to Robert Morris, who went to debtors' prison after he helped finance the Revolution. The square served as a burial ground for victims of the 1793 yellow fever epidemic and for 2,600 British and American soldiers who perished during the Revolution. The Square holds a Tomb of the Unknown Soldier, erected to the memory of unknown Revolutionary War soldiers. By the 1840s the square had gained prestige as the center of the city's most fashionable neighborhood. It later became the city's publishing center. During recent renovations to improve landscaping and repave walkways, construction workers were surprised to unearth a number of bones. ⊠ *Between 6th and 7th Sts. and Walnut and Locust Sts.*

CENTER CITY
City Hall and Environs

For a grand introduction to the heart of the downtown area, climb the few steps to the plaza in front of the Municipal Services Building at 15th Street and John F. Kennedy Boulevard for a great overview of the city. You'll be standing alongside a 10-ft-tall bronze statue of the late Frank L. Rizzo waving to the people. Rizzo, nicknamed the "Big Bambino," was the city's police commissioner, two-term mayor (in the 1970s), and a five-time mayoral candidate. He shaped the political scene just as the buildings that surround you—City Hall, the PSFS Building, the Art Museum, the skyscrapers at Liberty Place, Oldenburg's *Clothespin*, and more—shape its architectural landscape.

The story behind this skyline begins with Philadelphia's historic City Hall, which reaches to 40 stories and was the tallest structure in the metropolis until 1987. No law prohibited taller buildings, but the tradition sprang from a gentleman's agreement not to build higher. In May 1984, when a developer proposed building two office towers that would break the 491-ft barrier, it became evident how entrenched this tradition was: The proposal provoked a public outcry. The traditionalists contended the height limitation had made Philadelphia a city of human scale, given character to its streets and public places, and showed respect for tradition. The opposing camp thought that a dramatic new skyline would shatter the city's conservative image and encourage economic growth. After painstaking debate the go-ahead was granted. In short order, the midtown area became the hub of the city's commercial center, Market Street west of City Hall became a district of high-rise office buildings, and the area became a symbol of the city's ongoing transformation from a dying industrial town to a center for service industries. Here, too, are a number of museums, the excellent Reading Terminal Market and the convention center, and Chinatown.

Numbers in the text correspond to numbers in the margin and on the Center City and Along the Parkway map.

A Good Walk

Ask most locals where "downtown" or "Center City" is, and you'll find they agree that Victorian **City Hall** ① is at its heart. Take the elevator up to the tower for an incomparable bird's-eye view of the city. Leave City Hall by the north exit and cross John F. Kennedy Boulevard to the **Masonic Temple** ②, with its ornate interiors and collection of Masonic items. Two blocks north on Broad Street, at Cherry Street in a striking Victorian Gothic building, is the **Pennsylvania Academy of the Fine Arts** ③, filled with paintings by such artists as Winslow Homer and Andrew Wyeth. Head west on Cherry Street one block to 15th Street, turn left, and walk south three blocks to Market Street. This walk will take you from the classics to the avant-garde: Claes Oldenburg's 45-ft-high, 10-ton steel **Clothespin.** (From here you can take public transportation to a few of the city's more distant sites—the Insectarium, the American-Swedish Historical Museum, and Bartram's Garden—or you can drive to Bryn Athyn Cathedral.)

Two blocks west of the sculpture are **Liberty Place One and Two** ④; the food court between them makes a great stop for lunch. Exit the building at 16th and Chestnut; three blocks east at 13th Street is **Lord & Taylor** ⑤, formerly the John Wanamaker store, famous for its eagle and its nine-story grand court. Walk over to Market Street, turn right, and go one block to 12th Street. Here is the **Philadelphia Saving Fund Society (PSFS) Building,** an early (1930) skyscraper. On the same block, SEPTA's headquarters holds the **Transit Museum.** Two blocks north on 12th Street is the **Reading Terminal Market** ⑥, filled with vendors of all kinds of food. Across Arch Street is the **Pennsylvania Convention Center** ⑦, which houses a terrific collection of contemporary art. Walking two blocks east on Arch Street brings you to the 40-ft-tall Chinese

44

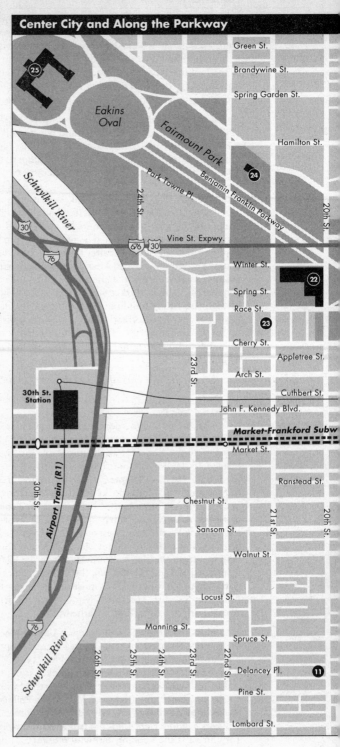

Center City and Along the Parkway

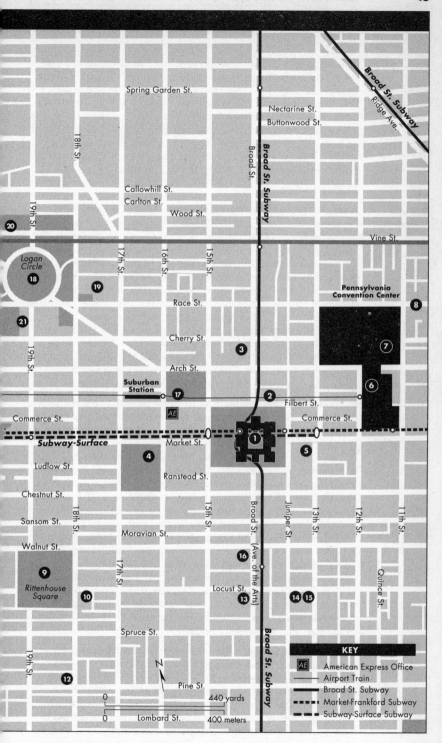

Spring Garden St.

Nectarine St.
Buttonwood St.

Broad St. Subway

Ridge Ave.

18th St.

Callowhill St.
Carlton St.
Wood St.

19th St.

Vine St.

20

17th St.

16th St.

15th St.

Logan
Circle

18

Pennsylvania
Convention Center

8

19

Race St.

7

21

Cherry St.

3

19th St.

Arch St.

Suburban
Station

17

2

Filbert St.

6

AE

Commerce St.

Commerce St.

Subway-Surface

Market St.

1

5

4

Ludlow St.

Ranstead St.

Chestnut St.

18th St.

Sansom St.

Moravian St.

15th St.

Broad St. (Ave. of the Arts)

Juniper St.

13th St.

12th St.

11th St.

Quince St.

Walnut St.

9

Rittenhouse
Square

10

17th St.

16

Locust St.

13

14 15

Spruce St.

19th St.

N

12

Pine St.

0   440 yards

0   400 meters

Lombard St.

Broad St. Subway

KEY

AE   American Express Office
— Airport Train
— Broad St. Subway
····· Market-Frankford Subway
- - - Subway-Surface Subway

Friendship Gate, the unofficial entrance to the restaurants and stores of **Chinatown** ⑧.

TIMING

To get a feel for the city at work, save this walk for a weekday, when the streets are bustling (on weekends the area can be quite deserted). Besides, the City Hall Observation Tower is open weekdays only, and both the Reading Terminal Market and the Masonic Temple, two don't-miss spots, are closed Sunday. You could complete this walk in 45 minutes, but if you want to sightsee, reserve about half a day, with an hour each at the Masonic Temple, City Hall Tower, and the Pennsylvania Academy of the Fine Arts. If you get an early start, you can finish with lunch at the Reading Terminal Market.

Sights to See

OFF THE
BEATEN PATH

AMERICAN-SWEDISH HISTORICAL MUSEUM – The Swedes settled the Delaware Valley in the mid-1600s before William Penn, but few traces remain other than Gloria Dei (Old Swedes') Church (☞ Southwark and South Philadelphia, *below*) and this museum. Modeled after a 17th-century Swedish manor house, the museum has 14 galleries that trace the history of Swedes in the United States. The John Ericsson Room honors the designer of the Civil War ironclad ship the *Monitor,* and the Jenny Lind Room contains memorabilia from the Swedish Nightingale's American tour of 1848–1851. Other rooms display handmade costumed Swedish peasant dolls, crafts, paintings, and drawings. To get here, you can pick up the subway just below the *Clothespin* sculpture, at 15th and Market streets. ✉ *1900 Pattison Ave.,* ☎ *215/389–1776. Take Broad St. subway south to Pattison Ave. Cross Broad St., walk 5 blocks west through the park to the museum.* ▨ *$5.* ☉ *Tues.–Fri. 10–4, weekends noon–4.*

BARTRAM'S GARDEN – Begun in 1728 by the pioneering botanist John Bartram (1699–1777), America's oldest surviving botanical garden has remained relatively unchanged while the surrounding areas have altered dramatically. The 44-acre oasis is tucked into a heavily industrialized and depressed corner of southwest Philadelphia. With stone columns and carvings by Bartram himself, the 18th-century farmhouse on the grounds reflects his unique vision of classical and Colonial architecture. The self-trained Bartram became botanist to King George III, traveling throughout the Colonies and returning with many unusual species. He corresponded and exchanged plants with botanists around the world. The house is a National Historic Landmark, and the trails extending to the Schuylkill River are part of the National Recreation Trails System. You can get the subway in front of the *Clothespin,* at 15th and Market streets. Note that you can get a map to tour the gardens only when the house is open. ✉ *54th St. and Lindbergh Blvd.,* ☎ *215/729–5281. 20-min ride on Trolley 36 from 15th and Market Sts., then right to the entrance.* ▨ *$3 for house tour; garden free.* ☉ *Garden, daily dawn–dusk. House May–Oct., Wed.–Sun. noon–4; Nov.–Apr., Wed.–Fri. noon–4.*

BRYN ATHYN CATHEDRAL – At one of the most beautiful spots in the Philadelphia area stands a spectacular cathedral built in 12th-century Romanesque and 14th-century Gothic styles. Atop a hill overlooking the Pennypack Valley, the cathedral is the Episcopal seat of the Church of the New Jerusalem, a sect based on the writings of the Swedish scientist and mystic Emanuel Swedenborg (1688–1772). The main patrons of the church are descendants of John Pitcairn, an industrialist who made his fortune in paint and plate glass. Construction of the cathedral began in 1914 and went on for decades. It was built according to the medieval guild system: all materials—wood, metal, glass, stone—were brought to craftspeople at the site, and everything was fashioned by hand. The stained glass includes two colors, striated ruby and cobalt blue, found nowhere else in the Americas. Also on the hill is the former home of Raymond and Mildred Pitcairn, **Glencairn** (☎ 215/938–2600; call for appointment), a neo-Romanesque building that's now a museum. From Broad Street in Center City, go north on Broad Street to Route 611, right on County Line Road, and south on Route 232 to the second traffic light; the cathedral will be on your right. ✉ *Rte. 232, Huntingdon Pike at Cathedral Rd., Bryn Athyn, 15 mi north of Center City,* ☎ *215/ 947–0266.* ✇ *Free.* ⊙ *Tues.–Sun. 1–4 for 30–min tours (sometimes preempted by special events); visitors also welcome at services Sun. 9:30 and 11.*

❽ Chinatown. Centered on 10th and Race streets just two blocks north of Market Street, Chinatown serves as the residential and commercial hub of the city's Chinese community. Along with more than 50 restaurants, Chinatown has grocery stores, souvenir and gift shops, martial arts studios, a fortune cookie store, bilingual street signs, and red-and-green pagoda-style telephone booths. One striking Chinatown site is the **Chinese Friendship Gate,** straddling 10th Street at Arch Street. This intricate and colorful 40-ft-tall arch—the largest authentic Chinese gate outside China—was created by Chinese artisans, who brought their own tools and construction materials. The citizens of Tianjin, Philadelphia's sister city in China, donated the building materials, including the ornamental tile. From February to May you can celebrate Chinese New Year with a 10-course banquet at the **Chinese Cultural Center** (✉ 125 N. 10th St., ☎ 215/923–6767). The center occupies an 1831 building of the Beijing Mandarin-palace style. ✉ *9th to 11th Sts., Arch to Vine Sts.*

★ **❶ City Hall.** Topped by a 37-ft bronze statue of William Penn, City Hall was Philadelphia's tallest building until 1987; you can study the trappings of government and also get a panoramic of the city here. With 642 rooms, it is the largest city hall in the country and the tallest masonry-bearing building in the world: no steel structure supports it. Designed by architect John McArthur Jr., the building took 30 years to build (from 1871 to 1900) and cost taxpayers more than $23 million. The result has been called a "Victorian wedding cake of Renaissance styles." Placed about the facade are hundreds of statues by Alexander Milne Calder, who also designed the statue of William Penn at the top (Calder's son and grandson were artists, too; ☞ Logan Circle *in* The Benjamin Franklin Parkway, *below*). Calder's 27-ton cast-iron statue of Penn is the largest single piece of sculpture on any building in the world.

Not only the geographic center of Penn's original city plan, City Hall is also the center of municipal and state government. Many of the magnificent interiors—splendidly decorated with mahogany paneling, gold-leaf ceilings, and marble pillars—are patterned after the Second Empire salons of part of the Louvre in Paris. On a tour each weekday at 12:30, you'll see the mayor's ornate reception room, Conversation Hall, the Supreme Court of Pennsylvania, and the City Council chambers (Room 400). You can attend these often heated City Council meetings, held each Thursday morning at 10.

To top off your visit, take the elevator from the 7th floor up the tower to the observation deck at the foot of William Penn's statue for a 30-mi view of the city and surroundings. The elevator holds only six people per trip and runs every 15 minutes; the least crowded time is early morning. ✉ *Broad and Market Sts. (tour office: East Portal, Room 121),* ☎ *215/686–1776 or 215/686–2840 for tour information.* ✇ *Free;*

donations welcome. ☉ *Tower: weekdays 9:30–4:15; 90-min building tour including tower, weekdays at 12:30.*

NEED A
BREAK?

Grab a pita sandwich and a fresh fruit cup from one of the **sidewalk vendors** along 15th Street around Market Street and munch and relax in Dilworth Plaza (on the west apron of City Hall) or John F. Kennedy Plaza (✉ 15th St. and John F. Kennedy Blvd.).

Clothespin. Claes Oldenburg's 45-ft-high, 10-ton steel sculpture stands in front of the Center Square Building. Lauded by some and scorned by others, this pop art piece contrasts with the traditional statuary so common in Philadelphia. ✉ *15th and Market Sts.*

OFF THE
BEATEN PATH

INSECTARIUM – Even if you hate bugs, you'll love this ugly, yet beautiful collection of more than 1 million creepy crawlers—tarantulas, giant centipedes, scorpions, assassin bugs, and metallic beetles that look like pieces of gold jewelry. About 25% of the insects are alive; the rest are mounted. The 18,000-square-ft museum recently acquired the largest butterfly and moth collection in North America, with 63,000 mounted specimens. Don't forget to check out the amazing bug gift shop. It's easier to drive here than to take public transportation; call the museum for directions, though you can pick up the subway in front of the *Clothespin.* ✉ *8046 Frankford Ave., Northeast Philadelphia,* ☎ *215/338–3000. By public transit: From 15th and Market St. station take the Market-Frankford subway to end (Bridge St.); transfer to SEPTA Bus 66 to Welsh Rd.* ▨ *$4.* ☉ *Mon.–Sat. 10–4.*

❹ **Liberty Place One and Two.** One Liberty Place is the 945-ft, 63-story office building designed by Helmut Jahn that propelled Philadelphia into the "ultra-high" skyscraper era. Built in 1987, it became the tallest structure in Philadelphia. The art deco–style structure, vaguely reminiscent of New York's Chrysler Building, is visible from almost everywhere in the city. In 1990 the adjacent 58-story tower, **Two Liberty Place,** opened. It held the elegant Ritz-Carlton Hotel, which in 1999 become the equally elegant St. Regis Philadelphia. Zeidler Roberts designed this second building. ✉ *One Liberty Place, 1650 Market St.;* ✉ *Two Liberty Place, 1601 Chestnut St.*

NEED A
BREAK?

The **Shops at Liberty Place** (✉ 1625 Chestnut St., between Liberty One and Liberty Two, ☎ 215/851–9055) houses a large international food court on the second level, above the upscale boutiques. You'll find anything from salad to sushi to those familiar Philly cheese steaks.

❺ **Lord & Taylor.** The former John Wanamaker department store, this building is almost as prominent a Philadelphia landmark as the Liberty Bell. Wanamaker began with a clothing store in 1861 and became one of America's most innovative and prominent retailers. The massive building, which occupies a city block with grace, was designed by the noted Chicago firm of D. H. Burnham and Company. Its focal point is the nine-story grand court with its 30,000-pipe organ—the largest ever built—and a 2,500-pound statue of an eagle, both remnants of the 1904 Louisiana Purchase Exposition in St. Louis. "Meet me at the Eagle" remains a popular way for Philadelphians to arrange a rendezvous. Happily, the new owners have kept the eagle and continue the famous Christmas sound-and-light show and the organ performances. ✉ *13th and Market Sts.,* ☎ *215/241–9000.* ☉ *Mon., Tues., Thurs., Fri. 10–7; Wed. 9–8; Sat. 9–7; Sun. noon–5; organ concerts Mon.–Sat. at 11:15 and 5:15.*

★ ❷ **Masonic Temple.** The temple is one of the city's architectural jewels, but it remains a hidden treasure even to many Philadelphians. Historically, Freemasons were skilled stoneworkers of the Middle Ages who possessed secret signs and passwords. Their worldwide fraternal order—the Free and Accepted Masons—included men in the building trades, plus many honorary members; the secret society prospered in Philadelphia during Colonial times. Brother James Windrim designed this elaborate temple as a home for the Grand Lodge of Free and Accepted Masons of Pennsylvania. The trowel used here at the laying of the cornerstone in 1868, while 10,000 brothers looked on, was the same one that Brother George Washington used to set the cornerstone of the U.S. Capitol. The temple's ornate interior consists of seven lavishly decorated lodge halls built to exemplify specific styles of architecture: Corinthian, Ionic, Italian Renaissance, Norman, Gothic, Oriental, and Egyptian. The Egyptian room, with its accurate hieroglyphics, is the most famous. The Temple also houses an interesting museum of Masonic items, including Benjamin Franklin's printing of the first book on Freemasonry published in America and Brother George Washington's Masonic Apron, which was embroidered by Madame Lafayette, wife of the famous marquis. ⊠ *1 N. Broad St.,* ☎ *215/988–1917.* 🖼 *Free.* ⊘ *45-min. tours Sept.–June, weekdays 10, 11, 1, 2, and 3, Sat. 10 and 11; July–Aug., weekdays 10, 11, 1, 2, and 3.*

★ ❸ **Pennsylvania Academy of the Fine Arts.** This High Victorian Gothic structure is a work of art in itself. Designed in 1876 by the noted, and sometimes eccentric, Philadelphia architects Frank Furness and George Hewitt, the multicolor stone-and-brick exterior is an extravagant blend of columns, friezes, and Richardsonian Romanesque and Moorish flourishes. The interior is just as lush, with rich hues of red, yellow, and blue and an impressive staircase. Inside, the oldest art institution in the United States (founded 1804) displays a fine collection that ranges from the Peale family, Gilbert Stuart, Benjamin West, and Winslow Homer to Andrew Wyeth and Red Grooms. *Fox Hunt* by Winslow Homer, *The Artist in His Museum* by Charles Willson Peale, and *Interior with Doorway* by Richard Diebenkorn are just a few notable works. The academy faculty has included Thomas Sully, Thomas Eakins, and Charles Willson Peale. The permanent collection is supplemented by constantly changing exhibitions of sculpture, paintings, and mixed-media artwork. The art school's classes are now held a block away at 1301 Cherry Street. ⊠ *118 N. Broad St., at Cherry St.,* ☎ *215/972–7600.* 🖼 *$5; free Sun. 3–5.* ⊘ *Mon.–Sat. 10–5, Sun. 11–5.*

❼ **Pennsylvania Convention Center.** Opened in June 1993 with galas, parties, and Vice President Al Gore cutting the ribbon, the convention center is helping rejuvenate Philadelphia's economy and fuel a hotel boom. It's big: With 313,000 square ft, the area of the main exhibition hall equals seven football fields. And it's beautiful: The 1.9 million square ft of space are punctuated by the largest permanent collection of contemporary art in a building of its kind. Many city and state artists are represented in the niches, nooks, and galleries built to house their multimedia works. To see the architectural highlight of the building—the Reading Terminal's magnificently restored four-story-high Victorian train shed, which has been transformed into the Convention Center's Grand Hall—enter the building through the century-old Italian Renaissance headhouse structure on Market Street between 11th and 12th streets and ride up the escalator. The Headhouse is also home to Philadelphia's Hard Rock Cafe. ⊠ *1101 Arch St.,* ☎ *215/ 418–4735.* 🖼 *Free.* ⊘ *45-min tours Tues. and Thurs. by reservation.*

PHILADELPHIA FLOWER SHOW: THE CITY IN BLOOM

I T TAKES ONE WEEK; 7,000 Belgian blocks; 3,500 volunteers; thousands of plumbers, carpenters and electricians; more than a million plants; and 50 tractor-trailer loads of mulch to transform the Pennsylvania Convention Center into the annual Philadelphia Flower Show, the world's largest indoor horticultural event. But the exhibitors—nursery owners, landscapers, and florists from the region and from Africa, Japan, and Europe—spend the better part of a year planning their displays. The astonishing, fragrant results of their efforts arrive in the city as a breath of spring in early March.

It's a fitting tribute to William Penn that Philadelphia hosts this extravaganza, for this was Penn's "greene countrie town," which he laid out on a grid punctuated with tree-lined streets, pocket parks, small squares, and large public parks. It's also appropriate that this city gave root to the Pennsylvania Horticultural Society (PHS), the nation's first such organization. In 1829, two years after its founding, the society hosted its first show at the Masonic Hall in an 82- by 69-foot exhibition space; 25 society members showed off their green thumbs.

Today the show fills 10 acres of exhibition space at the convention center and spills throughout the area as the city hosts a variety of Flower Show Week events. Along with the more than 60 major exhibits there are hands-on lectures; demonstrations of the latest garden gadgets; hundreds of vendors selling plants, birdhouses, topiaries, watering systems, botanical prints, and more; and an amateur division with more than 2,000 entries in 700 competitive categories—from pressed plants and miniature settings to spectacular orchids and jewelry designs that use flowers. In 1999, Flower Show attendance topped 280,000, 40% of whom were from out of town; the economic impact on the city was estimated to be about $25 million.

Each year, the show has a theme, and the show's designers think big—very big. One year an exhibit re-created a portion of the Wissahickon in Fairmount Park. Highlights from "The Art of Gardening," 1999's theme, included re-creations of four of the many formal gardens maintained by the National Trust for Historic Preservation, including the Kykuit gardens at the Rockefeller mansion in New York state, and a prehistoric landscape with "living fossils" of horsetail, gingko, and ferns, presided over by an apatosaurus. Nearby were an opulent Raj tent surrounded by Japanese crabapples; a meditative water garden; and an authentic 19th-century one-room schoolhouse, transported from rural Pennsylvania and nestled among native wildflowers. The theme for 2000 is "Marking Time: Gardens of the New Millennium.

In 1974, with revenues from the show, the PHS launched Philadelphia Green, which provides neighborhood groups in low and moderate income areas with the assistance needed to transform trash-strewn vacant lots into vegetable and flower gardens and to line streets with trees and plants in containers. The program has also revitalized public landscaping throughout the city. In September, PHS hosts the Philadelphia Harvest Show, a salute to the end of the growing season.

Many people plan trips to Philadelphia around the show, so be sure to make reservations early. If you just happen to be in the city during Flower Show Week, do not miss it. Wear good walking shoes, check your coat, and bring spending money for the many horticultural temptations. To avoid crowds (which can be daunting), take advantage of the show's evening hours. If you're not in town in early March, you can still appreciate the city's green thumb at the Philadelphia Zoo, Bartram's Garden, and the Morris Arboretum; in Fairmount Park; and farther afield at Longwood Gardens.

Philadelphia Saving Fund Society (PSFS) Building. In 1930, architects George Howe and William Lescaze wowed the world with their design for the PSFS Building, one of the city's first skyscrapers. This was America's first skyscraper to embrace modernism's International style; 70 years later, the structure is still modern-looking. The architects installed custom-designed Cartier clocks in every elevator lobby and even designed the wastebaskets. Loews Hotels has taken on the challenge of turning the 33-story building into a 585-room hotel (scheduled to open by mid-2000) while maintaining its architectural integrity. ⊠ *12 S. 12th St.*

★ ❻ **Reading Terminal Market.** The market is nothing short of a historical treasure and a food heaven to Philadelphians and visitors alike. One floor beneath the former Reading Railroad's 1891 train shed, the sprawling market has more than 80 food stalls and other shops. Some stalls change daily, offering items from hooked rugs and handmade jewelry to South American and African crafts. Here, amid the local color, you can sample Bassett's ice cream, Philadelphia's best; down a cheese steak, a bowl of snapper soup, or a soft pretzel; or nibble Greek, Mexican, and Indian specialties. From Wednesday through Saturday the Amish from Lancaster County cart in their goodies, including Lebanon bologna, shoofly pie, and scrapple. Many stalls have their own counters with seating; there's also a central eating area. If you want to cook, you can buy a large variety of fresh food from fruit and vegetable stands, butchers, fish stores, and Pennsylvania Dutch markets. The entire building is a National Historic Landmark, and the train shed is a National Engineering Landmark. ⊠ *12th and Filbert Sts.,* ☎ *215/922–2317.* ⊙ *Mon.–Sat. 8–6.*

Transit Museum. Located, appropriately enough, in the headquarters of the Southeastern Pennsylvania Transportation Authority (SEPTA), this museum showcases the history and development of public transportation in the region and its impact on social, political, and economic life. On display is a 1947 Presidents Conference Committee trolley, along with transit memorabilia and photographs. ⊠ *Concourse level, 1234 Market St.,* ☎ *215/580–7168.* ▣ *Free.* ⊙ *Mon.–Sat. 10–5.*

RITTENHOUSE SQUARE
Living the Good Life

Rittenhouse Square, at 18th and Walnuts streets, has long been one of the city's swankiest addresses. The square's entrances, plaza, pool, and fountains were designed in 1913 by Paul Cret, one of the people responsible for the Benjamin Franklin Parkway. The square was named in honor of one of the city's 18th-century stars: David Rittenhouse, president of the American Philosophical Society and a professor of astronomy at the University of Pennsylvania. The first house facing the square was erected in 1840, soon to be followed by other grand mansions. Almost all the private homes are now gone, replaced by hotels, apartments, and cultural institutions, and elegant restaurants and stylish cafés dot the neighborhood. The former home of banker George Childs Drexel was transformed into the Curtis Institute, alma mater of Leonard Bernstein and Gian Carlo Menotti. The former Samuel Price Wetherill mansion is now the Philadelphia Art Alliance, sponsor of exhibitions, drama, dance, and literary events.

The area south and west of the square is still largely residential and lovely, with cupolas and balconies, hitching posts and stained-glass windows. You can also find some small shops and two fine museum/library collections tucked in—the Civil War Library and Museum and the Rosenbach Museum. In the heart of the city there are green places, too. Peek in the streets behind these homes or through their wrought-iron gates, and you'll see beautiful gardens. On Delancey Place, blocks alternate narrow and wide. The wide blocks had the homes of the wealthy, while the smaller ones held dwellings for servants or stables (today these carriage houses are prized real estate). When he saw 18th Street and Delancey Place, author R. F. Delderfield, author of *God Is an Englishman,* said, "I never thought I'd see anything like this in America. It is like Dickensian London." Today the good life continues in Rittenhouse Square. Annual events include the Rittenhouse Square Flower Show and the Fine Arts Annual, an outdoor juried art show.

Numbers in the text correspond to numbers in the margin and on the Center City and Along the Parkway map.

A Good Walk

The lovely residential area around **Rittenhouse Square** ⑨ is dotted with small museums. A walk through this neighborhood logically begins at the square itself, on Walnut Street between 18th and 19th streets. East of the square are the former Barclay Hotel, celebrated for decades as the city's most fashionable hotel; the Philadelphia Art Alliance (✉ 251 S. 18th St.), housed in an 1890s mansion, with galleries open to the public; the environmentally smart Sheraton Rittenhouse Square; and the **Curtis Institute of Music** ⑩, which offers concerts to the public. West of the square you'll find a branch of the Free Library of Philadelphia, the Rittenhouse Hotel, and the Church of the Holy Trinity, presided over in the mid-19th century by Reverend Phillips Brooks, who achieved renown as the lyricist of *O Little Town of Bethlehem.*

Leave the square on its south side and continue south on 19th Street to **Delancey Place,** then turn right and take a look at this urban residential showcase with its grand houses. The 2000 block of Delancey wins the prize: At Number 2010 is the **Rosenbach Museum and Library** ⑪, a local gem, with paintings, manuscripts, and rare books. Heading east a block south of Delancey, you'll find the **Civil War Library and Museum** ⑫, at 18th and Pine streets. Back at Rittenhouse Square, an elegant tea time can be had in the tearoom at the Rittenhouse Hotel.

From Rittenhouse Square walk east on Locust Street four blocks to the **Academy of Music** ⑬, current home of the Philadelphia Orchestra. Cross Broad Street and continue east; within the first block you come across two renowned collections, the **Library Company of Philadelphia** ⑭ and the **Historical Society of Pennsylvania** ⑮. You could walk three blocks east to 10th and Locust streets to see Thomas Eakins's masterpiece, *The Gross Clinic,* in Thomas Jefferson University's Alumni Hall. Double back to Broad Street, which has been christened the **Avenue of the Arts.** One block south, at Broad and Spruce streets, construction is under way for the new Regional Performing Arts Center, set to open in fall 2001 as a new home for the Philadelphia Orchestra. As you walk along the west side of Broad between Spruce and Walnut streets, notice the more than 30 plaques in the sidewalk honoring some of those who contributed to Philadelphia's cultural history. Where else could Frankie Avalon and Dizzy Gillespie rub shoulders with Anna Moffo and Eugene Ormandy? A block north of the venerable Academy of Music is another grande dame of South Broad Street, the former Bellevue Stratford Hotel, now the **Park Hyatt Philadelphia at the Bellevue** ⑯. As you continue up Broad Street, you'll pass a French Renaissance–style building, the **Union League of Philadelphia.**

TIMING

This is one of the city's loveliest neighborhoods for strolling. Two hours would allow you enough time to wander through the Rittenhouse Square area and visit the Rosenbach Museum and Library (get there before 2:45). If you start midday, you could conclude with afternoon tea at the Rittenhouse.

Sights to See

⓭ Academy of Music. The only surviving European-style opera house in America is the current home of the Philadelphia Orchestra and the Pennsylvania Ballet. Designed by Napoleon Le Brun and Gustav Runge and completed in 1857, the building has a modest exterior; the builders ran out of money and couldn't put marble facing on the brick, as they had intended. The brick hides a lavish, neo-Baroque interior modeled after Milan's La Scala opera house, with gilt, carvings, murals on the ceiling, and a huge Victorian crystal chandelier. Friday-afternoon orchestra concerts are legendary for their audience of "Main Line matrons" from the wealthy suburbs. If you're willing to wait in line for "rush" tickets that go on sale an hour before curtain time and to sit in the cramped amphitheater four levels above the stage, you can take advantage of one of the music world's great bargains—the $5–$8 "nosebleed" seats. The academy is also home to the Opera Company of Philadelphia and the site of the Pennsylvania Ballet's Christmas production of *The Nutcracker.* Tours are occasionally given on designated weekdays at 2 by reservation. ⊠ *Broad and Locust Sts.,* ☎ *215/ 893–1999 for box office; 215/893–1935 for tours.*

NEED A BREAK?

Hot cocoa and s'mores? Espresso and biscotti? A martini and a chocolate layer cake brushed with Chambord liqueur and topped with fresh raspberries? Your choices are many at the fashionable, funky **Xando** (⊠ *235 S. 15th St.,* ☎ *215/893–9696).*

Avenue of the Arts. "Let us entertain you" could be the theme of the ambitious cultural development project that is transforming North and South Broad Street (☞ Chapter 6 *for* more information about some of these venues). New performance spaces are being built, old landmarks are being refurbished, and South Broad Street has been spruced up with landscaping, cast-iron lighting fixtures, and decorative sidewalk paving. Joining the Merriam Theater and the University of the Arts on South Broad Street are the Wilma Theater, a 300-seat theater for this innovative company; a cabaret-style theater for the Philadelphia Clef Club of Jazz and the Performing Arts; and the intimate Philadelphia Arts Bank at the University of the Arts. The latest addition is the Prince Music Theater, a venue for musical theater and film. The Regional Performing Arts Center, under construction at Broad and Spruce streets, will include a 2,500-seat concert hall, specifically designed for the Philadelphia Orchestra, and a recital hall. With a total capacity of 6,000 seats, the venue will be one of the nation's largest performing arts centers. Opening night is scheduled for the beginning of the orchestra's season in 2001. The Academy of Music is being extensively renovated and modernized. On North Broad Street, the Pennsylvania Academy of the Fine Arts (☞ Center City, *above*) has completed structural renovations; the Apollo of Temple, Temple University's multipurpose sports and concert complex, has opened; and the Freedom Theatre, the state's oldest African-American theater, has built a new auditorium in its majestic Italianate mansion.

⓬ Civil War Library and Museum. The museum is one of the country's premier collections of Civil War memorabilia pertaining to the Union. Artifacts include two life masks of Abraham Lincoln; dress uniforms and swords that belonged to generals Grant and Meade; plus many other weapons, uniforms, and personal effects of Civil War officers and enlisted men. The library has more than 12,000 volumes about the war. ⊠ *1805 Pine St.,* ☎ *215/735–8196.* ☒ *$5.* ☉ *Tues.–Sat. 11–4:30.*

⑩ Curtis Institute of Music. Graduates of this tuition-free school for outstanding students include Leonard Bernstein, Samuel Barber, Ned Rorem, and Anna Moffo. The school occupies four former private homes; the main building is in the mansion that belonged to banker George W. Childs Drexel. Built in 1893 by the distinguished Boston firm of Peabody and Stearns, it is notable for Romanesque and Renaissance architectural details. Free student and faculty concerts are given from October through May at 8, usually on Monday, Wednesday, and Friday evenings; their recital hot line lists events. ⊠ *1726 Locust St.,* ☎ *215/893–5261 for hot line.*

Delancey Place. This fine residential area southwest of Rittenhouse Square was once the address of Pearl S. Buck (⊠ 2019 Delancey Pl.) and Rudolf Serkin. At one corner (⊠ 320 S. 18th St.) there is an interesting old sea captain's house. At Number 2010 is the **Rosenbach Museum and Library** (☞ *below*). Cypress Street, just north of Delancey Place, and Panama Street (especially the 1900 block, one block south of Delancey) are two of the many intimate streets lined with trees and town houses characteristic of the area.

OFF THE
BEATEN PATH

THE GROSS CLINIC – Most art historians would put Thomas Eakins's magnificent medical painting *The Gross Clinic* (1875) on the list of top 10 American paintings; you can view it in the alumni hall of Thomas Jefferson University, a medical school. Eakins depicts Dr. Samuel D. Gross, Jefferson's celebrated surgeon and teacher, presiding over an operation for osteomyelitis in an amphitheater under a skylighted roof. His assistants are removing the bone, while the patient's mother stands off to the side. It's a dramatic piece in size (96 by 78 inches), composition (the light streaming into the murky room), and subject matter. The alumni hall is three blocks east of the Historical Society of Pennsylvania; request entry at the information desk. ⊠ *Jefferson Alumni Hall, 1020 Locust St.,* ☎ *215/955–6000.* ☒ *Free.* ☉ *Mon.–Sat. 10–4, Sun. noon–4.*

⑮ Historical Society of Pennsylvania. More than 500,000 books, 300,000 graphic works, and 15 million manuscript items are housed in this superlative special collections library with an emphasis on Colonial, early national, and Pennsylvania history. Founded in 1824, the society also owns one of the largest family history libraries in the nation. This is the place to go to trace your family roots. Notable items from the collection include the Penn family archives, President Buchanan's papers, a printer's proof of the Declaration of Independence, and the first draft of the Constitution. The library is open to anyone over 13 years old. ⊠ *1300 Locust St.,* ☎ *215/732–6200.* ☒ *$5 for use of library.* ☉ *Tues. and Thurs.–Sat. 10–4, Wed. 2–8.*

⑭ Library Company of Philadelphia. Founded in 1731, this is one of the oldest cultural institutions in the United States and the only major Colonial American library that has survived virtually intact, despite having moved from building to building. You can stop by and read the rare books, although nothing circulates. Ben Franklin and his Junto, a group of people who read and then discussed philosophical and political issues, started the Library Company; they also founded the American Philosophical Society. From 1774 to 1800 it functioned as the de facto Library of Congress, and until the late 19th century it was the city library. Ten signers of the Declaration of Independence were members, among them Robert Morris, Benjamin Rush, and Thomas McKean. The 400,000-volume collection includes 200,000 rare books. Among the first editions—many acquired when they were first published—are Melville's *Moby-Dick* and Whitman's *Leaves of Grass.* The library is particularly rich in Americana up to 1880, black history to 1915, the history of science, and women's history. Changing exhibits showcase the library's holdings. ⊠ *1314 Locust St.,* ☎ *215/546–3181.* 🖃 *Free.* ⏾ *Weekdays 9–4:45.*

⑯ Park Hyatt Philadelphia at the Bellevue. Though its name has been changed many times, this building will always be "the Bellevue" to Philadelphians. The hotel has had an important role in city life, much like the heroine of a long-running soap opera. The epitome of the opulent hotels characteristic of the early 1900s, the Bellevue Stratford was the city's leading hotel for decades. It closed in 1976 after the first outbreak of Legionnaires' disease, which spread through the building's air-conditioning system during an American Legion convention. Reopened as the Fairmont several years later, the hotel failed to regain its luster and closed again in 1986. When renovations were completed in 1989, this magnificent building debuted as home to a number of upscale shops (the Shops at the Bellevue), restaurants, and a food court, as well as the luxurious Hotel Atop the Bellevue. Although the hotel has been renamed, its character seems to have remained the same (☞ Chapter 4). ⊠ *Broad and Walnut Sts.,* ☎ *215/893–1776.*

⑨ Rittenhouse Square. Once grazing ground for cows and sheep, Philadelphia's most elegant square is reminiscent of a Parisian park. One of William Penn's original five city squares, the park was named in 1825 to honor David Rittenhouse, 18th-century astronomer, clock maker, and the first director of the United States Mint. Many of Philadelphia's movers, shakers, and celebrities have lived here. Extra paths were made for Dr. William White, a leader in beautifying the square, so he could walk directly from his home to the exclusive Rittenhouse Club across the square and lunch with the likes of Henry James. Until 1950 town houses bordered the square, but they have now been replaced on three sides by swank apartment buildings and hotels. Some great houses remain, including the celebrated former residence of Henry P. McIlhenny (on the southwest corner), once home to one of the world's great art collections, now on view at the Philadelphia Museum of Art. If you want to join the office workers who have lunch-hour picnics in the park, you'll find scores of restaurants and sandwich shops along Walnut, Sansom, and Chestnut streets east of the square. ⊠ *Walnut St. between 18th and 19th Sts.*

NEED A BREAK? From 2 to 5 daily, the **Mary Cassatt Tearoom** in the Rittenhouse (⊠ 210 W. Rittenhouse Sq., ☎ 215/546–9000) serves an elegant afternoon tea accompanied by tiny tea sandwiches and a tower of pastries. In warm weather you can dine alfresco in the hotel's cloistered garden.

★ ⑪ Rosenbach Museum and Library. This 1863 three-floor town house is furnished with Persian rugs and 18th-century British, French, and American antiques (plus an entire living room that once belonged to poet Marianne Moore), but the real treasures are the artworks, books, and manuscripts here. Amassed by Philadelphia collectors Philip H. and A. S. W. Rosenbach, the collection includes paintings by Canaletto, Sully, and Lawrence; drawings by Daumier, Fragonard, and Blake; book illustrations ranging from medieval illuminations to the works of Maurice Sendak; the only known copy of the first edition of Benjamin Franklin's *Poor Richard's Almanack;* and the library's most famous treasure—the original manuscript of James Joyce's *Ulysses.* The library has more than 130,000 manuscripts and 30,000 rare books. ✉ *2010 Delancey Pl.,* ☎ *215/732–1600.* ✇ *$3.50.* ☉ *Sept.–July, Tues.–Sun. 11–4. Guided 1-hr tour as visitors arrive; last tour at 2:45.*

Union League of Philadelphia. An elegant double staircase sweeps from Broad Street up to the entrance of this 1865 French Renaissance–style building; within lies a bastion of Philadelphia conservatism. The Union League is a private social club founded during the Civil War to support the Union—in a big way. The club contributed $100,000, then a huge sum. ✉ *140 S. Broad St.* ☉ *Closed to the public.*

THE BENJAMIN FRANKLIN PARKWAY

Museums and Marvels

The Benjamin Franklin Parkway is the city's Champs-Elysées, home to many great cultural institutions. Alive with colorful flowers, flags, and fountains, this 250-ft-wide boulevard stretches northwest from the John F. Kennedy Plaza to the Kelly (East) and West River drives. It is crowned by a Greco-Roman temple on a hilltop—the Philadelphia Museum of Art. French architects Jacques Greber and Paul Cret designed the parkway in the 1920s. Today a distinguished assemblage of museums, institutions, hotels, and apartment buildings line the road, competing with each other in grandeur.

Here you'll find the Free Library of Philadelphia and the Family Court, housed in buildings whose designs are both copied from the palaces on Paris's Place de la Concorde. A newer addition is the Four Seasons Hotel, though its dignified design has made it look like a local institution since the day it opened. A grand processional path, the parkway occasionally lets down its hair as the route for city parades and the site of many festivals and events, including the Thanksgiving and Columbus Day parades and the First Union U.S. Pro Cycling championship (☞ Festivals and Seasonal Events *in* Chapter 1).

Numbers in the text correspond to numbers in the margin and on the Center City and Along the Parkway map.

A Good Walk

Begin at John F. Kennedy Plaza, on the west side of City Hall. On the corner of 16th Street, in what looks like a UFO, is the **Philadelphia Visitors Center** ⑰, full of helpful maps and information. Note that by late 2000 or early 2001 this facility will close, to be replaced by the new Gateway Visitor Center, on 6th Street between Market and Arch. (If you'd prefer not to walk the length of the Benjamin Franklin Parkway, you could pick up one of Philadelphia Trolley Works's trolley buses here; the 90-minute narrated tour of the city includes stops at the parkway museums. Or you could board SEPTA Bus 44 to Merion, home of the Barnes Foundation, with its Impressionist and Postimpressionist paintings.) From the plaza walk northwest on the parkway about four blocks to **Logan Circle** ⑱ and its lovely fountain sculpture. Next visit the Italian Renaissance–style **Cathedral of Saints Peter and Paul** ⑲, at 18th Street.

Walking counterclockwise around Logan Circle, you'll see twin marble Greek Revival buildings off to your right. The nearer of the two is the city's Family Court; the other is the **Free Library of Philadelphia** ⑳. Cross Logan Circle to see the dinosaur exhibition and more at the **Academy of Natural Sciences** ㉑. From the academy walk west on Race Street to 20th Street and tour the hands-on exhibits at the **Franklin Institute Science Museum** ㉒. If it's a warm day, head outside to the **First**

Union Science Park, a play-and-learn area just behind the museum on 21st Street. If you have children under the age of seven, don't miss the interactive displays at the **Please Touch Museum** ㉓, just a half block south on 21st Street. If your kids are older and if you and they appreciate the macabre, it's worth walking a few blocks south to see the Mutter Museum's collection of skulls and specimens.

Head back to the north side of the parkway and walk northwest. On your right is the Youth Study Center (a detention center for juvenile offenders) with two striking tableaux depicting families. At the next corner, guarded by a bronze cast of the famous sculpture *The Thinker,* is the **Rodin Museum** ㉔. Just ahead, atop Faire Mount, the plateau at the end of Franklin Parkway, is the **Philadelphia Museum of Art** ㉕, with its world-class collections. Before you see the beauty at the art museum, you could choose to tour the "beast." Half a mile north on 21st Street, Eastern State Penitentiary is the unrestored building of what was once an influential prison and is now an offbeat attraction. From there, following Fairmount Avenue west toward the higher numbers is the quickest route back to the art museum.

TIMING

The parkway is at its most colorful in spring, when the trees and flowers are in bloom. It's a long 10-block walk from the Philadelphia Visitors Center at 16th Street to the Art Museum, so if the day's too hot or too cold, hail a taxi. Leave early in the morning and plan to spend an entire day—and possibly the evening—in this area. On Wednesday you can cap off your day of culture with dinner and entertainment at the Philadelphia Museum of Art. If it's a Friday or Saturday, save the Franklin Institute for mid-afternoon, head out to dinner in the neighborhood, and return for a film on the giant screen of the Omniverse Theater, followed by a rock-and-roll laser light show in Fels Planetarium (the last show is at midnight). How much time you spend at each museum depends on your interests; be aware that the art museum and the Rodin Museum are closed on Monday.

Sights to See

㉑ **Academy of Natural Sciences.** The world-famous dioramas of animals from around the world displayed in their natural habitats give this natural history museum an old-fashioned charm; the latest discoveries give it drawing power. The most popular attraction is Dinosaur Hall, with reconstructed skeletons of a Tyrannosaurus rex and the latest paleontological find—the giganotosaurus, the biggest meat-eating dinosaur ever discovered. Dinosaur Hall marks the first phase of a renovation that will add six new fossil dinosaur skeletons in Dinosaur Hall, an interactive paleontology lab, and other innovative hands-on dinosaur exhibits. Other drawing cards are The Dig, where you can dig for real fossils; the live tropical butterflies that flutter all around you in a tropical rain forest setting; the Live Animal Center, which cares for over 100 wild animals unable to survive on their own in the wild; and the children's nature museum, Outside In. If you're keeping track of Philadelphia firsts, note that the academy, the oldest science research institution in the Western Hemisphere and a world leader in the fields of natural science research, education, and exhibition, was founded in 1812; the present building dates from 1868. ✉ *19th St. and Benjamin Franklin Pkwy.,* ☎ *215/299–1000.* 🎟 *$8.50.* ☉ *Weekdays 10–4:30, weekends 10–5.*

OFF THE
BEATEN PATH

BARNES FOUNDATION – It used to be pretty much a secret that one of the world's greatest collections of Impressionist and Postimpressionist art— 175 Renoirs; 66 Cézannes (including his *Card Players*); 65 Matisses;

plus masterpieces by van Gogh, Degas, Picasso, and others—was on view in the little town of Merion, 8 mi west of Center City. That was the way Albert C. Barnes wanted it. The son of a Philadelphia butcher who made millions by inventing Argyrol (used to treat eye inflammations), Barnes considered his art collection an educational tool, and until a 1961 court order the collection was open only to students of the educational institution he had chartered. Now that the trustees of Lincoln University have taken over, Barnes's public-be-damned attitude is a thing of the past. Thanks to a successful worldwide tour of the collection (which allowed the trustees to renovate Barnes's French Renaissance–style mansion), the secret is out. The Gauguins, Tintorettos, and Degases are displayed as they have always been: wallpapered floor to ceiling and cheek by jowl with household tools, Amish chests, and New Mexican folk icons (a Matisse and an antique door latch shared similar aesthetics, according to Barnes). A bus right outside the **Philadelphia Visitors Center** (☞ *below*) will take you to these masterpieces. Reservations are strongly recommended; the foundation admits only 200 people on Friday and Saturday and 100 on Sunday. ✉ *300 Latches La., Merion,* ☎ *610/667–0290.* 💲 *$5.* ☉ *Sept.–June, Fri.–Sat. 9:30–5, Sun. 12:30–5; call to check hrs before you go. SEPTA Bus 44 runs from 15th St. and Kennedy Blvd. to Old Lancaster Rd. and Latches La., ½ block from the museum.*

⑲ Cathedral of Saints Peter and Paul. This is the basilica of the archdiocese of Philadelphia and the spiritual center for the Philadelphia area's 1.4 million Roman Catholics. Topped by a huge copper dome, it was built between 1846 and 1864 in the Italian Renaissance style. Many of the interior decorations were done by Constantino Brumidi, who painted the dome of the U.S. Capitol. Six Philadelphia bishops and archbishops are buried beneath the altar. ✉ *18th and Race Sts.,* ☎ *215/561–1313.* ☉ *Daily 7–3:30. Masses weekdays 7:15, 8, 12:05, 12:35; Sat. 12:05, 5:15; Sun. 8, 9:30, 11, 12:15, 5.*

OFF THE
BEATEN PATH

EASTERN STATE PENITENTIARY HISTORIC SITE – Designed by John Haviland and built in 1829, Eastern State was at the time the most expensive building in America; it influenced penal design around the world and was the model for some 300 prisons from China to South America. The massive hulk, with 30-ft-high, 12-ft-wide walls and a hub-and-spoke floor plan, was created to promote a revolutionary and controversial concept: the reform of prisoners through solitary confinement, in accordance with the Quaker belief that if prisoners had light from heaven (in their private exercise yard), the word of God (the Bible), and honest work, they would reflect and repent. Charles Dickens came to America in 1842 to see Niagara Falls and Eastern State; he became its most famous detractor, insisting that solitary confinement was cruel. Before it closed in 1971, the prison was home to Al Capone, Willie Sutton, and Pep the Dog, who killed the cat of a governor's wife. The guides on the hourly tours of the unrestored structure (you must wear hard hats) tell terrific anecdotes and take you on a visit to Death Row. The penitentiary, just a half mile north of the Rodin Museum, hosts changing art exhibitions, Haunted House tours around Halloween, and a Bastille Day celebration the Sunday before July 14, with a reenactment of the storming of the Bastille. ✉ *22nd St. and Fairmount Ave.,* ☎ *215/236–3300.* 💲 *$7; children under 7 not allowed.* ☉ *Early May–Memorial Day and Labor Day–Oct., weekends 10–5; Memorial Day–Labor Day, Wed.–Sun. 10–5.*

First Union Science Park. A cooperative venture between the Franklin Institute Science Museum and the Please Touch Museum, the park presents interactive displays in an outdoor setting—which means children get a chance to run around and play while they learn. Swings demonstrate the laws of gravity and energy, and golf illustrates physics in motion. ⊠ *21st St. between Winter and Race Sts.* ☜ *Free with admission to the Franklin Institute or the Please Touch Museum.* ⊙ *First Sat. in May–last Sun. in Oct., daily 9–4:30.*

★ ☙ ㉒ **Franklin Institute Science Museum.** Founded over 175 years ago to honor Benjamin Franklin, the institute is a science museum that is as clever as its namesake, thanks to an abundance of dazzling hands-on exhibits. To make the best use of your time, study the floor plan before you begin exploring. You can sit in the cockpit of a T-33 jet trainer, trace the route of a corpuscle through the world's largest artificial heart (15,000 times life size), and ride to nowhere on a 350-ton Baldwin steam locomotive. The many exhibits cover energy, motion, sound, physics, astronomy, aviation, ships, mechanics, electricity, time, and other scientific subjects. You'll also find a working weather station and the world's largest pinball machine. **Franklin–He's Electric** celebrates the genius of the museum's namesake, an inventor, scientist, and observer of the natural world. You'll see his actual lightning rod and explore the areas that fascinated him, from optics, aquatics, and electricity to meteorology, music, and medicine. The **Fels Planetarium** has shows about the stars, space exploration, comets, and other phenomena, plus laser light shows to rock-and-roll favorites on Friday and Saturday nights (the last show's at midnight). The **Mandell Center** includes the Cyberzone computer lab with 20 computers linked to the Web; Material Matters, a chemistry lesson; and an Omniverse Theater, with a 79-ft domed screen and a 56-speaker high-tech sound system. One don't-miss: the 30-ft statue of Benjamin Franklin. ⊠ *20th St. and Benjamin Franklin Pkwy.,* ☎ *215/448–1200; 215/448–1388 for laser show hot line.* ☜ *Ticket packages range from $9.75 to $16.75.* ⊙ *Daily 9:30–5. The Mandell Center and Omniverse Theater remain open until 9 Fri.–Sat.*

⓴ **Free Library of Philadelphia.** Philadelphia calls its vast public library system the "Fabulous Freebie." Founded in 1891, the central library has more than 1 million volumes. With its grand entrance hall, sweeping marble staircase, 30-ft ceilings, enormous reading rooms with long tables, and spiral staircases leading to balconies, this Greek Revival building looks the way libraries should. With more than 12,000 musical scores, the Edwin S. Fleisher Collection is the largest of its kind in the world. Tormented by a tune whose name you can't recall? Hum it to one of the Music Room's librarians, and he or she will track it down. The Department of Social Science and History has nearly 100,000 charts, maps, and guidebooks. The Newspaper Room stocks papers (back issues are on microfilm) from all major U.S. and foreign cities, some dating all the way to Colonial times. The Rare Book Room is a beautiful suite housing first editions of Dickens, ancient Sumerian clay tablets, illuminated medieval manuscripts, and more modern manuscripts, including Poe's *Murders in the Rue Morgue* and "The Raven."

With 100,000 books for children from preschool to eighth grade, the Children's Department houses the city's largest collection of children's books in a made-for-kids setting. Historical collections include copies of the Hardy Boys and Nancy Drew series, over which adults wax nostalgic. The foreign-language collection has children's books in more than 50 languages. The department also sponsors story hours and film festivals. ⊠ *19th St. and Benjamin Franklin Pkwy.,* ☎ *215/686–5322.* ⊙ *Mon.–Wed. 9–9, Thurs.–Fri. 9–6, Sat. 9–5, Sun. 1–5; late May–Sept., closed Sun.; tours of Rare Book Room weekdays at 11.*

NEED A
BREAK?
The rooftop cafeteria of the **Free Library** (✉ 19th St. and Benjamin Franklin Pkwy., ☎ 215/564–4170) provides inexpensive meals at indoor umbrellaed tables weekdays from 9 to 4; Saturday from 9 to 2.

⑱ Logan Circle. One of William Penn's five squares, Logan Circle was originally a burying ground and the site of a public execution by hanging in 1823. It found a fate better than death, though. In 1825 the square was named for James Logan, Penn's secretary; it later became a circle and is now one of the city's gems. The focal point of Logan Circle is the **Swann Fountain** of 1920, designed by Alexander Stirling Calder, son of Alexander Milne Calder, who created the William Penn statue atop City Hall. (You'll find many works by a third generation of the family, noted modern sculptor Alexander Calder, the mobile- and stabile maker, in the nearby **Philadelphia Museum of Art,** ☞ *below*.) The main figures in the fountain symbolize Philadelphia's three leading waterways: the Delaware and Schuylkill rivers and Wissahickon Creek. Around Logan Circle are some examples of Philadelphia's magnificent collection of outdoor art, including *General Galusha Pennypacker,* the Shakespeare Memorial (*Hamlet and the Fool,* by Alexander Stirling Calder), and *Jesus Breaking Bread.*

OFF THE
BEATEN PATH
MUTTER MUSEUM – Skulls, antique microscopes, and a cancerous tumor removed from President Grover Cleveland's mouth in 1893 form just part of the unusual medical collection in the Mutter Museum, in the College of Physicians of Philadelphia, a few blocks south of the Please Touch Museum. The museum has hundreds of anatomical and pathological specimens, medical instruments, and organs removed from patients, including a piece of John Wilkes Booth's neck tissue. The collection contains 139 skulls; items that belonged to Marie Curie, Louis Pasteur, and Joseph Lister; and a 7'6" skeleton, the tallest on public exhibition in the United States. ✉ 19 S. 22nd St., ☎ 215/563–3737. ☞ $8. ⊙ Tues.–Sat. 10–4.

★ ㉕ Philadelphia Museum of Art. The city's premier cultural attraction is one of the country's leading museums. Actually, one of the greatest treasures of the museum is the building itself. Constructed in 1928 of Minnesota dolomite, it's modeled after ancient Greek temples but on a grander scale. The museum was designed by Julian Francis Abele, the first African-American to graduate from the University of Pennsylvania School of Architecture. Covering 10 acres, it has 200 galleries and a collection of more than 300,000 works. You can enter the museum from the front or the rear; choose the front, and you can run up the 99 steps made famous in the movie *Rocky* (Rocky ran up only 72). From the expansive terrace look up to the pediment on your right, at a group of 13 glazed multicolor statues of classical gods. After passing Jacques Lipchitz's statue *Prometheus Strangling the Vulture,* climb the last flight of steps; before entering the museum, turn around to savor the impressive view down the parkway.

Once inside, you'll see the grand staircase and Saint-Gaudens's statue of *Diana*; she formerly graced New York's old Madison Square Garden. The museum has several outstanding permanent collections: The John G. Johnson Collection covers Western art from the Renaissance to the 19th century; the Arensberg and A. E. Gallatin collections contain modern and contemporary works by artists such as Brancusi, Braque, Matisse, and Picasso. Famous paintings in these collections include Van Eyck's *St. Francis Receiving the Stigmata,* Rubens's *Prometheus Bound,* Benjamin West's *Benjamin Franklin Drawing Electricity from the Sky,* van Gogh's *Sunflowers,* Cézanne's *The Large Bathers,* and Picasso's *Three Musicians.* Two important recent acquisitions are a John Singleton

Copley painting, *Portrait of Mr. and Mrs. Thomas Mifflin*, and a marble bust of Ben Franklin by Jean-Antoine Houdon.

The enigmatic Marcel Duchamp, whose varied creations influenced many 20th-century artists, is a specialty of the house; the museum has the world's most extensive collection of his works, including the world-famous *Nude Descending a Staircase* and *The Bride Stripped Bare by Her Bachelors, Even*. Among the American art worth seeking out is a fine selection of the works by 19th-century Philadelphia artist Thomas Eakins, including *The Concert Singer* and some notable portraits. The most spectacular "objects" in the museum are entire structures and great rooms moved lock, stock, and barrel from around the world: a 12th-century French cloister, a 16th-century Indian temple hall, a 16th-century Japanese Buddhist temple, a 17th-century Chinese palace hall, and a Japanese ceremonial teahouse. Among the other collections are costumes, Early American furniture, and Amish and Shaker crafts. An unusual touch—and one that children especially like—is the Kienbusch Collection of Arms and Armor.

Pick up a map of the museum at either of the two entrances and wander on your own, or you can select from a variety of guided tours. You'll have at least one or two special exhibitions to choose from, too. Every Wednesday evening, the museum throws a themed party including music, entertainment, films, tours, lectures, storytelling, demonstrations, poetry readings, food, and drink. The museum has a cafeteria and a restaurant. ⊠ *26th St. and Benjamin Franklin Pkwy.,* ☎ *215/763–8100 or 215/684–7500 for 24-hr taped message.* ⊡ *$8; free Sun. 10–1.* ☉ *Tues., Thurs.–Sun. 10–5, Wed. 10–8:45.*

⓱ Philadelphia Visitors Center. Here you can get maps, brochures about the city and surroundings, lists of restaurants and hotels, and information about current events. You can also pick up the Philadelphia Trolley Works trolley, the PHLASH downtown loop bus, or SEPTA's Bus 76, which takes you to the parkway museums and the zoo. Volunteers and staff members are on hand to answer questions. In the gift shop you can buy a Philadelphia T-shirt, a Liberty Bell necktie, or a bumper sticker showing an inscribed tombstone: "I'd rather be in Philadelphia." This center will be closing by late 2000 or early 2001; a new one will open on 6th Street between Market and Arch streets. ⊠ *16th St. and John F. Kennedy Blvd.,* ☎ *215/636–1666.* ☉ *Sept.–June, daily 9–5; July–Aug., daily 9–6.*

☾ ㉓ Please Touch Museum. Philadelphia's children's museum, one of the country's best, is designed for youngsters ages 1–7. Highlights include Alice's Adventures in Wonderland, a 2,300-square-ft re-creation of Wonderland that encourages children to develop problem-solving and literacy skills; Sendak, an interactive exhibit of oversize settings and creatures from books by celebrated author-illustrator Maurice Sendak; and SuperMarket Science, with large shopping and kitchen play settings and a lab where science and math-related demonstrations are held. The museum also has a child-size television studio, an exhibit on transportation, a farm-theme area for toddlers, and interactive theater shows. The museum will be moving to a new, larger facility on the Delaware River waterfront early in 2002. ⊠ *210 N. 21st St.,* ☎ *215/963–0667.* ⊡ *$6.95.* ☉ *Sept.–June, daily 9–4:30; July–Aug., daily 9–6.*

★ ㉔ Rodin Museum. This jewel of a museum holds the best collection outside France of the work of sculptor Auguste Rodin (1840–1917). You'll pass through Rodin's *Gates of Hell*—a 21-ft-high sculpture with more than 100 human and animal figures—into an exhibition hall where the sculptor's masterworks are made even more striking by the use of light and shadow. Here are the French master's *The Kiss, The Burghers of Calais,* and *Eternal Springtime*. A small room is devoted to one of Rodin's most famous sitters, the French novelist Balzac. Photographs by Edward Steichen showing Rodin at work round out the collection. The museum occupies a 20th-century building designed by French architects Jacques Greber and Paul Cret. ✉ *22nd St. and Benjamin Franklin Pkwy.,* ☎ *215/763–8100.* ☜ *$3 donation requested.* ☉ *Tues.–Sun. 10–5.*

FAIRMOUNT PARK
The Emerald City

Stretching from the edge of downtown to the city's northwest corner, Fairmount Park is the largest landscaped city park in the world. With more than 8,500 acres and 2 million trees (someone claims to have counted), the park winds along the banks of the Schuylkill River—which divides it into west and east sections—and through parts of the city. Quite a few city dwellers consider the park their backyard. On weekends the 4-mi stretch along Kelly Drive is crowded with joggers, bicycling moms and dads with children strapped into kiddie seats atop the back wheel, hand-holding senior citizens out for some fresh air, collegiate crew teams sculling along the river, and budding artists trying to capture the sylvan magic just as Thomas Eakins once did.

Fairmount Park encompasses beautiful natural areas—woodlands, meadows, rolling hills, two scenic waterways, and a forested 5½-mi gorge. It also contains tennis courts, ball fields, playgrounds, trails, exercise courses, several celebrated cultural institutions, and some beautiful and historic Early American country houses open to visitors. Philadelphia has more works of outdoor art than any other city in North America, and more than 200 of these works—including statues by Frederic Remington, Jacques Lipchitz, and Auguste Rodin—are scattered throughout Fairmount Park. Some sections of the park that border depressed urban neighborhoods are neglected, but it's better maintained along the Schuylkill.

The park was established in 1812 when the city purchased 5 acres behind Faire Mount, the hill upon which the Philadelphia Museum of Art now stands, for waterworks and public gardens. Through private bequests and public purchases (which continue today), it grew to its present size and stature.

The following tour highlights many of the park's treasures. You can tour by car (get a good city map), starting near the Philadelphia Museum of Art. Signs help point the way, and the historic houses have free parking. Before you set out, call **Park House Information** (☎ 215/ 684–7922) to find out which historic houses are open that day and what special events are planned. Another option is to take the narrated tour offered by Philadelphia Trolley Works (board it at the Philadelphia Visitors Center, Philadelphia Museum of Art, or the park houses). The trolley bus visits many of these sites, and you can get on and off all day (☞ Sightseeing *in* Smart Travel Tips A to Z).

Numbers in the text correspond to numbers in the margin and on the Fairmount Park map.

A Good Drive

Your visit can start where the park began, at **Faire Mount** ①. If it's a nice day, you could begin this outing with a short walk before you set off by car. Park behind the art museum and walk down the stairs. To

Fairmount Park

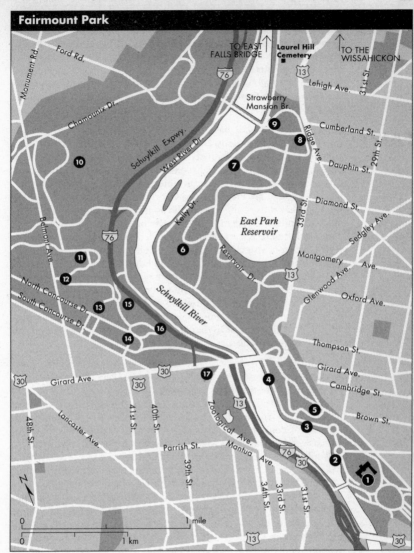

Belmont Plateau, **10**
Boathouse Row, **3**
Cedar Grove, **15**
Ellen Phillips Samuel
Memorial Sculpture
Garden, **4**
Faire Mount, **1**
Fairmount
Waterworks, **2**
Horticulture
Center, **11**
Japanese House, **12**
Laurel Hill, **7**

Lemon Hill, **5**
Memorial Hall, **13**
Mt. Pleasant, **6**
Philadelphia Zoo, **17**
Smith Civil War
Memorial, **14**
Strawberry
Mansion, **9**
Sweetbriar, **16**
Woodford, **8**

your right is the museum's Azalea Garden, designed in the English romantic style. Straight ahead, overlooking the Schuylkill River, is the **Fairmount Waterworks** ②, an elegant group of Greek Revival buildings. A few steps north of the Waterworks you'll see the Victorian structures of **Boathouse Row** ③; watch for rowers on the river here, too. Walking north along Kelly Drive, alongside the river, you soon reach the **Ellen Phillips Samuel Memorial Sculpture Garden** ④, with works by 16 artists.

Now's the time to walk back to your car for a driving tour of East Fairmount Park. Follow Kelly Drive to the end of Boathouse Row; turn right up the hill to a Federal-style country house, **Lemon Hill** ⑤. Head back to Kelly Drive, turn right, pass through the rock archway, and turn right again at the equestrian statue of Ulysses S. Grant. The first left takes you to **Mt. Pleasant** ⑥, a Georgian mansion. Continue along the road that runs to the right of the house (as you face it) past Rockland, a handsome Federal house that's currently closed. At the dead end turn left onto Reservoir Drive. You'll pass the redbrick Georgian-style Ormiston, also closed. Take the next left, Randolph Drive, to another Georgian house, **Laurel Hill** ⑦, on Edgely Drive, which becomes Dauphin Street. Just about 10 ft before reaching 33rd Street, turn left on Strawberry Mansion Drive, and you're at **Woodford** ⑧, which has an interesting collection of household goods. A quarter mile northwest of Woodford stands the house that gave its name to the nearby section of Philadelphia, **Strawberry Mansion** ⑨. It has furniture from three periods of its history.

If you're a fan of historic cemeteries, you can visit Laurel Hill Cemetery before you cross the river to West Fairmount Park. Drive back down the driveway of Strawberry Mansion, turn left at the stop sign, and follow the narrow road as it winds right to the light. Turn left onto Ridge Avenue and follow it to the entrance gate, which sits between eight Greek columns. To skip the cemetery and continue your tour, proceed down the Strawberry Mansion driveway to the stop sign, turn left, and follow the road as it loops down and around to the Strawberry Mansion Bridge. Cross the river and follow the road; when it splits, stay left. You'll come to Chamounix Drive, a long straightaway. Turn left and then left again on Belmont Mansion Drive for a fine view from **Belmont Plateau** ⑩. Follow Belmont Mansion Drive down the hill. Where it forks, stay to the left, cross Montgomery Drive, and bear left to reach the **Horticulture Center** ⑪ with its greenhouse and garden. Loop all the way around the Horticulture Center to visit the serene **Japanese House** ⑫ and its waterfall and gardens.

Drive back around the Horticulture Center and continue through the gates to Montgomery Drive. Turn left and then left again at the first light (Belmont Avenue). Turn left again on North Concourse Drive. On your left is **Memorial Hall** ⑬, a building from the 1876 Centennial Exposition. The two towers just ahead are part of the **Smith Civil War Memorial** ⑭. Turn left just past them to see furniture from over the centuries at **Cedar Grove** ⑮. Just south of Cedar Grove, atop a hill sloping down to the Schuylkill, is a Federal mansion, **Sweetbriar** ⑯. Continue past the house, make the first left, and turn left again at the stop sign onto Lansdowne Drive. Follow the signs straight ahead to the **Philadelphia Zoo** ⑰. If you enjoy hiking, you could continue on to the Wissahickon, in the northwest section of Fairmount Park.

TIMING

Any time but winter is a fine time to explore the great outdoors in Fairmount Park. In spring the cherry blossoms are lovely; in fall the changing leaves blaze with color. In winter you can explore the indoors, on

Christmas tours of the historic houses. If you leave the driving to the Philadelphia Trolley Works, your narrated tour will take just 40 minutes. If you drive, after you've explored Kelly Drive on foot, you'll need about two hours. Add another 20–30 minutes for each historic house you tour. Because each property keeps its own quirky schedule, it's hard to choose one day that's best for seeing the interiors, although a summer Saturday is your best bet. Animal lovers can spend half a day at the Philadelphia Zoo.

Sights to See

⑩ Belmont Plateau. Literally the high point of your park tour, Belmont Plateau has a view from 243 ft above river level. In front of you lie the park, the Schuylkill River winding down to the Philadelphia Museum of Art, and—4 mi away—the Philadelphia skyline. ⊠ *Belmont Mansion Dr., West Fairmount Park.*

❸ Boathouse Row. These architecturally varied 19th-century buildings—in Victorian Gothic, Gothic Revival, and Italianate styles—are home to the rowing clubs that make up the "Schuylkill Navy," an association of boating clubs organized in 1858. The view of the boathouses from the west side of the river is splendid—especially at night, when they're outlined with hundreds of small lights. The row's new Lloyd Hall has a gymnasium, bicycle and skate rentals in season, and a two-story café overlooking the river. ⊠ *Kelly Dr., East Fairmount Park.*

⑮ Cedar Grove. Five styles of furniture—Jacobean, William and Mary, Queen Anne, Chippendale, and Federal—reflect the accumulations of five generations of the Paschall-Morris family. The house stood in Frankford, in northeastern Philadelphia, for 180 years before being moved to this location in 1927. ⊠ *Lansdowne Dr. off N. Concourse Dr., West Fairmount Park,* ☎ *215/235–7469.* ⊡ *$2.50 or $3 for tour.* ☉ *Tues.–Sun. 10–5.*

❹ Ellen Phillips Samuel Memorial Sculpture Garden. Bronze and granite sculptures by 16 artists stand in a series of tableaux and groupings on riverside terraces. Portraying American themes and traits, they include *The Quaker,* by Harry Rosen; *Birth of a Nation,* by Henry Kreis; and *Spirit of Enterprise,* by Jacques Lipchitz. ⊠ *Kelly Dr., East Fairmount Park.*

❶ Faire Mount. This is now the site of the Philadelphia Museum of Art (☞ The Benjamin Franklin Parkway, *above*). In 1812 a reservoir was built here to distribute water throughout the city.

★ ❷ Fairmount Waterworks. Designed by Frederick Graff, this National Historic Engineering Landmark built in 1815 was the first steam-pumping station of its kind in the country. The notable assemblage of Greek Revival buildings—one of the city's most beautiful sights—is undergoing extensive renovation. A restaurant will be opening in the Engine House in spring 2001. ⊠ *Along the Schuylkill River,* ☎ *215/685–4908.* ⊡ *Free.* ☉ *Tours June–mid-Oct., weekends 1–3:30.*

⑪ Horticulture Center. On the Horticulture Center's 22 wooded acres are a butterfly garden, a greenhouse where plants and flowers used on city property are grown, and a pavilion in the trees for bird-watching from the woodland canopy. Don't miss the whimsical *Seaweed Girl* fountain in the display house. The center stands on the site of the 1876 Centennial Exposition's Horticultural Hall ⊠ *N. Horticultural Dr., West Fairmount Park,* ☎ *215/685–0096.* ⊡ *Free.* ☉ *Visitor center and greenhouses, daily 9–3; grounds, daily 7–6.*

⑫ Japanese House. This reconstructed 16th-century samurai's dwelling, built in Japan, was exhibited temporarily at the Museum of Modern Art in New York, then reassembled here in 1958. The architectural setting and the waterfall, gardens, Japanese trees, and pond make a serene contrast to the busy city. The house is called Shofu-So, which means "pine breeze villa." A recent renovation gave the home a roof made of the bark of hinoki, a cypress that grows only in the mountains of Japan. ⊠ *Lansdowne Dr. east of Belmont Ave., West Fairmount Park,* ☎ *215/878–5097.* 🖃 *$2.50.* ☺ *May–Oct., Tues.–Sun. 10–4.*

⑦ Laurel Hill. Built around 1767, this Georgian house on a laurel-covered hill overlooking the Schuylkill River once belonged to Dr. Philip Syng Physick (also owner of Society Hill's Physick House; ☞ Society Hill and Penn's Landing, *above*). On some Sunday evenings during the summer, Women for Greater Philadelphia sponsors candlelight chamber music concerts here. ⊠ *E. Edgely Dr., East Fairmount Park,* ☎ *215/235–1776.* 🖃 *$2.50.* ☺ *Late Apr.–early Dec., Wed.–Fri. 10–3:30.*

<table>
<tr><td>OFF THE
BEATEN PATH</td><td>**LAUREL HILL CEMETERY** – John Notman, architect of the Athenaeum and many other noted local buildings, designed Laurel Hill in 1836. The cemetery is an important example of an early rural burial ground and the first cemetery in America designed by an architect. Its rolling hills overlooking the Schuylkill River, its rare trees, and its monuments and mausoleums sculpted by greats such as Notman, Alexander Milne Calder, Alexander Stirling Calder, William Strickland, and Thomas U. Walter made it a popular picnic spot in the 19th century; today it's a great place for a stroll. Those buried in this 99-acre necropolis include prominent Philadelphians and Declaration of Independence signers. Burials still take place here. ⊠ *3822 Ridge Ave.,* ☎ *215/228–8200; 215/228–8817 for tours through the Friends of Laurel Hill Cemetery.* ☺ *Weekdays 8–4:30, Sat. 9–1:30.*</td></tr>
</table>

⑤ Lemon Hill. A beautiful example of a Federal-style country house, Lemon Hill was built in 1800 on a 350-acre farm. Its most distinctive features are oval parlors with concave doors and the entrance hall's checkerboard floor of Valley Forge marble. ⊠ *Poplar Dr., East Fairmount Park,* ☎ *215/232–4337.* 🖃 *$2.50.* ☺ *Apr.–mid-Dec., Wed.–Sun. 10–4.*

⑬ Memorial Hall. Architect Hermann J. Schwarzmann's grand stone building with a glass dome and Palladian windows served as an art museum during the Philadelphia Centennial Exposition, a celebration of the nation's 100th birthday. Close to 10 million people attended the exposition to see the novel exhibits of machinery, produce, and art sent by foreign countries. The hall, a notable example of beaux arts architecture, influenced the design of many American and European museums and government buildings. It is the only major building remaining from the event; you can walk in and look around. ⊠ *N. Concourse Dr., West Fairmount Park,* ☎ *215/685–0000.* ☺ *Weekdays 9–4.*

⑥ Mt. Pleasant. Built in 1761 by John Macpherson, a Scottish sea captain, Mt. Pleasant is one of the finest examples of Georgian architecture in the country. The historically accurate furnishings are culled from the Philadelphia Museum of Art's collection of Philadelphia Chippendale furniture. According to legend, Revolutionary War traitor Benedict Arnold once purchased this house as an engagement gift for Peggy Shippen, but he was banished before the deal was signed. ⊠ *Mt. Pleasant Dr., East Fairmount Park,* ☎ *215/235–7469.* 🖃 *$2.50.* ☺ *Tues.–Sun. 10–5.*

★ ⬤ **⑰ Philadelphia Zoo.** Chartered in 1859 and opened in 1874, America's first zoo is home to more than 2,000 animals representing six continents. It's small and well-landscaped enough to feel pleasantly intimate, and the naturalistic habitats allow you to get close enough to hear the animals breathe. At each exhibit an old-fashioned Talking Storybook provides narration when activated by an elephant-shape key. The newly renovated Amphibian and Reptile House houses 87 species, from 15-ft-long snakes to frogs the size of a dime. The new 2½-acre Primate Reserve is home to 11 primate species from around the world. Notable attractions include the zoo's rare white lions; Carnivore Kingdom, where meat eaters prowl just inches away; the Rare Animal House, with seriously ugly naked mole rats; a terrific Bird House; and the African Plains, stomping ground of giraffes and zebras. Children can climb inside a four-story tree, hatch from an egg, and ride a dinosaur in the Treehouse. The Children's Zoo offers pony rides and a barnyard animal petting area. Set in a lovely 42-acre Victorian garden, the zoo has trees dating from the 18th century. ⊠ *34th St. and Girard Ave., West Fairmount Park,* ☎ *215/243–1100.* ⌨ *$8.50; additional charge for Treehouse.* ☉ *Mar.–Nov., weekdays 9:30–4:45, weekends 9:30–5:45; Dec.–Feb., daily 10–4.*

⑭ Smith Civil War Memorial. Built from 1897 to 1912 with funds donated by wealthy foundry owner Richard Smith, the memorial honors Pennsylvania heroes of the Civil War. Among those immortalized in bronze are Generals Meade and Hancock—and Smith himself. At the base of each tower is a curved wall with a bench. If you sit at one end and listen to a person whispering at the other end, you'll understand why they're called the Whispering Benches. Unfortunately, the litter around the site reflects its location near an economically struggling neighborhood. ⊠ *N. Concourse Dr., West Fairmount Park.*

⑨ Strawberry Mansion. The largest mansion in Fairmount Park has furniture from the three main phases of its history: Federal, Regency, and Empire. In the parlor is a collection of rare Tucker porcelain; the attic holds fine antique dolls. ⊠ *Near 33rd and Dauphin Sts., East Fairmount Park,* ☎ *215/228–8364.* ⌨ *$2.50.* ☉ *Tues.–Sun. 10–4.*

⑯ Sweetbriar. This three-story Federal mansion dating from 1797 was the first year-round residence in what is now Fairmount Park. It was built by Samuel and Jean Breck to escape the yellow fever epidemic that ravaged the city. ⊠ *Lansdowne Dr. off N. Concourse Dr., West Fairmount Park,* ☎ *215/222–1333.* ⌨ *$2.50.* ☉ *Apr.–June, by appointment; July–Dec., Wed.–Sun. 10–4.*

OFF THE
BEATEN PATH

THE WISSAHICKON – Of the Philadelphia areas that William Penn encountered, the Wissahickon has changed the least. In the northwestern section of Fairmount Park, this gorge was carved out by the Wissahickon Creek—5½ mi of towering trees, cliffs, trails, and animals. You can easily visualize the Leni-Lenape who lived here and gave the creek its name. Many inns once stood along the banks of the Wissahickon; only two remain. One is now a police station; the other is the **Valley Green Inn** (⊠ Springfield Ave. and Wissahickon Creek, ☎ 215/247–1730), built in 1850. It is nestled in one of the loveliest parts of the Wissahickon gorge. You can sit on a bench alongside the creek, look at the stone bridge reflected in the water, and savor the tranquillity of this spot.

Forbidden Drive, a dirt-and-gravel pathway along the west side of the creek, is a haunt of joggers, bikers, horseback riders, fishermen, and nature lovers. There are foot trails along both sides of the creek and interesting statues along the route. Walking less than a half mile south of the Valley Green Inn brings you to Devil's Pool; Shakespeare Rock, with a quotation carved on its face; and Hermit's Cave, where German mystic Johannes Kelpius and his followers came in 1694 to await the millennium. A visit to Historic RittenhouseTown, America's first paper mill, requires a 3-mi hike south. To the north of the inn are Indian Rock and a covered bridge that was built around 1855, the last still standing within the boundaries of a major American city.

You'll need a car to get here: To reach Valley Green Inn from downtown, take the Schuylkill Expressway west to the Lincoln Drive–Wissahickon Park exit (Exit 32). Follow Lincoln Drive to Allen's Lane, then turn right. At Germantown Avenue turn left, go about a mile, turn left at Springfield Avenue, and follow it to the end. A map of the Wissahickon showing all the trails and sites can be purchased for $5 at the Valley Green Inn's snack-booth window, open daily in warmer months from 9 to 5, weekends only the rest of the year.

❽ **Woodford.** The Naomi Wood collection of antique household goods, including Colonial furniture, unusual clocks, and English delftware, can be seen in this fine Georgian mansion built about 1756. ⊠ *Near 33rd and Dauphin Sts., East Fairmount Park,* ☎ *215/229–6115.* ⌦ *$2.50.* ☉ *Tues.–Sun. 10–4.*

SOUTHWARK AND SOUTH PHILADELPHIA

Strutting South of South

Two of the city's most interesting neighborhoods lie south of South Street—Southwark and South Philadelphia. Southwark, stretching from Front to 6th Street and from South Street to Washington Avenue, was the center of the commercial and ship-building activity that made Philadelphia the biggest port in the Colonies and in the young United States. One of the oldest sections of the city, Southwark was already settled by the Swedes when the English arrived; the Swedish influence shows in street names such as Swanson, Christian, and Queen.

Directly south of Society Hill, Southwark is neither as glamorous nor as historically renowned as its neighbor. Chiseled in stone on one facade are these words: ON THIS SITE IN 1879, NOTHING HAPPENED! But like Society Hill, Southwark's Queen Village neighborhood has been gentrified by young professionals; the restoration attracted chic restaurants and interesting shops.

Through the years South Philadelphia has absorbed boatloads of immigrants—European Jews, Italians, and most recently, Asians. The city's Little Italy, it is a huge area of identical row houses with gleaming white marble steps, stretching south and west of Southwark. At the heart of the neighborhood, along 9th Street, is the outdoor Italian Market, packed with vendors hawking crabs and octopus, eggplants and tomatoes. From butcher shop windows hang skinned animals; cheese shops are crammed with barrels of olives. Sylvester Stallone walked along 9th Street in the films *Rocky* and *Rocky II*, and almost every campaigning president has visited the market on his swing through Philadelphia. It's a great photo op for them—and for you.

Although there are chic eateries in South Philadelphia, the majority of the neighborhood restaurants are not fancy (decor such as red-checked vinyl tablecloths and plastic grapes hanging from plastic vines is not uncommon), but the food can be terrific and—more important—authentic. You'll wonder if Mama is in the kitchen preparing a southern Italian specialty just for you. This is the neighborhood that gave the world Mario Lanza, Bobby Rydell, Frankie Avalon, and Fabian, and some area restaurants proudly display gold records earned by these neighborhood celebrities. Plenty of locals and visitors alike head for South

Philly's competing culinary shrines, Pat's King of Steaks and Geno's, both at the corner of 9th Street and Passyunk Avenue. One of their cheese steaks makes a perfect prelude to an evening spent at the city's sports complexes, at the southern end of South Philadelphia.

A Good Walk

A leisurely stroll through Southwark and South Philadelphia is a fun day's outing. From Bainbridge Street, proceed south (right turn) on 2nd Street, which old-timers call Two Street. The homes along these streets are the oldest in the city, dating from the mid-1700s. Even when their construction dates are not chiseled on the facades, the settling bricks above the overhangs, the crooked windows, and the shutters that don't hang straight all attest to their vintage. Turn east (left) on Catharine Street and then south (right) on Hancock Street, one of the most charming streets in the city. The tiny clapboard houses at Numbers 813 and 815 were built by a shipwright and are the last of their type. Detour onto Queen Street to see the old firehouse with gas lamps at Number 117. It has been beautifully converted to a single-family home.

Continue down Hancock to Christian Street; go east (left) about one block (under the I–95 overpass) to Swanson Street. Here is **Gloria Dei,** the oldest church in Pennsylvania. Return to 2nd Street by way of Christian Street and walk south (left turn), past a neighborhood landmark, the Shot Tower, where lead shot was made during the War of 1812. At Washington Avenue is the **Mummers Museum,** where you can get a feeling for this local institution. From the museum walk west on Washington Avenue to 9th Street and then proceed north to the five-block-long open-air **Italian Market.** At Christian Street walk east to 5th Street, half a block north to Queen Street, and then east again to the **Mario Lanza Museum,** with memorabilia and photos of the singer. Following 4th Street north will bring you back to South Street. Drygoods merchants line 4th Street south of South Street in an area called Fabric Row; you'll find an amazing variety of designer and ethnic textiles, upholstery, and draperies.

TIMING

It's best to visit this neighborhood Tuesday through Saturday, because the Italian Market and the Mummers Museum are closed Sunday and Monday (the Italian Market *is* open Sunday morning, though). Start early—the Italian Market winds down by mid-afternoon—and allow three–four hours.

Sights to See

Gloria Dei. One of the few remnants of the Swedes who settled Pennsylvania before William Penn, Gloria Dei (Old Swedes') Church was organized in 1642. Built in 1698, the church has numerous intriguing religious artifacts, such as a 1608 Bible once owned by Sweden's Queen Christina. The carvings on the lectern and balcony were salvaged from the congregation's first church, which was destroyed by fire. Models of two of the ships that transported the first Swedish settlers hang from the ceiling—right in the center of the church. Grouped around the church are the parish hall, the caretaker's house, the rectory, and the guild house. The church sits in the center of its graveyard; it forms a picture that is pleasing in its simplicity and tranquillity. ⊠ *916 Swanson St., near Christian St. and Columbus Blvd.,* ☎ *215/389–1513.* ▨ *Free.* ☉ *Daily 9–5, but call first.*

Italian Market. It's more Naples than Philadelphia: Vendors crowd the sidewalks and spill out onto the streets; live crabs and caged chickens wait for the kill; picture-perfect produce is piled high. The market dates back to the turn of the century, when it was founded by Italian immigrants. You'll find imported and domestic products, kitchenware, fresh pastas, cheeses, spices, meats, fruits and vegetables, and dry goods (☞ Chapter 7 *for* more information). These days the market has lost some of its charm; food stalls share the already crowded street with vendors selling bootleg CDs, logo T-shirts, and dollar-store bargains, but it's still enjoyable to stroll and to duck into a cheese or spice shop. ✉ *9th St. between Washington Ave. and Christian St.,* ☎ *215/922–5557.* ⏲ *Tues.–Sat., 9:30–late afternoon; Sun. 9:30–12:30.*

Mario Lanza Museum. In this museum devoted to the famous tenor and Hollywood star (1921–59), you'll find thousands of photos, memorabilia, videocassette showings of Lanza's films, and souvenirs for sale. Lanza was supposedly moving a piano into the Academy of Music when he seized the opportunity to sing from its stage—and was first discovered. Arturo Toscanini said that Lanza had perhaps the greatest natural voice of the century. Lanza's birthplace, at 634 Christian Street, is a few blocks away. ✉ *In the Settlement Music School, 416 Queen St.,* ☎ *215/468–3623.* ⏲ *Sept.–June, Mon.–Sat. 10–3:30; July–Aug., weekdays 10–3:30.*

NEED A BREAK? When your walking tour is over, reward yourself with a dessert that doubles as a work of art at the **Pink Rose Pastry Shop** (✉ 630 S. 4th St., ☎ 215/592–0565). Check out the white chocolate raspberry mousse cake.

Mummers Museum. Even if you aren't in Philadelphia on New Year's Day, you can still experience this unique local institution and phenomenon. Famous for extravagant sequin-and-feather costumes and string bands, the Mummers spend the year preparing for an all-day parade up Broad Street on January 1. The museum has costumes, photos of parades, and audiovisual displays of Mummerabilia. You can push buttons to compose your own Mummers medley, with banjos, saxophones, and xylophones, and you can dance the Mummers strut to the strains of "Oh, Dem Golden Slippers." A 45-inch screen shows filmed highlights of past parades.

Early English settlers brought to the Colonies their Christmastime custom of dressing in costume and performing pantomimes—the name Mummers derives from the German *mumme,* meaning "mask or disguise." In Philadelphia, families would host costume parties on New Year's Day; on January 1, 1876, the first individual groups paraded informally through the city. The parade caught on, and by 1901 the city officially sanctioned the parade and 42 Mummers clubs strutted for cash prizes.

In recent years the Mummers have staged a summer Mummers Parade around July 4 (during the city's Welcome America! celebration); in late February they present the "Show of Shows" at the Spectrum. The latter is a chance to hear the original 16 string bands perform indoors. The museum presents free outdoor concerts (weather permitting) on most Tuesday evenings 8–10 from May to September. ✉ *1100 S. 2nd St., at Washington Ave.,* ☎ *215/336–3050.* *$2.50.* ⏲ *Tues.–Sat. 9:30–5, Sun. noon–5.*

UNIVERSITY CITY

University City is the portion of West Philadelphia that includes the campuses of the University of Pennsylvania, Drexel University, and the Philadelphia College of Pharmacy and Science. It also has the University City Science Center (a leading think tank), the Annenberg Center performing arts complex (part of the University of Pennsylvania), an impressive collection of Victorian houses, and a variety of moderately priced restaurants, movie theaters, stores, and lively bars catering to more than 32,000 students and other residents. The neighborhood stretches from the Schuylkill River west to 44th Street and from the river north to Powelton Avenue.

This area was once the city's flourishing western suburbs, where wealthy Philadelphians built grand estates and established summer villages. It officially became part of the city in 1854. Twenty years later the University of Pennsylvania moved its campus here from the center of the city. The university moved into many of the historic homes, while others were adopted by fraternities. There are still many privately owned, architecturally exciting properties, particularly on Locust, Spruce, and Pine streets. Other areas of West Philadelphia beyond University City are, however, less prosperous today.

Penn has spruced up its campus with the Sansom Common development (between Walnut and Sansom streets, and 36th and 37th streets), which includes shops, a bookstore, and a new hotel, the Inn at Penn. To promote University City's visual and performing arts and its unique international restaurants, the University City District has created a monthly event, Go West! Go International! Third Thursdays, modeled after Old City's First Fridays. Museums and galleries host special events the third Thursday of the month (4 PM–8 PM) and stay open late, and restaurants offer special discounts and activities. Metered parking is free after 5 PM and a shuttle bus makes a continuous loop around the neighborhood. **Penn's Information Center** (☎ 215/898–1000) is at 34th and Walnut streets.

A Good Walk

This walk through University City takes in the Ivy League campus of the University of Pennsylvania, where ivy really does cling to many buildings. Begin at the University's **Institute of Contemporary Art,** at 36th and Sansom streets. Walk east (down the hill) on Sansom Street to 34th Street and turn right (south). At 220 South 34th Street is the historic Furness Building, which houses the **Arthur Ross Gallery** and the **Fisher Fine Arts Library.** When you exit the building, you're in the heart of the University of Pennsylvania campus at the edge of College Green (Blanche Levy Park). You'll see a statue of Benjamin Franklin, who founded the university in 1740, in the middle of the green. To your right, the huge Van Pelt Library stretches from 34th Street to 36th Street. In front of it is Claes Oldenburg's *Broken Button*. To your left is College Hall, an administration building said to be the inspiration for the scary Addams House in cartoonist Charles Addams's work. Where the walk splits, stay right. Just west of 36th Street, the Annenberg School of Communications and the Annenberg Center (☞ The Arts *in* Chapter 5) are to the right; the famed Wharton School of Economics, to the left. As you pass the intersection of 37th Street, say hello to the statue of Ben Franklin sitting on a bench. A footbridge takes you over 38th Street (turn around for a good view of Center City) to Superblock, three high-rise student dormitories. Locust Walk ends at 40th Street with the dental school and a row of stores and restaurants.

Follow Locust Walk back to 37th Street and walk south (right) to Spruce Street. The Gothic sprawl ahead of you is the Quad, the university's first dorm buildings. Designed by Cope and Stewardson in 1895, the Quad became the prototype of the collegiate Gothic style prevalent in campuses coast to coast. These dormitory buildings—awash with gargoyles and gables—easily conjure up the England of everyone's dreams. South of the Quad on Hamilton Walk, you're smack back in the 20th century, thanks to Louis Kahn's Alfred Newton Richards Medical Research Laboratories building, an award-winning masterpiece of this important architect. Kahn, a brilliant teacher and architectural theorist, did not leave many completed buildings.

Head back to Spruce Street and turn right (east) to 33rd Street to explore the **University Museum of Archaeology and Anthropology,** which holds everything from mummies to Mayan artifacts. Just across the street you see Franklin Field, the university's football stadium. Following 33rd Street north back to Walnut Street brings you to the Moore School of Engineering, home of the post–World War II era **ENIAC,** the world's first all-electronic general-purpose digital computer.

TIMING

University City is at its best when college is in session; it's the students rushing to classes who give this area its flavor. Allow half an hour each in the Arthur Ross Gallery and the Institute of Contemporary Art, two hours in the University Museum, and an hour exploring the campus. If your time is limited, skip all but the University Museum, a don't-miss for the archaeologically inclined.

Sights to See

Arthur Ross Gallery. Penn's official art gallery showcases treasures from the university's collections and traveling exhibitions. The gallery shares its historic landmark building, designed by Frank Furness, with the **Fisher Fine Arts Library** (☞ *below*). ⊠ *220 S. 34th St.,* ☎ *215/ 898–2083.* ☑ *Free.* ⊙ *Tues.–Fri. 10–5, weekends noon–5.*

ENIAC. Here's a chance for computer aficionados to see the place where the computer age dawned. During World War II engineers at the Moore School of Engineering at the University of Pennsylvania undertook a secret project to develop the world's first all-electronic, large-scale general-purpose digital computer. They called it ENIAC, an acronym for electronic numerical integrator and calculator. The largest electronic machine in the world, it weighed 30 tons and contained 18,000 vacuum tubes—one of which burned out every few seconds when ENIAC was first built. Although most of ENIAC is now in the Smithsonian Institution, a small portion is still on view at the Moore School. Photos and informative signs tell ENIAC's story. ⊠ *Moore School of Electrical Engineering, 200 S. 33rd St., enter on 33rd St. just below Walnut St.,* ☎ *215/898–2492.* ☑ *Free.* ⊙ *By appointment only.*

Fisher Fine Arts Library. One of the finest examples remaining of the work of Philadelphia architect Frank Furness, this was the most innovative library building in the country when it was completed in 1890. It was the first library to separate the reading room and the stacks. Peek into the catalog room, dominated by a huge fireplace, and the reading room, with study alcoves lit from the lead-glass windows above. The unusual exterior stirred controversy when it was built: Note the terra-cotta panels, short heavy columns, and gargoyles on the north end. ⊠ *220 S. 34th St.,* ☎ *215/898–8325.* ☑ *Free.* ⊙ *Late Aug.–May, Mon.–Thurs. 8:30 AM–midnight, Fri. 8:30–8, Sat. noon–8, Sun. noon–midnight; June–late Aug., variable weekday hours.*

NEED A
BREAK?
From 10 AM to 10 PM, you can refuel at **Moravian Cafes at Sansom Commons** (⊠ 3409 Walnut St.), a food court with the requisite pizza, ice cream, steak sandwich, salad, and coffee counters.

Institute of Contemporary Art. This museum, part of the University of Pennsylvania, has established a reputation for identifying promising artists and exhibiting them at a critical point in their careers. Among the artists who have had shows at ICA and later gone on to international prominence are Andy Warhol, Robert Mapplethorpe, and Laurie Anderson. ⊠ *118 S. 36th St., at Sansom St.,* ☎ *215/898–7108.* 📧 *$3.* ⊘ *Wed.–Fri. noon–8, weekends 11–5.*

★ ⑤ **University Museum of Archaeology and Anthropology.** Indiana Jones, look out! Rare treasures from the deepest jungles and ancient tombs make this one of the finest archaeological/anthropological museums in the world. The collection of more than a million objects, gathered largely during worldwide expeditions by University of Pennsylvania scholars, includes a 12-ton sphinx from Egypt, a crystal ball once owned by China's Dowager Empress, the world's oldest writing—Sumerian cuneiform clay tablets—and the 4,500-year-old golden jewels from the royal tombs of the kingdom of Ur. The museum has a superb collection of Chinese monumental (large-scale) art and more than 400 artifacts in its Ancient Greek World section. *Canaan and Ancient Israel* showcases ancient pottery, statuary, jewelry, weapons and more, with some artifacts dating from as early as 3000 BC, and includes a full-scale reconstruction of a house of the biblical period. Children run to *The Egyptian Mummy: Secrets and Science* and to *Living in Balance: The Universe of the Hopi, Zuni, Navajo, and Apache.* The museum has two gift shops and a café. ⊠ *33rd and Spruce Sts.,* ☎ *215/898–4000.* 📧 *$5 suggested donation.* ⊘ *Labor Day–Memorial Day, Tues.–Sat. 10–4:30, Sun. 1–5; Memorial Day–Labor Day, Tues.–Sat. 10–4:30.*

GERMANTOWN AND CHESTNUT HILL

Germantown, about 6 mi northwest of Center City, has been an integrated, progressive community since 13 German Quaker and Mennonite families moved here in 1683 and soon welcomed English, French, and other European settlers seeking religious freedom. The area has a tradition of free thinking—the first written protest against slavery came from its residents. Today it houses a wealth of still-occupied and exceptionally well-preserved architectural masterpieces.

The Germantown area is rich in history. It was the site of Philadelphia's first gristmill (1683) and America's first paper mill (1690). The American Colonies' first English-language Bible was printed here (1743). By the time of the Revolution, Germantown had become an industrial town. In 1777 Colonial troops under George Washington attacked part of the British force here and fought the Battle of Germantown in various skirmishes. After the Revolutionary War Germantown became a rural retreat for wealthy city residents who wanted to escape summer heat and disease. The Deshler-Morris House was the summer White House where President Washington and his family resided in 1793 and 1794, when the yellow fever epidemic drove them from the city.

Farther northwest is Chestnut Hill. Although it's part of the city, Chestnut Hill is more like the classy suburbs of the Main Line. When Germantown's second railroad, the Chestnut Hill Line, began operation west of Germantown Avenue in 1884, it spurred the development of Chestnut Hill. Beyond cobblestone Germantown Avenue, lined with restaurants, galleries, and boutiques, you'll find lovely examples of Colonial Revival and Queen Anne houses. The Woodmere Art Museum is in this neighborhood. For tours and information, contact the **Chestnut Hill Business Association** (⊠ 8426 Germantown Ave., ☎ 215/247–6696).

The best way to tour the area is by car. From Center City follow Kelly Drive to Midvale Avenue and turn right. Follow Midvale up the hill to Conrad Street and turn right, then make a left on Queen Lane, which ends at Grumblethorpe house. You can also reach Germantown from

MANAYUNK:
FROM MILL TOWN TO HOT SPOT

FOR MANY PEOPLE, MANAYUNK'S Main Street has replaced South Street as the "hippest street in town." In this former mill town along the banks of the Schuylkill River, just 7 mi northwest of Center City, more than 30 restaurants compete for attention with alfresco dining, creative menus, and valet parking. Most of the 80-plus stores are one-of-a-kind; among them are art galleries, antiques shops, and clothing boutiques. On the weekends you'll be strolling with hundreds of visitors—and fighting with them for parking spaces.

In the mid-1800s, when Philadelphia was one of the nation's leading industrial cities, Manayunk was a prosperous town; it became part of the city in 1854. It was home to a number of the city's 185 cotton mills, which provided raw material for the region's thriving paper and textile industries. The European immigrants who settled here to work in the mills built row houses in the steep hills overlooking the river. During the Civil War the mills switched to wool textiles to produce blankets for the troops. When they eventually closed because of competition with cheaper labor in southern mills, the town's fortunes declined.

Originally called Flat Rock, for the rock formations in this section of the Schuylkill River, the town was rechristened Manayunk, a Leni-Lenape word that translates as "where we go to drink." Today those words seem prophetic. In the mid-1980s the neighborhood was designated a historic district, and business owners saw a golden opportunity. Good fortune struck again in 1986, when the U.S. Pro Cycling championship picked Philadelphia as its home and included Manayunk's steep hills (now dubbed the "Wall") on its route.

These days, Manayunk is a stay-up-late, sleep-in-in-the-morning place, and to enjoy it, you should do the same. You could set out in the afternoon, explore the town, have a leisurely dinner, and still have plenty of time to shop or see a movie. Many stores stay open until 9 or 10 on Friday and Saturday nights. If you do come on a weekday, note that most stores don't open until noon.

If you're driving from Center City, follow I–76 west (the Schuylkill Expressway) to the Belmont Avenue exit. Turn right across the bridge and right again onto Main Street and park. You can also take the SEPTA R6 (Norristown) train from Market East, Suburban Station, or 30th Street Station downtown to the Manayunk station (on Cresson Street) and walk downhill to Main Street.

The blocks between 4400 to 3700 are lined with shops and restaurants. As you walk east, you'll pass some reminders of the town's former calling: Ma Jolie (No. 4340), a designer boutique, is housed in a historic 1912 bank building; the restaurant Edge (No. 4100) occupies an old textile mill; and the Farmers' Market set up shop in a former knitting mill. A right turn on Lock Street, just before the market, brings you to the towpath of the Manayunk Canal, built between 1817 and 1823. Along here barges once transported goods to and from the textile mills.

Manayunk's calendar is filled with popular events. On the first Friday night in June, the Main Street Stroll, a Victorian street festival with a costume parade and carnival games, kicks off the First Union U.S. Pro Cycling championship. On the last weekend in June, the Manayunk Arts Festival lines Main Street with arts and crafts and curbside food stands.

Center City via SEPTA Bus 23; pick it up at 11th and Market streets and get off at Queen Lane.

A Good Drive

You can follow Germantown Avenue from lower Germantown north to Chestnut Hill. Many homes you'll see were built when Germantown Avenue was a dirt road; today it's lined with cobblestones. At Queen Lane is John Wister's **Grumblethorpe,** built from stones quarried on the property. A few blocks north on Germantown Avenue is Market Square, a park that was once the site of a prison and its stocks and a focal point for trade. Facing Market Square on your left is the **Deshler-Morris House,** with fine antiques and lovely gardens; diagonally across the square in a row of beautifully restored redbrick buildings is the **Germantown Historical Society,** which offers a good introduction to the houses in the area. Drive north a half mile farther to the Quaker-style **Wyck** house, at the corner of Germantown Avenue and Walnut Lane.

Just before Pastorius Street is the tiny, historic Germantown Mennonite Church. On this site in 1708 the Mennonites established their first church in the New World. The little log church was replaced in 1770 by the current building. Turn left on Tulpehocken Street; at Number 200 West is the Victorian Gothic **Ebenezer Maxwell Mansion.** Continue north on Germantown Avenue past the Johnson House (⊠ 6306 Germantown Ave.), once a tannery, later a station on the Underground Railway. At Number 6401 is **Cliveden,** an elaborate house set at the end of a long, graceful driveway. Across the street is **Upsala,** a Federal-style home of the Johnson family (who also owned the Johnson House).

Adjacent to Germantown is the residential community of Mount Airy, and farther north, at the "top" of Germantown Avenue, is Chestnut Hill. The town's tony shopping district runs from Number 7900 to 8700. Half a mile north at Number 9201 is the **Woodmere Art Museum,** with works from the 19th and 20th centuries. From here, if it's a nice day, you could detour to the gardens of the Morris Arboretum or the natural setting of the Schuylkill Center for Environmental Education.

TIMING

Each historic house has its own schedule, so it's difficult to coordinate your visit to include all the sights. However, you could catch five homes open on a Thursday afternoon and four on Saturday or Sunday afternoon. You could then head to Chestnut Hill for dinner. Avoid this trip in winter, when most of the homes are closed.

Sights to See

★ **Cliveden.** Its unique history and fine architecture combine to make Cliveden, built in 1763 by Benjamin Chew (1722–1810), one of Germantown's treasures. The area's most elaborate country house is a shining example of Georgian style, with Palladian windows and an elegant entrance hall with pedimented door frames. The home was occupied by the British during the Revolution. On October 4, 1777, Washington's unsuccessful attempt to dislodge the British resulted in his defeat at the Battle of Germantown. You can still see bullet marks on the outside walls. Today a museum, Cliveden occupies a 6-acre plot, with outbuildings and a barn converted into offices and a gift shop. It remained in the Chew family until 1972, when it was donated to the National Trust for Historic Preservation. ⊠ *6401 Germantown Ave.,* ☎ *215/848–1777.* ▧ *$6.* ☉ *Apr.–Dec., Thurs.–Sun. noon–4.*

Deshler-Morris House. This is where President Washington lived in 1793–94, making it the seat of government of the new republic for a short time. Beautiful antiques accent the rooms, and, as one of the many Germantown houses built flush with the road, it has enchanting side and

back gardens. ✉ *5442 Germantown Ave.,* ☎ *215/596–1748.* ✉ *$1.*
☉ *Apr.–Nov., Tues.–Sat. 1–4; other times by appointment.*

Ebenezer Maxwell Mansion. Philadelphia's only mid-19th-century
house-museum is a Victorian Gothic extravaganza of elongated windows and arches. Its three-story tower is the incarnation of an old
haunted house. ✉ *200 W. Tulpehocken St.,* ☎ *215/438–1861.* ✉ *$4.*
☉ *Apr.–mid-Dec., Fri.–Sun. 1–4.*

Germantown Historical Society. The headquarters of the society has a
historical and genealogical library and a museum showcasing collections of industrial and decorative arts. It is also an orientation point
for anyone visiting the Germantown houses. ✉ *5501 Germantown Ave.,*
☎ *215/844–0514.* ✉ *$4.* ☉ *Tues. and Thurs. 10–4, Sun. 1–5.*

Grumblethorpe. Built by John Wister in 1744, this Georgian house is
one of Germantown's leading examples of early 18th-century architecture. ✉ *5267 Germantown Ave.,* ☎ *215/843–4820.* ✉ *$3.* ☉ *Apr.–
mid-Dec., Tues., Thurs., and Sun. 1–4.*

OFF THE
BEATEN PATH

MORRIS ARBORETUM – Begun in 1887 by siblings John and Lydia Morris
and bequeathed to the University of Pennsylvania in 1932, this 166-
acre arboretum typifies Victorian-era garden and landscape design with
its romantic winding paths, a hidden grotto, tropical ferns in a fernery,
and natural woodland. An eclectic retreat, the Morris also holds a rose
garden, English garden, Japanese garden, and meadows. It has 3,500
trees and shrubs from around the world, including one of the finest collections of Asian plants outside Asia. The arboretum is in the far northwest corner of the city, near the Woodmere Art Museum in Chestnut Hill.
✉ *Hillcrest Ave. between Germantown and Stenton Aves.,* ☎ *215/
247–5777. Chestnut Hill East or West commuter trains stop ½ mi away;
Bus L stops at the corner of Hillcrest and Germantown Aves.* ✉ *$6.* ☉
*Apr.–Oct., weekdays 10–4, weekends 10–5; Nov.–Mar., daily 10–4;
guided tours weekends at 2.*

SCHUYLKILL CENTER FOR ENVIRONMENTAL EDUCATION – This sanctuary consists of more than 500 acres of wildflowers, ferns, and thickets;
ponds, streams, and woodlands; 6 mi of winding trails; and the 8-acre
Pine Plantation. You may spot deer, hawks, Canada geese, red foxes,
and other animals. Hands-on exhibits in the Discovery Museum explain
the flora and fauna, and there are nature programs on weekends. The
bookstore and gift shop follow the nature theme. ✉ *8480 Hagy's Mill
Rd., Roxborough,* ☎ *215/482–7300. Bus 27 stops at Henry and Port
Royal Aves., 1 mi away.* ✉ *$3.* ☉ *Sept.–July, Mon.–Sat. 8:30–5, Sun.
1–5; Aug., Mon.–Sat. 8:30–5.*

Upsala. One of Germantown's best examples of Federal-style architecture, Upsala was built about 1755. The Johnsons, who owned the
house, were a well-to-do family of tanners. Continental troops set up
their cannons on Upsala's front lawn and shelled the British at **Cliveden** (☞ *above*). ✉ *6430 Germantown Ave.,* ☎ *215/842–1798.* ✉ *$4.*
☉ *Apr.–Nov., Thurs. and Sat. 1–4.*

Woodmere Art Museum. The art and artists of Philadelphia are showcased here, along with American and European art from the 19th and
20th centuries, in a fine collection of paintings and prints. Benjamin
West, Frederick Church, and Pennsylvania Impressionists such as Edward Redfield and Daniel Garber are represented. The museum also
has a lovely collection of decorative arts, including tapestries, sculptures, porcelains, ivories, and Japanese rugs. ✉ *9201 Germantown Ave.,*
☎ *215/247–0476.* ✉ *$5.* ☉ *Tues.–Sat. 10–5, Sun. 1–5.*

NEED A
BREAK? The British presence can still be felt in this area at **Best of British** (⊠ 8513 Germantown Ave., ☎ 215/242–8848), a cute Chestnut Hill tearoom where you can have lunch or enjoy tea with clotted cream. And since this is America, you can have your afternoon tea beginning at 9:30 AM.

Wyck. One of the most charming of Quaker-style houses, Wyck also has an old pump, barn, carriage house, and idyllic gardens. The house remained the property of the same Quaker family from 1736 to 1973. Known as the oldest house in Germantown, Wyck was used as a British field hospital after the Battle of Germantown. ⊠ *6026 Germantown Ave.,* ☎ *215/848–1690.* ⊠ *$5.* ☉ *Apr.–mid-Dec., Tues., Thurs., and Sat. 1–4; other times by appointment.*

3 DINING

Once known mainly for hoagies and snapper soup, Philadelphia has extended its culinary range to embrace the world. French food set the pace for years, but these chefs now share honors with stars from Italy and China. Distinctive ethnic restaurants and excellent seafood and steak houses round out the dining scene. Although revamped banks and brokerage houses hold a number of pricey dazzlers, simpler treasures abound, including the Reading Terminal Market.

By Barbara
Ann Rosenberg

WHETHER YOU WANT TO DINE at a fine French restaurant, sample innovative cuisine in a sophisticated setting, or just grab a quick but tasty lunch, Philadelphia has a welcome abundance of choices. The restaurant renaissance that put the city on the national culinary map began in the 1970s, largely a result of the influx of a creative new group of restaurateurs. Some started a sweeping trend by incorporating Asian flavors into otherwise familiar dishes. Others added their own personal visions to augment the city's formerly rather dreary repertoire of restaurant foodstuffs. An outstanding chef with exquisite credentials— Georges Perrier—came to the city, eventually opening his own fine dining venue, Le Bec-Fin, which was then, and is now, the most expensive in town. The number of restaurants and the range of their cuisines have continued to explode until Philadelphia dining options are now truly international in scope.

Over the years the city's restaurants have become more sophisticated in every way. Some have incorporated striking architectural details to augment the excitement of the food. In 1994, a new all-fish restaurant, Striped Bass, put a daring spin on the concept of what dining interiors should look like by moving into a handsomely renovated brokerage house. Other restaurants followed, metamorphosing turn-of-the-century banks into trendy dining locations or building contemporary spaces designed for smashing visual impact.

Modest ethnic restaurants of nearly every persuasion, from Vietnamese and Malaysian to Jamaican, also enhance the dining scene. Steak houses abound, both top-of-the-line and modestly priced establishments. And, in keeping with a nationwide trend, hotel dining has improved significantly. Philadelphia hotels now claim some of the best chefs in the business, including a number with national reputations. Italian food in Philadelphia has its own connotations, ranging from South Philadelphia home style to restaurants that rate among the city's most elegant.

No rundown of Philadelphia's dining scene would be complete without mention of celebrity chef Susanna Foo, who revolutionized Chinese food to include many of her own dishes, blending ingredients from other cultures without detracting from the essential integrity of her cuisine.

Then there is Manayunk, the former working-class city neighborhood transformed into a trendy, upscale destination drawing beautiful people (and even mere mortals) to eat, to shop, and to see and be seen. In Old City, too, many exciting new eateries have opened, rivaling those in Manayunk or elsewhere in glamour and style. And this doesn't even begin to consider other, somewhat unusual Philadelphia specialties for which locals feel a quirky but bona fide passion. Some of these local favorites have produced a number of long-standing rivalries for the title "the best of the best." Hoagies (Italian sandwiches) and cheese steaks fall into this category.

Bear in mind that Philadelphia is becoming a well-attended convention city, and so it's always wise to make reservations ahead and to reconfirm when you get to town. (Le Bec-Fin is generally booked several *months* ahead for Saturday night.) In general, you should tip 15% of the check (20% in the fanciest places), depending on the service.

In the listings, reservations are noted only when they're essential or when they are not accepted. Unless otherwise indicated, restaurants are open daily for lunch and dinner. Most of Philadelphia's restaurants can be classified as casual, but not, with the exception of inexpensive spots or the University City area, of the jeans and sneakers variety. Smart casual wear usually works except in the top hotel dining rooms and the most expensive places, where women will feel more comfortable in some version of basic black and men in ties and jackets. Dress is mentioned in reviews only when men are required to wear a jacket or a jacket and tie. For price-category information, *see* Dining *in* Smart Travel Tips A to Z.

DISTRICT BY DISTRICT

A neighborhood reference is provided along with the street address of each restaurant. Many of Philadelphia's fine restaurants are concentrated in the downtown area known locally as Center City, bounded by the Schuylkill and Delaware rivers, Vine Street to the north, and South Street to the south. To make finding restaurants easier, this large area has been subdivided geographically. Center City is used to describe the midtown area bounded roughly by the Schuylkill River to the west, 6th Street to the east, South Street to the south, and Vine Street to the north. Within this area is Chinatown, which lies between 9th and 11th streets and Vine and Arch streets. The neighborhood identified as the Historic Area takes in the eastern part of Center City and includes the area around Independence National Historical Park, with Old City and Society Hill to the north and south, respectively, of the national historical park. The boundaries of this area are 6th Street to the west, the Delaware River to the east, Vine Street to the north, and Bainbridge Street to the south.

Also included are a number of restaurants on or near the Benjamin Franklin Parkway, which leads diagonally from John F. Kennedy Plaza past Logan Circle and the Philadelphia Museum of Art to Kelly and West River drives. University City, west of the Schuylkill River around the University of Pennsylvania and Drexel University, has a number of restaurants. South Philadelphia lies south of Bainbridge Street; included here are a few places in Queen Village. Manayunk, 7 mi northwest of Center City along the Schuylkill, has some outstanding places to dine. A restaurant along City Line Avenue and a suburban spot are listed; a few additional suburban restaurants are mentioned in Chapter 8.

A good source for reasonably up-to-the-minute dining information is *Philadelphia*, a monthly magazine with restaurant listings. A couple of free weekly local papers such as the *City Paper* also have restaurant reviews and numerous listings. These "freebies" are available in metal sidewalk dispensers on nearly every Center City street corner.

American

$$-$$$ ✕ **City Tavern.** You can time-travel to the 18th century at this authentic re-creation of historic City Tavern, whose atmosphere suggests that founding fathers such as John Adams, George Washington, Thomas Jefferson, and the rest of the gang *might* have supped here (they didn't). It was in 1994, under the supervision of the National Park Service, that international consultant/restaurateur Walter Staib refurbished this spot to the specifications of the original 1773 tavern. The food—West Indies pepper pot soup, Martha Washington's turkey stew, honey pecan roast duckling—is prepared from period recipes and served on china with Colonial patterns by servers in period dress. ⊠ *138 S. 2nd St., Historic Area,* ☎ *215/413–1443. AE, D, DC, MC, V.*

American/Casual

$ ✕ **Where Else? Cafe.** Funky, charming, artsy, innovative: all these words happily describe this little spot that caters to neighborhood locals and anyone else who happens by en route to Antiques Row or wherever. Touches of the Caribbean, such as the exemplary Cuban sandwich (ham, chicken, cheese, lettuce, and tomato on a chewy roll, pressed down and grilled), share menu space with a triple-decker chicken melt and specials such as feather-light crab cakes. ✉ *301 S. 11th St., Center City,* ☎ *215/733–0482. No credit cards. Closed Mon.*

Belgian

$–$$ ✕ **Cuvée Notredame.** Michel Notredame, the jovial native Flemish chef-owner, is only too happy to discuss the menu and the French/Flemish overtones of the dishes served in a very European atmosphere, complete with lace curtains typical of Belgium. Mussels, a Belgian favorite, are prepared curried, with leeks or cream, or in several other ways; rabbit and other traditional foods of the country are available, along with a wide variety of Belgian beers. The owner is the Philadelphia originator of the $5 bar menu—with entrées from chicken livers to a small steamed lobster—served at lunch. ✉ *1701 Green St., Benjamin Franklin Pkwy.,* ☎ *215/765–2777. AE, DC, MC, V.*

$–$$ ✕ **Monk's.** Mussels are practically the national dish of Belgium. Whether cooked in classic style with wine and shallots or with cream, they are a high point at this casual, lively bar and restaurant, and the fries that accompany them draw raves from the regulars who crowd the place. Burgers, too, are menu favorites. Add to these an outstanding assortment of Belgian beers and you get the picture. ✉ *264 S. 16th St., Center City,* ☎ *215/545–7005. Reservations not accepted. MC, V. Closed Sun.*

Brunch

In Philadelphia, as elsewhere, many restaurants have latched on to the habit of serving copious amounts of food as a high point of the weekend. Several top-notch hotels have outstanding (and expensive) brunches that are virtual extravaganzas (☞ Chapter 4 for the addresses and telephone numbers of these hotels). Plenty of more laid-back, casual places are also great for socializing with a not-so-early Sunday coffee in hand.

The Wyndham Franklin Plaza has **Between Friends,** with a jazz- and champagne-embellished buffet brunch. **Founders** at the Park Hyatt Philadelphia at the Bellevue has a chef-attended brunch on Saturday, when guests can chat with him about the various dishes; caviar is one delicacy served at Sunday brunch. The Fountain restaurant and the Swan Lounge at the Four Seasons are both stunners. At the **Fountain** the price is determined by the cost of the served-at-the-table entrée, although the rest of the meal is an all-you-can-stuff buffet of delicacies. **Swan** includes the entrées on a succession of varied buffets at a fixed price. A group plays nonstop classical jazz during the feast. **Treetops** at the Rittenhouse hotel has an à la carte brunch in a lovely setting overlooking the elms of Rittenhouse Square.

Bridget Foy's Second Street Grill (✉ 200 South St., ☎ 215/922–1813) has a make-your-own-Bloody-Mary station as part of the fun. **Le Bus** (✉ 4266 Main St., ☎ 215/487–2663), in Manayunk, is a favorite for omelets and innovative egg preparations, with all the wonderful breads this supercasual, friendly place is known for. It's a mob scene, so go early. **Meiji-En** (✉ Pier 19 at Callowhill St., ☎ 215/592–7100), a riverside restaurant with stupendous views, serves waffles, eggs, and all the accoutrements from smoked salmon to fruit (and even some sushi) in a huge, bright room. A jazz duo or trio adds the finishing touch. An à la carte jazz brunch at **Zanzibar Blue** (✉ 200 S. Broad St., ☎ 215/732–5200) includes really good jazz along with eggs and other creditable food in a downstairs location at the Bellevue Building.

Dining

Arroyo Grill, **17**

Assagi Italiani, **62**

The Bards, **23**

Between Friends, **44**

Bookbinder's Seafood House, **38**

Brasserie Perrier, **43**

Bridget Foy's Second Street Grill, **73**

Buddakan, **83**

Chart House, **77**

Ciboulette, **31**

Circa, **41**

City Tavern, **79**

Continental Restaurant & Martini Bar, **87**

Cuvée Notredame, **45**

Deux Cheminées, **56**

DiPalma, **86**

Dock Street Brasserie, **11**

Fez, **68**

Fishmarket, **21**

Fish on Main, **5**

Fork, **84**

Founders, **31**

Fountain Restaurant, **10**

The Garden, **28**

Genji, **12, 20**

Gianna's, **64**

Girasole, **55**

Guru, **72**

H.K. Golden Phoenix, **50**

Hikaru, **2, 19, 67**

Jake's, **3**

Jamaican Jerk Hut, **30**

Jim's Steaks, **70**

Joseph Poon, **53**

Kansas City Prime, **6**

La Veranda, **88**

Le Bec-Fin, **42**

Le Bus, **4**

Le Colonial, **35**

Lee How Fook, **46**

The Marker, **8**

Meiji-En, **90**

Monk's, **29**

Monte Carlo Living Room, **75**

Morning Glory Diner, **61**

Morton's of Chicago, **39**

The Moshulu, **76**

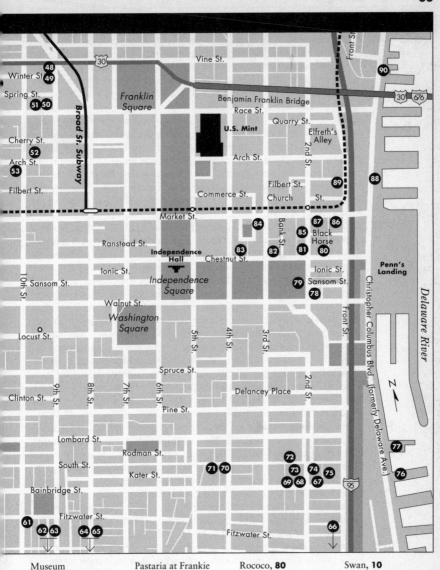

Museum Restaurant, **7**

Mustard Greens, **69**

Nam Phuong, **65**

Nan, **18**

Ocean City, **49**

Ocean Harbor, **51**

Old Original Bookbinder's, **78**

Overtures, **71**

Palm, **31**

Pamplona, **57**

Panorama, **89**

Pasión, **33**

Pastaria at Frankie and Luigi's, **60**

Penang, **52**

Philadelphia Fish & Company, **81**

Philippe on Locust, **27**

The Plough and the Stars, **82**

Prime Rib, **26**

Rachel's Nosheri, **22**

Reading Terminal Market, **54**

Restaurant School, **16**

Ristorante Primavera, **74**

Rococo, **80**

Rocco's, **54**

Rouge, **25**

Salumeria, **54**

Sang Kee Peking Duck House, **48**

Sansom Street Oyster House, **40**

Serrano, **85**

Sonoma, **1**

Striped Bass Restaurant and Bar, **37**

Sullivan's, **9**

Susanna Foo, **36**

Swan, **10**

Tequila's, **34**

Thai Singa House, **13**

Tony Luke's, **66**

Toto, **32**

Tre Scalini, **63**

Treetops, **24**

Vetri, **58**

Vietnam, **47**

Where Else? Cafe, **59**

White Dog Cafe, **15**

Zanzibar Blue, **31**

Zócalo, **14**

Chinese

$$–$$$$ ✕ **Susanna Foo.** The displays of unusual orchids and contemporary
★   Chinese artwork in this elegant restaurant provide a worthy setting for
food that has earned a national reputation. The chef has garnered all
manner of awards for her cuisine, which incorporates Western ingre-
dients into essentially Chinese food. Such favorites as Hundred-Cor-
ner Crab Cakes, lobster dumplings with coconut-lobster sauce, and
five-spice venison with Mongolian sauce, along with a battery of ex-
otic specials (such as foie gras), bring repeat business from a loyal co-
terie of regulars who compete for tables with out-of-towners. There is
a full bar and a thoughtfully chosen, pricey wine list as well as imported
beers. The restaurant's pastry chef favors desserts, many with butter
and cream, that are more often found in upscale French restaurants.
✉ *1512 Walnut St., Center City,* ☎ *215/545–2666. Reservations es-
sential. AE, DC, MC, V.*

$–$$ ✕ **Ocean Harbor and H. K. Golden Phoenix.** At lunchtime these sister
★   restaurants, just a block from each other on the same busy Chinatown
street, closely resemble Hong Kong teahouses, with multiple carts flying through their dining rooms full of dizzying selections of dim sum.
Besides the usual pork and shrimp dumplings, the chefs often incor-
porate specifically Chinese ingredients. You point at what you want
and it is transferred to your plate and charged to your bill. The bill is
in Chinese and prices of portions vary, but no matter how much it takes
to stuff your party, it ends up as a pretty reasonable meal. If you don't
know what's in the dim sum, ask for a description—sometimes you
get it. The clientele at lunch is mainly Chinese, and the restaurants are
crowded. Evenings are quieter and the menu is different, listing such
dishes as lobster with ginger and scallions. ✉ *Ocean Harbor: 1023 Race
St., Chinatown,* ☎ *215/574–1398. DC, MC, V.* ✉ *H. K. Golden
Phoenix: 911 Race St., Chinatown,* ☎ *215/629–4988. DC, MC, V.*

$–$$ ✕ **Joseph Poon.** Named for its owner-chef, who taps into a Chinese-
Italian fusion mode, this striking contemporary restaurant decorated
with jars of artistically arranged pasta is often the scene of special events
such as free weekly cooking classes. Peking duck pizza, Arch Street ciop-
pino (fish in a black bean, bourbon, and ginger sauce), and fried
spinach with five-spice powder and Parmesan are typical creations. Poon
is also a celebrity master carver of fruits and vegetables, and his handiwork frequently decorates his ample plates. ✉ *1002 Arch St., Chinatown,* ☎ *215/928–9333. AE, D, DC, MC, V. Closed Tues.*

$–$$ ✕ **Lee How Fook.** This restaurant has been serving Cantonese food to
loyal fans of the genre for years, even when that style took a tempo-
rary backseat to the craze for Szechuan and Hunan dishes. Small and
plain but clean, and just a block from the main Chinatown action, Lee
How Fook is rediscovered every few years by yet another reviewer who
extols its simple dishes, such as salt-baked shrimp or squid, beautifully
cooked and seasoned asparagus (in season), and a variety of noodle
dishes (except for the Singapore-style noodles, which, for whatever reason, are dry and lifeless in taste). ✉ *219 N. 11th St., Chinatown,* ☎
215/925–7266. No credit cards.

$ ✕ **Mustard Greens.** Light, bright, and airy describe the ambience as
well as the food at this outside Chinatown but thoroughly Chinese restaurant. It strongly appeals to neighborhood folks, who often chummily
exchange views on what is especially good. When soft shell crabs are
in season, there's no question—they are on nearly every table, enrobed
in greaseless, ethereal, tempura-light batter. A dish of lightly seasoned
chicken and apricots is also notable. Green beans, asparagus, and, of
course, greens are handled with finesse. Bill Wong, the "out front" part-

ner (the other is in the kitchen), charms all the guests. ✉ *622 S. 2nd St., Historic Area,* ☎ *215/627–0833. AE, MC, V.*

$ ✗ **Ocean City.** Lacquered ducks and roast pork cuts hang in the window of this restaurant on the eastern periphery of Chinatown, a large, bright place that covers all bases on its huge menu, although it leans heavily toward Cantonese. Fish tanks of creatures, including eels, meant for cooking line the entryway. Banquets for 10 or more people (reserve ahead) are an outstanding specialty. Order one of these, and course after course of well-known—and several lesser known but well-prepared—dishes comes flying to the table. A private ground-floor dining room holds 20, and the vast upstairs accommodates up to 500 people. ✉ *234 N. 9th St., Chinatown,* ☎ *215/829–0688. AE, MC, V.*

$ ✗ **Sang Kee Peking Duck House.** Until recently, this place was totally devoid of decor, unless you count the lacquered ducks and boneless pork loins hanging in the interior window. A renovation has doubled its size and brought in black metal chairs and Formica tables, but Sang Kee continues to dish up the most delicious noodle soups in town. It's possible to order egg or rice noodles in different widths and a selection of accompanying meats: duck, pork, beef brisket. And if you wish, you can have your soup with both noodles *and* overstuffed, tender wontons. Other traditional foods, besides the house specialty duck, are carried from the kitchen with more speed than style. Beer is available. ✉ *238 N. 9th St., Chinatown,* ☎ *215/925–7532. Reservations not accepted. No credit cards.*

Contemporary

$$$$ ✗ **Fountain Restaurant.** Dining at the Fountain is a glamorous and cos-
★ mopolitan experience, blending pleasant, polished service with elegance of appointments. The peak of the experience, however, is unquestionably the food. Chef Jean-Marie Lacroix and his staff are constantly experimenting to create culinary excitement that changes with the seasons. Among the favorites are potatoes lyonnaise with caviar cream; pot-au-feu of rabbit and artichokes; and sautéed venison medallions swaddled in homemade pasta. "Healthy menu" choices are equally delicious. The restaurant is tucked away off the lavish but understated lobby of the Four Seasons hotel—a culinary oasis for travelers and a favorite dining location for locals, as well. ✉ *1 Logan Sq., Benjamin Franklin Pkwy.,* ☎ *215/963–1500. Reservations essential. AE, D, DC, MC, V.*

$$$–$$$$ ✗ **The Garden.** A quintessential Philadelphia town house–turned–restaurant, the Garden nonetheless manages to convey the impression of France as you walk through the hallway into the bar or into the somewhat formal yet welcoming dining room. The restaurant takes its name from the charming back garden that has service (in appropriate weather) on a canopied deck or in the lower garden. Among owner-chef Kathleen Mulhern's specialties is exquisitely fresh grilled Dover sole equal to any served on the other side of the pond. She has earned a reputation for pristine ingredients, from beef and lamb to lobster, simply but elegantly prepared. Desserts are all homemade. Two cruvinets dispense glasses of selected red and white wines from an outstanding wine list. ✉ *1617 Spruce St., Center City,* ☎ *215/546–4455. AE, DC, MC, V. Closed Sun.; Sat. in July and Aug.*

$$$–$$$$ ✗ **Jake's.** Owner-chef Bruce Cooper (his wife is Jake) has garnered a
★ reputation for food that is innovative but somehow classic rather than quirky. The place displays the hottest in contemporary crafts, many from local art galleries that punctuate trendy Manayunk. Cooper has a particular affinity for scallops and transforms them into dishes that range from simple to complex—always tender, sweet, and perfectly cooked. His lump crab cakes and salmon are also outstanding. This is

one of the places that helped Manayunk achieve its reputation as a dining mecca. ✉ *4365 Main St., Manayunk,* ☎ *215/483–0444. AE, DC, MC, V.*

$$–$$$ ✗ **Circa.** This restaurant, now firmly entrenched on the dining scene, was the first of the lapsed banks with soaring arched ceilings to be transformed into a dining space. The food is as bright and lively as the people who flock here. You walk into an atmosphere punctuated by flickering votive candles; the greeter's station is a church pulpit, and pews do duty as benches in the bar. The lower floor, open only for dinner, includes the original bank vault. The master chef has a particular penchant for global cuisine made with anything from seafood to buffalo. Nut-crusted Australian rack of lamb, cardamom-spiked Muscovy duck breasts, and foie gras spaetzle are notably fancy, hearty dishes. ✉ *1518 Walnut St., Center City,* ☎ *215/545–6800. AE, D, MC, V.*

$$–$$$ ✗ **The Marker.** This restaurant in the Adam's Mark hotel has become increasingly popular as its menu has developed a more adventurous style under the tutelage of creative chef Vincent Alberici. Popular items include jumbo lump crab cakes with smoked red-pepper butter; herb- and mustard-crusted domestic rack of lamb carved table-side; and a flaky raspberry napoleon for dessert. The Library, a cozy room with a fireplace and built-in bookshelves, is a favorite seating choice, but there are two other larger, somewhat more formal areas as well. ✉ *City Line Ave. and Monument Rd., City Line Ave. area,* ☎ *215/581–5000. AE, D, DC, MC, V.*

$$–$$$ ✗ **Rococo.** An architectural dazzler, Rococo makes its home in the former turn-of-the-century Corn Exchange Bank. Executive chef Albert Paris and his sidekick Mustapha Rouissiya each brought their individual style of cooking to what became an instant hit for meeting and eating. The lively front bar gives way to a handsome, large, rather noisy dining room that extends up a flight of steps to an area for smokers. Sesame-crusted rare tuna, Asian rack of king prawns, and roast duck are high points of the menu, and many regulars make their meal out of a succession of appetizers such as spicy rock shrimp. ✉ *123 Chestnut St., Historic Area,* ☎ *215/629–1100. AE, D, DC, MC, V.*

$$ ✗ **The Moshulu.** Anchored at the foot of South Street, this huge, 100-year-old sailing ship is a landmark that juts out into the Delaware River. The dining room serves a large menu of contemporary global foods with flavors from many of the ports touched by the vessel during its travels. The restaurant has a great, comfortable bar, and the entire experience is akin to taking a voyage without leaving the port. ✉ *Pier 34, 735 S. Columbus Blvd., Historic Area,* ☎ *215/923–2500. AE, D, DC, MC, V.*

$$ ✗ **Museum Restaurant.** The venerable Philadelphia Museum of Art gives visitors an opportunity to feed their bodies while nourishing their souls at lunch as well as Wednesday-night dinner and Sunday brunch. Run by nationally renowned Restaurant Associates, the restaurant is bright, white, and hung with a rotating display of paintings. The chef's table (a buffet with unlimited returns) artfully arranges foodstuffs such as ham, salmon, green beans, Parmesan toasts, crisp salad, and a fine cheese board. The chef is from the Eastern Shore of Chesapeake Bay and has a special way with crab. Soups are sometimes scrumptious, and sandwiches are always fresh. When the weather is amenable, a cold buffet is presented under a large tent on a terrace with a glorious view of the city. ✉ *26th St. and Benjamin Franklin Pkwy.,* ☎ *215/763–8100. AE, DC, MC, V. Closed Mon. No dinner Thurs.–Tues.*

$$ ✗ **Restaurant School.** Here's the only place in Philadelphia where you have a chance to get somewhat haute cuisine (depending on which student chef is at the stove) and European service at a fraction of what you would pay at a fancy restaurant. It is managed and staffed entirely by students attending the city's Restaurant School. Each of the three dining rooms in a restored 1860 Victorian mansion has a different menu: American comfort food in one, Italian in another, and well-known-Philadelphia-chef-inspired in a third. In the latter, recipes are furnished by the chefs—Georges Perrier, Susanna Foo, and Philippe Chin—and cooked by the students. ⊠ *4207 Walnut St., University City,* ☎ *215/ 222–4200. AE, D, DC, MC, V. Closed Sun. and Mon.*

$$ ✕ **White Dog Cafe.** The name of this funkily decorated, eclectic town house restaurant near the Penn campus derives from the story of the 19th-century mystic Madame Blavatsky who claimed that while she was living in the house, a white dog lay across her ailing leg and cured it. Innovative restaurateur Judy Wicks took her inspiration from the tale and sponsors all manner of events that would make Madame Blavatsky proud. The restaurant specializes in locally grown products; seasonings can be overly ambitious, so choose carefully. The small, lively bar has a number of American beers on tap and in bottles; the wine list, too, is all-American. ⊠ *3420 Sansom St., University City,* ☎ *215/ 386–9224. AE, D, DC, MC, V.*

$–$$ ✕ **Fork.** Happy sounds emanate from the diners here—if you can hear them over the noise of the always lively bar patrons. A limited menu of tasty food is attractively served, such as the moderately priced rack of lamb that arrives with potatoes and a green vegetable, or roast pork with multiple vegetables. Fork counts many locals among its regulars. There's usually a wait for a table but not always a place to wait comfortably. Sit as far back in the restaurant as possible to watch the folks at work in the open kitchen. ⊠ *306 Market St., Historic Area,* ☎ *215/ 625–9425. AE, D, DC, MC, V. Closed Mon.*

$–$$ ✕ **Rouge.** This jewel box (with the name that changes to incorporate the last two digits of the current year) opens out onto Rittenhouse Square and is very much a "meet and greet and eat" kind of place, with subtle, smart decor that includes blown-glass fixtures. Ladies who lunch love it—ditto gentlemen whose offices are in the neighborhood—both for a midday repast and a chance to hook up with everybody after work at the busy bar or one of the sidewalk or window tables. Martinis are large but food portions can sometimes be small. The tuna tartare is excellent, as are the steak frites and herb-roasted chicken with potato puree. Many regulars opt for the outstanding $10 hamburger. ⊠ *205 S. 18th St., Center City,* ☎ *215/732–6622. Reservations not accepted. AE, MC, V.*

$–$$ ✕ **Sonoma.** The first of Chef Derek Davis's ventures as an entrepreneur became the cornerstone of his mini-empire in trendy Manayunk (☞ Fish on Main *in* Diners and Philly Food, *below*). The contemporary, airy design sets the stage for California-influenced food with Italian touches. The sandwiches on focaccia are standouts, as is the glazed chicken. Sonoma immediately earned a reputation as a hangout for those who are hip; the bar, which regularly stocks 135 varieties of vodka, cemented that reputation. ⊠ *4411 Main St., Manayunk,* ☎ *215/483– 9400. AE, D, DC, MC, V.*

$ ✕ **Continental Restaurant & Martini Bar.** Light fixtures that look like olives pierced with toothpicks are a tip-off to the theme at this cool martini watering hole and small-plate eatery ensconced in a classic diner shell in the center of Old City's action. This is another of Stephen Starr's trendy restaurants, and his executive chef Bradlee Bartram serves up trendy (but not outré) food to a crowd that knows the difference. Don't miss the addictive Szechuan french-fried potatoes with hot mustard sauce. Greaseless, crisp fried shrimp and squid is a winner, and the sesame seared tuna is fine. Reservations are accepted only for parties of six or more. ⊠ *138 Market St.,* ☎ *215/923–6069. AE, DC, MC, V.*

Delicatessens

$　✕ **Rachel's Nosheri.** All the trappings of standard deli fare are evident here, including jars of cucumbers in various stages of pickling. The menu lists smoked fish of all types, and smoked meats, too, for stuffed sandwiches and platters. The lively take-out business caters to the apartments and businesses in the area, but a neat complement of tables awaits those who prefer to devour their food on the premises. ✉ *120 S. 19th St., Center City,* ☎ *215/568–9565. No credit cards.*

Diners and Philly Food

Philadelphia's former mayor Ed Rendell gleefully enhanced the city's reputation as "the junk food capital of the country" by frequently appearing while stuffing his mouth with a hoagie or cheese steak. Hoagies, a Philadelphia spin on the traditional Italian sandwich (called a hero or sub in other cities), have been embraced by nearly everyone who tastes them. Soft pretzels—with mustard, to be authentic—are tolerated by many visitors, but the merits of Philadelphia cheese steaks (as served up at South Philly joints such as Pat's and Geno's, both at 9th Street and Passyunk Avenue) often elude anyone not to the city born. Nevertheless, lovers of Philly food will be happy to know that gift packages of everything *but* cheese steaks can be shipped by calling **Philadelphia Favorites to Go** (☎ 800/808–8646) or **A Taste of Philadelphia** (☎ 800/846–2443).

$–$$　✕ **Fish on Main.** With a startling amount of chrome-embellished decor that harks back to the '50s and forward farther into the 21st century, this huge diner is another in the Derek Davis empire of restaurants, all in Manayunk. The large daily selection of fish is served baked, grilled, fried, steamed, and raw. Some specialties are jumbo lump crab cakes, sautéed pompano, and roasted monkfish. Other eateries that display the chef's versatility and vitality are **Arroyo Grill** (✉ Main and Leverington St., Manayunk, ☎ 215/487–1400), strictly Southwestern in ambience and food preparation, with such dishes as fried oysters on tortillas with salsa; the sophisticated steak house **Kansas City Prime** (✉ 4417 Main St., Manayunk, ☎ 215/482–3700), the only place in the city that serves ultra-pricey, ultra-tender Kobe beef; and **Sonoma** (☞ Contemporary, *above*). ✉ *3720 Main St., Manayunk,* ☎ *215/483–7500. AE, D, DC, MC, V.*

$　✕ **Jim's Steaks.** You are sharply aware of the fact that you're coming up on Jim's from at least a block away, as the odor of mountains of frying onions comes rolling at you. Big, juicy, drippy sandwiches of "Philly steaks"—shaved beef piled high on long crusty rolls—come off the grill with amazing speed when the counter workers hit their stride, but be aware that no matter how hard you beg, they will not toast the rolls. Take extra napkins so you won't be wearing your sandwich as well as eating it. Jim's is mostly takeout, but some tables and chairs are upstairs. ✉ *400 South St.,* ☎ *215/928–1911. Reservations not accepted. No credit cards.*

$　✕ **Morning Glory Diner.** Although the Morning Glory bills itself as a diner and carries many of the requisite standbys, such as big mugs of steaming coffee, the place was fashioned from a couple of corner storefronts and departs from tradition in some other ways as well: big breakfasts come with mammoth homemade biscuits, but if you want toast, you pay extra. Huge sandwiches are served on crusty bread from a local South Philadelphia bakery. Tasty turkey meat loaf is a specialty—frequently topped off with nippy, homemade tomato-based catsup—that gives obeisance to the health consciousness of the owners. The accompanying home-fried potatoes, however, seem to deviate from that consciousness. ⊠ *735 S. 10th St., South Philadelphia,* ☎ *215/413–3999. No credit cards. Closed Mon.*

$ ✕ **Reading Terminal Market.** A Philadelphia treasure, the Reading
★ Terminal Market (☞ Center City *in* Chapter 2) contains a profusion
of more than 80 stalls, shops, lunch counters, and food emporiums in
a huge, exciting indoor market. You can choose from numerous raw
ingredients and prepared foods—Chinese, Greek, Mexican, Japanese,
Thai, Middle Eastern, Italian, soul food, vegetarian, and Pennsylvania Dutch. Food options include an extensive salad bar, seafood spots,
a deli, baked goods, specialty hoagie (☞ Rocco's *and* Salumeria,
below) and cheese-steak shops, a sushi bar, and the outstanding Bassett's ice-cream counter. Get here early to beat the daily lunch rush.
The Down Home Diner inside the market has farm-style breakfasts and
lunches (and dinner until 8, except Sunday). The market is open Monday–Saturday 8–6. ⊠ *12th and Arch Sts., Center City,* ☎ *215/922–
2317. Closed Sun.*

$ ✕ **Rocco's.** Fortunately for the hungry, one of Philadelphia's prime pur-
veyors of overstuffed hoagies has a convenient location at Reading Terminal Market (☞ *above*). The sandwiches can be made with a variety
of fillings, but the classic Italian hoagies earn the most fans. Freshly
sliced meats such as Genoa salami, *capicolla* (spiced ham), and others
join aged provolone and other cheeses in an overstuffed crisp roll specially baked to hold the assortment without spilling over. The simple
dressing is the finishing touch. Note: Rocco's closes at 6. ⊠ *Reading
Terminal Market, 12th and Arch Sts., Center City,* ☎ *215/238–1223.
No credit cards. Closed Sun.*

$ ✕ **Salumeria.** A local favorite, Salumeria specializes in hoagies that have
★ taken the basic sandwich one step up to a new level of consciousness.
This hoagie includes such ingredients as roasted pimientos and a house
dressing among its standard ingredients and offers house-marinated
artichoke hearts as an embellishment. Nobody can complain about gilding the lily, however, because these additions are somehow incorporated into a delicious whole. Salumeria closes at 6. ⊠ *Reading Terminal
Market, 12th and Arch Sts., Center City,* ☎ *215/592–8150. No credit
cards. Closed Sun.*

$ ✕ **Tony Luke's.** The location—at Front Street and Oregon Avenue, nearly
under I–95—earned such a reputation from truckers who stopped for
huge beef or pork sandwiches with Italian greens and cheese that locals finally caught on and adopted the dinerlike restaurant for their
own. The lines are long (though they move quickly) and seating (outside only, under cover) is relatively scarce; still, people flock here from
early morning to closing time for generous breakfasts and tasty sandwiches. For large orders, it's possible to call ahead and take food
home. ⊠ *39 E. Oregon Ave., South Philadelphia,* ☎ *215/551–5725.
Reservations not accepted. No credit cards. Closed Sun.*

Eclectic

$–$$ ✕ **Buddakan.** Softened by miles of fabric, this former post office has
★ been transformed into a stunning restaurant. A 10-ft-tall gilded Bud-
dha presides over the otherwise all-white, soaring space, seemingly ap-
proving of the mostly fusion food that pairs Asian ingredients with
various cooking styles. Chicken with cashews, tempura lump crab, and
sushi rolls are all superb. A long "community" table may provide access to dine with the likes of the mayor, other politicos, or anyone for-
tunate enough to snag this center stage space. Be prepared for major
din as the evening wears on. ⊠ *325 Chestnut St., Historic Area,* ☎
215/544–9940. Reservations essential. AE, DC, MC, V.

$-$$ ✗ **Nan.** Long before fusion was ever thought of as a way to describe food, this talented chef began a wholly different approach to his native Thai food, pairing it with French ingredients and techniques. Others followed his lead, and he took some time off to reflect. Now Kamul Phutlek is back in the swing, fascinating people with an intriguing mix of flavors that keeps University folk, Center City types, and suburban settlers clamoring for dishes such as crisp half-chicken with plum and tamarind sauce and escargots on puff pastry with duxelles and garlic butter. The three-course lunch is a downright bargain. Fruit tart is an ethereal dessert. ✉ *4000 Chestnut St., University City,* ☎ *215/382–0818. AE, MC, V. BYOB. Closed Sun.*

$ ✗ **Guru.** The chef calls his cooking Asian soul food, which is as handy a description as any of the tasty mélange of flavors in his Philippine roast chicken or shrimp and chorizo over noodles. Meaty ribs are served as an appetizer for one but will work for two, if anyone will give away a single bite. The decor is intended to be soothing, and if the New Age music isn't turned up too loud, conversation is possible, even pleasant, in this popular little space. ✉ *222 South St., Historic Area,* ☎ *215/413–9240. Reservations not accepted. AE, MC, V.*

French

$$$$ ✗ **Deux Cheminées.** This unique restaurant occupies two 19th-century mansions filled with Oriental rugs, paintings, and fine objects that create a supremely romantic setting for dining. The French food on the $75 prix-fixe menu is rather classic in style, with touches that owner-chef Fritz Blank feels are appropriate. Some signature dishes are rack of lamb with truffle sauce; a rich crab bisque with Scotch; and a risotto with black truffles, fontina cheese, and fresh shrimp. The service here is truly polished. ✉ *1221 Locust St., Center City,* ☎ *215/790–0200. AE, DC, MC, V. Closed Sun., Mon. No lunch.*

$$$$ ✗ **Le Bec-Fin.** For many years this outpost of Parisian and Lyonnais
★   food (with inspired touches from stellar owner-chef Georges Perrier) was judged the finest in the city and, oftentimes, the country. Despite some recent competition for that accolade, there are still sufficient plaudits to require an advance reservation of several *months* to garner a Saturday-night seat for the $118 per person fixed-price dinner. Expect to find this haute cuisine served in a luxurious setting of Louis XV furniture, apricot silk walls, and crystal chandeliers. *Galette de crabe* (a sublime crab cake) and salmon mille-feuille are popular signature dishes. It's possible to indulge in a more limited selection of some dishes by reserving ahead for a three-course lunch for a fairly modest $36. Le Bar Lyonnais, just downstairs from the main dining room, has smallish portions of some specialty dishes for relatively affordable prices. ✉ *1523 Walnut St., Center City,* ☎ *215/567–1000. Reservations essential. Jacket and tie. AE, D, DC, MC, V. Closed Sun.*

$$-$$$ ✗ **Brasserie Perrier.** To fulfill his dream of a "less formal place where
★   people can go to eat well and have a good time" (presumably without breaking the bank), Georges Perrier of Le Bec-Fin (☞ *above*) opened this large, exuberant, Americanized version of a brasserie, complete with a bar and striking modern-deco ambience. The menu lists contemporary food such as wild striped bass with ginger sauce and curried couscous as well as some traditional brasserie dishes such as *boudin blanc* (white-meat sausage) and *moules marinière* (mussels cooked in white wine). Chef Francesco Martorella also prepares four- and five-course tasting menus of his choice of foods (after consultation with the customer). This continues to be one of the most happening places in town—cheap by no means, but people concede they get their

money's worth. ⊠ *1619 Walnut St., Center City,* ☎ *215/568–3000. AE, DC, MC, V. No lunch Sat.*

\$\$–\$\$\$ ✕ **Ciboulette.** Bruce Lim, the owner-chef, has made his way through several incarnations of this high-ceilinged French restaurant on the second floor of the handsome Bellevue Building. His current style is to serve all his entrées in appetizer-size portions while maintaining the complexity of preparation. Black bass in *barigoule* consists of the fish with artichoke bottoms, fennel, and arugula. Some choices are intended to be kind to waistlines—or you can indulge in such pleasures as foie gras with mango or sinful desserts. ⊠ *200 S. Broad St., Center City,* ☎ *215/ 790–1210. AE, DC, MC, V.*

\$\$–\$\$\$
★ ✕ **Overtures.** A bit of Paris exists just off funky South Street. Not the food, exactly, since Overtures does not cook pure French but rather the inspired interpretations of the owner-chef, a genial man with definite ideas about how to operate his fine, moderately priced restaurant. Among the stylish decorative touches are extravagant flower arrangements, trompe l'oeil paintings, and black-and-white floor tiles. Although the menu changes periodically, there's always a lavender-scented rack of lamb, a genuine winner; and people who adore sweetbreads swear by Overtures' preparation. The Caesar salad may be the best in town. ⊠ *609–611 E. Passyunk Ave., Historic Area,* ☎ *215/ 627–3455. AE, DC, MC, V. BYOB.*

\$\$–\$\$\$ ✕ **Philippe on Locust.** Philippe is Philippe Chin, who made his reputation as a hotel chef and then as the owner-chef of Chanterelles on Spruce Street. Chef Chin is now turning out his mix of classic and somewhat new food, a kind of French fusion, in a building that was for many years one of the city's classiest private clubs. The decor has been entirely redone as hip rather than stuffy, and you have a choice of menus and food styles between the dining room and the bar. Maine lobster bisque is served with lemongrass-cognac essence, and braised lamb shank strudel comes with moussaka. ⊠ *1614 Locust St., Center City,* ☎ *215/ 735–7551. AE, DC, MC, V. Closed Sun.*

\$–\$\$ ✕ **Dock Street Brasserie.** All the makings of a classic brasserie (which actually means "brewery" in French) are here: the machinery for producing the beer and the large, exuberant space in which to drink it. Olivier de St. Martin, a chef from the north of France whose family home nuzzles up to Alsace—where brasseries began—metamorphosed the menu to include the dishes for which that region is famous. Hearty favorites such as *choucroute* (sauerkraut cooked with white wine, juniper berries, assorted sausages, and duck confit) and cassoulet dominate, although there are still standards such as steaks, fish, and burgers. Several flavors of the house-specialty boutique beer are available on a daily basis, along with a full bar. ⊠ *2 Logan Sq., Benjamin Franklin Pkwy.,* ☎ *215/496–0413. AE, MC, V.*

Irish

\$–\$\$ ✕ **The Plough and the Stars.** The animated, first-floor dining room and bar of this renovated bank feels like a genuine Irish pub. A long bar with a dozen spigots is consistently busy drawing many imported and a few local brews, all served up at the correct temperature—not really cold, but cooler than room temperature. In winter people crowd up to a blazing fireplace on stools set around tables. It's possible to munch on good Irish smoked salmon on grainy bread while imbibing; you can also head to the upstairs dining room for some respite from the crush and taste a variety of worldly appetizers, salads, and main courses. Irish afternoon tea, with sandwiches, scones, and pastries, is a winner and a change from the more delicate English spread. ⊠ *123 Chestnut St. (entrance on 2nd St.), Historic Area,* ☎ *215/733–0300. AE, DC, MC, V.*

$ The Bards. The pictures on the wall commemorate some notable Irish writers such as George Bernard Shaw and James Joyce. The food, too, testifies to the authenticity of this pub-restaurant, which features a full range of Irish specialties and full-bodied beers to accompany them. The front-of-the house bar is lively at all hours, and the dining room, a bit farther back, is also busy, with contented people chowing down on such pub grub as shepherd's pie (at lunch), potato cakes, Irish smoked salmon, and liver and Irish bacon. *2013 Walnut St., Center City,* ☎ *215/569–9585. AE, DC, MC, V.*

Italian

$$–$$$$ ✕ Monte Carlo Living Room. Two mirrored, candlelighted dining rooms
  ★   with crystal chandeliers create a refined atmosphere for sublime Italian cuisine. Chef Nunzio Patruno applies his deft touch to foods of his entire country and to all forms of protein, but fish and shellfish dishes seem to bring out his very best instincts. Homemade pastas, such as black pasta with seafood and tomato or thin pasta with sautéed lobster, brandy, and cream, are ethereal. If the chef is available to create a special menu ($65), by all means consider the possibility. Dancing in a plush private club upstairs is free to diners. The Wednesday night buffet in the club is excellent. ⊠ *150 South St., Historic Area,* ☎ *215/ 925–2220. Reservations essential. Jacket required. AE, MC, V.*

$$–$$$ ✕ Assagi Italiani. Dark wood trims the stucco walls at this casual, reasonably priced restaurant, and the white tile floors are fashioned after a Roman *ristorante.* The menu lists assorted small-plate samplings of pastas with a variety of sauces tasting of the Old World; osso bucco is a winner, too. A new item, available by reservation for six or more, is a traditional roast suckling pig dinner for $40 per person. The wine list is excellent. ⊠ *935 Ellsworth St., South Philadelphia,* ☎ *215/ 339–0700. AE, DC, MC, V. Closed Mon.*

$$–$$$ ✕ DiPalma. Rosewood walls and sophisticated appointments set the tone for the service and food. Lobster cannelloni, carefully wrapped in delicate leaves of squid ink pasta, is a favorite starter, and such main courses as grilled langoustines and rack of tiny lamb chops in a wine sauce follow with a flourish. It's no wonder that serious business discussions seem to dominate the tables during the week; on weekends, friends gather here to enjoy the decor and heady food. ⊠ *114 Market St., Historic Area,* ☎ *215/733–0545. AE, D, DC, MC, V. No lunch Sun.–Mon.*

$$–$$$ ✕ La Veranda. Gaze out the window of this riverside restaurant and you'll see a charming marina of pleasure boats. Gaze at your plate and you'll find the food of Italy, prepared the way the Centofanti family favored at its original restaurant, near the Trevi Fountain in Rome. The antipasti of vegetables or seafood are outstanding; so are the pastas. Owner/chef Roberto relies on the best local and imported ingredients to replicate the flavors of the old country. Check out the Caviar Ristorante upstairs for the best views and snappy table-side preparations. ⊠ *Pier 3, Penn's Landing (between Market and Arch Sts.), Historic Area,* ☎ *215/351–1898. Reservations essential. AE, DC, MC, V.*

$$–$$$ ✕ Ristorante Primavera. Get here early: this popular Italian bistro, owned by the same people as the Monte Carlo Living Room (☞ *above*), seats only 36 and takes no reservations. Cozy touches include soft track lighting, exposed brick walls, and pink table linens. *Insalata di frutti di mare* (seafood antipasto) is an excellent light appetizer. Pastas and appetizers are the high points of the menu, but the veal chop is always delicious. The wine list is small but thoughtfully chosen. ⊠ *146 South St., Historic Area,* ☎ *215/925–7832. Reservations not accepted. No credit cards.*

$$–$$$ ✕ **Toto.** This space directly across from the side door of the Academy of Music was formerly home to DiLullo Centro, but with a management change the price points have dropped and the fare at this beautiful restaurant has been somewhat simplified while retaining the essential elegance of dishes such as striped bass in broth with shrimp and mussels. The bar area, brightened with white leather upholstery and a marble-top community table, is a favorite meeting place before and after the theater and concerts for tasty, thoroughly Italian small-plate specialties such as *grigliata* (marinated, grilled meats and mushrooms) and *frittura* (fried fish and vegetables). ⊠ *1407 Locust St., Center City,* ☎ *215/546–2000. AE, MC, V.*

$$ ✕ **Gianna's.** Named for the proprietor and her niece, this immaculate glass-block-decorated, retro-feeling restaurant is on an equally immaculate, classic South Philadelphia block, with free parking next door. The recipes are mostly derived from the family, including some unusual dishes such as finely chopped antipasto and warm bruschetta piled high with tomatoes, onions, olive oil, and herbs. Bolognese sauce served on a choice of pasta is a treasured Old World recipe. ⊠ *721 Wharton St., South Philadelphia,* ☎ *215/468–4605. AE, MC, V.*

$$ ✕ **Panorama.** The name refers to a lovely inside mural rather than a window view from this lively Old City restaurant with the largest wine cruvinet (a wine storage system) in the world. Besides 120 wines available by the glass, there is a huge selection of well-chosen bottles. You can sip them in Il Bar or in the main dining room. The food is authentic northern Italian, simple and hearty, with special attention to such antipasti as ricotta and goat cheese in a potato crust, served with tomato sauce. The ambience is either ultranoisy or animated, depending on your tolerance level. ⊠ *14 N. Front St., Historic Area,* ☎ *215/922–7800. Reservations essential. AE, DC, MC, V.*

$$ ✕ **Pastaria at Frankie and Luigi's.** Arias from classic operas, sung mostly by fresh-faced young people who are in training or have done professional stints around Philadelphia and other cities, accompany somewhat unusually prepared but unquestionably Italian dishes. Chicken breasts are cooked with sundried tomatoes and artichokes, and salmon with linguine has a caper and wine sauce. The two-story restaurant fills up quickly; wise diners try to show up early since no reservations are accepted. ⊠ *1547–1549 S. 13th St., South Philadelphia,* ☎ *215/755–8900. Reservations not accepted. No credit cards. BYOB. Closed Mon.*

$$ ✕ **Tre Scalini.** "Three little steps" are exactly what it takes to enter this restaurant in South Philadelphia, a locus of down-home Italian ambience with a plethora of plastic hanging plants. The food, too, is more home style than professional kitchen, yet it is unmistakably carefully prepared, including such unusual (for South Philadelphia) appetizers as a tangle of wild mushrooms, beautifully sautéed with garlic and served on their own. Otherwise, simple pasta preparations are best; main courses suffer by comparison. ⊠ *1533 S. 11th St., South Philadelphia,* ☎ *215/551–3870. MC, V.*

$$ ✕ **Vetri.** Owner-chef Mark Vetri blew into town directly from New York, where his former Bella Blu had garnered all sorts of kudos. The auspicious, although tiny, space in which he chose to settle was formerly home to such stellar restaurants as Le Bec-Fin. The magic of the location seems to be working again as Vetri's sensitive palate and deft hands turn out featherlight green gnocchi. Shellfish soup and a strange-sounding but exquisite dessert known as chocolate polenta soufflé continue to delight patrons who vie for the limited number of tables. ⊠ *1312 Spruce St., Center City,* ☎ *215/732–3478. Reservations essential. AE, DC, MC, V. Closed Sun.*

$–$$ ✕ **Girasole.** Sunflowers (*girasole*, in Italian) adorn every surface of this bright, cheery bastion of northern Italian specialties, a favorite of former maestro Ricardo Muti and many Philadelphia Orchestra members. A wood-burning oven turns out thin-crusted pizzas that could have been flown over from the homeland and pastas that float from the plate. Veal is a particular specialty; try it with mushrooms. ⊠ *1305 Locust St., Center City,* ☎ *215/ 985–4659. AE, D, DC, MC, V.*

Jamaican

$ ✕ **Jamaican Jerk Hut.** The scintillating flavors of the beautiful island of Jamaica are all here, tasting at least as good as on their original turf. The tiny storefront, overseen by the chef-owner Nicola Shirley, who decided to apply her culinary school training to the tastes of her homeland, is primarily takeout. There are a couple of doll-size tables where people sit to wait for their orders, but you can eat in a charming back garden when the weather permits. Pork or chicken jerk is lovingly tended over an authentic pit; the curries and *roti* (pancakes with fillings such as curried chickpeas or chicken) are exemplary. And it all costs, as they say, a "fish cake." ⊠ *1436 South St., Center City,* ☎ *215/545–8644. No credit cards. Closed Sun.*

Japanese

$$ ✕ **Meiji-En.** A thoroughly Japanese *tepenyaki* room and a sushi bar co-exist with a huge, bright dining room that has been transmogrified into an American family dining place serving a selection of foods for every member of the family. You'll find everything from sushi to blintzes and smoked salmon at brunch. The view from the huge windows overlooking the Delaware River across to New Jersey is inspiring (even though the most imposing building on the other shore is a prison). *Pier 19, N. Columbus Blvd. at Callowhill St., Historic Area,* ☎ *215/592–7100. AE, D, DC, MC, V.*

$–$$ ✕ **Genji.** This classic Japanese place has been around University City for many years; at one time the majority of its following came from the nearby college crowd, both students and faculty. Now nearly everybody who is addicted to the cult of raw fish in its many guises trots both to this senior location, out of loyalty and because of regard for its familiar decor, and to its newer, even more simple Center City space. Attractive plates of all the standard raw and cooked Japanese dishes make their way to the tables. The presentation is so enticing, in fact, that it is difficult to keep from running up the tab. ⊠ *4002 Spruce St., University City,* ☎ *215/387–1583;* ⊠ *1720 Sansom St., Center City,* ☎ *215/564–1720. AE, DC, MC, V.*

$–$$ ✕ **Hikaru.** If one location is good for people who find watching the preparation of Japanese food intriguing, then three must be even better (and certainly convenient). Each location—Center City, Manayunk, South Street—has its aficionados; sushi is a good bet at any of them, and teriyaki and tempura dishes are available. Reviews by some persnickety folks occasionally give these places mundane marks and call the food commercial. ⊠ *108 S. 18th St., Center City,* ☎ *215/496–9950;* ⊠ *438 Main St., Manayunk,* ☎ *215/487–3500;* ⊠ *607 S. 2nd St., Historic Area,* ☎ *215/627–7110. AE, D, DC, MC, V.*

Latin

$$$ ✕ **Pasión.** The rich red entryway sets the tone for the culinary passion inside this smallish restaurant, and a tented ceiling floats over warm-hued walls that accent the character of the room. Argentine chef Guillermo Pernot's food draws on his intimacy with several South American and

Caribbean food styles. He certainly doesn't hold back on the intensity of any of the seasonings. Chilean sea bass is cooked with wild mushrooms and tamarind sauce; seviche of several kinds of fish is a specialty. ✉ *211 S. 15th St., Center City,* ☎ *215/875–9895. AE, DC, MC, V.*

Malaysian

$ ✕ **Penang.** The Asian and high-tech decor—bamboo and exposed pipes—of this one-of-a-kind in Philadelphia (although there are New York locations) is indicative of the surprising mix of flavors in this perennially bustling restaurant. A taste of India creeps into a scintillating appetizer of a handkerchief-thin crepe with a small dipping dish of flavorful chicken curry. Other dishes come redolent with tastes from several other Asian countries. The staff tries to be helpful in explaining unfamiliar dishes; giant shrimp with coconut or curry is a favorite among people unaccustomed to other menu items. Soups with various types of noodles are unusual, tasty, and filling. Try to forgo popular meal times in order to avoid long lines. ✉ *117 N. 10th St., Chinatown,* ☎ *215/413–2531. Reservations not accepted. No credit cards.*

Mediterranean

$$ ✕ **Serrano.** This simply decorated restaurant has been around for several years, tweaking its menu before settling on lusty home-style food from the shores of the Mediterranean. Try some of the many eggplant-based preparations: baba ghanoush, eggplant Parmesan, or *imam biyaldi,* a Turkish dish with onions, garlic, tomatoes, and pine nuts. The chef is familiar with all the tastes of the area and serves them pure or in various combinations that seem to work out well. ✉ *20 S. 2nd St., Historic Area,* ☎ *215/928–0720. AE, D, DC, MC, V.*

Mexican

$$ ✕ **Zócalo.** The freshly fine-tuned menu at this innovative contemporary Mexican outpost in University City continues to experiment with some favorite preparations such as guacamole and empanadas. A tasty Mayan appetizer, *xik-l-pak,* is a pumpkinseed salsa with *habanero* chile, cilantro, and tomato. Main courses range from venison and swordfish tacos to vegetable tostadas. At the bar, the lively crowd munches on appetizers and sips from an ever-expanding stock of tequila. The simple decor is punctuated by shows of Mexican artifacts and contemporary art. ✉ *3600 Lancaster Ave., University City,* ☎ *215/895–0139. AE, D, DC, MC, V.*

$–$$ ✕ **Tequila's.** Chef Carlos Molina makes Tequila's a prime Center City
★ choice for Mexican food—not just standards such as enchiladas but authentic south-of-the border dishes such as chilies *rellenos,* moderately spicy *poblano* peppers stuffed either with cheese or ground meat mixed with raisins and nuts and baked in a tomato sauce or fried in a light batter. The chef also prepares fowl in multi-ingredient mole sauces or occasionally a delicious *pozole,* a pork and hominy dish. The decor is clearly Mexican, with alcoves containing Mexican glassware and ceramics. You can choose from a dozen different Mexican beers and 15 brands of tequila. ✉ *1511 Locust St., Center City,* ☎ *215/546–0181. AE, DC, MC, V.*

Moroccan

$$ ✕ **Fez.** If you want your dining experience to be a bit exotic, Fez—with its Moroccan decor and its menu of Moroccan food, cooked by a Middle Eastern chef—may fill the bill. The Queen Village location is cramped, but don't take it all too seriously and just enter into the

spirit of eating with your hands (after having them washed by a waiter with water from an ornate kettle). The best main-course choices are the lamb with honey and almonds or chicken with olives, both available on the $20 fixed-price banquet. Sometimes a belly dancer performs; call ahead for information. ⊠ *620 S. 2nd St., Historic Area,* ☎ *215/925–5367. AE, D, DC, MC, V. No lunch.*

Seafood

$$$–$$$$ ✕ **Striped Bass Restaurant and Bar.** The opening of this all-seafood
   ★   restaurant in 1994 caused the biggest splash on Philadelphia's dining scene in more than a decade. Capitalizing on the existing grandeur of a former brokerage house with soaring marble pillars, restaurateur-trendsetter Neil Stein created a visually stunning room with striking appointments that accent the 28-ft ceilings and muslin-draped windows. A spectacular 16-ft sculpture of a leaping striped bass overhangs the exhibition kitchen. A stellar new chef, Terence Fuery from New York's Le Bernardin, should boost the restaurant to—or beyond—its former glory. There is an extensive raw bar of pristine shellfish. ⊠ *1500 Walnut St., Center City,* ☎ *215/732–4444. Reservations essential. AE, MC, V.*

$$–$$$$ ✕ **Chart House.** Most people come here for the atmosphere, although the rather ordinary food has been jazzed up. The Penn's Landing location of this national chain has dramatic Delaware River views; the nautical theme includes ultramodern paintings, sculptures, and striking architecture, with a waterfall that descends from the lobby to the lounge. All fish is flown in from its home ports fresh daily; coconut shrimp with plum and mustard sauces and twin lobsters are good choices. Teriyaki beef medallions are another crowd-pleaser. Mud pie, the house dessert, is an ultrarich concoction of coffee ice cream with a chocolate crust topped with fudge and whipped cream. ⊠ *555 S. Columbus Blvd., at Lombard Circle, Historic Area,* ☎ *215/625–8383. AE, D, DC, MC, V.*

$$–$$$$ ✕ **Old Original Bookbinder's.** Today the city's most famous restaurant has become more of a landmark (the original opened in 1865) than an essential stop for serious diners. On the walls hang photos of Elizabeth Taylor and other celebrities and politicians with former owner John Taxin, whose daughter and grandson are the current owners. The restaurant is often criticized for being overpriced (entrées range from $22 to $30), and you'll spring for the top end and then some if you're in the mood for lobster. Still, Bookbinder's remains a haunt of politicians and athletes who want to see and be seen. ⊠ *125 Walnut St., Historic Area,* ☎ *215/925–7027. AE, D, DC, MC, V.*

$$–$$$ ✕ **Bookbinder's Seafood House.** This Bookbinder's restaurant is the one that causes all the confusion: it is actually owned by a member of the original family, who sold the larger Old Original Bookbinder's (☞ *above*) to new owners in the 1940s. The typical seafood restaurant decor includes stuffed swordfish on the walls and fishing nets dangling from the ceiling. The fare is equally predictable, with a few daily specials that deviate from the standard dishes. The famous snapper soup is always good; broiled local fish are a dependable choice. ⊠ *215 S. 15th St., Center City,* ☎ *215/545–1137. AE, D, DC, MC, V.*

$–$$ ✕ **Fishmarket.** This new restaurant, retail store, and oyster bar occupies the corner where wunderkind Neil Stein opened his original Fishmarket (precursor of his current empire, which includes Striped Bass) in 1972. Wood hutches, exposed brickwork, sand-color walls, and painted floors create an appealing contrast of urban textures and rustic seaside references. Big bowls of steamed mussels and clams are offered, along with a shellfish boil for two that includes lobster, clams, mussels, shrimp, and a variety of fish. The restaurant also has selections from the first Fishmarket, such as crab quiche and shrimp, tomato, and cheese pie. There are prepared dishes to take home as well as top quality fish. ⊠ *122 S. 18th St., Center City,* ☎ *215/569–9080. AE, DC, MC, V.*

$–$$ ✕ **Philadelphia Fish & Company.** A new chef, Anthony Bonnett, is in command of the solid, imaginative menu at this Old City oasis for seafood lovers. Barbecue shrimp with cheddar grits and collard greens, crab and potato pancakes, and grilled tuna are favorites here. Outdoor dining and drinking take place in season on a deck that overlooks busy Chestnut Street and is good for people-watching—and traffic noise. ⊠ *207 Chestnut St., Historic Area,* ☎ *215/625–8605. AE, D, DC, MC, V.*

$–$$ ✕ **Sansom Street Oyster House.** Old-timey and reasonably priced, this seafood house just goes on and on with its ample servings of simply prepared fish and shellfish. An active raw bar at the front of the restaurant serves whichever oysters—and clams—are in the market. An enormous collection of antique oyster plates serves as decoration. ⊠ *1516 Sansom St., Center City,* ☎ *215/567–7683. AE, D, DC, MC, V.*

Spanish

$–$$ ✕ **Pamplona.** Decorated with a huge faux-Picasso mural that overlooks the lively dining room, this Center City outpost promises tapas, the Spanish snacks. The renditions here, however, are often like the mural—charming but not exactly like the originals. Nevertheless, you can tailor your intake and expenditure by the number and relative costliness of your selections. Try the grilled mushrooms filled with parsley and ham, potato omelets cooked in olive oil, or the popular shrimp in garlic sauce. ⊠ *225 S. 12th St., Center City,* ☎ *215/627–9059. No credit cards.*

Steak

$$$–$$$$ ✕ **Prime Rib.** The glamorous atmosphere of black-leather steak-house poshness combined with the clubby feel of a longstanding classic restaurant immediately let you know you're in for some serious eating. Habitués (of whom there are many) admire the gigantic portions of dry aged prime beef, sparkling fresh seafood (also served in more than generous quantity), delicious potato skins, and other sit-up-and-take-notice dishes that keep this handsome restaurant full. ⊠ *Warwick Hotel, 1701 Locust St., Center City,* ☎ *215/772–1701. Reservations essential. Jackets required. D, MC, V.*

$$–$$$$ ✕ **Palm.** The city's branch of the celebrated Palm group holds forth in a light, bright, busy space off the lobby of the Park Hyatt at the Bellevue. The pure steak-house ambience comes complete with bare floors, harried waiters, and huge steaks, chops, and salads whizzing by. Nearly in the shadow of City Hall and the surrounding courts, this is deal-making territory, and local movers and shakers are frequently seen chatting it up at lunch and dinner. Caricatures of nearly everyone who is anyone in the city are on the walls, and it's fun to match up the people with their likenesses. The flavorful New York strip steak is fine at dinner, and the stupendous steak sandwich (*no* relation to a Philly cheese steak) is a lunchtime value. ⊠ *200 S. Broad St., Center City,* ☎ *215/ 546–7256. AE, D, DC, MC, V.*

$$$ ✕ **Morton's of Chicago.** This classy steak house, now at a second-floor location a few steps from Broad Street, attracts many visitors familiar with Morton's other outposts of top-quality red meat and humongous lobsters as well as a devoted coterie of local businesspeople. Etched glass and wood dividers provide a semblance of privacy in the large dining room, and there is an intimate stand-up bar. The house specialty, a juicy, tasty 24-ounce porterhouse, puts the most determined carnivore to the test. Other fine cuts of meat are available, too, presented

for selection from a cart that is wheeled to the table. Pristine whole fish and lobsters are priced by the pound. The excellent vegetable portions are large—really enough for two—and are ordered à la carte. ✉ *1411 Walnut St., Center City*, ☎ *215/557–0724. AE, DC, MC, V.*

$$ ✕ **Sullivan's.** In case you'd ever question the origin of the name of the restaurant, numerous photos of the legendary John L. Sullivan, bare-knuckle boxer of heroic reputation, adorn the walls of this large Kansas City–style steak house in King of Prussia Mall. The beef is routinely served in outlandishly sized portions that auger well for leftover roast beef or steak hash at home. The meat is carefully selected USDA choice beef; a large chunk of iceberg lettuce with blue cheese dressing is included in the price of beef entrées, and side dishes usually feed two. ✉ *700 W. DeKalb Pike, King of Prussia*, ☎ *610/878–9025. AE, D, DC, MC, V. Closed Sun.*

Thai

$–$$ ✕ **Thai Singa House.** Simple and unprepossessing, this pleasant family-run Thai outpost in University City cooks all the usual dishes plus an array of more unusual (for this country, at least) ones, such as venison and wild boar. Pad Thai, a noodle-dish staple that's a good choice if you're not certain you love Thai food, is particularly well prepared, with an authenticity of texture and a fine meld of flavors. The family is fun to talk to, and the proprietor and his wife are helpful both to novices and to experts exploring unfamiliar dishes on the menu. ✉ *3939 Chestnut St., University City*, ☎ *215/382–8001. AE, D, DC, MC, V.*

Vietnamese

$–$$ ✕ **Le Colonial.** Bamboo and cane furniture with batik-patterned upholstery and Oriental rugs set the tone in this outpost of a small chain that includes restaurants in New York and Chicago. As you enter, you fall immediately into the ambience of the French colonial period of Vietnam's past, evoked in sepia-tone photographs. The food is beautifully conceived and served on lovely china, but often the cost is considerably more than in other places that serve similar cuisine. *Ca chien* is crisp, seared whole red snapper; *bo sate* is filet mignon rubbed with spices and served with yams and string beans. The upstairs bar is particularly pleasant; a few lucky people can eat up there. ✉ *1623 Walnut St., Center City* ☎ *215/851–1623. AE, D, DC, MC, V.*

$ ✕ **Nam Phuong.** Family pictures and watercolors of the homeland are the simple decorations at this authentic Vietnamese winner in an area that's now rapidly changing into what locals refer to as Little Saigon. Neat and friendly, the restaurant has a menu with all the staple dishes, as well as daily specials that are often unusual, sometimes more expensive, and frequently delicious. Someone is usually available to explain the more obscure items. Appealing choices include *bo* (beef) sautéed with lemongrass and curry, and *tom* (shrimp) in black bean sauce. ✉ *746 Christian St., South Philadelphia*, ☎ *215/529–4002. AE, DC, MC, V.*

$ ✕ **Vietnam.** This family-run restaurant next to a busy police station serves up an extensive selection of Vietnamese food. Restaurateurs from many much fancier eateries often find one another here, comparing notes on which dishes are particularly tasty that day. The crisp spring rolls, squid with black bean sauce, and soups with rice noodles are good picks. Occasionally, however, it seems as if the chef himself is "out to lunch." It's cheap enough, however, to forgive an occasional lapse without damaging the budget. If the first couple of courses don't measure up to expectations on a particular day, it's possible to leave and head to any of the similar places nearby to finish your meal. ✉ *221 N. 11th St., Chinatown*, ☎ *215/592–1163. No credit cards.*

4 LODGING

From primly historic digs with four-poster
beds to hotels that favor such grand gestures
as room-service foie gras, Philadelphia has
lodgings for every style of travel. Thanks to
the Pennsylvania Convention Center and a
hotel-building boom, some midprice chains
have moved into town or have spruced up
their accommodations. If you have greater
expectations, you need look no further than
the city's handful of swank hotels, each with
its own gracious character.

By Barbara
Ann Rosenberg

PHILADELPHIA HOTELS RUN THE GAMUT from world class to commonplace, from a plush 1,400-room hotel with every amenity to some appealingly personal bed-and-breakfast inns. Although there are many utilitarian hotels and national chains, both in town and in the area close to the airport, other lodgings are unique experiences. Aside from an increasing number of bed-and-breakfasts and a few hostels, the city still has a relatively small pool of moderately priced hotels in the center of the city; many are expensive.

The number of rooms in the metropolitan area has increased dramatically over the past couple of years because of the demand created by the Pennsylvania Convention Center (and the Republican National Convention, set for July 2000), but it is still occasionally difficult to find a place to stay. Advance reservations are usually advised. The city has no central reservation office.

According to the Philadelphia Convention and Visitors Bureau, some 4,000 new rooms have been added to the roster in anticipation of the millennium. New developments include a 600-room Loews hotel, under construction at press time in the Pennsylvania Savings Fund Society (PSFS) Building, a 1932 modernist skyscraper at 12th and Market streets. Another significant new hotel (opened in summer 1999) is the Courtyard by Marriott, with 500 rooms, just a block from the Pennsylvania Convention Center. Several others are in various stages of construction; among the hotels not completed at press time are the Hyatt at Penn's Landing, Hilton Garden, Ritz-Carlton Philadelphia, and a Sofitel.

Hotels are listed geographically, according to six neighborhoods. The Historic Area, on the east side of downtown, centers on Independence Hall and extends to the Delaware River. Old City and Society Hill lodgings are included here. Center City encompasses the heart of the downtown business district, centered around Broad Street and Market Street; Rittenhouse Square hotels are in this section. The Benjamin Franklin Parkway/Museum Area runs along the Benjamin Franklin Parkway from 16th Street to the Philadelphia Museum of Art. Several hotels are in University City, near the campus of the University of Pennsylvania and Drexel in West Philadelphia. Additional hotels are clustered near Philadelphia International Airport, about 8 mi south (a 20-minute drive) of Center City. Two are in the City Line Avenue area, northwest of downtown. Other options can be found in outlying areas, including Valley Forge and Bucks County (☞ Chapters 8 *and* 9).

Philadelphia has no off-season rates, but many hotels offer discount packages for weekends, when demand from businesspeople and groups subsides. Besides substantially reduced rates, these packages often include an assortment of freebies, such as breakfast, parking, cocktails or champagne, and the use of exercise facilities. Tickets to popular museum shows have become part of many special packages, too. Always ask about special packages and rates when making a reservation. Most downtown hotels charge an average of $15 a day for parking when it is not included as a package feature. Accommodations are ranked according to the price categories described in Lodging *in* Smart Travel Tips A to Z.

B&B Reservation Services

Bed-and-breakfast establishments in Philadelphia can be appealing for a number of reasons, such as a warm welcome reflecting the personal touch of the owner, or antique-filled rooms. These sometimes (but not

In case you want to see the world.

At American Express, we're here to make your journey a smooth one. So we have over 1,700 travel service locations in over 130 countries ready to help. What else would you expect from the world's largest travel agency?

do more

Travel

Call 1 800 AXP-3429 or visit
www.americanexpress.com/travel

In case you want to be welcomed there.

We're here to see that you're always welcomed at establishments everywhere. That's why millions of people carry the American Express® Card – for peace of mind, confidence, and security, around the world or just around the corner.

do more

Cards

To apply, call 1 800 THE-CARD
or visit www.americanexpress.com

In case you're running low.

We're here to help with more than 190,000 Express Cash locations around the world. In order to enroll, just call American Express at 1 800 CASH-NOW before you start your vacation.

do more   AMERICAN EXPRESS

Express Cash

And in case you'd rather be safe than sorry.

We're here with American Express® Travelers Cheques. They're the safe way to carry money on your vacation, because if they're ever lost or stolen you can get a refund, practically anywhere or anytime. To find the nearest place to buy Travelers Cheques, call 1 800 495-1153. Another way we help you do more.

do more **AMERICAN EXPRESS**

Travelers Cheques

always) less expensive alternatives to hotels offer considerable diversity depending on amenities. Breakfasts range from simple to hearty to elegant. Be aware that some B&Bs welcome children and pets, but others do not. A number of B&Bs are listed in this chapter, and reservation services can help you find others in or near the center of the city or in a variety of other neighborhoods from urban to rural.

$–$$$$ 🏠 **Bed and Breakfast Connections–Philadelphia.** This reservation service represents more than 100 inspected host homes and inns including a Colonial town house, a converted 1880s bank-style barn, and an 18th-century farmhouse on the Main Line. ✉ *Box 21, Devon 19333,* ☎ *610/687–3565 or 800/448–3619. AE, MC, V.*

$–$$ 🏠 **Association of B&Bs in Philadelphia, Valley Forge, and Brandywine.** You can choose from 300 rooms in town and country settings in the areas listed in the association's name, as well as in Bucks and Lancaster counties. ✉ *Box 562, Valley Forge 19481,* ☎ *610/783–7838 or 800/344–0123,* ☏ *610/783–7783. AE, D, DC, MC, V.*

Historic Area

$$$$ 🏠 **Sheraton Society Hill.** Conveniently located for visits to the Historic District, this redbrick neo-Colonial building is two blocks from Penn's Landing, three blocks from Head House Square, and three blocks from Independence Hall. The hotel's pleasant four-story atrium lobby, filled with trees and plants, is framed by archways and balconies and lighted by wrought-iron lanterns. Rooms are furnished traditionally in shades of blue or green and have modern conveniences such as voice mail and coffeemakers. The fourth-floor rooms facing east toward the Delaware River have the best view. ✉ *1 Dock St., 19106,* ☎ *215/238–6000,* ☏ *215/922–2709. 365 rooms, 17 suites. Restaurant, bar, in-room data ports, minibars, room service, indoor pool, health club, parking (fee). AE, D, DC, MC, V.*

$$$ 🏠 **Omni Hotel at Independence Park.** With attractive if not exactly posh accommodations in the historic district, the Omni has the feel of a much smaller hotel. An ornate fireplace dominates the lobby; you can have cocktails in the adjoining lounge in front of floor-to-ceiling windows overlooking a meticulously groomed park and city streets. The spacious rooms are decorated in pretty floral prints but are otherwise undistinguished; many have park views. The health club includes a lap pool, exercise pool, sauna, and whirlpool. This is a pleasant location for visiting the art galleries and cafés of Old City as well as the Liberty Bell, Independence Hall, and other historic attractions. ✉ *4th and Chestnut Sts., 19106,* ☎ *215/925–0000,* ☏ *215/925–1263. 147 rooms, 3 suites. Restaurant, lobby lounge, no-smoking rooms, 2 indoor pools, health club, concierge, business services, parking (fee).*

$$–$$$ 🏠 **Best Western Independence Park Hotel.** From the rooms facing busy Chestnut Street you'll hear the clop-clop of carriage horses as well as the roar of city buses. Things do quiet down during normal sleeping hours, though. The five-story building is a former dry goods warehouse, built in 1856; it opened in 1988 as a hotel. The high-ceiling guest rooms are modern but have Colonial touches and come in standard and deluxe (deluxe includes king-size bed and parlor). VCRs and videos can be rented for a small charge. Complimentary Continental breakfast and afternoon tea are served in a courtyard dining room with a glass ceiling. ✉ *235 Chestnut St., 19106,* ☎ *215/922–4443 or 800/624–2988,* ☏ *215/922–4487. 36 rooms. In-room data ports, parking (fee). AE, D, DC, MC, V. CP.*

$$–$$$ 🏠 **Holiday Inn Independence Mall.** The "Independence Mall" in the name is no exaggeration; the hotel lies in America's "most historic square mile." It was recently refurbished and is looking considerably fresher

Lodging

Abigail Corby Carriage House, **12**

Adam's Mark, **4**

Airport Hilton, **38**

Alexander Inn, **23**

Bank Street Hostel, **32**

Best Western Center City, **1**

Best Western Independence Park Hotel, **33**

Chamounix Mansion, **3**

Comfort Inn at Penn's Landing, **29**

Crowne Plaza Philadelphia City Center, **10**

DoubleTree Hotel, **21**

Four Seasons, **7**

Hawthorn Suites, **27**

Holiday Inn City Line, **5**

Holiday Inn Express Midtown, **22**

Holiday Inn Independence Mall, **28**

Holiday Inn Philadelphia International Airport, **40**

Hotel Sofitel Philadelphia, **17**

Inn at Penn, **8**

KormanSuites Hotel, **2**

Latham, **16**

Omni Hotel at Independence Park, **31**

Park Hyatt Philadelphia at the Bellevue, **20**

Penn Tower, **9**

Penn's View Inn, **30**

Philadelphia Airport Marriott, **36**

Philadelphia Downtown Courtyard, **25**

Philadelphia Marriott, **26**

The Rittenhouse, **11**

Rittenhouse Bed and Breakfast, **14**

Ritz-Carlton Philadelphia, **19**

St. Regis Philadelphia, **18**

Sheraton Philadelphia Airport Hotel, **39**

Sheraton Rittenhouse Square, **13**

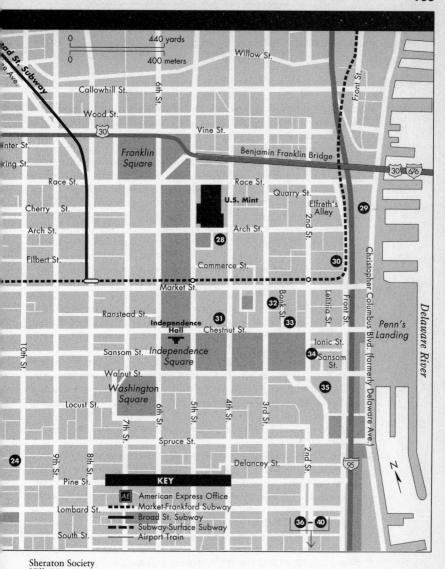

than it has in the past few years. Multicolor coverlets, tall lamps, work desks, and amenities such as irons and ironing boards help create a generally pleasant ambience. ⊠ *4th and Arch Sts., 19106,* ☎ *215/923–8660 or 800/843–2355,* ℻ *215/923–4633. 364 rooms, 7 suites. 2 restaurants, bar, in-room data ports, pool, parking (fee). AE, D, DC, MC, V.*

$$–$$$ ⊡ **Penn's View Inn.** This cosmopolitan little hotel on the fringe of Old
★   City, formerly the city's oldest warehouse district and now an enclave of artists' galleries and studios, has its own brand of urban charm. Housed in a refurbished 19th-century commercial building, Penn's View Inn is owned by an Italian-born restaurateur well regarded for his good taste and high quality. The owner also runs Panorama (☞ Italian *in* Chapter 3), the downstairs eatery and extensive wine bar. Guest rooms are done in subdued tapestry; six deluxe rooms have a whirlpool bath and fireplace. Most windows overlook the Delaware River. Accommodations are comfortable and rather European, with Chippendale-style furniture, floral wallpaper, and queen beds. Street noise can be a concern. ⊠ *14 N. Front St., 19106,* ☎ *215/922–7600 or 800/ 331–7634,* ℻ *215/922–7642. 28 rooms. Restaurant, bar, parking (fee). AE, DC, MC, V. CP.*

$$ ⊡ **Comfort Inn at Penn's Landing.** The reasonable price is the most noteworthy draw here, with complimentary Continental breakfast as an additional lure at this 10-story hotel. Decor is contemporary, with oak furniture and a mauve color scheme. A bar helps enliven the small, nondescript lobby. Tucked between the Benjamin Franklin Bridge, Delaware Avenue, and I–95, the location has more noise than charm—but if you have a room on an upper floor facing the river, you'll enjoy a good view of the Benjamin Franklin Bridge lighted up at night. A nice plus is the courtesy van service to Center City; foot power will bring you to the nearby Betsy Ross House, historic Elfreth's Alley, and shops or to the RiverLink ferry to the New Jersey State Aquarium in Camden. ⊠ *100 N. Columbus Blvd., 19106,* ☎ *215/627–7900,* ℻ *215/238– 0809. 185 rooms. Lobby lounge, no-smoking rooms, parking (fee). AE, D, DC, MC, V. CP.*

$–$$ ⊡ **Thomas Bond House.** It doesn't get any more Colonial than this: you can spend the night in the heart of Old City the way Philadelphians did in the 18th century. Built in 1769 by a prominent local physician, this four-story house, now a B&B, has undergone a faithful, meticulous restoration of everything from its molding and wall sconces to the millwork and flooring. Rooms have reproduction period furnishings (there are also a few antiques) including four-poster beds, and two have marble fireplaces. ⊠ *129 S. 2nd St., 19106,* ☎ *215/923–8523 or 800/ 845–2663,* ℻ *215/923–8504. 10 rooms, 2 suites. Breakfast room. AE, D, DC, MC, V. CP weekdays, BP weekends.*

Center City

$$$$ ⊡ **The Rittenhouse.** This small luxury hotel, in a building with con-
★   dominium residences on several floors, takes full advantage of its Rittenhouse Square location: many of the rooms and both restaurants overlook the city's classiest park. The expansive white-marble lobby leads to the Mary Cassatt Tearoom and Lounge and a cloistered garden. The 33-story building's sawtooth design gives the guest rooms their unusual shape, with nooks and alcoves. Each room has a very large, luxurious bathroom done in golden brown marble, with a TV and a scale; many have whirlpool tubs. Posh amentities include three telephones, an entertainment center in an armoire, a fully stocked minibar, and a king-size bed. Ninth-floor rooms facing the square have the best views. ⊠ *210 W. Rittenhouse Sq., 19103,* ☎ *215/546–9000 or 800/635–1042,* ℻ *215/732–3364. 87 rooms, 11 suites. 2 restaurants,*

bar, minibars, no-smoking floors, room service, health club, concierge, business services, parking (fee). AE, D, DC, MC, V.

$$$$ 🖭 **Ritz-Carlton Philadelphia.** In a startling act, the Ritz announced in mid-1999 that it was changing its location to a building just a few blocks east of its previous site (now the St. Regis Philadelphia). The new 30-story, 330-room hotel, set to open in May 2000, will occupy the neo-classical former Mellon Bank building catercorner to City Hall in the heart of Center City. The bank's spectacular rotunda will house public spaces including two restaurants; an adjoining tower will hold guest rooms. The new Ritz will live up to the standards of the chain with special Ritz toiletries, complimentary shoe shines, and more. ⊠ *10 Avenue of the Arts (S. Broad St.) 19107,* 🕾 *215/735–7700,* FAX *215/735–7710. 330 rooms. 2 restaurants, bar, minibars, room service, concierge, business services, parking (fee). AE, D, DC, MC, V.*

$$$$ 🖭 **St. Regis Philadelphia.** Without skipping a beat, the St. Regis took
★ over in 1999 a location that was formerly the Ritz-Carlton. Originally opened in 1990, the 15-story structure is nestled between the twin blue towers of tall, tall Liberty Place (and adjacent to the Shops at Liberty Place—more than 70 stores, boutiques, and restaurants). At press time the St. Regis was still putting its imprimatur on the hotel to bring it up to its own elegant style, although rooms are still decorated in what can be called luxury Colonial. Breakfronts full of gorgeous china and fine paintings set the tone in the public areas. Guest rooms all have specially designed "Heavenly" beds with all-cotton sheets, two or more king-size down pillows (or non-allergic fillings), new 27-inch TVs, "hands-free" phones at desks with a fax/copier/printer, and Bijan toiletries. The two Astor Floors have butler service. ⊠ *17th and Chestnut Sts. at Liberty Pl., 19103,* 🕾 *215/563–1600,* FAX *215/567–2822. 275 rooms, 15 suites. Restaurant, bar, lobby lounge, room service, health club, baby-sitting, concierge, concierge floors, parking (fee). AE, D, DC, MC, V.*

$$$–$$$$ 🖭 **Hotel Sofitel Philadelphia.** At press time this French chain was preparing to open its first hotel in Philadelphia in February 2000; all indications, including project renderings, pointed to an elegant new option. Conversion and expansion of the former Philadelphia Stock Exchange Building at 17th and Sansom Streets has created a luxurious 14-story hotel with a facade of limestone and tinted glass. The simplicity of Shaker quilts inspired the lobby floor, done in seven kinds of granite and marble that introduce the hotel's interior color palate of blues, black, and neutral tones; the reception desk is made of blue Brazilian granite. A striking lighting fixture of steel and Murano glass hangs over the main staircase. Guest rooms, which could not be seen at press time, seem sleekly modern yet comfortable. Chez Colette, a contemporary brasserie that is a trademark of Sofitel, pays homage to the French writer. Cherry walls trimmed with satin chrome hold artwork, letters, and other Colette memorabilia. ⊠ *122 S. 17 St., 19103,* 🕾 *215/569–8300,* FAX *not available at press time. 235 rooms, 65 suites. Brasserie, lobby lounge, in-room data ports, no-smoking rooms, minibars, exercise room, meeting rooms, parking (fee). AE, D, DC, MC, V.*

$$$–$$$$ 🖭 **Park Hyatt Philadelphia at the Bellevue.** A Philadelphia institution for more than 90 years, the elegant Bellevue hotel is now managed by Hyatt, with its lower floors transformed into the upscale Shops at the Bellevue (including Tiffany's and Polo/Ralph Lauren), offices, and a food court with a wide range of choices. The Barrymore Room, topped by a 30-ft stained-glass dome, is great for tea and cocktails; Founders, the hotel's posh restaurant, has views of the city from its 19th-floor location. Both these spaces rank among the most visually impressive in town. From the champagne toast or hot cider (in winter) available at registration to the telephones in the bathrooms, a stay at the Park

Hyatt promises luxury. Rooms are large, done in light, bright prints, and possess the high ceilings and moldings typical of older hotels; each has an entertainment center with color TV, stereo, and VCR. Guests have free use of the Sporting Club, the poshest health club in town. ⊠ *Broad and Walnut Sts., 19102,* ☏ *215/893–1776 or 800/233–1234,* ℻ *215/732–8518. 170 rooms. Restaurant, bar, lobby lounge, room service, in-room data ports, minibars, shops, concierge, parking (fee). AE, D, DC, MC, V.*

$$$–$$$$ 🆃 **Sheraton Rittenhouse Square.** A "green" haven in a very tony setting, this innovative hotel on the city's prettiest square has won attention by billing itself as the "first environmentally smart hotel in the United States." Built inside a former apartment house, the Sheraton has indeed been creative in many ways. A huge bamboo stand in the lobby helps oxygenate the air, and filtered fresh air circulates in the guest rooms at all times. Furniture in the rooms was made from recycled wooden pallets, and all the carpeting comes from 100% recycled surplus synthetic fiber; sheets and bedspreads are organic cotton. In keeping with the organic theme, the hotel's color scheme is a soothing beige, sand, tan, and peach. If you hadn't guessed already, no smoking is permitted anywhere in the hotel. Potcheen is an Irish-oriented sports pub, and the Square Bar is a fancy Italian small-plate restaurant that overlooks the square; both draw lively crowds. ⊠ *227 S. 18th St., 19103,* ☏ *215/ 546–9400,* ℻ *215/893–0955. 193 rooms, 7 suites. Restaurant, pub, in-room data ports, exercise room, meeting rooms, parking (fee). AE, D, DC, MC, V.*

$$–$$$$ 🆃 **Warwick Hotel & Towers.** The spacious guest rooms in this centrally located, freshly renovated landmark 1929 hotel come in three distinct categories—standard, deluxe, and the large Towers rooms. The Towers section includes four floors, two of which are concierge levels where additional amenities are provided. All guest rooms are pleasant and bright, with a floral motif. Bathrooms are marble or tile, and all rooms have individual climate control, voice messaging, a large desk, and free newspaper delivery. The hotel's lobby is large and open, with a balcony; the Towers has a concierge lounge. The Circles off the Square restaurant serves a fine mix of traditional dishes and contemporary creations that appeals to locals as well as hotel guests. ⊠ *1701 Locust St., 19103,* ☏ *215/735–6000 or 800/523–4210,* ℻ *215/790–7766. 523 rooms, 46 suites. 2 restaurants, bar, coffee shop, in-room data ports, concierge floor, exercise room, sauna, parking (fee). AE, DC, MC, V.*

$$$ 🆃 **Philadelphia Downtown Courtyard.** Marriott's largest Courtyard, this new hotel is housed in the historic City Hall Annex, and original brass, copper, and bronze details on the elevators and staircases have been refurbished. The hotel is just across the street from its sister property, the Philadelphia Marriott (☞ *below*); both help service the Pennsylvania Convention Center. The hotels share some facilities such as meeting rooms. Each pleasantly comfortable room (smaller than those in the Marriott), decorated in muted shades of red, green, and gold, has a full-size work desk and two telephones among its amenities. ⊠ *21 N. Juniper St., 19107,* ☏ *215/625–6139 or 800/321–2211,* ℻ *215/ 625–6101. 500 rooms, 16 suites. Restaurant, lobby lounge, indoor pool, in-room data ports, exercise room, laundry service, business services, parking (fee). AE, D, DC, MC, V.*

$$$ 🆃 **Philadelphia Marriott.** If you like big, bustling hotels, this is the place for you. Opened in 1995 and expanded in 1999, this convention hotel—the biggest in Pennsylvania—takes up an entire city block and has so many corridors that sometimes even the staff gets lost. For an intrinsically impersonal type of place, the Marriott tries to meet special needs (iron and ironing board in each room, 24-hour workout room, children's menu from room service); it also offers some of the lowest rates in its price category. The five-story lobby atrium has a water sculpture, piano music (live and taped), and greenery (real and fake). The more than 1,400 guest rooms are big, beige, and bland; half come with two queen beds, the rest with kings; all have extra counter space in the bathrooms. You can request, at no additional cost, one of the 250 "rooms that work," with an adjustable work table and extra lighting and outlets. ⊠ *1201 Market St., 19107,* ☎ *215/625–2900 or 800/320–5744,* FAX *215/625–6000. 1,408 rooms, 76 suites. 2 restaurants, 2 lobby lounges, sports bar, room service, indoor pool, health club, concierge, business services, parking (fee). AE, D, DC, MC, V.*

$$–$$$ 🖬 **Crowne Plaza Philadelphia City Center.** This upscale Holiday Inn is centrally located between Benjamin Franklin Parkway, Rittenhouse Square, and City Hall. The 25-floor hotel has good-size guest rooms with a green-and-beige color scheme and contemporary decor. Rooms designated Select have extra amenities, including voice mail, irons and ironing boards, coffeemakers, cable TV, hair dryers, and *USA Today.* The Elephant and Castle serves indifferent British food but is a convenient place for a drink. ⊠ *1800 Market St., 19103,* ☎ *215/561–7500,* FAX *215/561–4484. 443 rooms, 2 suites. Restaurant, bar, in-room data ports, no-smoking floors, pool, exercise room, parking (fee). AE, D, DC, MC, V.*

$$–$$$ 🖬 **DoubleTree Hotel.** The hotel's sawtooth design gives each room a peaked bay window with a whopping 180° view. East-side rooms get a panoramic view of the city, the Delaware River, and New Jersey. You can also sit in the four-story atrium lobby lounge and observe one of the busiest corners of Philly's shopping and theater district, directly across the street from the handsome Academy of Music. Guest rooms are decorated in earth tones and have modern furnishings. Cafe Academy has all the attributes of an independent dining room, with fine contemporary food (great crab cakes) and pleasant service. ⊠ *Broad St. at Locust St., 19107,* ☎ *215/893–1600,* FAX *215/893–1663. 419 rooms, 8 suites. 2 restaurants, lobby lounge, indoor pool, sauna, health club, racquetball, parking (fee). AE, D, DC, MC, V.*

$$–$$$ 🖬 **Latham.** When this hotel opened early in the 20th century, it was reportedly the finest hostelry in America for business travelers. It remains a small, elegant hotel with a European accent, although it lacks such basics as a dining room (a Continental or buffet breakfast is served, however). Doormen clad in vests and riding boots welcome you to the small lobby. All the freshly renovated rooms, done in hunter green or more contemporary black and tan, have marble-top bureaus and Louis XV–style writing desks, full-wall mirrors, hair dryers, coffeemakers, makeup mirrors, and terry robes; bathrooms have marble showers and floors. The hotel is one block from Rittenhouse Square. ⊠ *135 S. 17th St., 19103,* ☎ *215/563–7474 or 800/528–4261,* FAX *215/ 568–0110. 139 rooms. Breakfast room, exercise room, business services, parking (fee). AE, D, DC, MC, V. BP.*

$$–$$$ 🖬 **Ten Eleven Clinton.** Connected by a courtyard, these two 1836 Federal ★ houses on a beautiful historic street contain nicely furnished apartment/suites suitable for all manner of uses, from corporate retreats to romantic getaways. Room styles vary from traditional to southwestern. The location is within easy walking distance of entertainment as well as the old homes of Society Hill and the shops of Antiques Row on Pine Street. ⊠ *1011 Clinton St., 19107,* ☎ *215/923–8144,* FAX *215/ 923–5757. 7 suites. Kitchenettes, in-room data ports. AE, MC, V. CP.*

$$ 🖬 **Alexander Inn.** The nicely rehabbed rooms at this bed-and-breakfast inn, which occupies a turn-of-the-century redbrick hotel, are close to the Pennsylvania Convention Center, the Avenue of the Arts, and most Center City attractions. The rooms and furnishings have an art

deco feeling; all rooms have color TVs. The deluxe Continental break-fast buffet includes fresh baked muffins and a variety of fruits and juices. ⊠ *Spruce and 12th Sts., 19107,* ☎ *215/923–1004 or 877/253–9466,* FAX *215/923–1004. 48 rooms. In-room data ports, exercise room, busi-ness services. AE, D, DC, MC, V. CP.*

$$ 🛏 **Holiday Inn Express Midtown.** Rooms are more spacious than av-erage here—perhaps because they're older (this Holiday Inn opened in 1964). All have contemporary furnishings and a light, floral motif. Rooms facing south to Walnut Street have the best views, though these are not outstanding. The location is excellent: one block from the Broad Street subway, near the theater and shopping district, and three blocks from the Pennsylvania Convention Center. Guests have free ac-cess to a nearby health club. ⊠ *1305 Walnut St., 19107,* ☎ *215/735–9300 or 800/564–3869. 166 rooms. No-smoking rooms, pool, park-ing (fee). AE, D, DC, MC, V. CP.*

$–$$ 🛏 **Abigail Corby Carriage House.** The innkeeper at this B&B tucked away on a quiet street in the middle of Center City is a font of infor-mation on just about anything that goes on in town. The rooms here can be converted into two suites. A refrigerator and cupboards are full of complimentary snacks and breads that your heart—or tummy—might desire all day and into the evening, such as ice cream, fruit, and cook-ies or muffins. ⊠ *1935 Manning St., 19103,* ☎ *215/735–1881,* FAX *215/790–0732. 6 rooms. No credit cards. BP.*

$–$$ 🛏 **Hawthorn Suites.** A recently remodeled factory building, this utili-tarian hotel has many of the necessities for short or extended stays as standard amenities. On the edge of Chinatown, it overlooks the Schuylkill Expressway and is convenient to the Pennsylvania Con-vention Center. The hotel is just a few steps from Reading Terminal Market and Independence Mall. It's also near many Vietnamese, Thai, and Chinese eateries, some of which stay open late for dinner. The newly built but undistinguished pale green suites have a full-size kitchen, din-ing area, and two televisions. ⊠ *1100 Vine St., 19107,* ☎ *215/829–8300 or 800/527–1133,* FAX *215/829–8104. 225 suites. Bar, café, ex-ercise room, parking (fee). CP.*

$–$$ 🛏 **Rittenhouse Bed and Breakfast.** A stay here is like stepping into a
★   country manor house—but you're actually in the heart of Center City, close to the best shopping, dining, and elegant Rittenhouse Square. This B&B is loaded with pampering touches, such as concierge service, a choice of pillow and comforter types, oversize towels, turndown ser-vice, robes, and 25-inch TVs with VCR. Some rooms have whirlpool baths, balconies, or fireplaces. Continental breakfast includes spe-cialty breads from the best bakeries in town, with a choice of bever-ages. ⊠ *1715 Rittenhouse Sq., 19103,* ☎ *215/545–1755,* FAX *215/923–8504. 8 rooms, 2 suites. Breakfast room, in-room data ports, con-cierge. AE, D, DC, MC, V. CP.*

Benjamin Franklin Parkway/Museum Area

$$$$ 🛏 **Four Seasons.** With its exemplary service, impeccable maintenance,
★   and high-quality food, this luxurious member of the worldwide chain ranks consistently among the best hotels in the United States. The big, square, granite hotel is somewhat forbidding from the outside until you reach the front, embellished with highly polished brass and a portico, as well as solicitous doormen. It shares with other Four Seasons the long, long walk from the elevators to some of the guest rooms; you may feel you're just as close to the area's museums and shopping as to your room. Guest room furniture is rather formal Federal style, just right for Philadelphia. Other Four Seasons amenities include a multi-lingual concierge. The Fountain Restaurant (☞ Contemporary *in*

Chapter 3) is one of the best in town and the Swan Lounge one of the liveliest at cocktail time and late evening. Weather permitting, the Swann Courtyard Cafe is an excellent spot for lunch and drinks. ⊠ *1 Logan Sq., 19103,* ☎ *215/963–1500 or 800/332–3442,* FAX *215/963–9506. 371 rooms. 2 restaurants, outdoor café, room service, 6 no-smoking floors, indoor pool, sauna, steam room, exercise room, concierge, parking (fee). AE, D, DC, MC, V.*

$$$ 🏨 **Wyndham Franklin Plaza.** This was Philadelphia's biggest and most active meetings location until the Philadelphia Marriott opened in 1995 (just across from the Pennsylvania Convention Center), but people who are willing to travel a few blocks farther still enjoy this facility. All public areas and guest rooms have been renovated and brightened up; rooms are done in soft green. Although it is still primarily a convention hotel, the Wyndham now caters to individual travelers with a variety of added amenities and services. Rooms have full-length mirrors, cable TV, voice mail, coffeemakers, and hair dryers. The 70-ft atrium lobby encompasses restaurants and numerous sitting areas. ⊠ *17th and Race Sts., 19103,* ☎ *215/448–2000 or 800/822–4200,* FAX *215/448–2864. 720 rooms, 38 suites. 2 restaurants, bar, no-smoking rooms, room service, indoor pool, barbershop, beauty salon, exercise room, coin laundry, concierge, parking (fee). AE, D, DC, MC, V.*

$$–$$$ 🏨 **KormanSuites Hotel.** The abstract neon sculpture on the roof of this comfortable hotel and corporate apartment complex serves as a colorful landmark in the Philadelphia skyline. Just a few blocks off the Benjamin Franklin Parkway, the business- and family-oriented all-suite facility offers striking city views from most of the spacious rooms. About half of the accommodations have washer-dryers; otherwise there's one on each floor. Larger suites have fully equipped kitchens with a table and chairs, dishes, and a stove and refrigerator; smaller ones have coffeemakers and microwaves. The hotel restaurant, Tuscan Twenty, specializes in Italian food and also serves a large selection of single-malt scotches. Complimentary shuttle bus in the Center City area is available six days a week. ⊠ *2001 Hamilton St., 19130,* ☎ *215/569–7000,* FAX *215/469–0138. 100 suites. Restaurant, lounge, pool, beauty salon, health club, business services, free parking.*

$$ 🏨 **Best Western Center City.** A bit far from the heart of Center City but within an easy walk of the Philadelphia Museum of Art and the Rodin Museum, this old-timer (in relative terms) of a motel was renovated and redecorated a few years ago, with rooms done in royal blue and peach. The best views from the guest rooms face south toward the flag-draped Benjamin Franklin Parkway and the downtown skyline. This is still a relative bargain in a city where prices have been rising quickly. ⊠ *501 N. 22nd St., 19130,* ☎ *215/568–8300,* FAX *215/557–0259. 179 rooms, 4 suites. Restaurant, sports bar, pool, free parking. AE, D, DC, MC, V.*

University City

This area just across the Schuylkill River in West Philadelphia is a 5- to 10-minute drive or taxi ride from Center City. The hotels are somewhat less posh (but also less expensive) than those downtown, but compensate to a degree by being close to the University of Pennsylvania and Drexel University.

$$$–$$$$ 🏨 **Penn Tower.** The University of Pennsylvania purchased and improved this 21-floor former Hilton in 1987, converting half the space to medical offices. It is on the eastern edge of the campus, close to the University Museum, Franklin Field, the 30th Street Station, Drexel University, and University Hospital. Guest rooms, with traditional mahogany furnishings and cable TV, have excellent views east to Center City and

west across campus. The exercise facility on the concierge level is available free to guests on those floors, and to others at a nominal charge. ⊠ *34th St. and Civic Center Blvd., 19104,* ☎ *215/387–8333 or 800/ 356–7366,* FAX *215/386–8306. 85 rooms, 2 suites. Restaurant, bar, in-room data ports, room service, parking (fee). AE, D, DC, MC, V.*

$$–$$$ 🏨 **Inn at Penn.** Part of the Sansom Common redevelopment on the University of Pennsylvania campus, this new hotel (opened in fall 1999) aims for a residential ambience and is a welcome addition for anyone seeking to stay in University City. Nice elements include tiles from Moravian Tile Works, a grand staircase and book-lined living room, and a green, burgundy, and yellow color scheme throughout. The amenities are totally 21st century: two phone lines in each room, data ports offering Internet and PennNet access, and pampering touches such as plush terry robes and daily newspapers. There's a small fitness room, or you can use the University Gymnasium for a fee. The full-service Ivy Grill restaurant is convenient. ⊠ *3600 Sansom St.,* ☎ *215/222–0200,* FAX *215/823–6229. 238 rooms, 26 suites. Restaurant, in-room data ports, exercise room, parking (fee). AE, D, DC, MC, V.*

Airport District

A 20-minute drive or taxi ride from most sight-seeing and entertainment, these hotels about 8 mi south of Center City are somewhat less expensive than those downtown. Although some are within sight of industrial parks, they all have a convenient location near the airport—a plus for business travelers.

$$$ 🏨 **Philadelphia Airport Marriott.** Opened in 1995, this sprawling hotel in the Marriott style has a skybridge connecting directly to Terminal B at Philadelphia International Airport. Rooms have dark wood and blue and green color schemes. Business travelers are accommodated with voice mail, data ports, and a speakerphone. Weekend packages are a good value here. ⊠ *Arrivals Rd., 19153,* ☎ *215/492–9000 or 800/228–9290,* FAX *215/492–6799. 419 rooms, 5 suites. Restaurant, lounge, in-room data ports, indoor pool, exercise room, business services, meeting rooms, free parking.*

$$–$$$ 🏨 **Airport Hilton.** You can take a swim in the lobby pool of this Hilton before jumping on a free shuttle bus for the ride to your airport terminal. During the week this is mostly a business travelers' hotel, but weekends bring honeymooners and vacationing couples—and substantially lower rates. Rooms have wood-and-wicker dressing tables and bureaus, as well as cable TV. This was one of the earliest of the airport hotels, and it has remained pleasant and not noisy. ⊠ *4509 Island Ave., 19153,* ☎ *215/365–4150 or 800/445–8667,* FAX *215/365–3002. 328 rooms, 3 suites. Restaurant, sports bar, room service, indoor pool, sauna, exercise room, free parking. AE, D, DC, MC, V.*

$$–$$$ 🏨 **Westin Suites, Philadelphia Airport.** A glass-wall elevator whisks you
★   to your floor at this all-suite hotel where front balconies overlook the light-flooded atrium lobby and restaurant. Suites are standard or deluxe; deluxe have a larger living room and a better view. Each accommodation has a king-size bed in the bedroom and a queen-size fold-out in the living room, three telephones, two remote-control TV/clock radios, and coffeemakers, plus complimentary daily newspapers. Some rooms have extra aids for business travelers, including speakerphones with data ports. ⊠ *4101 Island Ave., 19153,* ☎ *215/365–6600 or 800/ 937–8461,* FAX *215/492–8471. 251 suites. Restaurant, lobby lounge, 1 indoor and 1 outdoor pool, exercise room, airport shuttle, free parking. AE, D, DC, MC, V.*

$$ ⚅ **Holiday Inn Philadelphia International Airport.** The lobby sets a traditional tone, with green marble, gold-trimmed dark colors, and fireplaces. The slightly oversize guest rooms have pastel color schemes with dark cherry wood furniture. There are good weekend rates here, depending on availability. The hotel is 3 mi south of the airport. ⊠ *45 Industrial Hwy., Rte. 291, Essington 19029,* ☎ *610/521–2400,* ℻ *610/ 521–1605. 307 rooms. Restaurant, pool, exercise room, airport shuttle, free parking. AE, D, DC, MC, V.*

$$ ⚅ **Sheraton Philadelphia Airport Hotel.** Even though this hotel is surrounded by highways and is across the street from the airport, special construction makes it a quiet place. The neutral decor is inviting. The five-story L-shape building has pleasant, spacious rooms with two double beds or one king- size bed. ⊠ *4101 Island Ave., 19153,* ☎ *215/492– 0400 or 800/325–2525,* ℻ *215/365–6035. 177 rooms. Café, no-smoking rooms, pool, airport shuttle, free parking. AE, D, DC, MC, V.*

City Line Avenue

If you prefer to stay outside the bustle of downtown and park for free, two hotels here may be a good choice. City Line Avenue is only a 10-minute ride on the Schuylkill Expressway to Center City under favorable conditions; however, the expressway is frequently heavily congested at rush hour.

$$–$$$ ⚅ **Adam's Mark.** At 23 stories, the Adam's Mark is one of the tallest hotels in Philadelphia: request a room on the upper floors facing south toward Fairmount Park and the downtown skyline for the best views. The ample rooms are geared primarily to the business traveler, with tailored striped fabrics that are serviceable but without particular charm. The big attraction here is the nighttime activity: Quincy's, a lively nightclub, plus two restaurants (one, rather formal, serving excellent, eclectic food, and the other resembling a bright coffee shop) and a sports bar. Lines can form early for the action at the clubs, particularly when there's major talent in town. ⊠ *City Ave. and Monument Rd., 19131,* ☎ *215/581–5000 or 800/444–2326,* ℻ *215/581–5089. 459 rooms, 56 suites. 2 restaurants, sports bar, 1 indoor and 1 outdoor pool, health club, nightclub, free parking. AE, D, DC, MC, V.*

$$ ⚅ **Holiday Inn City Line.** This eight-story Holiday Inn is perfectly ordinary, but it's a good value in a choice location. You could stay here to save money and just walk across the parking lot to all the eateries and nightspots of the Adam's Mark hotel (☞ *above*). A five-minute walk takes you to five other restaurants. In the lobby you can sink into an overstuffed easy chair and watch swimmers in the glass-enclosed pool. ⊠ *4100 Presidential Blvd., 19131,* ☎ *215/477–0200 or 800/642– 8982,* ℻ *215/473–5510. 343 rooms. Restaurant, 1 indoor pool and 1 outdoor pool, exercise room, business services, meeting rooms, free parking. AE, D, DC, MC, V.*

Hostels

Hostels provide dormitory-style accommodations for less than you'd pay to park your car at a downtown hotel. They also offer a sense of adventure and a chance to share living, eating, and sleeping quarters with travelers from all over the world. The **American Youth Hostel Regional Office and Travel Center** is at 624 South 3rd Street (☎ 215/925–6004).

$ ⚅ **Bank Street Hostel.** A member of Hostel International, Bank Street opened in 1992 and, at $16 (members) to $19 (nonmembers) a night, is a downtown-Philly lodging bargain. Independently owned by David Herskowitz, it is on the cusp of Old City in a 140-year-old manufacturing building that has been combined with two neighboring buildings. Guests gather around the pool table and the 48-inch TV. ⊠ *32 S. Bank St., 19106,* ☎ *215/922–0222 or 800/392–4678. 3 rooms for 70 people, with shared baths. No credit cards.*

$ 🏠 **Chamounix Mansion.** Here's the cheapest place to stay in Philadelphia—$11 a night for American Youth Hostel members, and $14 for nonmembers. Set on a wooded bluff overlooking the Schuylkill River—and, unfortunately, the Schuylkill Expressway—the hostel feels like it's out in the country, though it's in Fairmount Park. The restored 1802 Quaker country estate is loaded with character. Flags line the entrance hall; period rooms have antiques; walls display old maps, sketches, and paintings. There's a self-service kitchen. Chamounix Mansion is hard to find and not too convenient for public transportation; call for directions. ⊠ *Chamounix Dr., 19131,* ☎ *215/878–3676 or 800/379–0017,* FAX *215/871–4313. 6 rooms for 48 people, with shared baths. MC, V. Closed Dec. 15–Jan. 15.*

5 NIGHTLIFE AND THE ARTS

Philadelphia seems to have a rhythm of its own. Whether you're listening to the Philadelphia Orchestra while picnicking on the lawn at the Mann Center for the Performing Arts, or having a jazz brunch at Zanzibar Blue, music adds depth to the Philadelphia experience. This is a city of neighborhoods, and you can find entertainment in all of them. From Broadway shows at the Forrest Theater to performance art and poetry readings at the Painted Bride, there's always something new to explore.

Updated by
Robert
DiGiacomo

THEATER, DANCE, AND MUSIC from rock to opera: Philadelphia has plenty going on after dark. The city's Avenue of the Arts cultural district on North and South Broad Street is one significant sign of the new energy in town. Of the arts facilities on the avenue, some are long-standing, such as the Academy of Music and the Merriam Theater; others, including the Wilma Theater and the Prince Music Theater, are more recent additions. Adding further excitement to the Avenue of the Arts is the long-awaited construction of the $200 million Regional Performing Arts Center, a project that will include a new hall for the Philadelphia Orchestra and a smaller recital space; the new facility is scheduled to open in fall 2001.

The Avenue of the Arts spaces are providing forums for an ever wider range of talents, both traditional and innovative, from local artists to international stars. On a lighter note, you can relax by partying on the Delaware River or checking out some of the city's fine jazz.

NIGHTLIFE

In today's Philadelphia you can listen to a chanteuse in a chic basement nightclub, dance till 3 AM in a smoky bistro, and watch street jugglers, mimes, and magicians on a Society Hill corner. South Street between Front and 9th streets is still hip, with one-of-a-kind shops, bookstores, galleries, restaurants, and bars that attract the young and the restless in droves. Today, however, those in the know head to the trendy bars and clubs of the Old City, where the crowd is chic and upscale. Over the past few years Main Street in Manayunk, in the northwest section of the city, has become a smaller, tamer version of South Street. More than a dozen clubs have also opened up along the Delaware River waterfront, most near the Benjamin Franklin Bridge; a water taxi shuttles revelers between them. Besides its club scene, Philadelphia also has larger venues for rock, pop, and jazz concerts (☞ Concerts *in* The Arts, *below*).

Bars and clubs can change hands or go out of business faster than a soft pretzel goes stale. Many places are open until 2 AM; cover charges vary from free to $12. Some may not be open every night, so call ahead. A few places do not accept credit cards, so carry some cash. For current information check the entertainment pages of the *Philadelphia Inquirer*, the *Philadelphia Daily News*, and *Philadelphia* magazine. For Penn's Landing events, call ☎ 215/923–4992.

Bars and Brew Pubs

The Bards. An authentic Irish pub, the Bards (☞ Irish *in* Chapter 3) has an Irish crowd, Irish food, and great Irish music sessions on Sunday from 5 to 9. ⊠ *2013 Walnut St.,* ☎ *215/569–9585.*

Beaujolais. The long, narrow bar of this popular Rittenhouse area bistro serves as a gathering spot for twenty- and thirtysomething professionals. The bar menu is served until 12:30 AM. ⊠ *261 S. 20th St.,* ☎ *215/732–8000.*

Copacabana. Need a break from the bustle of South Street? This popular hangout serves up some of the city's best margaritas, along with satisfying bar food such as hamburgers and veggie burgers topped with guacamole or salsa, and spicy Spanish fries with jalapeño peppers and fried onions. Floor-to-ceiling windows in the first floor bar give you great views of the parade of characters outside. ⊠ *344 South St.,* ☎ *215/923–6180.*

Copa, Too. The younger sibling of the popular South Street Copacabana (☞ *above*) attracts a slightly older crowd in their early thirties and is quite crowded for after-work happy hour. Besides margaritas and bar food, Copa, Too offers a vast selection of beers—some 100 varieties are available on tap and by the bottle. ⊠ *263 S. 15th St.,* ☎ *215/735–0848.*

Dirty Frank's. Frank is long gone, but this place is still dirty, cheap, and a Philadelphia classic. An incongruous mixture of students, artists, journalists, and resident characters crowd around the horseshoe-shape bar and engage in friendly mayhem. It's open Monday–Saturday. ⊠ *347 S. 13th St.,* ☎ *215/732–5010.*

Dock Street Brasserie. This brewery (☞ French *in* Chapter 3) occupies a large, lively space. You can choose hearty Alsatian dishes with your beer or standards such as steaks and burgers. Several flavors of the house-specialty boutique beer are available on a daily basis. ⊠ *2 Logan Sq.,* ☎ *215/496–0413.*

The Plough and the Stars. An upscale Irish pub-restaurant (☞ Irish *in* Chapter 3) in the historic Corn Exchange Building seemingly transports you from New World Philadelphia to Old Country Dublin with a mere lifting of a glass of Guinness. Dozens of brews are on tap or sold by the bottle, and the restaurant serves up Irish-style nouvelle comfort food. Shepherd's pie is a winner, but you won't find corned beef and cabbage here. ⊠ *123 Chestnut St., entrance on 2nd St.,* ☎ *215/733–0300.*

Woody's. Philadelphia's most popular gay bar has a large disco and two video bars. ⊠ *202 S. 13th St.,* ☎ *215/545–1893.*

Comedy Clubs

Comedy Sportz. Anything goes during this once-a-week night of improvisational comedy. Two teams compete each Saturday night at 10 at the 70-seat Brick Playhouse, and the audience is also welcome to participate. ⊠ *623 South St. (above Montserrat Restaurant),* ☎ *215/985–2844.*

David Brenner's Laugh House. This 250-seat club is co-owned by Brenner, who was born in the city. It showcases local and national acts Thursday through Saturday. ⊠ *221 South St.,* ☎ *215/440–4242.*

Dance Clubs

Dave & Buster's. Call this a big amusement park for the somewhat grown-up. A short list of what's going on—besides music and dancing—includes two restaurants, five bars, pool tables, pinball and video games, just-for-fun blackjack and poker, and a virtual reality shooting game. An outdoor deck overlooks the Delaware River. ⊠ *Pier 19 N, 325 N. Columbus Blvd.,* ☎ *215/413–1951.*

Edge. Finished that Manayunk shopping spree? Stick around for a meal, have a cigar in the lounge, relax on the outdoor deck, and dance to today's tunes, spun by a DJ. The restaurant and nightclub are open Tuesday–Sunday. ⊠ *4100 Main St., Manayunk,* ☎ *215/483–4100.*

Five Spot. This sleek throwback to the era of the supper club is frequented by a stylish, retro crowd that enjoys a stiff martini and knows how to swing its way around a dance floor. There's live music (big band, Latin, and swing) Tuesday–Sunday. Latin dance lessons are given on Thursday at 7; Friday at 8 is the time for beginners to learn how to swing. ⊠ *5 S. Bank St.,* ☎ *215/574–0070.*

Katmandu. Large and usually crowded, this Delaware waterfront spot is an indoor/outdoor Caribbean restaurant and bar that has live music nightly—world, reggae, rock—and a "Wild Island" dance party on Saturday night. It's open from May to mid-October. ⊠ *Pier 25, N. Columbus Blvd. south of Spring Garden St.,* ☎ *215/629–7400.*

Maui Entertainment Complex. If your idea of heaven is ersatz tropical ambience, beach volleyball, and waitresses in cutoffs and bikini tops hawking drinks to a crowd in their twenties, this place is for you. On the city's biggest dance floor you can dance both indoors and out to live bands (rock, alternative, progressive) and to radio DJ dance-party broadcasts. Maui is open Thursday–Sunday. ⊠ *Pier 53 N, 1143 N. Columbus Blvd.,* ☎ *215/423–8116.*

Monte Carlo Living Room. The DJ at this sophisticated watering hole (☞ Italian *in* Chapter 3) plays Top-40 hits, European sounds, and South American music for a mostly thirties–fifties crowd. A jacket and tie are required. All the furnishings, from the tapestries to the paintings, are European. It's open Wednesday–Saturday. ⊠ *150 South St.,* ☎ *215/ 925–2220.*

The Moshulu. This restored restaurant ship (☞ Contemporary *in* Chapter 3) has fine riverfront views and an area for dancing from Wednesday through Saturday. ⊠ *735 S. Columbus Blvd.,* ☎ *215/923–2500.*

Polly Esther's and Culture Club. The music and decor of the '70s take center stage at this hot spot, part of a national chain. The bar is painted to look like the Partridge family's bus, *Charlie's Angels* photographs adorn one wall, and there's a *Saturday Night Fever*–style disco floor. It's open Thursday through Saturday. ⊠ *1201 Race St., next to the Pennsylvania Convention Center,* ☎ *215/851–0776.*

Rock Lobster. From May to September you can join the party at this riverfront tent that resembles a yacht club. The over-thirty set comes for reasonably priced meals and plenty of live music and dancing. ⊠ *Pier 13–14, 221 N. Columbus Blvd.,* ☎ *215/627–7625.*

Shampoo. The look of this trendy club—retro furniture and Pop Art—reflects the origins of its name: the 1975 Warren Beatty movie about a hairdresser with a complicated love life. A former warehouse has been transformed into a mega-club with eight bars and three dance floors. On Wednesdays, Thursdays, Saturdays, and Sundays, the crowd is a fashionable mix of gays and straights; "Shaft" Fridays are predominantly gay and often feature guest DJs and performers from New York, including Lady Bunny of "Wigstock" fame. ⊠ *417 N. 8th St. (entrance on Willow St.),* ☎ *215/922–7500.*

Jazz, Blues, and Cabaret

Philadelphia has a rich jazz and blues heritage that includes such greats as the late, legendary jazz saxophonist John Coltrane and current players like Grover Washington, Jr. That legacy continues today in clubs around town. The Peco Energy Jazz Festival in February and the Mellon Jazz Festival in June (☞ Concerts *in* The Arts, *below*) are popular events.

You can call the **Philadelphia Clef Club of Jazz & Performing Arts** (☞ *below*) for information. The monthly *Jazz Philadelphia* (☎ 215/473–4273) is available at the Philadelphia Visitors Center (⊠ 16th St. and John F. Kennedy Blvd.).

Chris' Jazz Cafe. An intimate hangout just off the Avenue of the Arts, Chris' showcases top local talent Monday–Saturday in a cigar- and pipe-friendly environment. ⊠ *1421 Sansom St.,* ☎ *215/568–3131.*

Liberties. This handsomely restored Victorian pub has jazz Friday and Saturday. ⊠ *705 N. 2nd St.,* ☎ *215/238–0660.*

Ortlieb's Jazz Haus. You'll hear good jazz in this 100-year-old bar. Celebrated jazz organist Shirley Scott and her quartet occasionally perform. There's music nightly from Monday through Saturday; Tuesday night includes a jam session for local musicians. ✉ *847 N. 3rd St.,* ☎ *215/922–1035.*

Philadelphia Clef Club of Jazz & Performing Arts. Dedicated solely to jazz, including its history and instruction, the organization also has a 250-seat cabaret-style theater for concert performances. ✉ *736–738 S. Broad St.,* ☎ *215/893–9912.*

Upstairs at Frangelica. Established and up-and-coming cabaret artists perform in an intimate space on the second floor of the Frangelica restaurant. ✉ *200 S. 12th St.,* ☎ *215/731–9930.*

Warmdaddy's. This rustic, down-home blues club and restaurant, owned by the people who run Zanzibar Blue (☞ *below*), serves up live blues and southern cuisine every night except Monday. The Sunday gospel brunch from noon to 3 costs $20 per person. ✉ *4–6 S. Front St., at Front and Market Sts.,* ☎ *215/627–8400 for reservations; 215/627–2500 for hours and upcoming performances.*

Zanzibar Blue. A hip restaurant and bar adjoins the hottest jazz room in town. The best local talent plays on weeknights; nationally known names take the stage on weekends. There's a jazz brunch on Sunday from 11 to 2 for $20 per person. ✉ *Downstairs at the Bellevue, Broad and Walnut Sts.,* ☎ *215/732–4500 for reservations; 215/732–5200 for hours and upcoming performances.*

Lounges

Brasserie Perrier. The bar and banquette at Georges Perrier's (of Le Bec-Fin fame) more casual bistro (☞ French *in* Chapter 3) attract a sophisticated, after-work crowd. ✉ *1619 Walnut St.,* ☎ *215/568–3000.*

Continental Restaurant & Martini Bar. This retro former diner (☞ Contemporary *in* Chapter 3) draws a hip, twentysomething crowd to its swank setting for cocktails and a tapas-style dinner menu. The design, including lighting fixtures resembling olives with toothpicks through them and lots of stainless steel, is worth checking out. ✉ *138 Market St.,* ☎ *215/923–6069.*

Friday, Saturday, Sunday. One of Philadelphia's most intimate and romantic spaces is tucked away on the second floor of this neighborhood restaurant. Tiny white lights, strategically placed mirrors, and a tank full of exotic tropical fish add just the right touches of comfort and sophistication. ✉ *261 S. 21st St.,* ☎ *215/546–4232.*

Happy Rooster. Owner "Doc" Ulitsky provides the best selection of after-dinner drinks and liqueurs in the city. French, Russian, and Gypsy music plays in the background. It's open Monday–Saturday. ✉ *118 S. 16th St.,* ☎ *215/563–1481.*

Il Bar. The wine bar at Panorama (☞ Italian *in* Chapter 3) in the Penn's View Inn stands out for its 120-bottle selection, curved bar, and romantic atmosphere. It's open seven nights a week, with a separate entrance from the restaurant. ✉ *14 N. Front St.,* ☎ *215/922–7800.*

Inn Philadelphia. This meticulously restored Colonial-style restaurant on a quaint side street is best appreciated for its warm, convivial bar-lounge. It's a good place to stop for a cocktail before dinner or a nightcap on your way home. Live piano music is a plus on weekends, and there's seating in the "Secret Garden" in warm months. ✉ *251–253 S. Camac St.,* ☎ *215/732–8630.*

Library Lounge. Handsome and wood-paneled, this space on the 19th floor of the venerable Bellevue hotel (now a Park Hyatt) harkens to the days when gentlemen left the ladies behind to retire to the library, but all are welcome here. Oriental carpets, shelves lined with leather-bound volumes, and a roaring fire complete the scene. ✉ *Broad and Walnut Sts.,* ☎ *215/893–1776.*

Rouge. With lovely Rittenhouse Square as its backdrop, this French-style bistro (☞ Contemporary *in* Chapter 3) from celebrity restaurateur Neil Stein is the place to see and be seen, especially for the city's over-35 set. Noisy and crowded on weekend nights, it's best enjoyed in the warmer weather when the wall of French windows is thrown open and the party spills out into the street. ⊠ *205 S. 18th St.,* ☎ *215/732–6622.*

Swann Lounge. You can listen to a jazz trio on Thursday night and dance on Friday and Saturday nights in this extremely elegant hotel lounge. A Sunday brunch with Dixieland music is also offered. ⊠ *Four Seasons Hotel, 18th St. and Benjamin Franklin Pkwy.,* ☎ *215/963–1500.*

Performance Arts Center

Painted Bride Art Center. By day it's a contemporary art gallery showing bold, challenging works. By night it's a multidisciplinary, multicultural performance center, with performance art, prose and poetry readings, folk and new music, jazz, dance, and avant-garde theater. The gallery is open Tuesday–Friday 10–6, Saturday noon–6; call for the performance schedule. ⊠ *230 Vine St.,* ☎ *215/925–9914.*

Rock and Pop

Electric Factory. Electric Factory Concerts, which presents major rock concerts at various venues in the city, now has its own smaller rock club. ⊠ *421 N. 7th St.,* ☎ *215/568–3222.*

The Khyber. Small and loud, this Old City spot has lots of action. The music is all live, including alternative and rock performed by national and local talent. With more than 100 brands of beer, it has one of the best selections in town. The Khyber is open Monday–Saturday. ⊠ *56 S. 2nd St.,* ☎ *215/238–5888.*

Theatre of Living Arts. The TLA, a former independent movie house, is a South Street institution that helped launch John Waters's film career; it was the longtime home of *The Rocky Horror Picture Show.* Today the TLA presents concerts by a range of rock, blues, and adult alternative acts, including Lucinda Williams and Michelle Shocked. ⊠ *334 South St.,* ☎ *215/922–1011.*

Tin Angel Acoustic Cafe. Local and national musicians hold forth at a 105-seat acoustic cabaret above the Serrano restaurant (patrons get preferred seating; ☞ Mediterranean *in* Chapter 3). You can sit at candlelit tables or at the bar and hear music from blues to folk. Tickets are required except for Wednesday's open-mike evenings. ⊠ *20 S. 2nd St.,* ☎ *215/928–0978.*

Trocadero. This spacious rock-and-roll club in Chinatown occupies a former burlesque house where W. C. Fields and Mae West performed. A lot of the old decor remains: mirrors, pillars, and balconies surround the dance floor. Most every up-and-coming band that's passing through Philly plays here to an under-thirty crowd. On other nights local DJs host dance parties. ⊠ *1003 Arch St.,* ☎ *215/922–5483.*

THE ARTS

Of all the performing arts, it is music for which Philadelphia is most renowned and the Philadelphia Orchestra of which its residents are most proud. Considered one of the world's best symphony orchestras, it rose to fame under the batons of former conductors Leopold Stokowski, Eugene Ormandy, and Riccardo Muti. The orchestra performs at the Academy of Music, built in 1857 and modeled after La Scala. Orchestra concerts during the September–May season are still among the city's premier social events. If you can get tickets, go. You'll see some of the city's finest performers in an opulent setting, with many Philadelphians dressed to match the occasion. The Opera Company of Philadelphia also performs at the Academy.

There is no shortage of live entertainment, ranging from the Philly Pops to the Mellon Jazz Festival. There are also summer concerts of popular and classical music at the Robin Hood Dell East and at Fairmount Park's Mann Center for the Performing Arts. Many rock groups stop in Philadelphia on their national tours, playing at the First Union Center and First Union Spectrum; the Keswick Theatre, in suburban Glenside; or the E-Centre in Camden.

Of course, Philly holds a special place in pop music history. *American Bandstand,* hosted by Dick Clark, began here as a local dance show. When it went national in 1957, it gave a boost to many hometown boys, including Fabian, Bobby Rydell, Frankie Avalon, and Chubby Checker. The city's rock-and-roll tradition began in 1955 with Bill Haley and the Comets. In the 1970s the Philadelphia Sound—a polished blend of disco, pop, and rhythm and blues—came alive through Kenny Gamble and Leon Huff; its lush sound has been kept alive by chart toppers such as Hall and Oates, Patti LaBelle, Boyz II Men, and rapper/actor Will Smith.

Until the early 1980s Philadelphia was considered an important tryout town for theatrical productions headed to New York. (Today, due to high production costs, few Broadway shows even have out-of-town tryouts on that scale.) But the rich theatrical tradition continues here. The city serves as a major stop for touring productions of shows from *Les Misérables* to *Rent,* and the local theater scene, which suppports more than two dozen regional and local companies, is thriving.

For information on the city's art scene, including art and crafts galleries, *see* Art and Crafts Galleries in Chapter 7.

Information and Tickets

For current performances and listings, the best guides to Philly's performing arts are the "Guide to the Lively Arts" in the daily *Philadelphia Inquirer,* the "Weekend" section of the Friday *Inquirer,* and the "Friday" section of the *Philadelphia Daily News.* Two free weekly papers, the *City Paper* and the *Philadelphia Weekly,* have extensive listings of concerts and clubs; they are available free in news boxes all over downtown.

The **Philadelphia Visitors Center** (⊠ 16th St. and John F. Kennedy Blvd., (☎ 215/636–1666) has information about performances. **UpStages** (⊠ 1412 Chestnut St., ☎ 215/569–9700) has tickets for many cultural events. Discount tickets, often reduced up to 50%, are offered on the day of the performance. The **Philadelphia Arts Bank** (⊠ 601 S. Broad St., at South St.) has regular-price tickets for performances on a given day. **TicketMaster** (☎ 215/336–2000) sells tickets to rock concerts and other performing arts events.

Prices for performing arts events vary widely. Tickets for rock or pop concerts range from $10 or $15 for a small venue such as the Tin Angel or lawn seats at the Mann Center, to $75 and up for good seats at the First Union Center to see the Rolling Stones; theater tickets can go from $15 for local productions to $70 for touring productions of Broadway shows; Philadelphia Orchestra tickets range from $10 for the amphitheater to $120 for the best box seats.

Concerts

All-Star Forum. This organization brings visiting orchestras, recitals by stars such as Itzhak Perlman and Isaac Stern, ballets, and special musical events to the Academy of Music. ☎ *215/735–7506.*

Blockbuster-Sony Music Entertainment Centre. The E-Centre, across the Delaware River in Camden, programs everything from symphonies to rock and roll in a space that can seat 1,600 or up to 25,000 people. ✉ *1 Harbor Blvd., on the waterfront, Camden,* ☎ *609/635–1445 for ticket information and directions.*

Concerto Soloists of Philadelphia. Directed by Marc Mostovoy, this prestigious group performs chamber music from October to May at the Pennsylvania Convention Center (✉ 13th and Cherry Sts., ☎ 215/418–4989). Sunday afternoon concerts take place from October to May at the Church of the Holy Trinity (✉ 19th and Walnut Sts., ☎ *215/545–5451).*

Curtis Institute of Music. Free concerts are given three times a week from October through May at 8 PM at this tuition-free music school for outstanding students. (Curtis alumni have included such luminaries as Leonard Bernstein, Samuel Barber, and Anna Moffo.) The recital hot line lists events. ✉ *1726 Locust St.,* ☎ *215/893–5261 for hot line.*

First Union Spectrum and First Union Center. Rock concerts are often staged in these enormous sports facilities on the south side of the city. ✉ *S. Broad St. and Pattison Ave., off I–95,* ☎ *215/336–3600.*

Keswick Theatre. A 1,900-seat former vaudeville house with fine acoustics hosts rock, jazz, and country music concerts as well as musicals; call for directions. ✉ *Easton Rd. and Keswick Ave., Glenside,* ☎ *215/572–7650.*

Mann Center for the Performing Arts. In June and July noted soloists and guest conductors perform with the Philadelphia Orchestra in an outdoor amphitheater. In addition to regular seats, there is free seating on the lawn (bring a blanket), but you must reserve this by sending in a form well in advance. ✉ *West Fairmount Park, George's Hill near 52nd St. and Parkside Ave.,* ☎ *215/878–7707 for box office.*

Mellon Jazz Festival. A series of 40 concerts and events (most free or with low ticket prices) are presented in June at locations around town. Look for top names in jazz, such as Pat Martino, Wynton Marsalis, and Chick Corea. ☎ *610/667–3559.*

Philadelphia Chamber Music Society. A classical music series of 40 concerts is given at the Pennsylvania Convention Center (✉ 13th and Cherry Sts., ☎ 215/418–4989) from October to May. ☎ *215/569–8587 or 215/569–8080.*

Philadelphia Folk Festival. First held in 1962, the oldest continuously running folk festival in the country takes place each year for three days during the last week in August. Doc Watson, Taj Mahal, Joan Baez, and Judy Collins are just a few of the artists who have performed here. ✉ *Old Pool Farm, near Schwenksville,* ☎ *215/242–0150 or 800/556–3655.*

Philadelphia Orchestra. The world-renowned ensemble performs at the Academy of Music from September to May. Musical director Wolfgang Sawallisch, who favors the German repertoire, will be emphasizing 20th-century composers for the 1999–2000 season, the orchestra's 100th anniversary. In summer the orchestra appears at the Mann Center for the Performing Arts (☞ *above*). ✉ *Broad and Locust Sts.,* ☎ *215/893–1999.*

Philly Pops. Conducted by Peter Nero, this group performs at the Academy of Music from October to May and occasionally at other local events. ☎ *215/735–7506.*

Robin Hood Dell East. The Dell is the site for rhythm-and-blues and soul music concerts on Monday and Wednesday evenings in July and August. ✉ *Strawberry Mansion Dr., East Fairmount Park,* ☎ *215/685–9560.*

Dance

Pennsylvania Ballet. This company, under artistic director Roy Kaiser, dances on the stages of the Academy of Music (✉ Broad and Locust Sts.) and the Merriam Theater (✉ 250 S. Broad St.) from October to June. The *Nutcracker* production at Christmastime is a city favorite. ☎ *215/551–7000.*

The **Philadelphia Dance Alliance** (☎ 215/564–5270) is a good source of information on dance concerts and local companies.

Philadelphia Dance Company. Modern dance performances are presented in September at the Philadelphia Arts Bank (✉ 601 S. Broad St., ☎ 215/545–0590) and in May at the Annenberg Center (✉ 3680 Walnut St., ☎ 215/898–6791). *Philadanco;* ☎ *215/387–8200.*

Film

Upcoming developments for later in 2000 and 2001 include a new multiplex theater at the Pavilion at Market East (✉ 8th and Market Sts.) and an IMAX theater and a multiplex at Penn's Landing. Avoid what's left of the first-run theaters on Chestnut Street west of Broad Street—they're often frequented by rowdy urban youths.

International Gay and Lesbian Film Festival. Organized by Theatre of Living Arts Video founder Raymond Murray, who has written several books on film, this festival is held annually in early July in venues around the city. ✉ ☎ *215/733–0608.*

International House. I-House on the University of Pennsylvania campus presents international film series throughout the year and also sponsors the popular Philadelphia Festival of World Cinema (☞ *below*).

Philadelphia Festival of World Cinema. Sponsored by International House (☞ *above*), this 12-day event in May is filled with screenings, seminars, and events attended by critics, scholars, filmmakers, and cinema buffs. ✉ *3701 Chestnut St.,* ☎ *215/895–6593.*

Ritz Five and Ritz at the Bourse. These are the finest movie theaters in town for independent and foreign films. Both have comfortable seats, clean surroundings, first-rate sound systems, and courteous audiences and staff. ✉ *Ritz Five, 214 Walnut St.;* ✉ *Ritz at the Bourse, 4th St. north of Chestnut St.;* ☎ *215/923–7900 for both.*

The Roxy. Philly's classic film repertory house offers a unique mix of new and classic films. ✉ *2023 Sansom St.,* ☎ *215/923–6699.*

United Artists Main Street 6 Theatre. Manayunk now has a multiplex to complement its shopping and dining options. ✉ *3720 Main St., Manayunk,* ☎ *215/482–6230.*

United Artist Riverview Plaza. Showing first-run commercial releases, this renovated cinema (✉ 1400 S. Columbus Blvd., ☎ 215/755–2219) is a modern, 19-screen multiplex.

Opera

Opera Company of Philadelphia. The company stages four productions a year, between October and April, at the Academy of Music; some operas have international stars. All performances are in the original language, with computerized English "supertitles" above the stage. ✉ *510 Walnut St.,* ☎ *215/928–2110.*

Savoy Company. The oldest Gilbert and Sullivan company in the country stages one G&S operetta each May or June at the Academy of Music and at Longwood Gardens in Kennett Square. ☎ *215/735–7161.*

Theater

Annenberg Center. The performing arts complex on the University of Pennsylvania campus has four stages, from the 120-seat Studio to the 970-seat Zellerbach Theater. Something is going on almost all the time—including productions of musical comedy, drama, dance, and children's theater. ✉ *3680 Walnut St.,* ☎ *215/898–6791.*

Arden Theatre Company. The Arden, formed in 1988, has gained a reputation for innovative theatrical productions. Its home is in Old City. ✉ *400 N. 2nd St.,* ☎ *215/922–8900.*

Brick Playhouse. This fairly new theater group, with a space above the Montserrat Restaurant that seats 70, develops and produces new works by local playwrights and performance artists. ✉ *623 South St.,* ☎ *215/592–1183.*

Forrest Theater. Here you can see productions of major Broadway shows, such as *Cats, La Cage aux Folles, Les Misérables,* and *Phantom of the Opera.* ✉ *1114 Walnut St.,* ☎ *215/923–1515.*

Freedom Theatre. The oldest and most active African-American theater in Pennsylvania is nationally renowned. Performances are scheduled from September through June. ✉ *1346 N. Broad St.,* ☎ *215/978–8497.*

Merriam Theater. Formerly the Schubert and part of the University of the Arts, the Merriam presents Broadway tours and student productions of musicals and dramas. ✉ *250 S. Broad St.,* ☎ *215/732–5446.*

Philadelphia Arts Bank. A number of nonprofit arts groups use the 230-seat theater owned by the University of the Arts. The Arts Bank is part of the Avenue of the Arts development. ✉ *601 S. Broad St., at South St.,* ☎ *215/545–0590.*

Philadelphia Theater Company. Philadelphia and world premieres of works by contemporary American playwrights are performed here. The company also produces Stages, a program showcasing new plays by American playwrights. ✉ *1714 Delancey St., at Plays and Players,* ☎ *215/735–0630 for theater; 568–1920 for PTC office.*

Prince Music Theater. Formerly known as the American Music Theater Festival, this organization—named in honor of legendary Broadway director-producer Harold Prince—presents new, original musicals and a cabaret series with national acts, including Andrea Marcovicci. The organization is also home to the Sharon Pinkenson Film Project (named after the city's longtime film office director), intended as a venue for independent film. ✉ *1412 Chestnut St.,* ☎ *215/893–1570.*

Society Hill Playhouse. The main stage is for contemporary works; the Second Space Cabaret Theater has musical comedies. ✉ *507 S. 8th St.,* ☎ *215/923–0210.*

Walnut Street Theatre. Founded in 1809, this is the oldest English-speaking theater in continuous use in the United States. The schedule includes musicals, comedies, and dramas in a lovely 1,052-seat auditorium where almost every seat is a good one. Smaller stages showcase workshop productions of new plays and are rented by other theater companies. ✉ *9th and Walnut Sts.,* ☎ *215/574–3550.*

Wilma Theater. Under artistic director Blanka Zizka, the Wilma has gained favorable critical notices for innovative presentations of American and European drama. Its season runs from September to June. ✉ *Broad and Spruce Sts.,* ☎ *215/546–7824.*

6 OUTDOOR ACTIVITIES AND SPORTS

Philadelphians are well-known sports fanatics. You can barely concentrate on a Phillies game when the fans are shouting at or cheering on the players, which is part of the fun, of course. Recreational athletes take full advantage of the city's natural resources, including its parks and rivers. Kelly and West River drives in Fairmount Park are quite a sight on spring weekends, when there is no car traffic and all the bikers, in-line skaters, and walkers are out enjoying the cherry blossoms.

Updated by
Robert
DiGiacomo

PHILADELPHIA SPORTS FANS have lots to cheer about. Their professional teams—the Eagles (football), the Phillies (baseball), the Flyers (ice hockey), and the 76ers (basketball)—are all popular and occasionally make it to the playoffs. Crowds are the norm at the 700,000-square-ft First Union Center sports complex and at Veterans Stadium: Philadelphians buy more tickets to pro sporting events than do residents of any other U.S. city. At press time, two new facilities for professional baseball and football were under development, with projected completion dates in 2001 or 2002.

There are many other sports attractions in the city, but two activities—and images—come immediately to mind. The first is one immortalized in a canvas by Thomas Eakins, Philadelphia's greatest painter, of an oarsman rowing on the Schuylkill River in an elegant single scull. Today, the scene that Eakins depicted in the 19th century is still enacted every week when scores of sculls are launched from Boathouse Row, a string of Victorian boathouses along Kelly Drive that are home to the city's many rowing clubs.

The second image, of course, is that of boxer Rocky Balboa, pungently captured by Sylvester Stallone in the film *Rocky* and its sequels. Had Rocky been a real Philadelphia boxer, he would have fought at the Blue Horizon (☞ Boxing *in* Spectator Sports, *below*), the legendary fight club. You can also see Rocky himself—immortalized in bronze—in front of the First Union Spectrum at Broad Street and Pattison Avenue.

Participant Sports and Fitness

Philadelphia has a wide variety of places for athletes to test their skills, whether the sport is biking, jogging, or tennis.

Biking

One popular treat for cyclists is to ride the paved path along the east side of the **Schuylkill River,** cross East Falls Bridge, and return on the west side of the river. The path begins behind the Philadelphia Museum of Art and is parallel to Kelly Drive. This 8-mi loop is about an hour of casually paced biking. **Forbidden Drive,** a 5½-mi dirt-and-gravel bridle path along a stream in the Wissahickon (☞ Fairmount Park *in* Chapter 2), is a great ride.

The **Bicycle Club of Philadelphia** (☎ 215/735–2453) organizes bike tours, from afternoon outings to weeklong events. Bike rentals, as well as in-line skates, are available from May through September, Wednesday–Friday 4–8 and weekends 9–6, at **Lloyd Hall** (☎ 215/765–3123), a new addition at the eastern end of Boathouse Row. There's also a café. You can rent bikes ($15 a day) from **Bike Line** (✉ 13th and Locust Sts., ☎ 215/735–1503).

Fishing

On the banks of Wissahickon Creek and Pennypack Creek, you'll find good trout fishing in attractive natural settings; call **Fairmount Park** (☎ 215/685–0000) for information. Both creeks are stocked for the mid-April–December season. You'll need a **license** ($12.50–$25.50), available at some local sporting goods stores and at Kmart (✉ 424 Oregon Ave., ☎ 215/336–1778).

Golf

Philadelphia has six 18-hole courses that are open to the public. Cobb's Creek is the most challenging; Roosevelt is the easiest.

For golfers who love lots of action, **Cobb's Creek** and **Karakung** (⊠ 7200 Lansdowne Ave., ☎ 215/877–8707) are two adjacent courses. Cobb's Creek plays in and around the creek itself, making for lovely vistas and challenging shots. Karakung has hilly fairways and smaller greens. Both are par 71. Greens fees are $16–$22 weekdays, $19–$26 weekends and holidays.

Franklin D. Roosevelt (⊠ 20th St. and Pattison Ave., ☎ 215/462–8997) is a flat, relatively easy par 69; it's particularly recommended for beginners. Greens fees are $18 weekdays, $21 weekends.

J. F. Byrne (⊠ 9500 Leon St., ☎ 215/632–8666), a short but semichallenging course with small greens and water on six holes, is rated par 67. Greens fees are $16 weekdays, $20 weekends.

With lots of hills, trees, and the Frankford Creek running through it, **Juniata** (⊠ L and Cayuga Sts., ☎ 215/743–4060) is an impressive par 66. Greens fees are $16 weekdays, $19 weekends.

Narrow tree-lined fairways make **Walnut Lane** (⊠ 800 Walnut La., ☎ 215/482–3370), a short (4,500 yards) course, into a semichallenging par 62. Greens fees are $15 weekdays, $18 weekends.

Outside Philadelphia, the privately owned **Valley Forge Golf Club** (⊠ 401 N. Gulph Rd., King of Prussia, ☎ 610/337–1776), near Valley Forge National Historic Park, is open to the public. Trees, doglegs, and small greens make this course (6,266 yards, par 71) a challenging one. Greens fees are $19 weekdays, $23 weekends.

Health Clubs

Some downtown clubs allow nonmembers (with photo IDs) to have day guest privileges for $10–$15. Three good facilities are **Central YMCA** (⊠ 1425 Arch St., ☎ 215/557–0082); **Rittenhouse Square Fitness Club** (⊠ 2002 Rittenhouse Sq., ☎ 215/985–4095); and **12th Street Gym** (⊠ 204 S. 12th St., ☎ 215/985–4092).

Hiking

There are 25 mi of fine solo walks or hikes in Fairmount Park and 54 mi in the unspoiled Wissahickon (☞ Fairmount Park *in* Chapter 2), a northern section of the park; call **Fairmount Park** (☎ 215/685–0000) for information. Despite the bucolic quality of these areas, it's important to remember that you are in an urban setting and should take appropriate precautions. If you're alone, keep to the main paths along Kelly Drive and West River Drive, or consider joining a hiking group.

Hiking takes on an added dimension if you opt for some of the organized hikes in the area. You can meet hikers at the **Batona Hiking Club** (☎ 215/659–3921) on Sunday morning at a central Philadelphia location (such as Broad and Arch streets) and carpool to hiking areas within a two-hour drive of the city, including the Appalachian Trail, the Delaware Water Gap, and the New Jersey Pine Barrens. Hikes range from 7 mi to 12 mi and tend to be more strenuous than those of the other clubs.

The Department of Recreation sponsors the **Wanderlust Hiking Club** (☎ 215/580–4847). Relatively easy hikes of 5–8 mi, many through Fairmount Park and Pennypack Park, begin every Saturday afternoon at 1:30. Check the "Weekend" section of the Friday Philadelphia *Inquirer* for locations each week.

Horseback Riding

Of the numerous bridle paths coursing through Philadelphia, the most popular are the trails of the Wissahickon in the northwest, Pennypack Park in the northeast, and Cobb's Creek Park in the southwest. One riding academy that has instruction, trail rides, and rentals is **Circle K Stables** (⊠ 4220 Holmesburg Ave., ☎ 215/335–9975), which charges $30 per hour for lessons, $20 per hour to rent. **Ashford Farms** (⊠ River Rd., Miquon, ☎ 610/825–9838), just over the northwestern border of the city, has trail ride fees of $25 per hour and lessons for $30–$40 per hour.

Ice-Skating

You can skate outdoors—with the Delaware River and Benjamin Franklin Bridge as a backdrop—daily from November to March at the **Blue Cross RiverRink** (⊠ Penn's Landing, Columbus Blvd. at Chestnut St., ☎ 215/925–7465). The **University of Pennsylvania Class of 1923 Ice Rink** (⊠ 3130 Walnut St., ☎ 215/898–1923) is open to the public from September to April.

Jogging

Joggers can be seen on streets all over the city, but probably no area is favored more than Kelly and West River drives, a scenic 8-mi route along the Schuylkill River (☞ Biking, *above*). Then, of course, there are the steps of the art museum itself, host to Rocky-like runners who raise their arms in salute during early morning jaunts. For information about jogging and running in the city, contact the **Northeast Road-runners of Philadelphia** (c/o Gerard Nolan, ⊠ 3904 I St., 19124, ☎ 215/535–7335).

Fairmount Park (☎ 215/685–0000)—especially along the river drives and Wissahickon Creek—is a natural for joggers and runners. Forbidden Drive along the Wissahickon offers more than 5 mi of soft-surface trail along a picturesque creek in a secluded valley. Only runners, walkers, bikers, and horses can use the trail—no motor vehicles are allowed.

Pennypack Park (⊠ Pine Rd. and Bloomfield Ave., ☎ 215/214–2524 or 215/685–0000), in the northeast section of the city, has an 8-mi macadam trail along Pennypack Creek. Those interested in the ultimate in running—through wide-open spaces on bike trails, horse trails, and grassy hills and dales—have to head outside Philadelphia to **Valley Forge National Park** (☞ Valley Forge *in* Chapter 8).

From dawn to dusk the south walkway of the **Benjamin Franklin Bridge** provides a tough but rewarding 3½-mi round-trip run with a terrific view of the Delaware River waterfront.

Tennis

Fairmount Park has more than 100 free public courts, but many players must bring their own nets. Courts are first-come, first-served. Call the **Department of Recreation** (☎ 215/686–1776) for information.

Among the main courts are **Chamounix Tennis Courts** (⊠ Chamounix Dr., off Belmont Mansion Dr., West Fairmount Park). The **West Park Tennis Courts** (⊠ George's Hill, near 52nd and Parkside) are adjacent to the Mann Center, West Fairmount Park.

Spectator Sports

Whether their teams win or lose, Philadelphians remain avid sports fans who support both professional and collegiate teams. The major-league sports teams play their home games in Veterans Stadium, the impressive First Union Center, or the newly named First Union Spectrum. These venues are all located around Broad Street and Pattison Avenue, near I–95, at the southern edge of the city. The Broad Street subway stops nearby at Pattison Avenue; Bus C also runs down Broad Street. The Phillies and the Eagles play at Veterans Stadium (separate new stadiums are planned for the teams by 2001 or 2002); the 76ers and the

Flyers call the First Union Center home. Some collegiate games are played in these stadiums, too; others are played on the campuses of the various colleges and universities.

Tickets to professional baseball, basketball, football, and hockey games are available at Veterans Stadium or the First Union Spectrum through **TicketMaster** (☎ 215/336–2000), at ticket agencies, and by mail and phone from the respective teams. You should plan to buy tickets as early as possible to avoid disappointment.

Baseball
The **Philadelphia Phillies** play from April to October at Veterans Stadium (✉ 3501 S. Broad St., ☎ 215/463–1000). Tickets cost $6–$20.

Basketball
The **Philadelphia 76ers** play at the First Union Center (✉ Broad St. at I–95, ☎ 215/339–7676) from November to April. Tickets are $14–$65.

Collegiate Big Five basketball (✉ Big Five Office; Hutchinson Gym, 220 S. 32nd St., ☎ 215/898–4747) features teams from LaSalle, St. Joseph's, Temple, the University of Pennsylvania, and Villanova. The season runs from December to March.

Bicycling
One of the world's top four bicycling events, the **First Union U.S. Pro Cycling Championship** (☎ 215/973–7425) is held here each June. The 156-mi race starts and finishes at Benjamin Franklin Parkway, with 10 loops including the infamous Manayunk Wall.

Boxing
The **Blue Horizon** (✉ 1314 N. Broad St., ☎ 215/763–0500) is the city's legendary fight club. It has more than a thousand seats, but every one is close to the action.

Football
The **Philadelphia Eagles** can be seen in action at Veterans Stadium (✉ 3501 S. Broad St., ☎ 215/463–5500) from September to January. Many seats go to season ticket holders; individual tickets are $40.

Hockey
The **Philadelphia Flyers** of the NHL hit the ice at First Union Center (✉ Broad St. at I–95., ☎ 215/755–9700) from October to April. Tickets are $34–$75.

The energetic **Philadelphia Phantoms,** the city's minor-league hockey team, are the Flyers' AHL affiliate. You can see them at the First Union Spectrum (✉ Broad St. and Pattison Ave., ☎ 215/465–4522) from October to May. Seats cost a reasonable $12–$16.

Horse Racing
Thoroughbred racing takes place at **Philadelphia Park** (✉ Street Rd., Bensalem, ☎ 215/639–9000). Post time is usually at 12:35 PM in the winter, 1:05 PM in the summer, Saturday–Tuesday year-round. At **Garden State Park** (✉ Rte. 70, Cherry Hill, NJ, ☎ 609/488–8400) the post time is 7:30 PM Friday and Saturday. Thoroughbred racing runs from March through May, harness racing from August through December. For offtrack betting, the **Turf Club Center City** (✉ 1635 Market St., ☎ 215/246–1556) is open daily from 11:30 through the last race, usually about midnight.

Lacrosse
The **Philadelphia Wings,** an indoor lacrosse team, have won several major indoor Lacrosse League championships in recent years. The team plays at the First Union Center (✉ Broad St. at I–95, ☎ 215/389–

9464); the season runs from January through March. Tickets cost $13–$25.

Rowing

The elegant boathouses, the regattas, the placid Schuylkill River, and a climate that allows an average of 360 rowing days a year all make Philadelphia the rowing capital of the world. From February to October you can watch single and team races out on the river, usually from 5 AM to dusk. Dozens of major meets are held here, including the largest rowing event in the country, the **Dad Vail Regatta** (☎ 215/248–2600). This May event includes up to 500 sculls from more than 100 colleges. Free shuttle buses for spectators provide transportation from remote parking areas. The May **Stotesbury Cup Regatta** (☎ 215/332–8531) includes more than 2,500 students from 110 schools. More than a thousand individual and club member rowers compete in the **Independence Day Regatta** (☎ 215/332–8531), held around July 4.

Soccer

Philadelphia Kixx, the city's first national professional soccer team, continues to draw crowds of exuberant fans at the First Union Spectrum (⊠ Broad St. and Pattison Ave., ☎ 888/888–5499). You can catch the team in action from October through April; tickets are $10–$20.

Tennis

The **Advanta Tennis Championships** take place at Villanova University (☎ 610/828–5777 or 888/367–6789) in suburban Villanova, usually in November. More than 60 of the world's top women pros compete in this final tune-up before the season-ending Chase Championships in New York.

Track and Field

The **Penn Relays** (☎ 215/898–6145), the world's largest and oldest amateur track meet, held the last week of April at the University of Pennsylvania's Franklin Field, stars world-class performers in track and field. The **Philadelphia Distance Run** (☎ 610/293–0786), the nation's top half-marathon, takes place in September. The **Philadelphia Marathon** (☎ 215/685–0054) runs through Center City and along the Schuylkill River and is held the Sunday before Thanksgiving. The **Broad Street Run** (☎ 215/563–6184), a 10-miler down Broad Street, is a May event.

7 SHOPPING

Philadelphia's shopping scene is much like the city itself: a harmonious combination of the old and the new. Whether you're picking up a souvenir at the Bourse after seeing the historic sights surrounding Independence Mall, or browsing in the very modern Shops at Liberty Place, there's something to suit all tastes. The choice is yours: check out the latest art trends at a chic Old City gallery, or hunt for fine cheese and olive oil in the Italian Market.

FOR CONSUMERS WITH CONSUMING PASSIONS, Philadelphia holds a vast array of goodies. Diamond baubles, bangles, and beads from Bailey, Banks, and Biddle? A photojournalist vest from Banana Republic? High-style Italian shoes from Bottino? A $500 reproduction of the inkwell used in the signing of the Declaration of Independence? Or for that matter, a $1 mini–Liberty Bell? For things homey or haute, Philadelphia can be a great shopping town.

Updated by
Janis
Pomerantz

The city has an upscale shopping district centered on 17th and Walnut streets; Jewelers' Row and Antiques Row; the first downtown indoor shopping mall in the United States; and an outdoor food market that covers five city blocks. Bargains are available, too—from discount stores, street vendors, and factory outlets (for the lowdown on Philly thrift stores, check out the book *The Thrift Shop Maniac's Guided Tours,* by Nancy Berman).

Local stores have sales throughout the year. If you're looking for a particular item, check the daily newspapers. Most stores accept traveler's checks and Visa, MasterCard, and American Express; Diners Club and Discover are less widely accepted. Policies on personal checks vary. Pennsylvania has a 6% sales tax, and the city adds another 1%. These taxes do not apply to clothing, medicine, and food bought in stores. For shopping hours, *see* Business Hours *in* Smart Travel Tips A to Z.

Blitz Tours

Philadelphia makes the old new again with its plethora of antiques and art and crafts stores in both the old and newer parts of the city. Get ready to move around by foot or by bus, and save enough strength to lug all your packages home from these themed shopping itineraries. For further information about these stores, *see* the individual listings.

Antiques

Begin your shopping in the generally expensive shops on Pine Street between 9th and 12th streets, long known as Antiques Row. Start at 9th Street and don't miss great stores such as **M. Finkel and Daughter** (⊠ 936 Pine St.), for furniture and needlework from the late 18th and early 19th century, and **G. B. Schaffer Antiques** (⊠ 1014 Pine St.), for stained glass, silver, and a large selection of paintings and prints. Then head toward the heart of Center City and a general shopping area by walking four blocks north to Chestnut Street. Continue west to **Freeman Fine Arts** (⊠ 1808 Chestnut St.), an auction house one block away from the upscale Shops at Liberty Place, to hunt for that one-of-a-kind, hard-to-find piece. Stop by on Monday or Tuesday to browse; return to bid at noon on Wednesday. You'll find plenty of places to eat in this area. Walk a block south on 19th Street to Rittenhouse Square and stroll through the park for a taste of the good life in the city. A number of antiques shops can be found around this elegant area, known as Rittenhouse Row. Visit **Metro Antiques** (⊠ 257 S. 20th St.), between Locust and Spruce streets, for sterling silver, period jewelry, and decorative collectibles. Another shop here is **Niederkorn Silver** (⊠ 2005 Locust St.), which specializes in decorative items such as antique silver picture frames.

Art and Crafts Galleries

Philadelphia is a great place to shop for art and crafts, particularly in the heart of Center City and in Old City. Begin downtown, amid the major shopping streets such as Chestnut and Walnut. Between 16th and 18th streets you'll find some wonderful galleries for contemporary art, such as the paintings at **Schmidt/Dean Gallery** (⊠ 1636 Walnut St.) and prints at **Works on Paper** (⊠ 1611 Walnut St.). You can find contemporary art in trendy Old City as well, by venturing down Chestnut Street by foot or bus to Third Street. On First Fridays (☞ Art and Crafts Galleries *in* Specialty Stores, *below*), the galleries here are open for browsing and refreshments. The area is fun for shopping at any time, however, and has plenty of places to eat. Stop by **Paul Cava Fine Art** (⊠ 54 N. 3rd St.), just north of Market Street, for vintage and contemporary photography. Head over to **The Works** (⊠ 303 Cherry St.) for a great selection of contemporary prints and to the **Snyderman Gallery,** at the same address, for handmade furniture and glass pieces.

Shopping Districts and Malls

Pine Street from 9th Street to 12th Street has long been Philadelphia's **Antiques Row.** The three-block area has dozens of antiques stores and curio shops, many specializing in expensive period furniture and Colonial heirlooms.

Across the street from the Liberty Bell is the **Bourse** (⊠ 21 S. 5th St., between Market and Chestnut Sts., ☎ 215/625–0300), an elegantly restored 1895 commodities exchange building. The six-story skylighted atrium contains a few fun shops catering to tourists, such as Best of Philadelphia, as well as a festive international food court.

The **Chestnut Street Transitway,** which extends from 8th to 18th streets, is somewhat seedy after dark but buzzes with urban vitality during the day. It has stores that sell rare and used books, custom tailors, sporting goods stores, pinball arcades, and discount drugstores.

What attraction could there be in the cultural wasteland of northeast Philadelphia that rivals the Liberty Bell and the zoo in popularity? **Franklin Mills Mall** (⊠ off I–95 at Exit 24, Rte. 63, Woodhaven Rd., ☎ 215/632–1500), with 1.7 million square ft, 200 stores, and two food courts, could be nicknamed the Disneyland of bargain shopping. Discount outlet stores include Ann Taylor, Saks Fifth Avenue Clearinghouse, and Last Call from Neiman Marcus. The mall, about 20 mi from downtown, is nearly a mile in length, and the parking lot holds almost 9,000 cars. You will get lost. For a break, you can visit one of the 14 theaters in the GCC Franklin Mills multiplex (☎ 215/281–2750) here.

A block north of Chestnut Street is Philadelphia's landmark effort at urban-renewal-cum-shopping, the **Gallery at Market East** (⊠ Market St. between 8th and 11th Sts., ☎ 215/925–7162), America's first enclosed downtown shopping mall. The four-level glass-roof structure near the Pennsylvania Convention Center contains 150 mid-price retailers. It includes 40 food outlets and two department stores—JCPenney (☎ 215/238–9100) and Strawbridge's (☎ 215/629–6000), which has somewhat higher-quality merchandise.

If you want local color, nothing compares with South Philadelphia's **Italian Market.** On both sides of 9th Street from Christian Street to Washington Street and spilling out onto the surrounding blocks, hundreds of outdoor stalls and indoor stores sell such food items as spices, cheeses, pastas, fruits, vegetables, and freshly slaughtered poultry and beef, not to mention household items, clothing, shoes, and other goods. It's crowded and filled with the aromas of everything from fresh garlic to imported salami. The vendors can be less than hospitable, but the food is fresh and the prices are reasonable. Food shops include the Spice Corner, DiBruno Brothers House of Cheese, Claudio's, and Talluto's Authentic Italian Foods. Fante's is well-known for cookware. The market's hours are Tuesday–Saturday 9–5:30; some vendors open earlier, and others close around 3:30. Some shops are open Sunday from 9:30 to 12:30.

Jewelers' Row, centered on Sansom Street between 7th and 8th streets, is one of the world's oldest and largest markets of precious stones: more than 350 retailers, wholesalers, and craftspeople operate here. The 700 block of Sansom Street is a brick-paved enclave occupied almost exclusively by jewelers.

Lord & Taylor (✉ between 13th, Juniper, Market, and Chestnut Sts., ☎ 215/241–9000) displays the chain's classic merchandise in the spacious former John Wanamaker department store, a Philadelphia landmark. Its focal point is the nine-story grand court with its 30,000-pipe organ—the largest ever built—and a 2,500-pound statue of an eagle, both remnants of the 1904 Louisiana Purchase Exposition in St. Louis. The new owners have continued the famous Christmas sound-and-light show and the organ performances.

For browsing, a visit to the historic and newly hip **Manayunk** neighborhood (☎ 215/482–9565) is worth the 7-mi trip from Center City. Clothes and crafts are the highlights; for antiques, art galleries, clothing, and gifts and souvenirs, *see* the listings in Specialty Stores, *below*. Many stores are on Main Street from number 4400 to 3900. For background on this area, *see* Manayunk *in* Chapter 2; for some of the area's good dining options, *see* Chapter 3.

Market Place East (✉ Market St. between 7th and 8th Sts., ☎ 215/592–8905), across from the Gallery, is in a historic building saved from the wrecker's ball at the 11th hour. The century-old former Lit Brothers department store went through a $75 million renovation to emerge as an office building with a five-level atrium full of moderately priced stores and restaurants.

Serious shoppers will want to make a trip to **The Plaza & The Court at King of Prussia** (✉ Rte. 202 at the Schuylkill Expressway, ☎ 610/265–5727 for the Plaza, 610/337–1210 for the Court; ☞ Valley Forge *in* Chapter 8), the largest retail shopping complex on the East Coast. The two malls are an elegant place to stroll and shop; the 365 specialty shops and eight department stores include Nordstrom, Neiman Marcus, Lord & Taylor, and Bloomingdale's. The mall is about 20 mi from downtown; SEPTA Bus 124 or 125 runs here from 17th Street and John F. Kennedy Boulevard.

At 16th and Chestnut streets you'll find the upscale **Shops at Liberty Place** (✉ 1625 Chestnut St., ☎ 215/851–9055), the city's newest shopping complex, with popular stores including Benetton, Barami, the Coach Store, Speedo Authentic Fitness, the Body Shop, and Country Road Australia. More than 60 stores and restaurants are arranged in two circular levels within a strikingly handsome 90-ft glass-roof atrium.

The elegant **Shops at the Bellevue** (✉ Broad and Walnut St.) include Polo/Ralph Lauren, with the designer's classic styles; the chic clothes of Nicole Miller; Tiffany & Co.; Cigars by Cubans; and a Williams-Sonoma cookware store. Also in the handsome historic building are several restaurants.

If you've finally decided on that new tattoo or need supplies for your next witches' sabbath, head to **South Street,** just south of Society Hill. One of the city's main entertainment strips is also one of its major shopping areas, with most shops open in the evening. From Front Street near the Delaware River to 9th Street you'll find more than 300 unusual stores—high-fashion clothing, New Age books and health food, avant-garde art galleries—and 100 restaurants. You'll find a few of the national chains, but 95% of the stores are individually owned, selling things you won't find in the mall back home.

Most shop-till-you-droppers first head for the main shopping area of **Walnut Street,** between Broad Street and Rittenhouse Square, and the intersecting streets just north and south. These blocks are filled with boutiques, art galleries, jewelers, fine clothing stores, and many other unusual shops. At Broad and Walnut streets are the upscale Shops at the Bellevue (☞ *above*). On 18th Street in the block north of Rittenhouse Square, you'll find entrepreneurs both indoors and out: the aesthetically pleasing, earthy home and clothing store Anthropologie, a sidewalk vendor selling handmade Peruvian shawls, street artist Joe Barker painting watercolors of Philadelphia cityscapes, and a shop—Scoop De Ville—that sells more than 40 flavors of frozen yogurt.

Specialty Stores

Antiques
Many dealers in higher-priced wares cluster on Antiques Row—Pine Street between 9th and 12th streets. Some hip, less expensive shops, carrying newer treasures such as '50s and '60s designs, are clustered off South Street, on Bainbridge Street between 4th and 9th streets. Call to check hours, as dealers may open late or be closed a few days a week.

Antique Marketplace. The 100 antiques and collectibles dealers with stalls in this brick building display vintage clothes, toys, glassware, furniture, and more. ⊠ *3797 Main St., Manayunk,* ☎ *215/482–4499.*

Architectural Antiques Exchange. Victorian embellishments from saloons and apothecary shops, stained and beveled glass, gargoyles, and advertising memorabilia entice the shoppers here. ⊠ *715 N. 2nd St.,* ☎ *215/922–3669.*

Calderwood Gallery. Art nouveau and art deco furniture, glass, bronzes, and rugs tempt discerning collectors at this fine establishment. ⊠ *1427 Walnut St.,* ☎ *215/568–7475.*

Freeman Fine Arts. This is not only the city's most prominent auction house but also America's oldest (founded in 1805). Examine furniture, china, prints, and paintings on Monday and Tuesday; bid for them on Wednesday. Freeman's auctioned one of the original flyers on which the Declaration of Independence was printed and posted throughout the city. It sold for $404,000 in 1968. ⊠ *1808 Chestnut St.,* ☎ *215/563–9275.*

G. B. Schaffer Antiques. Fine 18th-, 19th-, and early 20th-century American furnishings, stained glass, silver, porcelain, paintings, and prints are the specialties here. ⊠ *1014 Pine St.,* ☎ *215/923–2263.*

Gargoyles. You can wander through 11,000 square ft of displays of antiques and reproduction decorative and architectural pieces—archways, mantels, entranceways, carousel horses, stained-glass windows, and ornate mirrors. ⊠ *512 S. 3rd St.,* ☎ *215/629–1700.*

M. Finkel and Daughter. Late 18th- and early 19th-century American furniture, quilts, needlework, samplers, and folk art make this an important outpost for Americana buffs. ⊠ *936 Pine St.,* ☎ *215/627–7797.*

Metro Antiques. The store displays a wide variety of objects: sterling silver pieces, art deco jewelry, bar glassware, and African masks and statues. ⊠ *257 S. 20th St.,* ☎ *215/545–3555.*

Niederkorn Silver. A fine selection of silver items, including jewelry, pieces for the desk and dresser, and a nice selection of baby silver, make this a worthwhile stop. ⊠ *2005 Locust St.,* ☎ *215/567–2606.*

Olde City Antiques & Collectibles. Four floors carry consignments of antique and reproduction furniture, rugs, paintings, and glassware. ⊠ *33 S. 2nd St.,* ☎ *215/413–1944.*

South Street Antiques Market. An indoor center about half a block below South Street holds the stalls of 25 dealers who sell everything from furniture, paintings, and stained glass to jewelry and '50s collectibles. It's closed Monday and Tuesday. ⊠ *615 S. 6th St.,* ☎ *215/592–0256.*

Vintage Instruments. Antique strings and woodwinds are displayed; the store specializes in violins and also carries American fretted instruments—banjos, guitars, and mandolins. ⊠ *1529 Pine St.,* ☎ *215/545–1100.*

W. Graham Arader. This is the flagship store of a highly respected chain that stocks the world's largest selection of 16th- to 19th-century prints and maps, specializing in botanicals, birds, and the American West. ⊠ *1308 Walnut St.,* ☎ *215/735–8811.*

Art and Crafts Galleries

For current shows in Philadelphia's numerous galleries, see the listings in *Philadelphia* magazine or the Weekend section of the Friday *Philadelphia Inquirer.* Many galleries are near Rittenhouse Square; others are on South Street or scattered about downtown. In recent years Old City has become the hottest gallery area. One evening a month, on what is called First Friday, you can wander 2nd and 3rd streets above Market Street going from gallery to gallery. It's like a refined block party, with refreshments and performance artists.

American Pie Contemporary Crafts and Judaica. Artists from around the country produce the handcrafted jewelry, blown glass, and Judaica items such as menorahs and seder plates shown here. ⊠ *127 S. 18th St.,* ☎ *215/751–2752;* ⊠ *327 South St.,* ☎ *215/922–2226;* ⊠ *4303 Main St., Manayunk,* ☎ *215/487–0226.*

Clay Studio. A nonprofit organization runs the gallery and conducts classes as well as an outreach program to inner city schools. There are clay works and pottery by well-known artists; the gallery has juried shows and group exhibits. ⊠ *139 N. 2nd St.,* ☎ *215/925–3453.*

David David Gallery. American and European paintings, drawings, and watercolors from the 16th to the 20th centuries are on display. ⊠ *260 S. 18th St.,* ☎ *215/735–2922.*

Fabric Workshop and Museum. A nonprofit arts organization runs this center and store dedicated to creating new work in fabric and other materials, working with emerging and nationally and internationally recognized artists. ⊠ *1315 Cherry St.,* ☎ *215/568–1111.*

Fleisher Ollman Gallery. You'll find fine works by 20th-century self-taught American artists here. ⊠ *211 S. 17th St.,* ☎ *215/545–7562.*

Helen Drutt. This gallery presents contemporary American and European artists, with a focus on ceramics and jewelry. ⊠ *1721 Walnut St.,* ☎ *215/735–1625.*

I. Brewster. The specialty here is contemporary paintings and prints by such artists as Louis Icart, Erté, Andy Warhol, and Red Grooms. ⊠ *1628 Walnut St.,* ☎ *215/731–9200.*

Gilbert Luber Gallery. Japanese antique and contemporary prints and Thai and Balinese artifacts are offered. ⊠ *1220 Walnut St.,* ☎ *215/732–2996.*

Gross McCleaf Gallery. This is a good place to see works by both prominent and emerging artists, with an emphasis on Philadelphia painters. ⊠ *127 S. 16th St.,* ☎ *215/665–8138.*

Locks Gallery. Shows present works by an impressive assortment of contemporary regional, national, and international painters, sculptors, and mixed-media artists. ⊠ *600 Washington Sq. S,* ☎ *215/629–1000.*

Muse Gallery. Established in 1978 by the Muse Foundation for the Visual Arts, Muse Gallery is a women's cooperative in Old City committed to increasing the visibility of women's artwork and presenting experimental work in a variety of media. ⊠ *60 N. 2nd St.,* ☎ *215/627–5310.*

Newman Galleries. This gallery carries a range of works from 19th-century paintings to contemporary lithographs and sculpture. It's strong on 20th-century painters from the Bucks County area. ✉ *1625 Walnut St.,* ☎ *215/563–1779.*

Nexus Foundation for Today's Art. A group of artists started this non-profit organization in 1975. The emphasis is on experimental art as well as new directions in traditional media. ✉ *137 N. 2nd St.,* ☎ *215/629–1103.*

Paul Cava Fine Art. Vintage and contemporary photography and contemporary art distinguish this Old City gallery. ✉ *54 N. 3rd St.,* ☎ *215/922–2126.*

Schmidt/Dean Gallery. Contemporary paintings, sculpture, prints, and photographs are shown; the specialty is work by Philadelphia artists. ✉ *1636 Walnut St.,* ☎ *215/546–7212;* ✉ *1721 Spruce St.,* ☎ *215/546–9577.*

School Gallery of the Pennsylvania Academy of the Fine Arts. Stop here to see rotating exhibits of works by faculty, alumni, and students in the school's attractively renovated building near the Pennsylvania Convention Center. ✉ *1301 Cherry St.,* ☎ *215/972–7600.*

Schwarz Gallery. Eighteenth- to 20th-century American and European paintings are the focus, with an emphasis on Philadelphia artists of the past. ✉ *1806 Chestnut St.,* ☎ *215/563–4887.*

Snyderman Gallery. One-of-a-kind handmade furniture pieces and glass objects are displayed at this Old City gallery. ✉ *303 Cherry St.,* ☎ *215/238–9576.*

University of the Arts' Rosenwald-Wolf Gallery. The school's gallery presents works by faculty and students, and local, national, and international artists. ✉ *333 S. Broad St.,* ☎ *215/875–1116.*

The Works. This Old City gallery showcases contemporary American crafts in wood, fiber, ceramics, and metals. ✉ *303 Cherry St.,* ☎ *215/922–7775.*

Works on Paper. The contemporary prints here have won the gallery a reputation as one of the city's best. ✉ *1611 Walnut St.,* ☎ *215/988–9999.*

Bookstores

AIA Bookstore. Run by the Philadelphia chapter of the American Institute of Architects (AIA), this shop specializes in books on architectural theory, building construction, interior design, and furnishings. It also sells architectural drawings and watercolors, blueprint posters, international magazines, home furnishings, and unusual gifts. ✉ *117 S. 17th St.,* ☎ *215/569–3188.*

Barnes & Noble. This beautiful new location of the chain stocks a very good selection of regional books and maps in its extensive travel section; the children's section is also quite large. Author readings and children's programs are regular features, and the store has a café. ✉ *1805 Walnut St.,* ☎ *215/665–0716.*

Borders. Some locals find this the friendliest bookstore in Philadelphia. You can sit on a couch, listen to live guitar music, and read for hours. The 110,000 titles and more than half million books are spread over three levels. There's a second-floor espresso bar, and Saturday-morning children's programs are held at 11:30. ✉ *1727 Walnut St.,* ☎ *215/568–7400.*

Giovanni's Room. Focusing on books dealing with feminist, gay, and lesbian topics, this well-regarded store stocks an extensive inventory and sponsors many author appearances. ✉ *345 S. 12th St.,* ☎ *215/923–2960.*

How-to-Do-It Bookshop. Want to build a computer, grow rutabagas, groom your poodle? If there's a book telling you how to do something, chances are this unique place (with more than 40,000 titles) will have it. ⊠ *1608 Sansom St.,* ☎ *215/563–1516.*

Joseph Fox. This small bookstore specializes in art, architecture, and design. ⊠ *1724 Sansom St.,* ☎ *215/563–4184.*

Rittenhouse Bookstore. Known as the best medical bookstore in Philadelphia, this establishment may be able to get the book you want overnight if you can't find it in stock. ⊠ *1706 Rittenhouse Sq.,* ☎ *215/ 545–6072.*

Robin's Bookstore. Not the biggest bookstore in town and maybe not the best, but it's definitely the sentimental favorite of devotees of literature, poetry, and minority studies. Owner Larry Robin has been promoting literature and fighting literary censorship for more than 30 years. Book fans are drawn to its frequent poetry readings and book signings by local authors. ⊠ *108 S. 13th St.,* ☎ *215/735–9600.*

Tower Books. Famous for its magazine selection, the biggest in the city, this is a great place to browse on a Saturday night; so is its companion music store, Tower Records (☞ *below*), farther up South Street. You'll be mesmerized by the huge travel section. ⊠ *425 South St.,* ☎ *215/925–9909.*

University of Pennsylvania Barnes and Noble Bookstore. With more than 60,000 popular and scholarly titles, this bookstore is especially strong in business, computers, psychology, and sociology. The Middle East section may be the only place in town to buy a book on Kurdish grammar. ⊠ *3729 Locust Walk,* ☎ *215/898–7595.*

Whodunit. The city's only store specializing in mysteries, spy stories, and adventure books also stocks out-of-print mysteries. Owner Art Bourgeau has published six mysteries and a nonfiction book on mystery writing. ⊠ *1931 Chestnut St.,* ☎ *215/567–1478.*

RARE AND USED BOOKS

Bauman Rare Books. An antiquarian bookstore with volumes dating as far back as the 15th century, this is a treasure trove for collectors in the fields of law, science, literature, travel, and exploration. Bauman's also has a print and map collection. ⊠ *1215 Locust St.,* ☎ *215/ 546–6466.*

Book Trader. You'll find great browsing on the two floors of this eclectic used-book store, though prices are on the high side. It's open daily 10 AM–midnight. ⊠ *501 South St.,* ☎ *215/925–0219.*

Hibberd's. Rare and used books, remainders, and a large selection of unusual art books are the sizable draws for book aficionados. ⊠ *1306 Walnut St.,* ☎ *215/546–8811.*

William H. Allen Bookseller. This store carries one of the city's best collections of used and scholarly books; specialties are history, literature, and philosophy. Note the extensive collection of books on ancient Greece and Rome, in English and the original Greek or Latin. ⊠ *2031 Walnut St.,* ☎ *215/563–3398.*

Cameras and Photographic Equipment

Kosmin's Camera Exchange. Come here for film, motion picture equipment, slide projectors, screens, darkroom supplies, and a half dozen brands of cameras. ⊠ *927 Arch St.,* ☎ *215/627–8231.*

Mid-City Camera. This major stock house carries a large line of darkroom equipment and all major camera brands in all formats. It also buys and sells used cameras and has a service department and rentals. ⊠ *1316 Walnut St.,* ☎ *215/735–2522.*

Roth Camera Repairs. If you have camera trouble, here's the place to go. The store prides itself on extra-quick service. ⊠ *1015 Chestnut St., Jefferson Bldg. lobby, Room 102,* ☎ *215/922–2498.*

Clothing

CHILDREN'S CLOTHING

Born Yesterday. The selection of clothing and toys for tots includes handmade goods, imported fashions, and styles you won't find elsewhere. ⊠ *1901 Walnut St.,* ☎ *215/568–6556.*

Children's Boutique. This store carries a look between conservative and classic in infant to preteen clothes. You can buy complete wardrobes, specialty gifts, and handmade items. ⊠ *1717 Walnut St.,* ☎ *215/563–3881.*

Kamikaze Kids. Unique designer fashions for infants to preteens are showcased in a child-friendly atmosphere, with cloud-painted walls and play areas). ⊠ *527 S. 4th St.,* ☎ *215/574–9800.*

MEN'S AND WOMEN'S

Banana Republic. This store is part of the chain that helped make famous—and still sells—the photojournalist vest (with a plethora of pockets) and the Kenya convertible pants (with hidden zippers that convert them into shorts). ⊠ *1716 Walnut St.,* ☎ *215/735–2247.*

Burberrys Ltd. Named after Thomas Burberry, who designed the trench coat in the mid-1850s, this British-owned establishment stocks British raincoats, overcoats, sport coats, and cashmere sweaters. Quality is high, and so are prices. ⊠ *1705 Walnut St.,* ☎ *215/557–7400.*

Hats in the Belfry. Designer hats, practical hats, formal hats, silly hats, Panama hats, baseball caps, and more add the finishing touch to your outfit. ⊠ *245 South St.,* ☎ *215/922–6770.*

Neo Deco. Shop here for European-style contemporary clothing and accessories: sportswear, shoes, and jewelry. ⊠ *414 South St.,* ☎ *215/928–0627;* ⊠ *4409 Main St., Manayunk,* ☎ *215/487–7757.*

Nicole Miller. This successful designer for men and women even produced a T-shirt for a city tourist campaign. The men's line includes golf apparel and a notable selection of ties. The women's section has sportswear and evening wear, in addition to loads of the designer's signature scarves and handbags. ⊠ *Shops at the Bellevue, Broad and Walnut Sts.,* ☎ *215/546–5007;* ⊠ *4249 Main St., Manayunk,* ☎ *215/930–0307.*

Polo/Ralph Lauren. The city's entry in the Lauren retail empire of classically styled apparel carries the designer's women's, men's, boys', and home collections. ⊠ *Shops at the Bellevue, Broad and Walnut Sts.,* ☎ *215/985–2800.*

Urban Outfitters. What started out as a storefront selling used jeans to students in West Philadelphia is now a trend-setting chain on campuses across the country. The new Center City location sells hip clothing, books, unusual toys, and apartment accessories. ⊠ *1627 Walnut St.,* ☎ *215/569–3131.*

Zipperhead. As you enter this place, chances are you'll have to step around a teenager and his parents arguing about whether to go in. For almost 20 years this has been the alternative clothing landmark for the spiked-hair-and-nose-ring set. Offerings here include motorcycle jackets, rock band T-shirts, and hard-to-find body jewelry for those hard-to-pierce places. ⊠ *407 South St.,* ☎ *215/928–1123.*

MEN'S CLOTHING

Allure. Classic and stylish Italian clothing and furnishings draw a cosmopolitan crowd. Brioni, Pal Zileri, Verri, Donna Karan, and Canali are some of the designers here. ⊠ *4358-B Main St., Manayunk,* ☎ *215/482–5299.*

Boyd's. The largest single-store men's clothier in the country has nine shops that present the traditional English look, avant-garde Italian imports, and dozens of other styles and designers. The store has shops for extra tall, large, and short men; an excellent café for lunch; valet parking; and 60 tailors on the premises. Women will find a small selection of high-quality designer clothes, too. ⊠ *1818 Chestnut St.,* ☎ *215/564–9000.*

Brooks Brothers. The oldest men's clothing store in America (founded in New York in 1818), Brooks is synonymous with Ivy League business clothing: conservative suits, button-down shirts, and striped ties. ⊠ *1513 Walnut St.,* ☎ *215/564–4100.*

Structure. This hip, stylish store has relatively decent prices for casual clothes, such as silk shirts and baggy pleated pants in bold colors. Sales can yield real bargains. ⊠ *Shops at Liberty Place, 1625 Chestnut St.,* ☎ *215/851–0835.*

Wayne Edwards. You'll find exclusive lines of classic contemporary clothing from Italy, Japan, France, and the United States. Barbera, Palzileri, and Armani are representative designers. ⊠ *1521 Walnut St.,* ☎ *215/563–6801.*

WOMEN'S CLOTHING

Asta De Blue. A boutique in a brownstone off Rittenhouse Square is a hot place for upbeat urban-contemporary clothing, jewelry, accessories, and gifts. Key collections include Zelda, Harari, Lilith, and Tse. The owners say they have the largest collection of Arche footwear outside Manhattan. ⊠ *265 S. 20th St.,* ☎ *215/732–0550.*

Knit Wit. High-fashion clothes and accessories from sportswear to cocktail dresses are the focus here. Alberta Ferretti, Anna Molinari, and Vestimenta are among the designers. ⊠ *1721 Walnut St.,* ☎ *215/564–4760.*

Ma Jolie. Spacious and lovely, this boutique is run by three sisters, native Philadelphians. It specializes in clothing that is comfortable and flattering to all sizes, including suits, evening dresses, and sweaters. Children's clothes and toys are also sold; the mezzanine has a café and gift shop. The new Walnut Street location is near the Penn campus in West Philadelphia. ⊠ *4340 Main St., Manayunk,* ☎ *215/483–8850;* ⊠ *3661 Walnut St.,* ☎ *215/222–2272.*

Plage Tahiti. A leading showcase for promising young high-fashion designers carries a wide selection of chic and charming swimwear. ⊠ *128 S. 17th St.,* ☎ *215/569–9139.*

Toby Lerner. Expensive high-fashion apparel with strong classic lines, plus a full line of shoes, is the store's strength. Look for designs by Narciso Rodriguez, Richard Tyler, and Missoni. ⊠ *117 S. 17th St.,* ☎ *215/568–5760.*

Discount Shopping

Franklin Mills Mall (☞ Shopping Districts and Malls, *above*) is the big draw, but a number of other spots are downtown.

Cambridge Clothing Factory Outlet. This is a manufacturers' outlet for men, with 10 national brands starting at 40% off retail. Out-of-towners can get immediate alterations. ⊠ *1520 Sansom St., 2nd floor,* ☎ *215/568–8248.*

Daffy's. Housed in an attractive Egyptian deco–style building, Daffy's carries higher-end American and European designs for men, women, and children at 40%–75% off list (sometimes even more with special markdowns). The fourth floor holds women's designer suits and evening wear from designers such as Moschino, Jean-Paul Gaultier, and Les Copines. ⊠ *1700 Chestnut St.,* ☎ *215/963–9996.*

Thos. David Factory Store. Upstairs they make it; downstairs they sell it. High-quality men's and women's business clothing and sportswear are sold at almost wholesale prices. ⊠ *401 Race St.,* ☎ *215/922–4659.*

Food

The Italian Market (☞ Shopping Districts and Malls, *above*) is a classic Philly experience and the Reading Terminal Market (☞ Diners and

Philly Food *in* Chapter 3) is a city gem, but you'll find other good food options, too.

Chef's Market. Philly's ultimate gourmet supermarket prepares 60–70 entrées every day, stocks several hundred kinds of cheeses, sells goods from its own bakery, and is a fish market and meat market as well. Packaged items include 150 varieties of imported jams, 40 olive oils, and 60 flavored vinegars. ⊠ *231 South St.,* ☎ *215/925–8360.*

Caviar Assouline. Looking for that very special food gift? This stylish store carries imported and American caviar, smoked seafood, truffles, foie gras, Valrhona chocolate, and more. If you can't decide, pick up a catalog and order by mail from home. ⊠ *505 Vine St.,* ☎ *215/627–3517.*

Fante's. One of the oldest gourmet supply stores in the country has the largest selection of coffeemakers and cooking equipment in the United States. Family owned since 1906, Fante's is famous for oddball kitchen gadgets such as truffle shavers and pineapple peelers; restaurants and bakeries all over the country and overseas order from the store. It's in the Italian Market, so you can combine a visit here with other food shopping. ⊠ *1006 S. 9th St.,* ☎ *215/922–5557.*

Godiva Chocolatier. At $3 for a single piece of hand-dipped fruit to $32 for a one-pound box in the classic gold packaging, it doesn't get any sweeter than this. ⊠ *Shops at Liberty Place, 1625 Chestnut St.,* ☎ *215/ 963–0810.*

Kitchen Kapers. This is a good source for fine cookware, French copper, cutlery, coffees, and teas. ⊠ *213 S. 17th St.,* ☎ *215/546–8059.*

Gifts and Souvenirs

Best of Philadelphia. Here's a fun place for cheap Philly souvenirs: on display are more than 100 different items, including earrings, flags, jigsaw puzzles, coloring books, Ben Franklin key chains, T-shirts, and, of course, Liberty Bells. ⊠ *Bourse Bldg., 21 S. 5th St.,* ☎ *215/629– 0533.*

Hand of Aries. You'll find everything for the discriminating witch— books, candles, incense, tarot cards, ritual robes, capes, and long dresses (black only). The store is closed Monday and Tuesday. ⊠ *620 S. 4th St.,* ☎ *215/923–5264.*

Holt's Tobacconist. The city's oldest (1898) and largest purveyor of tobacco, cigars, and lighters, Holt's also has the city's largest selection of writing instruments. ⊠ *1522 Walnut St.,* ☎ *215/732–8500.*

Touches. Upscale shoppers come to this attractive shop for its handmade shawls, handbags, belts, unusual jewelry, and children's gifts. ⊠ *225 S. 15th St.,* ☎ *215/546–1221.*

Warner Bros. Studio Store. For those who love Bugs, Sylvester, Daffy, and Tweety on their mugs, T-shirts, key chains, puzzles, and golf club covers, this is the place. The store's gallery of animation art has 'toon lithographs for $150 and original cells for up to $2,400. ⊠ *Shops at Liberty Place, 1625 Chestnut St.,* ☎ *215/981–0680.*

Xenos Candy and Gifts. Asher chocolates and Philly souvenirs from key chains to T-shirts are stocked here, near the sites of the historic district. ⊠ *231 Chestnut St.,* ☎ *215/922–1445.*

Home Decor

Anthropologie. Filled with exotic gift items, candles, ethnic crafts, jewelry, and accessories, this new store also stocks lovely items for the bed, bath, and tabletop. You'll find comfortable cotton clothing for women, too. ⊠ *1801 Walnut St.,* ☎ *not available at press time.*

Country Floors. Decorators love the ceramic and terra-cotta handpainted tiles from the United States and all over Europe (mostly for floors and walls, but individual tiles can make great decorative art). ⊠ *1706 Locust St.,* ☎ *215/545–1040.*

Home Grown. Unique tableware, including ceramic serving pieces from around the United States and Europe, is the focus of an upscale home accessories shop that carries everything from Calvin Klein dinnerware to Mackenzie Childs pottery. ⊠ *4321 Main St., Manayunk,* ☎ *215/482–1910.*

Urban Objects. This store carries an eclectic collection of contemporary gifts, home accessories, antiques and reproductions of antiques, lamps, and pictures. Many objects are imported from Europe and Asia but are reasonably priced. ⊠ *1724 Sansom St.,* ☎ *215/557–9474.*

Jewelry

Philadelphia is an excellent town for shopping for jewelry from antique to contemporary, with good choices on Jewelers' Row (☞ Shopping Districts and Malls, *above*) and beyond.

Bailey, Banks & Biddle. This old-line store, in business since 1832, is known for diamond and gold jewelry, objets d'art, silver, and crystal. ⊠ *16th and Chestnut Sts.,* ☎ *215/564–6200.*

Harry Sable. Harry "king of the wedding bands" Sable has been selling engagement rings, diamond rings, gold jewelry, and watches for more than 50 years. ⊠ *8th and Sansom Sts.,* ☎ *215/627–4014.*

J. E. Caldwell. A local landmark since 1839, the store is adorned with antique handblown crystal chandeliers by Baccarat, making it as elegant as the jewels it sells. Along with traditional and modern jewelry, Caldwell has one of the city's largest selections of giftware and stationery. ⊠ *1339 Chestnut St.,* ☎ *215/864–7800.*

Jack Kellmer Co. Diamonds and gold jewelry are offered at below retail price. ⊠ *717 Chestnut St.,* ☎ *215/627–8350.*

Lagos–The Store. Here you'll find the largest selection of Lagos jewelry, handcrafted and designed in Philadelphia by Ann and Steven Lagos. Lagos is famous for its "golden wheat" collection of 22-karat contemporary gold jewelry, sold in the boutiques of upscale department stores; this is its only retail store. ⊠ *200 S. 17th St.,* ☎ *215/735–4630.*

Richard Kenneth. On display is jewelry from the late-Georgian, Victorian, art nouveau, art deco, and '40s-retro periods. Kenneth also specializes in repairs and appraisals. ⊠ *202 S. 17th St.,* ☎ *215/545–3355.*

Tiffany & Co. This is the local branch of the store, famous for its exquisite gems, fine crystal and china, and, of course, its signature blue gift box. ⊠ *Shops at the Bellevue, 1414 Walnut St.,* ☎ *215/735–1919.*

Luggage and Leather Goods

Robinson Luggage. The shop carries popular, moderate to expensive brands of luggage, leather, and travel accessories. The selection of briefcases and attaché cases is the largest in the Delaware Valley. ⊠ *201 S. Broad St.,* ☎ *215/735–9859.*

Music

HMV. Known for the huge selection of music in its vast 25,000-square-ft store, HMV also has helpful staff and listening booths. ⊠ *1510 Walnut St.,* ☎ *215/875–5100.*

Theodor Presser. The best selection of sheet music in Center City draws musicians from far and wide. The store specializes in classical but also carries pop and will special order anything. ⊠ *1718 Chestnut St.,* ☎ *215/568–0964.*

Tower Records. Open 9 AM to midnight 365 days a year, Tower stocks more than 250,000 CDs and tapes—the largest selection in the city. You can watch music videos on the 20 screens on three floors. Classical music lovers head to the annex across the street. ⊠ *610 South St.,* ☎ *215/574–9888.*

Perfumes

Body Shop de le Parfumier. This "scent boutique" for men and women imports new fragrances, some not yet available elsewhere in the United States. The shop also carries cosmetics, perfume bottles, discontinued scents, and accessories. ✉ *Bourse Bldg., 21 S. 5th St.,* ☎ *215/922–7660.*

Parfumerie Douglas Cosmetics. A wide selection of major brands of perfume, cosmetics, and beauty accessories are found here. ✉ *Shops at Liberty Place, 1625 Chestnut St.,* ☎ *215/569–0770.*

Shoes

Beige. You'll find a good selection of women's Italian leather shoes in sizes 4–12, priced toward the high end. ✉ *1715 Walnut St.,* ☎ *215/564–2395.*

Bottino. Men's shoes and accessories are the stars here, all handmade and imported from Italy. Some very big feet get shod here, including those of regular customers Michael Jordan and Sylvester Stallone. ✉ *121 S. 18th St.,* ☎ *215/854–0907.*

Sherman Brothers Shoes. This off-price retailer of men's shoes has name-brand merchandise and excellent service. The store carries 28 lines of shoes and stocks extra-wide and extra-narrow widths, as well as sizes up to 16. ✉ *1520 Sansom St.,* ☎ *215/561–4550.*

Strega. There's a wide range of looks for men here, including some exclusive footwear and many top Italian designers. ✉ *1521 Walnut St.,* ☎ *215/563–6801.*

Sporting Goods

City Sports. Besides sports equipment from in-line skates to bike helmets, the store carries plenty of brand-name active wear and its own line of clothing. ✉ *1608 Walnut St.,* ☎ *215/985–5860.*

Everyone's Racquet. As you might guess, this store's specialty is goods related to racket sports: tennis, racquetball, badminton, squash. Next-day racket-stringing service is available. ✉ *132 S. 17th St.,* ☎ *215/665–1221.*

The Original I. Goldberg. This army-navy-and-everything store is hip and practical, with an emphasis on sporting apparel and camping gear. Goldberg's is crammed with government-surplus, military-style clothing, jeans and work clothes, unusual footwear, and exclusive foreign imports. Rummaging here is a sport in itself. ✉ *902 Chestnut St.,* ☎ *215/925–9393.*

Rittenhouse Sports. The focus is on shoes and gear for triathlon sports—running, swimming, and cycling—but the store also stocks aerobic and workout shoes and gear. ✉ *126 S. 18th St.,* ☎ *215/569–9957.*

Wine and Liquor

Pennsylvania liquor stores (☎ 215/560–5316) are state operated. State stores (as they're known) are generally open Monday and Tuesday 11–7, Wednesday–Saturday 9–9. You may find chilled beer at delis and gourmet shops.

Wine and Spirits Shoppe. This shop carries one of the best selections of fine wines and liquors in the city. ✉ *819 Chestnut St.,* ☎ *215/560–6190.*

8 SIDE TRIPS FROM PHILADELPHIA

The Brandywine Valley

Valley Forge

I**T'S EASY TO** expand your view of the Philadelphia area by taking one or more easy day trips less than two hours from the city. Head southwest from Philadelphia, and in less than an hour you can be immersed in a whole new world. Make that worlds: First you can see the verdant hills and ancient barns of the Brandywine Valley, home to three generations of Wyeths and other artists inspired by the rural landscapes outside their windows. Then you can visit the extravagant realm of du Pont country, including Winterthur, an important repository of American decorative furnishings, over the border in Delaware. Or you can visit the Revolutionary War battlefield of Brandywine, at Chadds Ford. These attractions are favorites of Philadelphians, and area B&Bs and inns make the Brandywine appealing as an overnight or weekend trip as well as a day excursion.

Updated by
Anne
Dubuisson
Anderson

The historical park at Valley Forge adds another dimension to the revolutionary story that began in Independence Hall. Not far away, the town called King of Prussia dates to that period, but today it's primarily synonymous with shopping, thanks to two huge upscale malls just a half hour from Philadelphia and easily accessible by public transportation.

Pleasures and Pastimes

Dining

It seems that most restaurants in the Brandywine Valley serve what is called Continental-American cuisine, with creative contemporary touches at the better establishments. Most also present local specialties—fresh seafood from the Chesapeake Bay and dishes made with Kennett Square mushrooms. For price-category information *see* Dining *in* Smart Travel Tips A to Z.

Gardens

Anyone who has ever admired the simple beauty of spring's first crocus will thrill to the horticultural splendors of the greater Philadelphia area. The Brandywine area is home to some of America's most spectacular botanic sights, including the renowned Longwood Gardens. While touring the Hagley Museum and Library, as well as nearby Winterthur, take time to step outside and appreciate the gorgeous natural backgrounds designed to complement the architecture. The grounds of Rockwood, a rural Gothic manor in Wilmington, Delaware, have splendid landscaping.

Spring, of course, is the most obvious time to visit these glorious oases, but other seasons can be rewarding too: Longwood Gardens, a treat at any time of year, has one of the world's largest conservatories, and Rockwood has a similarly stunning, though smaller, Victorian cast-iron-and-glass garden room. At the Brandywine River Museum, the Brandywine Conservancy's Wildflower and Native Plant Gardens are a riot of fall colors, as are the grounds surrounding the French-inspired parterres of the Hagley Museum and Library.

Lodging

Many Brandywine Valley accommodations call themselves bed-and-breakfasts because they provide beds and serve breakfast, but they are far from the typical B&B—which is usually a room in a private home—and are more accurately characterized as inns or small hotels. For price-category information *see* Lodging *in* Smart Travel Tips A to Z.

THE BRANDYWINE VALLEY

Chances are that you may experience a strong sense of déjà vu during a journey to the Brandywine Valley. When Andrew Wyeth immortalized the special landscape of the valley—creating some of the most beloved works in 20th-century American art—he caused many people to flock to this valley and fall in love with its peaceful byways, and he made its vistas instantly recognizable. Using colors quintessentially Brandywine—the earthen brown of its hills, gray slate of its stone farmhouses, and dark green of its spruce trees—the famous American realist artist captured the unique personality of the valley: decidedly private, unostentatiously beautiful. Although parts of the valley have become suburban and U.S. 1 is lined with the usual sprawl of strip malls and gas stations, enough places still exist off the main paths to make you feel that you have discovered a tucked-away treasure.

KINGDOM OF THE DU PONTS

The Brandywine Valley actually incorporates parts of three counties in two states: Chester and Delaware counties in Pennsylvania and New Castle County in Delaware. Winding through this scenic region (about 25 mi southwest of Philadelphia), the Brandywine River flows lazily from West Chester, Pennsylvania, to Wilmington, Delaware. Although in spots it's more a creek than a river, it has nourished many of the valley's economic and artistic endeavors. Although paintings of the Wyeth family distilled the region's mystery, it was the regal du Pont family that provided more than a bit of its magnificence, recontouring the land with grand gardens, mansions, and mills. Their kingdom was established by the family patriarch, Pierre-Samuel du Pont, who had escaped with his family from post-Revolutionary France and settled in northern Delaware. The Du Pont company was founded in 1802 by his son Éleuthère Irénée (E. I.), who made the family fortune, first in gunpowder and iron and later in chemicals and textiles.

E. I. and five generations of du Ponts lived in Eleutherian Mills, the stately family home on the grounds of a black-powder mill that has been transformed into the Hagley Museum. The home, from which Mrs. Henry du Pont was driven after accidental blasts at the powder works, was closed in 1921. Louise du Pont Crowninshield, a great-granddaughter of E. I., restored the house fully before opening it to the public. Louise's relatives were busy, too. Henry Francis du Pont was filling his country estate, Winterthur, with furniture by Duncan Phyfe, silver by Paul Revere, splendid decorative objects, and entire interior woodwork fittings salvaged from homes built between 1640 and 1860.

Pierre du Pont (cousin of Henry Francis) devoted his life to horticulture. He bought a 1,000-acre 19th-century arboretum and created Longwood Gardens, where he entertained his many friends and relatives. Today 350 acres of the meticulously landscaped gardens are open to the public. Displays range from a tropical rain forest to a desert; acres of heated conservatories, where flowers are in bloom year-round, create eternal summer. Pierre also built the grand Hotel Du Pont in downtown Wilmington adjacent to company headquarters. No expense was spared; more than 18 French and Italian craftspeople labored for two years, carving, gilding, and painting. Alfred I. du Pont's country estate, Nemours, was named after the family's ancestral home in north-central France. It encompasses 300 acres of French gardens and a mansion in Louis XVI style.

WYETH COUNTRY

Although Andrew Wyeth is the most famous local artist, the area's artistic tradition began long before, when artist-illustrator Howard Pyle started a school in Wilmington in 1900. He had more than 100 students, including Andrew's father, N. C. Wyeth; Frank Schoonover; Jessie Willcox Smith; Maxfield Parrish; and Harvey Dunn. It was this tradition that inspired Andrew and his son Jamie.

In 1967 local residents formed the Brandywine Conservancy to prevent industrialization of the area and pollution of the river; their actions included significant land purchases. In 1971 the organization opened the Brandywine River Museum in a preserved 19th-century gristmill. It celebrates the Brandywine School of artists in a setting much in tune with their world.

OTHER PLEASURES

The valley is also the site of one of the more dramatic turns in the American Revolution, the Battle of Brandywine, and an offbeat museum that celebrates the mushroom. Antiques shops, fine restaurants, and cozy country inns dot the region. Your best bet is to rent a car and explore on your own with the help of a map (☞ Visitor Information *in* Brandywine Valley A to Z, *below*).

If you start early enough, you can tour the valley's top three attractions—the Brandywine River Museum, Longwood Gardens, and Winterthur—in one day. You'd have to limit your time at each stop, however. If you have more time to spend in the valley, you can visit additional sites in Pennsylvania and then move on to Wilmington.

Numbers in the text correspond to numbers in the margin and on the Brandywine Valley map.

West Chester

30 mi west of Philadelphia.

The county seat of Chester since 1786, this historic mile-square city holds distinctive 18th- and 19th-century architecture, with fine examples of Greek Revival and Victorian styles. A small but vital downtown offers shopping possibilities as well as restaurants and bars serving everything from classic American fare to the latest microbrews. Fine examples of classical architecutre, including the Chester County Courthouse and Market Street Station, can be found near the intersection of High and Gay streets.

A good place to begin a visit, the **Chester County Historical Society** (⊠ 225 N. High St., ☎ 610/692–4800) is a one-time opera house where Buffalo Bill performed; a history center has exhibits about the region.

Dining and Lodging

$$$–$$$$ ✕ **Dilworthtown Inn.** Fresh seafood from the Chesapeake Bay, confit of duck spring rolls, and smoked pheasant are among the entrées at this longtime area favorite for romantic dining. The 15 candlelit dining rooms are individually decorated. A garden across the road supplies many of the vegetables and herbs. The wine cellar stocks more than 860 different vintages. ⊠ *Old Wilmington Pike and Bronton's Bridge Rd., Dilworthtown, south of West Chester,* ☎ *610/399–1390. AE, D, DC, MC, V. No lunch.*

$ ✕ **Magnolia Grill.** Before or after a visit to the adjacent Chester County Book Company (☞ Shopping, *below*), you can partake of crawfish étouffée, jambalaya, and other New Orleans favorites in this bustling café. Breakfasts, including omelets and beignets, are served all day. ⊠ *975 Paoli Pike, West Goshen Shopping Center,* ☎ *610/696–1661. AE, D, MC, V.*

$$–$$$$ ⬚ **Whitewing Farm Bed & Breakfast.** Although it has a West Chester address, this B&B is adjacent to Longwood Gardens and within minutes of other attractions. Despite this, the tranquillity and elegance of

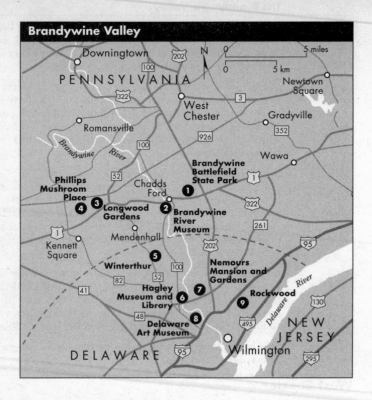

Brandywine Valley

these accommodations will make you feel as if you're miles away from the action. Nestled among 43 acres are four houses for guests, including a gatehouse suite, a renovated stable, and a guest house by a large pond. Bedrooms are formally but comfortably decorated in English country style, and all have marble-floor baths. The main house has a porch, cozy sitting rooms, and a billiard room. In good weather, full country breakfasts (stuffed French toast or pancakes with raspberry sauce) are served on the terrace overlooking the pond. ⊠ *370 Valley Rd., 19382,* ☎ *610/388–2664,* 𝖥𝖠𝖷 *610/388–3650. 7 rooms, 1 suite. Pool, putting green, tennis court, billiards, fishing. No credit cards. BP.*

Shopping

Chester County Book Company (⊠ 975 Paoli Pike, West Goshen Shopping Center, ☎ 610/696–1661), one of the country's largest independently owned bookstores, stocks more than 300,000 titles, including new, antique, and collectible books. The travel and children's sections are particularly expansive.

Chadds Ford

11 mi south of West Chester, 30 mi southwest of Philadelphia.

A Revolutionary War battlefield park and a museum celebrating area artists make this historic town appealing. There are some pretty side roads to explore as well. The **Chaddsford Winery** (⊠ U.S. 1, ☎ 610/388–6221), in a restored barn, offers tastings and tours of its wine-making facilities.

❶ **Brandywine Battlefield State Park** is near the site of the Battle of Brandywine, where British general William Howe and his troops defeated George Washington on September 11, 1777. The Continental Army then fled to Chester, leaving Philadelphia vulnerable to British troops. The visitor center has audiovisual materials and displays about the battle that are a good introduction to the area's history. On the site are two restored Quaker farmhouses that once sheltered Washington and Lafayette. The 50-acre park is a fine place for a picnic. ⊠ *U.S. 1,* ☎ *610/459–3342.* ⌨ *Park free; house tours $3.50.* ◷ *Tues.–Sat. 9–5, Sun. noon–6.*

★ ❷ In a converted Civil War–era gristmill, the **Brandywine River Museum** showcases the art of Chadds Ford native Andrew Wyeth, a major American realist painter, and his family: his father, N. C. Wyeth, illustrator of many children's classics; and his son Jamie. The collection also emphasizes still lifes, landscape paintings, and American illustration, with works by such artists as Howard Pyle and Maxfield Parrish. The glass-walled lobby overlooks the river and countryside that inspired the Brandywine School earlier in the century. The museum uses a system of filters, baffles, and blinds to direct natural light. Outside the museum, you can visit a garden with regional wildflowers and follow a 1-mi nature trail along the river.

The N. C. Wyeth Studio, where N. C. painted, is open part of the year; this highlight gives an intimate feeling for his artistic process and is worth the extra fee. The 1911 studio, set on a hill, holds many of the props N. C. used in creating his illustrations. A shuttle (departures every 50 minutes) takes you from the museum to the studio for a 30-minute guided tour. ⊠ *U.S. 1 and Rte. 100,* ☎ *610/388–2700.* ⌨ *$5; $2.50 additional for studio.* ◷ *Museum: daily 9:30–4:30; studio: Apr.–Oct., Wed.–Sun. 10–3:15.*

OFF THE
BEATEN PATH
ROUTE 100 – For a scenic, curving route to Wilmington, or just a pretty drive, follow Route 100 south from Chadds Ford. This is the countryside captured in the works of the Wyeths and other artists, and if you take time to study their paintings at the Brandywine River Museum before you begin, you'll see the land in a new light. You can also drive Route 100 north toward West Chester. If you do, stop at **Baldwin's Book Barn** (⊠ 865 Lenape Rd./Rte. 100, ☎ 610/696–0816), an old barn packed with enticing rare and used books, prints, and maps.

Dining and Lodging

$$–$$$ ✕ **Chadds Ford Inn.** Across the highway from the Brandywine River Museum, the inn was once a lively rest stop on the Wilmington-Philadelphia-Lancaster commerce route. The inn now welcomes you to a Colonial-period dining room, complete with candlelight, stone hearths, and Wyeth prints. Entrées such as bow-tie pasta with duck sausage and wild mushrooms and sautéed pork cutlets with apple cider and sweet potatoes are served up in generous portions. ⊠ *Rte. 100 and U.S. 1,* ☎ *610/388–7361. AE, DC, MC, V.*

$–$$ ✕ **Hank's Place.** The locals flock to this very casual outpost for hearty breakfasts, lunches, and early dinners (Hank's closes at 7). ⊠ *U.S. 1 and Rte. 100,* ☎ *610/388–7061. No credit cards. No dinner Sun.*

$$ ⌷ **Brandywine River Hotel.** This small, modern two-story hotel across the highway from the Brandywine River Museum has tasteful Queen Anne furnishings, classic English chintz, and florals that create a homey feeling. Suites have fireplaces and whirlpool baths. Request a room that overlooks the surrounding pasture. The hotel's restaurant, the Chadds Ford Inn (☞ *above*) is adjacent. Ask about special packages. ⊠ *Rte. 100 and U.S. 1, 19317,* ☎ *610/388–1200. 30 rooms, 10 suites. Restaurant, exercise room, business services, meeting rooms. AE, D, DC, MC, V. CP.*

Kennett Square

7 mi west of Chadds Ford.

This town has a long history that has left its downtown full of interesting buildings in different styles, but most people come here to visit Longwood Gardens and perhaps to stop at the mushroom museum that celebrates one of the area's most important businesses.

★ ❸ **Longwood Gardens,** 3 mi northeast of Kennett Square, has established an international reputation for its immaculate, colorful display gardens full of flowers and blossoming shrubs. In 1906 Pierre Samuel du Pont (1870–1945) bought a simple Quaker farm, famous for its trees, and turned it into the ultimate early 20th-century estate garden. Seasonal attractions include magnolias and azaleas in spring; roses and water lilies in summer; fall foliage and chrysanthemums; and winter camellias, orchids, and palms. You can stroll in the Italian water garden or explore a meadow full of wildflowers on the garden's 350 acres. Bad weather is no problem here, as 4 acres of exotic foliage, cacti, ferns, and bonsai are housed in heated conservatories; it's easy to spend an hour or more touring these. The Heritage exhibit in the 1730 Peirce–du Pont House traces the last 300 years of evolution, historical and horticultural, of the Longwood area. The spectacular illuminated fountain displays on Tuesday, Thursday, and Saturday evenings in summer are very popular; the gardens stay open until almost 10. The cafeteria (open year-round) and dining room (closed January–March) serve pleasant, reasonably priced meals. ⊠ *U.S. 1,* ☎ *610/388–1000.* ☞ *$12 ($8 Tues.).* ☉ *Apr.–Oct., daily 9–6; Nov.–Mar., daily 9–5; plus some evenings in summer and Thanksgiving–Christmas.*

❹ **Phillips Mushroom Place** is a small museum devoted exclusively to a fungus—the mushroom. Mushrooms are eastern Pennsylvania's number-one cash crop, and most are grown in Kennett Square, which labels itself the "mushroom capital of the world." The history, lore, and growing process of mushrooms is explained with dioramas, exhibits, a growing wall, and a 13-minute film. The gift shop sells a mushroom gift pack suitable for mailing. ⊠ *909 E. Baltimore Pike (U.S. 1),* ☎ *610/388–6082.* ☞ *$1.25.* ☉ *Daily 10–6.*

Dining and Lodging

$$–$$$$ ✗ **Mendenhall Inn.** Continental and American cuisine is served in this 1790s Quaker mill building, which still has its old beams intact. Seafood, prime rib, and game are specialties. For lunch request a table with a courtyard view; at Saturday dinner ask for the pleasant Mill Room upstairs. ⊠ *Rte. 52, Mendenhall, 1 mi south of U.S. 1, 3 mi east of Kennett Square,* ☎ *610/388–1181. Reservations essential. Jacket and tie. AE, D, DC, MC, V.*

$$–$$$ 🏨 **Fairville Inn.** Ole and Patti Retlev's inn, halfway between Longwood Gardens and Winterthur, has bright, airy rooms furnished with Queen Anne and Hepplewhite reproductions. There's a main house, built in 1826; a remodeled barn; and a carriage house. Request a room in the back of the property, away from traffic. The main house has a striking living room with a large fireplace. The Fairville serves a complimentary light breakfast and afternoon tea. Note that this inn is not suitable for children under 10 and is totally no-smoking. ⊠ *506 Rte. 52 (Kennett Pike), Mendenhall 19357,* ☎ *610/388–5900,* 🖷 *610/ 388–5902. 13 rooms, 2 suites. AE, D, MC, V. BP.*

$$ 🏨 **Meadow Spring Farm.** Anne Hicks's farmhouse is a gallery for her family's antiques, dolls, teddy bears, and Santas. Rooms have Amish quilts and televisions. A full country breakfast is served daily on the glassed-in porch. Children are welcome here, and they will particularly enjoy the farm animals. ⊠ *201 E. Street Rd., 19348,* ☎ *610/444–3903. 6 rooms, 4 with bath. Pool, hot tub, fishing, recreation room. No credit cards. BP.*

Wilmington

15 mi southeast of Kennett Square.

Although it's small in comparison to big-city neighbors such as Philadelphia, Wilmington should not be overlooked. Delaware's commercial hub and largest city has handsome architecture—with good examples of styles such as Federal, Greek Revival, Queen Anne, and art deco—and abundant cultural attractions. Wilmington began in 1638 as a Swedish settlement and later was populated by employees of various du Pont family businesses and nearby poultry ranches. Outside the compact city center are several outstanding museums, including some that are legacies of the du Ponts.

★ ❺ Henry Francis du Pont (1880–1969) housed his 89,000 objects of American decorative art in a sprawling nine-story mansion called **Winterthur**; today the collection is recognized as one of the nation's finest. The 1640–1860 furniture, silver, paintings, and textiles are displayed in 175 period room settings in the original house. A selection of these can be seen on guided tours. The museum also has galleries with permanent displays and changing exhibitions of decorative arts and crafts that you can study at your own pace. Surrounding the museum are 966 acres of landscaped lawns and gardens, which you can visit on a 30-minute narrated tram ride or on your own. Garden lectures are given on Sunday in the spring when the azaleas, peonies, and magnolias are flowering. Winterthur's Yuletide Tour (November 15–December 31) showcases the holiday traditions of early America. A gift shop, cafeteria, and restaurant are also on the grounds. ⊠ *Rte. 52, 5 mi south of U.S. 1,* ☎ *302/888–4600.* ⊠ *$8–$21 (depending on tour selected, but all include garden tram).* ☉ *Mon.–Sat. 9–5, Sun. noon–5; garden open until dusk.*

❻ A restored mid-19th-century mill community on 240 landscaped acres, the **Hagley Museum and Library** offers a glimpse of the du Ponts at work and an enlightening look at the development of early industrial America. This is the site of the first du Pont black-powder mills, built by E. I. du Pont. Exhibits, including a restored workers' community complete with schoolhouse, depict the dangerous work of the early explosives industry. One building holds dioramas and working models. Admission includes a bus ride with stops at Eleutherian Mills, an 1803 Georgian-style home furnished by five generations of du Ponts, and a French Renaissance–style garden. Allow about two hours for your visit. The coffee shop is open for lunch except in winter. ⊠ *Rte. 141 between Rte. 100 and U.S. 202,* ☎ *302/658–2400.* ⊠ *$9.75.* ☉ *Mar. 15–Dec., daily 9:30–4:30; Jan.–Mar. 14, weekends 9:30–4:30; winter tours, weekdays at 1:30.*

❼ For a look at how the very wealthy and tasteful lived, visit **Nemours Mansion and Gardens,** a 300-acre country estate built for Alfred I. du Pont in 1910. This modified Louis XVI château showcases 102 rooms of European and American furnishings, rare rugs, tapestries, and art dating to the 15th century. The gardens, reminiscent of those at Versailles, are landscaped with fountains, pools, and statuary. The estate can only be seen on the guided two-hour tours. Visitors must be over 16 years old. ⊠ *1600 Rockland Rd., between Rte. 141 and U.S. 202,* ☎ *302/651–6912.* ⊠ *$10;* ☉ *May–Nov.; tours Tues.–Sat. at 9, 11, 1, and 3; Sun. at 11, 1, and 3 (reservations required).*

The **Wilmington Public Library,** located downtown catercorner to the Hotel Du Pont, holds a wonderful bounty among its shelves: 14 of 17 canvases, plus the jacket and endpaper paintings, done by N. C. Wyeth in 1920 to illustrate Daniel Defoe's *Robinson Crusoe.* ⊠ *10th and Market Sts.,* ☎ *302/571–7415.* ⊘ *Mon.–Thurs. 9–8, Fri.–Sat. 9–5.*

❽ A medium-size treat for art lovers, the **Delaware Art Museum** has several notable strengths, including a good collection of paintings by Howard Pyle (1853–1911), a Wilmington native known as the "father of American illustration," and his students—N. C. Wyeth, Frank Schoonover, and Maxfield Parrish. Pyle's work has an appealingly direct realism. Other American artists represented are Benjamin West, Winslow Homer, Edward Glackens, and Edward Hopper. The museum also houses the largest American collection of 19th-century English pre-Raphaelite paintings and decorative arts and a children's participatory gallery. ⊠ *2301 Kentmere Pkwy.,* ☎ *302/571–9590.* ⊠ *$5.* ⊘ *Tues., Thurs.–Sat. 9–4, Wed. 9–9, Sun. 10–4.*

❾ **Rockwood,** a quietly elegant English-style country house and a fine example of rural Gothic architecture, stands in contrast to the opulent, French-inspired du Pont homes in the area. Built in 1851 by Joseph Shipley, a Quaker banker, the house is now a museum filled with 19th-century decorative arts and furnishings. Sixty acres of rambling grounds surround the house. The mansion can be visited by guided tour only. ⊠ *610 Shipley Rd.,* ☎ *302/761–4340.* ⊠ *$5.* ⊘ *Jan.–Feb., Tues.–Sat. 11–3; Mar.–Dec., Tues.–Sun. 11–3.*

The **First USA Riverfront Arts Center,** which hosts major touring art exhibitions with an international focus, was constructed as the first step in the ongoing revitalization of Wilmington's waterfront. It has no permanent displays. Tickets for exhibitions must be purchased in advance for a specific date and entry time. ⊠ *800 S. Madison St.,* ☎ *302/777–1600.* ⊠ *Varies with exhibition.* ⊘ *Call for exhibit schedule and times.*

Dining and Lodging

$$$–$$$$ ✕ **Green Room.** For years Philadelphians and locals have trekked here
★ to celebrate special occasions in the famous Hotel Du Pont restaurant. Such delicacies as lobster risotto, sesame-crusted tuna with lemongrass broth, and rack of lamb with dried cherries can be savored in Edwardian splendor under a gold-encrusted ceiling with massive Spanish chandeliers and high French windows. Harp music accompanies formal dinners. You can also try the hotel's dark-paneled Brandywine Room; the menu is similar, and paintings by artists including N. C. Wyeth line the walls. ⊠ *Hotel Du Pont, 11th and Market Sts.,* ☎ *302/594–3100. Reservations essential. Jacket required. AE, D, DC, MC, V.*

$$–$$$ ✕ **Deep Blue.** Ultra-modern, airy, and convivial, this bar and bistro presents a contrast to the formal Hotel Du Pont across the street. Oysters, tuna, salmon, and crabs are the stars of imaginatively seasoned and beautifully presented dishes. The bar features a wide selection of microbrews on tap. A jazz band entertains on Thursday night. ⊠ *111 W. 11th St.,* ☎ *302/777–2040. AE, D, DC, MC, V.*

$$–$$$$ ▥ **Hotel Du Pont.** Built in 1913 by Pierre-Samuel du Pont, the hotel is an elegant 12-story building with an old-world feel. The lobby has a spectacular decorative ceiling, polished marble walls, and carved paneling. The spacious, formal guest rooms, done in soothing earth tones, have high ceilings, 18th-century reproduction furnishings, and original art. ⊠ *11th and Market Sts., 19801,* ☎ *302/594–3100 or 800/441–9019,* FAX *302/594–3108. 216 rooms. 3 restaurants, lobby lounge, exercise room, theater. AE, D, DC, MC, V.*

$ 🖫 **Boulevard Bed and Breakfast.** Charles and Judy Powell welcome you to their large, comfortable 1913 home, adorned with neo-Georgian elements such as fluted columns. There's nothing formal or fussy in the rooms, which have reading chairs, desks, and floral wallpaper. This reasonably priced B&B is in one of Wilmington's fine older neighborhoods near downtown. A full breakfast is served on an enclosed side porch. ⊠ *1909 Baynard Blvd., 19802,* ☏ *302/656–9700. 6 rooms. AE, MC, V. BP.*

Brandywine Valley A to Z

Arriving and Departing

BY BUS
From Philadelphia, **Greyhound Lines** (☏ 215/931–4075 or 800/231–2222) operates out of the terminal at 10th and Filbert streets, just north of the Market East commuter rail station. There are about 10 daily departures to the Wilmington terminal at 101 North French Street. The trip takes one hour.

BY CAR
Take U.S. 1 south from Philadelphia; the Brandywine Valley is about 25 mi from Philadelphia, and many attractions are on U.S. 1. To reach Wilmington, pick up U.S. 202 south just past Concordville or take I–95 south from Philadelphia.

BY TRAIN
Amtrak (☏ 215/824–1600 or 800/872–7245) has frequent service from Philadelphia's 30th Street Station to Wilmington's station at Martin Luther King Jr. Boulevard and French Street on the edge of downtown. It's a 25-minute ride.

Getting Around
Driving is the best way to see the area's spread-out attractions.

Contacts and Resources

B&B RESERVATION AGENCIES
This is a popular area for B&Bs; for information *see* Chapter 4.

CANOEING
Northbrook Canoe Company (⊠ 1819 Beagle Rd., West Chester, ☏ 610/793–2279) has a variety of scenic canoe trips on the Brandywine River.

GUIDED TOURS
Brandywine Tours (⊠ 20 Woodland Dr., Glen Mills 19342, ☏ 610/358–5445) will pick you up at your Philadelphia hotel on Wednesday, Friday, or Saturday morning for full-day excursions in a 15-person van.

Colonial Pathways (⊠ Box 879, Chadds Ford 19317, ☏ 610/388–2654) offers full-day bus tours through the Brandywine Valley.

VISITOR INFORMATION
The **Brandywine Valley Tourist Information Center** (⊠ U.S. 1 north of Kennett Square, ☏ 610/388–2900 or 800/228–9933), in the Longwood Progressive Meeting House at the entrance to Longwood Gardens, has information on attractions, lodging, and restaurants. It's open daily 10–6 from May to September and 10–5 from October to April. The Brandywine information center is run by the **Chester County Tourist Bureau,** which has its main office at the Government Services Center (⊠ 601 Westtown Rd., Suite 170, West Chester 19382, ☏ 610/344–6365).

For good road maps and guides, contact the **Delaware County Convention and Visitors Bureau** (⊠ 200 E. State St., Suite 100, Media 19063, ☏ 610/565–3679 or 610/565–3666 for tape of events). The **Greater**

Wilmington Convention and Visitors Bureau (⊠ 100 W. 10 St., Wilmington, DE 19801, ☎ 302/652–4088) has maps and information.

VALLEY FORGE

The monuments, markers, huts, and headquarters in Valley Forge National Historical Park illuminate a decisive period in American history. The park, with its quiet beauty that seems to whisper of the past, preserves the area where George Washington's Continental Army endured the bitter winter of 1777–78. If the weather is fine, consider renting a bicycle or packing a lunch and picnicking in the park.

Other nearby attractions are Mill Grove, the home of naturalist John James Audubon; the studio and residence of craftsman Wharton Esherick; and The Plaza & The Court, a vast shopping complex.

Numbers in the text correspond to numbers in the margin and on the Valley Forge map.

Valley Forge

20 mi northeast of downtown Philadelphia.

Near the suburban village of Valley Forge is a major site of the Revolutionary War. The town was named because of an iron forge built in the 1740s.

★ ❶ **Valley Forge National Historical Park,** administered by the National Park Service, is the location of the 1777–78 winter encampment of General George Washington and the Continental Army. Stop first at the visitor center to see the 18-minute orientation film (shown every 30 minutes), view exhibits, and pick up a map for a 10-mi self-guided auto tour of the attractions in the 3,600-acre park. From June through September you can also purchase an auto-tour cassette tape for $8. Stops include reconstructed huts of the Muhlenberg Brigade and the National Memorial Arch, which pays tribute to the soldiers who suffered through the brutal winter. Other sites are the bronze equestrian statue of General Anthony Wayne, in the area where his Pennsylvania troops were encamped; Artillery Park, where the soldiers stored their cannons; and the Isaac Potts House, which served as Washington's headquarters.

The park is quiet today, but in 1777 the army had just lost the nearby battles of Brandywine, White Horse, and Germantown. While the British occupied Philadelphia, Washington's soldiers were forced to endure horrid conditions here—blizzards, inadequate food and clothing, damp quarters, and disease. Many men deserted, and although no battle was fought at Valley Forge, 2,000 American soldiers died.

The troops did win one victory that winter—a war of will. The forces slowly regained strength and confidence under the leadership of Prussian drillmaster Friedrich von Steuben. In June 1778 Washington led his troops away from Valley Forge in search of the British. Fortified, the Continental Army was able to carry on the fight for five years more.

The park contains 6 mi of jogging and bicycling paths and hiking trails, and you can picnic at any of three designated areas. A leisurely visit to the park will take no more than half a day. ⊠ *Rtes. 23 and 363, Box 953, Valley Forge 19481,* ☎ *610/783–1077.* 🖃 *Washington's headquarters $2.* ☉ *Daily 9–5.*

❷ The **Valley Forge Historical Society Museum** tells the Valley Forge story with military equipment and Colonial artifacts as well as a large collection of items that belonged to Martha and George Washington. The

Mill Grove, **4**
The Plaza & The Court, **5**
Valley Forge Historical Society Museum, **2**
Valley Forge National Historical Park, **1**
Wharton Esherick Museum, **3**

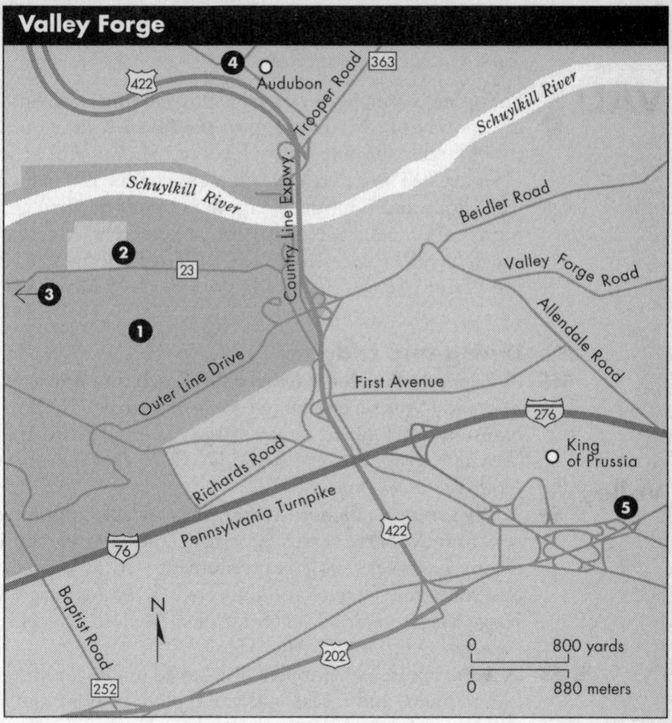

nearby Chapel Cabin Shop sells homemade goodies such as Martha's 16-Bean Soup and fudge. ✉ *Alongside the Washington Memorial Chapel on Rte. 23,* ☎ *610/783–0535.* 🎟 *$1.50.* ⏲ *Apr.–Dec., Mon.–Sat. 10–5, Sun. 1–5; Jan.– Mar., Wed.–Sat. 10–4, Sun. 1–4.*

3 The **Wharton Esherick Museum** preserves the former home and studio of the "Dean of American Craftsmen." Best known for his sculptural furniture, Esherick (1887–1970) shaped a new aesthetic in decorative arts by bridging art with furniture. The museum houses 200 examples of his work—paintings, woodcuts, furniture, and wood sculptures. The studio, in which everything from the light switches to the spiral staircase is hand-carved, is one of his monumental achievements. The museum is on the Horseshoe Trail, 2 mi west of Valley Forge National Historical Park. ✉ *1520 Horseshoe Trail,* ☎ *610/644–5822.* 🎟 *$6.* ⏲ *Mar.–Dec., Sat. 10–5, Sun. 1–5 for hourly guided tours (reservations required). Group tours (at least 5 people) weekdays.*

Audubon

2 mi north of Valley Forge.

Audubon is linked to the renowned American naturalist of the same
4 name. **Mill Grove** was the first American home of Haitian-born artist and naturalist John James Audubon (1785–1851). Built in 1762, the house is now a museum displaying Audubon's major works, including reproductions, original prints, his paintings of birds and wildlife, and a double-elephant folio of his *Birds of America*. The attic has been restored to a studio and taxidermy room. The Audubon Wildlife Sanctuary has 175 acres with 5 mi of hiking trails here. ✉ *Audubon and Pawlings Rds.,* ☎ *610/666–5593.* 🎟 *Free.* ⏲ *Museum: Tues.–Sat. 10–4, Sun. 1–4. Grounds: Tues.–Sun. dawn–dusk.*

King of Prussia

5 mi southeast of Audubon.

❺ Shopping is a main draw in this busy suburban town. For lunch or an afternoon of browsing, head to **The Plaza & The Court,** one of the nation's largest shopping complexes (☞ Shopping Districts and Malls *in* Chapter 7). These two adjacent malls contain more than 35 restaurants, 350 shops and boutiques, and nine major department stores, including Bloomingdale's, Nordstrom, and Neiman Marcus. ⊠ *Rte. 202 at the Schuylkill Expressway, 160 N. Gulph Rd.,* ☎ *610/265–5727 for the Plaza; 610/337–1210 for the Court.* ☉ *Mon.–Sat. 10–9:30, Sun. 11–5.*

Dining and Lodging

$$$ ✕ **Kennedy Supplee Restaurant.** French and northern Italian cuisine is served in the seven dining rooms of a circa 1852 Italian Renaissance mansion overlooking Valley Forge National Historical Park. ⊠ *1100 W. Valley Forge Rd.,* ☎ *610/337–3777. Jacket required. AE, MC, V. No lunch weekends.*

$$ ✕ **Lily Langtry's Dinner Theater.** This lavishly appointed Victorian-era restaurant/cabaret serves American and Continental dishes, but the campy Las Vegas–style entertainment—corny comedians, showgirls, and some fine singers and dancers—is the real draw here. ⊠ *Valley Forge Sheraton Hotel, 1160 1st Ave.,* ☎ *610/337–5459. Reservations required. AE, D, DC, MC, V.*

$–$$ ✕ **Jefferson House.** Bouillabaise, baked jumbo lump crab, Black Angus filet mignon, and a seasonal game plate of boar and venison are the specialties at this elegant, stately Georgian mansion on 11 acres of lush grounds. After dinner, you can stroll around the duck pond and Italian gazebos. ⊠ *2519 DeKalb Pike, Norristown, 4 mi northeast of King of Prussia,* ☎ *610/275–3407. AE, DC, MC, V.*

$$ ☷ **Valley Forge Sheraton Hotel and Convention Center.** Two bustling high-rises cater to groups and couples escaping to whirlpool bath–equipped fantasy theme suites—a prehistoric cave, a wild-and-woolly jungle, the outer-space-like "Outer Limits." Regular rooms and executive suites are contemporary in style. The hotel offers excellent champagne-and-dinner-theater packages at Lily Langtry's Dinner Theater (☞ *above*). ⊠ *1160 1st Ave., 19406,* ☎ *610/337–2000 or 800/325–3535,* ℻ *610/768–3222. 398 rooms, 50 suites, 40 fantasy suites. 4 restaurants, piano bar, pool, health club, comedy club, theater, convention center. AE, D, DC, MC, V.*

Valley Forge A to Z

Arriving and Departing

BY BUS

On weekdays **SEPTA** (☎ 215/580–7800) Bus 125 leaves from 16th Street and John F. Kennedy Boulevard (departing hourly starting at 5:30 AM) for King of Prussia (including The Plaza & the Court) and continues on to Valley Forge National Historical Park. On Saturday transfer at the plaza to the Royersford, Bus 99, which goes through the park. Bus 99 departs hourly. On Sunday Bus 99 does not run; Bus 125 goes as far as the Valley Forge Sheraton Hotel, less than a mile from the park but along busy roads.

BY CAR

Take the Schuylkill Expressway (I–76) west from Philadelphia to Exit 25 (Goddard Boulevard). Take Route 363 to North Gulph Road and follow signs to Valley Forge National Historical Park. Exit 25 also provides easy access to the Plaza & the Court shopping complex.

Getting Around

You can get to several sites, such as Valley Forge National Historical Park and The Plaza & The Court, by bus, but a car is helpful for touring the large park and for traveling between sights.

Contacts and Resources

B&B RESERVATION AGENCIES

This is a popular area for B&Bs; for information *see* Chapter 4.

GUIDED TOURS

The **Valley Forge National Historical Park Bus Tour** (☎ 610/783–1077), a narrated minibus tour, originates from the park's visitor center (✉ Rte. 23 and N. Gulph Rd.). Passengers can visit sites and reboard. Tours run from June through September; times vary. The cost is $5.50.

VISITOR INFORMATION

Valley Forge Convention and Visitors Bureau (✉ 600 W. Germantown Pike, Suite 130, Plymouth Meeting 19462, ☎ 610/834–1550 or 800/441–3549). Call or write for information packet. **Valley Forge Country Funline** (☎ 610/834–8844) has information about special events and exhibits.

9 BUCKS COUNTY

It's no wonder so many artists have found glorious inspiration in this Delaware River valley countryside. Despite inevitable pockets of development, the area remains a feast of lyrical landscapes—canal and river vistas, rolling hills, ancient stone barns—with plenty of low-key diversions. Quiet little towns, important historic sites, charming overnight inns, dozens of antiques shops, and one of the most dramatic drives in the state continue to make Bucks County the classic weekend getaway from Philadelphia.

BUCKS COUNTY, about an hour's drive northeast of Philadelphia, could have remained 625 square mi of sleepy countryside full of old stone farmhouses, lush rolling hills, and covered bridges if it hadn't been discovered in the '30s by New York's Beautiful Brainy People. Such luminaries as writers Dorothy Parker and S. J. Perelman and lyricist Oscar Hammerstein II bought country homes here, a short drive from Manhattan. Pulitzer Prize– and Nobel Prize–winning author Pearl S. Buck chose to live in the area because it was "a region where the landscapes were varied, where farm and industry lived side by side, where the sea was near at hand, mountains not far away, and city and countryside were not enemies." Author James A. Michener, who won the 1947 Pulitzer Prize for his *Tales of the South Pacific,* was raised and worked in Doylestown. The region quickly gained a nickname: the Genius Belt.

Updated by
Robert
DiGiacomo

Over the years Bucks County has become known for art colonies and antiques, summer theater, and country inns. And although parts of the county have fallen prey to urban sprawl and hyperdevelopment, many areas of central and upper Bucks County remain as bucolic as ever. One of Bucks County's agrarian pursuits is a cottage vineyard industry. Five local wineries have opened their doors for tours and tastings.

A BIT OF HISTORY

Named after England's Buckinghamshire, Bucks County was opened to European settlement by William Penn in 1681 under a land grant from Charles II. The county's most celebrated town, New Hope, was settled in the early 1700s as the industrial village of Coryell's Ferry. (One of the original gristmills is now the home of the Bucks County Playhouse.) The town was the Pennsylvania terminal for stagecoach traffic and Delaware River ferry traffic. Barges hauled coal along the 60-mi Delaware Canal until 1931.

Commerce built up New Hope, but art helped sustain it. An art colony took root in the late 19th century and was revitalized first in the 1930s by New York theater folk and more recently with the formation of the New Hope–Lambertville Gallery Association, a cooperative network of gallery owners, artists, and the community. Today artists from New York and other areas are again relocating to the region. The James A. Michener Art Museum, showcasing 19th- and 20th-century American art, occupies the renovated former Bucks County jail.

INNS AND ADVENTURES

Although you can see all the major attractions in a day-long whirlwind tour of Bucks County, many people plan overnight stays at some of the prettiest inns in the Mid-Atlantic region. A number of houses and mills, some dating back to a half century before the Revolution, are now bed-and-breakfasts and excellent restaurants. A hearty meal, blissful sleep, and a day spent driving leisurely along River Road (Route 32) are what make visits to Bucks County most enjoyable.

Among the leading destinations is New Hope, a hodgepodge of old stone houses, narrow streets and alleys, pretty courtyards, and charming restaurants. Summer weekends can be frantic here, with traffic jams along Main Street and shoppers thronging the tiny boutiques and galleries. The Delaware Canal threads through town, and you can glide lazily along it in a mule-pulled barge.

Doylestown, the county seat, was an important coach stop during the 18th century. Today the town is best known as the home of Henry Chapman Mercer, curator of American and Prehistoric Archaeology at the

University of Pennsylvania Museum, master potter, self-taught architect, and writer of Gothic tales. When Mercer died in 1930, he left a legacy of artistic creativity, along with a magnificently bizarre castle named Fonthill, a museum displaying 50,000 implements and tools, and a pottery and tile works that still makes Mercer tiles.

The county is also a treasure trove for Colonial history buffs. Among the most interesting sites is Pennsbury Manor, a careful reconstruction of the brick Georgian-style mansion and estate William Penn built for himself in the late 1600s. On the banks of the Delaware, the 500-acre Washington Crossing Historic Park is situated where George Washington and his troops crossed the icy river on Christmas night 1776 to surprise the Hessian mercenaries at Trenton, New Jersey.

The Delaware River and the canal that follows its path offer opportunities for canoeing, kayaking, and fishing. Thousands float down the river each year in inner tubes or on rubber rafts. Joggers, hikers, bicyclists, cross-country skiers, and horseback riders take full advantage of the 60-mi canal towpath.

The town of Lahaska is the center of shopping in Bucks County. The bargain-price American treasures that made the area an antiques-hunter's paradise are now few and far between, but there is good prowling between New Hope and Doylestown all along U.S. 202. In the 75 shops in Peddler's Village in Lahaska, you can find fine furniture, handcrafted chandeliers, hand-woven wicker, and homespun fabrics.

A premier family attraction in Langhorne is Sesame Place, a theme park based on the public television series. There are shows starring Bert and Ernie, water play such as Big Bird's Rambling River raft ride, a computer gallery, and lots of colorful structures on which to climb and jump.

Pleasures and Pastimes

Antiques
Bucks County has long been known for antiques shops full of everything from fine examples of early American craftsmanship to fun kitsch. You'll find formal and country furnishings plus American, European, and Asian antiques. Many shops are along a 4-mi stretch of U.S. 202 between Lahaska and New Hope and on intersecting country roads. You can walk across the bridge from New Hope to Lambertville, New Jersey, for dozens more shops full of treasures that include armoires from Provence, Depression glass, and vintage 20th-century toy rocket ships. Shops are generally open on weekends, with weekday hours by appointment only: It's best to call first.

Covered Bridges
Twelve covered bridges are all that remain of the 36 originally built in Bucks County. Although the romantically inclined call them "kissing bridges" or "wishing bridges," the roofs were actually intended to protect the supporting beams from the ravages of the weather. The bridges are examples of the lattice-type construction of overlapping triangles, without arches or upright beams. They are delightful to stumble upon, but if you're serious about seeing them, contact the Bucks County Conference and Visitors Bureau (☞ Visitor Information *in* Bucks County A to Z, *below*). Locations of the bridges are printed on the back of the map that comes with the county's Visitors Guide.

Dining
Bucks County has no regional specialties to call its own, but you will discover some very sophisticated restaurants as well as casual country

spots. What makes dining here unique are the enchanting settings, ranging from a French-style auberge to Colonial-era manor. Fine meals of French or contemporary American fare are served in restored mills, pre-Revolutionary taverns, stagecoach stops, small cafés, and elegant Victorian mansions. For price-category information *see* Dining *in* Smart Travel Tips A to Z.

Lodging

Bucks County has relatively limited lodging options for families; larger inns, hotels and motels, and campgrounds are the best bets. It does offer numerous choices to couples. Accommodations ranging from modest to elegant can be found in historic inns, small hotels, and bed-and-breakfasts. Most hostelries include breakfast with their room rates. Plan and reserve early—as much as three months ahead for summer and fall weekends. You should also ask about minimum stays; many accommodations require a two-night minimum stay on weekends and a three-night minimum on holiday weekends. Many inns prohibit or restrict smoking. Since some inns are historic homes furnished with fine antiques, the owners may not accept children or may have age restrictions. For price-category information *see* Lodging *in* Smart Travel Tips A to Z.

Outdoor Activities and Sports

One of the best ways to experience the beauty of Bucks is to stroll along the grassy towpath of the Delaware Canal, one of Pennsylvania's most picturesque byways. Dotted with fieldstone bridge-tender houses and clapboard toll-collector offices—now private studios and homes—and shaded by magnificent trees, the path runs parallel to the Delaware River and River Road (Route 32). Constructed in 1832 to allow access for coal barges, the canal and towpath are known today as the Delaware Canal State Park. You can enjoy the 60-mi towpath for biking, hiking, jogging, and in the winter, cross-country skiing. In winter the canal freezes over to form a great ice-skating rink. Tubing or canoeing the Delaware River rates as another popular activity. County parks have plenty of places for hiking, fishing, and boating.

Exploring Bucks County

Many Bucks County sights are contained within the triangle formed by the towns of New Hope, Doylestown, and Newtown. Other interesting places are along River Road (Route 32) from Pennsbury Manor north to pretty river villages such as Erwinna. Lambertville, New Jersey, a five-minute walk across the Delaware River bridge from New Hope, functions as an appealing adjunct to Bucks County, replete with inns, restaurants, and engrossing antiques shops.

Numbers in the text correspond to numbers in the margin and on the Bucks County map.

Great Itineraries

It's entirely possible to "do" Bucks County as a day trip from Philadelphia, but a few days more will allow you to sample many of the area's pleasures. If you have young children along, you may want to spend half a day at Sesame Place in the southern part of the county rather than at some of the nearby historic attractions.

IF YOU HAVE 1 DAY

Start in **Doylestown** ⑤ at Fonthill, the fantastic mansion built by local Renaissance man Henry Chapman Mercer. As lunchtime approaches, wend your way along U.S. 202, stopping at any antiques shops displaying wares along the roadside, usually indicating they're open for business. Have lunch in **New Hope** ⑦, take a quick stroll through town to check out the eclectic boutiques and gracious historic build-

Bucks County

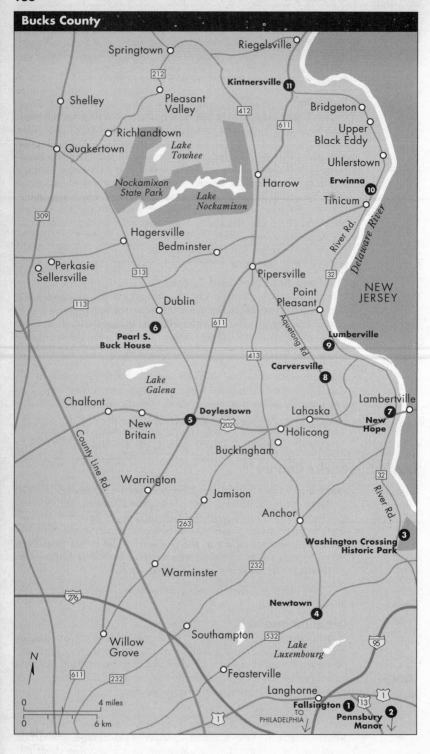

Riegelsville

Springtown

Kintnersville 11

212

Shelley

Pleasant
Valley

412

611

Bridgeton

Upper
Black Eddy

Richlandtown

*Lake
Towhee*

Quakertown

Uhlerstown

Erwinna 10

*Nockamixon
State Park*

Harrow

Tinicum

*Lake
Nockamixon*

309

Hagersville

Bedminster

313

Perkasie

Sellersville

Pipersville

32

River Rd.

NEW
JERSEY

Point
Pleasant

Delaware River

113

Dublin

611

Lumberville 9

**Pearl S.
Buck House** 6

413

Aquetong Rd.

Carversville 8

*Lake
Galena*

Chalfont

Doylestown 5

202

Lahaska

Lambertville

New
Britain

Holicong

**New
Hope** 7

Buckingham

Warrington

Jamison

263

Anchor

32

River Rd.

3

**Washington Crossing
Historic Park**

Warminster

232

276

Newtown

4

Willow
Grove

Southampton

532

*Lake
Luxembourg*

95

N

611

232

Feasterville

Langhorne

13

1

0   4 miles

0   6 km

Fallsington 1

TO
PHILADELPHIA

**Pennsbury
Manor** 2

1

ings, and then head north on River Road (Route 32) for a stirring drive along the Delaware River up to **Lumberville** ⑨ or **Erwinna** ⑩. Have dinner at one of the inns in these towns.

IF YOU HAVE 2 DAYS

At your starting point in **Washington Crossing Historic Park** ③, you can see where George Washington set off across the river with his troops on that fateful Christmas night in 1776. Then drive up River Road (Route 32) to ⊞ **New Hope** ⑦ and have lunch, perhaps outside. In the afternoon head west to explore Mercer Mile in **Doylestown** ⑤ and return to New Hope to spend the night at an inn. On Day 2 check out **Lambertville**'s antiques shops across the river and then drive upriver in Pennsylvania on River Road for about 17 mi. Stop to stretch your legs along the way with a stroll on the scenic Delaware Canal towpath. Have dinner and spend the night at an inn in ⊞ **Erwinna** ⑩ or ⊞ **Kintnersville** ⑪.

IF YOU HAVE 3 DAYS

Drive up River Road to ⊞ **Erwinna** ⑩. In season—roughly from May to October—even the mildly athletic will enjoy an 11-mi canoe trip south on the Delaware River, beginning at the rental facility Bucks County River Country Canoe and Tube, in **Point Pleasant.** It's a terrific way to appreciate the area's natural splendors and get some fresh-air exercise. Afterward you're justified in lounging for a few hours on the veranda of your inn with a good book. As an alternative, rent bikes in **Lumberville** ⑨ and take a ride on the river's bucolic towpath.

On Day 2 drive downriver to ⊞ **New Hope** ⑦ for breakfast at Mother's. Shop and see the town, then head west on U.S. 202. Visit the museums on Mercer Mile in **Doylestown** ⑤. If you enjoy art, linger in Doylestown and spend the afternoon at the James A. Michener Art Museum, where many paintings by the Pennsylvania Impressionists are on permanent display. Another choice is to spend the afternoon at Peddler's Village in **Lahaska;** check out its boutiques full of delicious nonessentials. Back in New Hope for the evening, consider dinner and window-shopping just across the river in **Lambertville.**

History buffs can fill their plate on Day 3 by starting out with a tour of the pre-Revolutionary village of **Fallsington** ① and **Pennsbury Manor** ②, William Penn's country retreat, both near Morrisville in the southern part of the county. Have lunch in **Newtown** ④, ideal for strolling and browsing. Drive toward the river in the afternoon, and you'll end up at **Washington Crossing Historic Park** ③, where a visitor center, two historic buildings, and a walk through the glorious parkland can easily occupy the rest of the day.

When to Tour Bucks County

Spring, summer, or fall—each time of year has its own pleasures and seasonal festivals. Summer and fall weekends are very busy, so make reservations well ahead and be ready for some crowds; a weekday trip could be more relaxing. Winter has its appeal here, too, especially around the holidays; the snow-covered buildings and fields are lovely.

Langhorne

25 mi northeast of Philadelphia.

For years families have visited this town because of a popular TV-theme attraction. The good times roll, crawl, climb, and jump at **Sesame Place,** a recreation park with 15 water rides and more than 50 play activities designed for children ages 2 to 13. The highlight for most is Sesame Neighborhood, a replica of the beloved street on the public-TV show. Kids can also go wild playing on Cookie Mountain and discovering

Ernie's Bed Bounce. This is the largest water park in the Philadelphia area, with slides and rides for all ages, so don't forget your bathing suit. The Vapor Trail is a roller coaster with Super Grover as its mascot. ⊠ *100 Sesame Rd., off Oxford Valley Rd. near junction of U.S. 1 and I–95,* ☎ *215/752–7070.* ⊠ *$29.95; parking $6.* ☉ *Mid-May–mid-Sept., daily; early May and mid-Sept.–mid-Oct., weekends. Peak season hrs (July–Aug.) 9–8; call for spring and fall hrs.*

Fallsington

❶ *2 mi east of Langhorne.*

Fallsington, the pre-Revolutionary village where William Penn attended Quaker meetings, displays 300 years of American architecture, from a simple 17th-century log cabin to the Victorian excesses of the late 1800s. Ninety period homes are found in the village, which is listed on the National Register of Historic Places. Many private homes are open to the public on the second Saturday in October.

Three historic buildings—a tavern, a log cabin, and a house—have been restored and opened for guided tours by **Historic Fallsington Inc.** ⊠ *4 Yardley Ave., off Tyburn Rd. W off U.S. 13,* ☎ *215/295–6567.* ⊠ *$3.50.* ☉ *May–Oct., Mon.–Sat. 10–4, Sun. 1–4.*

Morrisville

3 mi east of Fallsington.

The reason to visit this town across the river from Trenton, New Jersey lies a few miles south of the town itself. On a gentle rise 150 yards
❷ from the Delaware River, **Pennsbury Manor** is a 1938–39 reconstruction of the Georgian-style mansion and plantation William Penn built in the 1680s as his country estate. Living-history demonstrations on 43 of the estate's original 8,400 acres provide a glimpse of everyday life in 17th-century America. The property, including formal gardens, orchards, an icehouse, a smokehouse, and a bake-and-brew house, helps paint a picture of the life of an English gentleman 300 years ago. The plantation also shows that although history portrays Penn as a dour Quaker, as governor of the colony he enjoyed the good life by importing the finest provisions and keeping a vast retinue of servants. These extravagances led to financial difficulties that resulted in Penn spending nine months in a debtor's prison. The house can be seen only on the tour. ⊠ *400 Pennsbury Memorial Rd., Tyburn Rd. E off U.S. 13, between Morrisville and Bristol,* ☎ *215/946–0400.* ⊠ *$5.* ☉ *Tues.–Sat. 9–5, Sun. noon–5. Tours are weekdays at 10, 11:30, 1:30, 3:30; Sat. at 11, 12:30, 2, 3:30; Sun. at 12:30, 1:30, 2:30, 3:30.*

Washington Crossing Historic Park

❸ *7 mi north of Fallsington.*

It was here, at what is now a lovely Delaware River Park, that on Christmas night in 1776 General Washington and 2,400 of his men crossed the Delaware River, surprised the mercenary Hessian solders, and captured Trenton. A 1917 granite statue of Washington marks the point from which the soldiers embarked that snowy night. Memorials and attractions are divided between the Lower and the Upper Park, which are about 5 mi apart.

In the Lower Park, the fieldstone **Memorial Building and Visitors Center,** on Route 32, 7 mi south of New Hope, displays a reproduction of Emanuel Leutze's famous painting of the crossing (the original hangs in the Metropolitan Museum of Art in New York). Descendants of men who made that crossing sometimes come to gaze upon the painting and point out the resemblance between themselves and the soldiers in the boat. It's a vain exercise: Leutze was in Düsseldorf, Germany, when he painted the figures, and for his models he used either young men from villages along the Rhine River or American artists living abroad. But past and present do merge—magically—during the annual Christmas Day reenactment of the crossing, when locals don Colonial uniforms and brave the elements in small boats (at nearby restaurants later in the day, you may discover troops, still in uniform, enjoying their holiday bird). The **McConkey Ferry Inn** is where Washington and his staff had Christmas dinner while waiting to cross the river. It's near the Memorial Building. You also can tour the **Taylor Mansion**, a completely restored 19th-century residence in the Lower Park.

In the Upper Park, about 5 mi north of the Memorial Building on Route 32, stop at the landmark **Bowman's Hill Tower**, named after a surgeon who sailed with Captain Kidd. Washington used the hill as a lookout point. You can get a much better view of the countryside than he did by riding the elevator up the 110-ft-tall memorial tower. It's open April–November, Tuesday–Sunday 10–4:30.

A half mile north of Bowman's Hill Tower, the 100-acre **Wildflower Preserve** (☎ 215/862–2924) showcases hundreds of species of wildflowers, trees, shrubs, and ferns native to Pennsylvania. Take the guided tour (offered April–October for $3 per person) or follow the short trails, which are clearly marked to bring you back to your starting point. At the same location, the **Platt Bird Collection** displays more than 100 stuffed birds and 600 eggs. The **Thompson-Neely House**, an 18th-century farmhouse, is furnished just as it was when the Colonial leaders planned the attack on Trenton its kitchen.

✉ *Rtes. 532 and 32,* ☎ *215/493–4076.* ✆ *Grounds $1 per car. 45-min walking tour of 5 historic park buildings plus tower: $4, available at the visitor center, Thompson–Neely House, and Bowman's Hill Tower.* ☉ *Tours: Tues.–Sat. 9, 10, 11, 1, 2, 3; Sun. noon, 1, 2, 3. Park: Tues.–Sat. 9–5, Sun. noon–5.*

Newtown

4 *6 mi west of Washington Crossing Historic Park.*

Until the 1980s, Newtown was a busy village serving the commercial needs of the surrounding rural community. Today it's the bustling center of sprawling suburban development. Still, the town takes pride in its many 18th- and 19th-century homes and inns; the downtown historic district is on the National Register of Historic Places.

The **Newtown Historic Association** has regional antiques and a double-sided tavern painting by renowned local artist Edward Hicks. An association brochure provides a walking tour of the town. ✉ *Court St. and Center Ave.,* ☎ *215/968–4004.* ✆ *Free.* ☉ *June–Aug., Sun. 2–4.*

Dining and Lodging

$$$–$$$$ ✗ **Jean Pierre's.** Owner-chef Jean Pierre Tardy, formerly executive
★ chef at Philadelphia's distinguished Le Bec-Fin, prepares classic French cuisine in a country French setting. Salmon stuffed with lobster and herb-encrusted rack of lamb with a rosemary lamb *jus* (sauce) are two of the chef's favorites. ✉ *101 S. State St.,* ☎ *215/968–6201. Reservations essential. AE, D, DC, MC, V. Closed Mon. No lunch Sat.*

$$ ✗▥ **Temperance House.** This meticulously restored 1772 inn and hostelry also contains a restaurant ($$–$$$$) that serves an eclectic mix of fine Continental, nouvelle American, and Cajun cuisine. Home-

made soup stocks and an in-house charcuterie ensure an appealing range of dishes, including apple-smoked duckling and shrimp and andouille sausage étouffée. You can listen to live jazz Thursday, Friday, and Saturday nights; Dixieland jazz accompanies brunch on Sunday. Each guest room is decorated with a different style of furniture: the Benetz Suite has bent willow and twig furniture; the Edward Hicks Suite has rich period mahogany, a working fireplace, and walls stenciled in a pattern derived from a "Peaceable Kingdom" mosaic tile. Continental breakfast is served in the dining room. ⊠ *5–11 S. State St., 18940,* ☎ *215/ 860–0474. 13 rooms. Restaurant. AE, DC, MC, V. CP.*

Buckingham

8 mi north of Newtown.

This village, which dates to the Colonial era, remains primarily rural and is still the site of many large farms. One of the area's wineries is found here.

The **Buckingham Valley Vineyard & Winery** is a small family-owned operation that produces distinguished estate-bottled varietal wines. It was one of the state's first farm wineries. The vineyards and wine cellars are open to tours and tastings. ⊠ *1521 Rte. 413, 2 mi south of U.S. 202,* ☎ *215/794–7188.* ▨ *Free self-guided tour.* ☉ *Tues.–Sat. 11– 6, Sun. noon–4. Winter hours may vary.*

Shopping

At **Brown Brothers** (⊠ Rte. 413 south of Rte. 263, ☎ 215/794–7630) three or four auctioneers simultaneously conduct auctions in various categories—jewelry, silver, linens, tools, books, frames, furniture, and box lots. ☉ *Sept.–May, Sat. 8–3; June–Aug., Thurs. 3–9:30.*

Doylestown

⑤ *5 mi west of Buckingham, 12 mi north of Newtown.*

Doylestown, the county seat, is a showcase of American architecture, with stately Federal brick buildings on Lawyers' Row and plenty of gracious Queen Anne, Second Empire, and Italianate homes. The historic district, with its nearly 1,200 buildings, is listed on the National Register of Historic Places. A brochure available at the **Central Bucks Chamber of Commerce** (☞ Visitor Information *in* Bucks County A to Z, *below*) and at area B&Bs, inns, and bookstores maps out three walking tours highlighting the architecture and history of Doylestown. The town has interesting shops and restaurants and is also home to the James A. Michener Art Museum.

The most unusual buildings in Doylestown are those created by Henry Chapman Mercer. Bucks County has seen its share of eccentrics, but even in such august company Henry Mercer stands out. Expert in prehistoric archaeology, a homespun architect, and writer of Gothic tales, Mercer is best remembered for the three brilliantly theatrical structures, including his home and the Mercer Museum, found on what is known as **Mercer Mile.** All are constructed with reinforced concrete, using a technique perfected by Mercer in the early part of this century.

★ You almost expect to see a dragon puffing smoke outside **Fonthill,** Henry Chapman Mercer's storybook home and surely one of the most unique abodes in the country. Mercer, a Harvard-educated millionaire, designed the house in 1910, modeling it after a 13th-century Rhenish castle. Outside, the stone mansion bristles with turrets and balconies. Inside, the multilevel structure is truly mazelike: Mercer built his castle from the inside out—without using blueprints—and Gothic doorways, sudden

Finally, a travel companion that doesn't snore on the plane or eat all your peanuts.

When traveling, your MCI WorldCom Card is the best way to keep in touch. Our operators speak your language, so they'll be able to connect you back home—no matter where your travels take you. Plus, your MCI WorldCom Card is easy to use, and even earns you frequent flyer miles every time you use it. When you add in our great rates, you get something even more valuable: peace-of-mind. So go ahead. Travel the world. MCI WorldCom just brought it a whole lot closer.

You can even sign up today at www.mci.com/worldphone or ask your operator to make a collect call to 1-410-314-2938.

EASY TO CALL WORLDWIDE

1 Just dial the WorldPhone access number of the country you're calling from.
2 Dial or give the operator your MCI WorldCom Card number.
3 Dial or give the number you're calling.

Australia ♦	
To call using OPTUS	1-800-551-111
To call using TELSTRA	1-800-881-100
Bahamas/Bermuda	1-800-888-8000
British Virgin Islands	1-800-888-8000
Costa Rica ♦	0-800-012-2222
Denmark	8001-0022
Norway ♦	800 -19912
India	000-127
For collect access	000-126
United States/Canada	1-800-888-8000

For your complete WorldPhone calling guide, dial the
WorldPhone access number for the country you're in and ask the
operator for Customer Service. In the U.S. call 1-800-431-5402.

♦ Public phones may require deposit of coin or phone card for dial tone.

EARN FREQUENT FLYER MILES

AmericanAirlines
A Advantage

Continental Airlines
OnePass

▲ Delta Air Lines
SkyMiles

▬ MILEAGE PLUS.
United Airlines

US AIRWAYS
DIVIDEND MILES

Distinctive guides packed with up-to-date expert advice
and smart choices for every type of traveler.

Fodor's. For the world of ways you travel.

stairways, dead-ends, and inglenooks follow one after the other, all creating a fairy tale effect. Fonthill's wealth of books, prints, and Victorian engravings is enhanced by the setting: The ceilings and walls are embedded with tiles from Mercer's own kilns and with ancient tiles from around the world. As a final touch, every chamber has a different shape. ⊠ *E. Court St. and Swamp Rd. (Rte. 313),* ☎ *215/348–9461.* 🎫 *$5.* ☉ *Mon.–Sat. 10–5, Sun. noon–5. Hr-long guided tours.*

The **Moravian Pottery and Tile Works,** on the grounds of the Fonthill estate (☞ *above*), still produces unique Arts and Crafts–style picture tiles. These "Mercer" tiles adorn such structures as Graumann's Chinese Theater in Hollywood and the Harvard Lampoon Building. As author and Bucks County resident James Michener described them, "Using scenes from the Bible, mythology, and history, Henry Chapman Mercer produced wonderfully archaic tiles about 12 or 14 inches square in powerful earth colors that glowed with intensity and unforgettable imagery." Reproductions of Mercer's tiles can be purchased in the Tile Works Shop. The factory, built in 1912, resembles a Spanish mission. ⊠ *130 Swamp Rd. (Rte. 313),* ☎ *215/345–6722.* 🎫 *$3.* ☉ *Daily 10–4:45. 45-min self-guided tours every ½ hr; last tour at 4.*

The **Mercer Museum,** opened in 1916, displays Mercer's collection of tools, representing every craft and including more than 50,000 objects from before the age of steam. An archaeologist, Mercer worried that the rapid advance of progress would wipe out evidence of America's productivity before the industrial revolution. Consequently, from 1895 to 1915 he scoured the back roads of eastern Pennsylvania buying folk art, tools, and articles of everyday life. This must be one of the most incredible attics in the world: The four-story central court is crammed with log sleds, cheese presses, fire engines, boats, and bean hullers, most suspended by wires from the walls and ceiling. The **Spruance Library,** on the third floor, holds 20,000 volumes on Bucks County history. ⊠ *84 S. Pine St.,* ☎ *215/345–0210.* 🎫 *$5.* ☉ *Mon. and Wed.–Sat. 10–5, Tues. 10–9, Sun. noon–5; self-guided tours.*

The **James A. Michener Art Museum,** across the street from the Mercer Museum, has a permanent collection and changing exhibitions (photography, crafts, textiles, sculpture, and painting) that focus on 19th- and 20th-century American art and Bucks County art. It was endowed by the late best-selling novelist, a native of Doylestown. The Pennsylvania Impressionists, who worked in the area in the early part of the century, are represented by such artists as Edward Redfield and Daniel Garber.

The museum occupies the buildings and grounds of the former Bucks County Jail, which dates from 1884. A 23-ft-high fieldstone wall surrounds seven exhibition galleries, an outdoor sculpture garden, and a Gothic-style warden's house. There is also a re-creation of Michener's Doylestown study. The Mari Sabusawa–designed Michener Wing has a library, archives, and a room with 12 interactive exhibits, each honoring a prominent Bucks County arts figure such as Pearl S. Buck and Oscar Hammerstein II. ⊠ *138 S. Pine St.,* ☎ *215/340–9800.* 🎫 *$5.* ☉ *Tues.–Fri. 10–4:30, weekends 10–5.*

The **National Shrine of Our Lady of Czestochowa,** a Polish spiritual center, has drawn millions of pilgrims, including Pope John Paul II, many U.S. presidents, and Lech Wałesa, since its opening in 1966. The complex includes a modern church with huge panels of stained glass depicting the history of Christianity in Poland and the United States. The gift shop and bookstore sell religious gifts, many imported from Poland, and the cafeteria serves hot Polish and American food on Sunday. ⊠ *Ferry Rd. off Rte. 313,* ☎ *215/345–0600.* 🎫 *Free.* ☉ *Daily 9–4:30.*

Dining and Lodging

$$–$$$$ ✕ **Cafe Arielle.** This nouvelle French bistro serves delicious grilled
★ seafood dishes (including tuna steak), prime meats, and pistachio-encrusted
rack of lamb. The setting is appealing, with country French furnishings
and striking artwork. ✉ *100 S. Main St., in the Doylestown Agricul-
tural Works,* ☎ *215/345–5930. AE, DC, MC, V. Closed Mon.–Tues.*

$$–$$$ ✕ **Russell's 96 West.** Chef-proprietor Russell Palmer artistically pre-
sents classical French cuisine—with an accent on southern France—in
a restored 1846 town house. The seasonally changing menu may in-
clude rack of lamb, roasted breast of duck in a sweet apricot glaze,
and Maine salmon with a reduction sauce of roasted shallots and red
wine. Vegetables are bought from local organic farmers. Dinner and
the lighter lunch are also served on the patio in warm weather. ✉ *96
W. State St.,* ☎ *215/345–8746. AE, D, DC, MC, V. Closed Sun.*

$$ ✕🏠 **Sign of the Sorrel Horse.** Catering to weary (and hungry) travelers, this inn has one of the finest restaurants in the area. The 1714 grist-
mill houses the formal Escoffier Room ($$–$$$$; jacket preferred). Chef
Jon Atkin grows his own herbs and does wonders with fresh game dishes.
His wife, Monique, oversees the dining rooms and his son, Christian,
combs area stores for the best varietal wines. For espresso and desserts,
repair to the Waterwheel Lounge. If you plan to stay the night, you'll
be put up in a 1714 gristmill that once supplied flour for Washington's
army and lodged Lafayette. Today it is decorated in the style of a French
auberge. Period antiques fill the guest rooms; one has a fireplace, and
one has a whirlpool bath. ✉ *4424 Old Easton Rd., 18901,* ☎ *215/
230–9999,* 🖷 *215/230–8053. 6 rooms. Restaurant. AE, DC, MC, V.
Inn and restaurant closed Mon.–Tues. CP.*

$$$ 🏠 **Pine Tree Farm.** This Colonial farmhouse dating to 1730 has been
decorated with cheerful country antiques set in the light and airy
rooms. Room 1, the largest room and a favorite, has a white twig bed
and a dressing table in the bathroom. The glass-enclosed garden room
in the rear of the house overlooks 16 acres of pine trees, a pond, and
the pool. Breakfast, served poolside in summer, may include Grand
Marnier French toast and fresh-baked muffins; lighter fare is also
available. This B&B is no-smoking. ✉ *2155 Lower State Rd., 18901,*
☎ *215/348–0632. 4 rooms. Pool. AE, MC, V. BP.*

$$–$$$ 🏠 **Inn at Fordhook Farm.** The Burpee family (of seed catalog fame) coun-
try estate is now a B&B set on 60 lovely acres and loaded with family memorabilia and antiques. Built in 1760 and purchased in 1888 by
W. Atlee Burpee, the house has spacious high-ceiling bedrooms (two
with Mercer tile fireplaces) brightened with floral prints, a large Federal-style living room, and a dining room with another tile fireplace.
The full country breakfast, with oatmeal-buttermilk pancakes and
cream-cheese-filled French toast, is served in the Burpee family dining
room. The carriage house, with its dark wood paneling and vaulted
cathedral ceiling, is a more modern alternative to the main house. ✉
105 New Britain Rd., 18901, ☎ *215/345–1766,* 🖷 *215/345–1791. 7
rooms, 5 with bath. Badminton, croquet. AE, MC, V. BP.*

$$ 🏠 **Highland Farms.** If only this house could talk . . . or rather, sing.
★ This Bucks County estate was the home of lyricist Oscar Hammerstein
II from 1941 to 1960. Not far from the field where the *Oklahoma!*
co-creator could enjoy what he originally called "corn as high as an
elephant's eye," this pretty 1840s Federal-style country home often hosted
the greats of Broadway and even Hollywood. Today antiques and
Hammerstein family memorabilia furnish the house elegantly. A four-
course country breakfast is served in the formal dining room or on the
brick patio overlooking the 60-ft pool; at night you can settle in with
a film from the video library stocked with Rodgers and Hammerstein

favorites. ⊠ *70 East Rd., 18901,* ☎ *215/340–1354. 4 rooms. Pool, tennis court, library. AE, MC, V. BP.*

$–$$ 🏨 **Doylestown Inn.** In the middle of town at the crossroads of Route 611 and U.S. 202, this Victorian hotel dates to 1902. At press time, the inn was set to reopen in early 2000 after a major renovation. Dark woods and traditional furniture will set the tone in the guest rooms, some of which will have whirlpool tubs and fireplaces. Mercer tiles are found in the lobby. The restaurant serves casual American fare. ⊠ *18 W. State St.,* ☎ *215/345–6610,* FAX *215/345–4017. 19 rooms. Restaurant, in-room data ports, minibars, meeting rooms. AE, D, DC, MC, V.*

Perkasie

6 mi north of Doylestown.

Outside this small town (but closer to Dublin) is the home of writer Pearl S. Buck (1892–1973). Two of the area's covered bridges are ❻ nearby, too. The **Pearl S. Buck House** is filled with the writer's collection of Asian and American antiques and personal belongings. Green Hills Farm, Buck's country home (built in 1835), is where she wrote nearly 100 novels, children's books, and works of nonfiction while raising seven adopted children and caring for many others. The house still bears the imprint of the girl who grew up in China and became the first American woman to win both the Nobel and Pulitzer prizes. Buck is best known for her novel *The Good Earth.* Pearl S. Buck International, which supports displaced children in Asia, has offices on the 60-acre property. ⊠ *520 Dublin Rd., off Rte. 313,* ☎ *215/249–0100 or 800/220–2825.* 🎫 *$5.* ☉ *Mar.–Dec., farmhouse tours Tues.–Sat. 11, 1, and 2; Sun. 1 and 2.*

Outdoor Activities and Sports

Haycock Riding Stables (⊠ 1035 Old Bethlehem Rd., off Rte. 313, ☎ 215/257–6271) escorts riders on one- and two-hour trips through lovely Nockamixon State Park, 4 mi to the north; reservations are needed.

New Hope

❼ *18 mi southeast of Perkasie, 40 mi northeast of Philadelphia.*

The cosmopolitan village of New Hope is a mecca for artists, shoppers, and lovers of old homes—and hordes of day-trippers and backpackers on summer weekends. The town, listed on the National Register of Historic Places, is easy to explore on foot; the most interesting sights and stores are clustered along four blocks of Main Street and on the cross streets—Mechanic, Ferry, and Bridge streets—which lead to the river. Unfortunately, lower Main Street has succumbed to tourist blight (do try Gerenser's Exotic Ice Cream, at 22 South Main, though), but if you take a walk on Ferry Street or along the towpath, there's plenty of charm. For a good orientation to New Hope, take the Bucks County Carriages horse-drawn tour (☞ Guided Tours *in* Bucks County A to Z, *below*), which starts by the cannon alongside the Logan Inn. And if you're eager for more country charm and more antiques, you can take Bridge Street over the Delaware River to Lambertville (☞ *below*) in New Jersey.

The **Parry Mansion,** a stone house built in 1784, is notable because the furnishings reflect decorative changes from 1775 to the Victorian era—including candles, whitewashed walls, oil lamps, and wallpaper. Wealthy lumber-mill owner Benjamin Parry built the house, which was occupied by five generations of his family. ⊠ *S. Main and Ferry Sts.,* ☎ *215/862–5652 or 215/862–5460.* 🎫 *$5.* ☉ *May–Dec., Fri.–Sat. 1–5.*

Beginning in 1832, coal barges plied the Delaware Canal. Today the canal is a state park, and you can ride a mule-pulled barge from the **New Hope Canal Boat Company.** The one-hour narrated excursion travels past Revolutionary-era cottages, gardens, and artists' workshops. A barge historian/folk singer is aboard. ⊠ *New and S. Main Sts.,* ☎ *215/862–2842.* ☞ *$7.95.* ☉ *Apr., Fri.–Sun. 12:30, 3; May–Oct., daily noon, 1:30, 3, 4:30.*

The **New Hope & Ivyland Rail Road** makes a 9-mi, 50-minute scenic run from New Hope to Lahaska. The train crosses a trestle used in the rescue scenes in the old "Perils of Pauline" movies. The New Hope depot is an 1891 Victorian gem. Theme rides, which require reservations, include Saturday evening dinner trains, Santa trains at Christmas, and Sunday brunch trains. ⊠ *W. Bridge and Stockton Sts.,* ☎ *215/862–2332.* ☞ *$9.50.* ☉ *May–Oct., daily; Nov., Fri.–Sun.; Dec., Thurs.–Sun.; Jan.–Apr., weekends and holidays; trains run hourly 11–4.*

Dining and Lodging

$$$$ ✕ **La Bonne Auberge.** Some critics consider this to be Bucks County's
  ★ most elite and expensive restaurant, thanks to the owners—chef Gerard Caronello, a native of Lyon, France, and his wife, Rozanne, of Great Britain. The consistently classic French cuisine is served in a pre-Revolutionary farmhouse. The Terrace Room, used for dining, has a modern country French ambience. Some specialties are grilled salmon with a light lobster sauce and rack of lamb. The five-course table d'hôte menu, available Wednesday and Thursday evenings in addition to the regular menu, is a bargain. The restaurant is within a residential development called Village 2; when you call for reservations, travel directions will be provided. ⊠ *Village 2 off Mechanic St.,* ☎ *215/862–2462. Reservations essential. Jacket required. AE, MC, V. Closed Mon.–Tues.*

$$–$$$ ✕ **Martine's.** Reminiscent of an English pub with its beam ceiling, plaster-over-stone walls, and fireplace, Martine's has an eclectic menu that includes filet mignon au poivre, pasta, duckling, and steamed seafood mélange. Try the French onion soup. Outdoor dining is on a small patio. ⊠ *7 E. Ferry St.,* ☎ *215/862–2966. AE, MC, V.*

$$–$$$ ✕ **Odette's.** In 1961 Parisian actress Odette Myrtil Logan converted a former canal lock house into a restaurant. The atmosphere is French country bistro; the cuisine, Continental, with a menu that changes seasonally. Sunday brunch is buffet style. You may want to request a table at one of the dining rooms with a river view. Entertainment consists of a nightly session around the piano bar, legendary among local show-tune buffs, plus regular appearances by nationally known cabaret performers. ⊠ *S. River Rd., ½ mi south of Bridge St.,* ☎ *215/862–2432. AE, DC, MC, V.*

$$ ✕ **Mother's.** One of New Hope's most popular dining spots, Mother's main claim is still its truly sinful desserts, such as chocolate mousse pie and apple walnut cake. Homemade soups, pastas, and unusual pizzas are offered on the extensive menu, but your best bet for good food is to visit for breakfast. In summer meals are also served in the garden. Expect to wait; it's often crowded here. ⊠ *34 N. Main St.,* ☎ *215/ 862–9354. AE, D, MC, V.*

$–$$ ✕ **Havana Bar and Restaurant.** Grilled specialties enhance the American regional and contemporary fare at the Havana. Menu items include sesame onion rings, a grilled eggplant and Brie sandwich, and a nouvelle hamburger with Gorgonzola cheese and spiced walnuts. The bar is enlivened by jazz bands from Thursday through Sunday nights and by karaoke on Monday night. The view of Main Street is ideal for people-watching, especially from the outdoor patio. ⊠ *105 S. Main St.,* ☎ *215/862–9897. AE, D, DC, MC, V.*

$$ ✕🏨 **Hotel du Village.** Flower-filled grounds surrounding the large, old stone boarding school create the feeling of an English manor house. The guest rooms have country furniture, and a Continental breakfast is served in the parlor. You can feast on country French fare in the restaurant (closed Monday and Tuesday; no lunch), either in a Tudor-style room or on the sunporch. Chef-owner Omar Arbani prepares tournedos Henri IV, a beef fillet with béarnaise sauce; sweetbreads with mushrooms in Madeira sauce; and fillet of sole in curried butter, all topped off by extravagant desserts. ⊠ *2535 N. River Rd. (Rte. 32), 18938,* ☎ *215/862–5164 or 215/862–9911,* 𝖥𝖠𝖷 *215/862–9788. 20 rooms. Pool, 2 tennis courts. AE, DC. CP.*

$$ ✕🏨 **Logan Inn.** Established in 1727 as an extension of the Ferry Tavern, this inn accommodated passengers who used the Delaware River ferry to Lambertville. George Washington is said to have stayed here at least five times—and one can only imagine what he would think of the crowds of shoppers who stroll right outside the inn, smack dab in the busiest part of town. Rooms have original and reproduction Colonial and Victorian furnishings and canopy beds; some have river views. Full or Continental breakfast on the tented patio is included. As for the friendly restaurant ($$–$$$), the Logan serves three menus: lunch (11–3:30), dinner (4–closing), and a popular all-day tavern menu, with such favorites as nachos, buffalo wings, salads, and burgers. ⊠ *10 W. Ferry St., 18938,* ☎ *215/862–2300. 16 rooms. Restaurant. AE, D, DC, MC, V. CP.*

$$–$$$$ 🏨 **Mansion Inn.** Romantic luxury and calm surround you inside this ★ elegant 1865 Second Empire–style Victorian inn, although busy Main Street is just steps away from the massive front door. Even the pool and English garden feel pleasantly private. Depression glass, local art, antiques, and comfortable furniture fill the inviting, high-ceiling yellow and beige sitting rooms. Guest rooms (two in a separate building) have antique pieces, plush linens, and modern baths, some with fireplaces and whirlpool tubs. Breakfast includes everything from fresh muffins and fruit to an egg dish or French toast. There's a two-night minimum on weekends, three on holidays; no smoking is allowed. ⊠ *9 S. Main St., 18938,* ☎ *215/862–1231,* 𝖥𝖠𝖷 *215/862–0277. 5 rooms, 4 suites. Breakfast room, air-conditioning, pool. AE, MC, V. BP.*

$$–$$$ 🏨 **Whitehall Inn.** Guest rooms at the 18th-century manor house of what was once a gentleman's horse farm are furnished with period antiques, canopy beds, and patterned wallpaper; four also have fireplaces. You get a bowl of fresh fruit and a bottle of mineral water upon arrival and will find chocolate truffles and velour robes in your room. A spacious parlor has sofas and rocking chairs facing a fireplace. The four-course candlelit gourmet breakfast is served at tables set with white linen, English china, and heirloom silver; in the afternoon, high tea is served. Smoking is not allowed. ⊠ *1370 Pineville Rd., 18938,* ☎ *215/598–7945 or 888/379–4483. 5 rooms. Pool. AE, D, DC, MC, V. BP.*

$–$$$ 🏨 **Wedgwood Inn.** Three buildings comprise the Wedgwood Inn B&B ★ lodgings: a blue "painted lady" 1870 Victorian house with a gabled roof, porch, and a porte cochere; a Federal-style 1840 stone manor house; and the Aaron Burr House, another 1870 Victorian building. Just steps from Main Street, the inn has landscaped grounds with gazebos and gardens. Wedgwood pottery, antiques, fireplaces, and wood-burning stoves add to the charm. Five rooms have two-person whirlpool tubs. A Continental-plus breakfast is served on the sunporch, gazebo, or your room. For a fee you can have tennis and pool privileges at a nearby club. The inn is no-smoking. ⊠ *111 W. Bridge St., 18938,* ☎ *215/862–2570. 15 rooms, 4 suites. Concierge. AE, MC, V. CP.*

$$ ☒ **Best Western New Hope Inn.** This serviceable motel is a few minutes from New Hope and 30 minutes from Sesame Place. It's handy for single-night accommodations on busy fall weekends, when the country inns are often fully booked. ☒ *6426 Lower York Rd. (Rte. 202), 18938,* ☏ *215/862–5221 or 800/467–3202,* FAX *215/862–5847. 159 rooms. Restaurant, lobby lounge, pool, tennis court. AE, D, DC, MC, V.*

Nightlife and the Arts

The **Bucks County Playhouse** (☒ 70 S. Main St., ☏ 215/862–2041), housed in a historic mill, stages Broadway musical revivals. Recent shows have included *She Loves Me* and *West Side Story*. The season runs from April through December.

Outdoor Activities and Sports

New Hope Cyclery (☒ 186 Old York Rd., ☏ 215/862–6888) rents mountain bikes for $31 per day. The staff can direct you to scenic bike routes.

West End Farm (☒ River Rd. in Phillips Mill, north of New Hope, ☏ 215/862–5883) offers one-hour escorted rides on horseback along the Delaware Canal; call to make a reservation.

Shopping

New Hope's streets are lined with shops selling crafts and handmade accessories, art, antiques, campy vintage items, and contemporary wares.

ANTIQUES

Hobensack & Keller (☒ Bridge St., New Hope, ☏ 215/862–2406) stocks antique and authentic reproduction garden ornaments, cast-iron furniture, fencing, and Oriental rugs. **Olde Hope Antiques** (☒ U.S. 202 and Reeder Rd., ☏ 215/862–5055) carries hooked rugs, Pennsylvania German textiles, hand-painted furniture, and folk art. **Katy Kane** (☒ 34 W. Ferry St., New Hope, ☏ 215/862–5873) is the place for antique, vintage, and designer clothing; accessories; and fine linens: the shop is open by appointment only.The **Pink House** (☒ W. Bridge St., ☏ 215/862–5947) has magnificent European 18th- and 19th-century furnishings and textiles.

ART GALLERIES

Many artists live in Bucks County, and more than 30 galleries in New Hope and neighboring Lambertville (across the river in New Jersey) showcase paintings, prints, and sculpture. The New Hope Information Center (☞ Bucks County A to Z, *below*) can tell you about other galleries. The **Golden Door Gallery** (☒ 52 S. Main St., ☏ 215/862–5529) displays works by Bucks County painters, sculptors, and printmakers, as well as by artists from other parts of the country.

BOOKSTORE

The crowded shelves at **Farley's Bookshop** (☒ 44 S. Main St., ☏ 215/862–2452) hold plenty of choices, including books about the area.

Lambertville

Across the Delaware River from New Hope.

If you're interested in all that New Hope has to offer but prefer it in a lower key, this New Jersey village is just a walk or short drive away, over the Delaware River; use the bridge on New Hope's Bridge Street. You'll find more charm and even better antiques, as well as a delightfully chic assemblage of shops, galleries, Federal and Victorian houses, and fine restaurants. The **Hamilton Grill Room** (☒ 8½ Coryell St., ☏ 609/397–4343) a Mediterranean eatery, is one good dining choice. For an overnight stay, try the **Historic Lambertville House** (☒ 32 Bridge St., ☏ 609/397–0200), a historic lodging with 25 rooms.

Lahaska

3 mi west of New Hope.

Shopping packs in the crowds here, primarily because of the boutiques at Peddler's Village (☞ Shopping, *below*). If bargains are your goal, you can also find outlets here. Along U.S. 202 between New Hope and Lahaska you'll see many antiques shops.

Dining and Lodging

$$-$$$ ✕ **Jenny's Bistro.** American regional cuisine is served in a Victorian or a country French room. Lobster ravioli and filet Chesterfield (filet mignon with cheddar cheese, bacon, and horseradish sauce) are favorites. You can hear piano music Friday and Saturday nights. ⊠ *U.S. 202, Peddler's Village,* ☎ *215/794–4020. AE, D, DC, MC, V. No dinner Mon.*

$-$$ ✕ **Spotted Hog.** This casual country bistro in the Golden Plough Inn (☞ *below*) serves American cuisine such as New York strip steak, grilled chicken with melted Monterey Jack cheese in an oyster sherry sauce, Philadelphia cheese steaks, and interesting pizzas. The bar stocks 35 American microbrewery beers. The Spotted Hog is the only restaurant in Peddler's Village to serve breakfast. ⊠ *Peddler's Village, Rte. 202 and Street Rd.,* ☎ *215/794–4030. AE, D, DC, MC, V.*

$$-$$$ ⌂ **Barley Sheaf Farm.** If Bucks County was once known as the Ge-
★ nius Belt, this famous estate was probably its buckle. Home to playwright George S. Kaufman—author of and collaborator on such jewels as *Dinner at Eight* and *You Can't Take It with You*—the house was then called Cherchez la Farm. The inn's 30-acre parklike setting includes the 1740 fieldstone mansion, a duck pond, a pool, and a meadow full of sheep. You retire to bedrooms decorated with country antiques, brass, and four-poster beds. A hearty breakfast is served on the glass-enclosed sunporch. Rooms in the adjacent cottage are smaller but share the same country decor. Barley Sheaf Farm is in Holicong, a mile west of Lahaska. ⊠ *5281 York Rd. (U.S. 202), Holicong 18928,* ☎ *215/794–5104,* FAX *215/794–5332. 12 rooms. Pool, badminton, croquet, meeting rooms. AE, MC, V. BP.*

$$-$$$ ⌂ **Golden Plough Inn.** Nestled within Peddler's Village, this inn has
★ 22 spacious guest rooms, many with four-poster beds, rich fabrics, and cozy window seats that beautifully evoke 19th-century Bucks County. All rooms come with air-conditioning, remote control TV, a small refrigerator, and a complimentary bottle of champagne, and some have a fireplace or whirlpool bath. Forty-three other guest rooms are scattered about the village—in an 18th-century farmhouse, a historic carriage house, and in Merchant's Row. There is a complimentary Continental breakfast or a credit toward breakfast on the à la carte menu at the Spotted Hog (☞ *above*). ⊠ *Peddler's Village, Rte. 202 and Street Rd., 18931,* ☎ *215/794–4004,* FAX *215/794–4008. 65 rooms. Restaurant. AE, D, DC, MC, V. CP.*

$$ ⌂ **Ash Mill Farm.** This country B&B is a handsome 18th-century fieldstone manor house set on 10 acres. High ceilings, ornate moldings, and deep-sill windows add character to the parlor; rooms have family antiques, reproductions, and thoughtful extras such as hair dryers and down comforters on canopy or four-poster beds. A full country breakfast is served, and afternoon refreshments are available. The porch has a view of resident sheep. This B&B is just south of Lahaska. ⊠ *5358 York Rd. (Rte. 202), Holicong 18928,* ☎ *215/794–5373. 3 rooms, 2 suites. MC, V. BP.*

Shopping

Peddler's Village (⊠ U.S. 202 and Rte. 263, ☎ 215/794–4000) began in the early 1960s, when Earl Jamison bought a 6-acre chicken farm, moved local 18th-century houses to the site, and opened a Carmel, California–inspired collection of specialty shops and restaurants. Today the 75 shops in the 42-acre village peddle books, cookware, toys, leather goods, clothes, jewelry, contemporary crafts, art prints, candles, and other decorative items. The Grand Carousel, a restored 1922 Philadelphia Toboggan Company creation, still operates. Crowd-drawing seasonal events include the Strawberry Festival and display, in May; the Teddy Bear's Picnic, in July; and the Scarecrow Festival, in September. On the grounds is the Golden Plough Inn (☞ Dining and Lodging, *above*).

Penn's Purchase Factory Outlet Stores (✉ 5881 York Rd., at U.S. 202, ☎ 215/794–0300) includes more than 40 stores selling name-brand merchandise at 20%–60% off regular retail prices. You'll find Adidas, Coach, Easy Spirit, Geoffrey Beene, Izod, Jonathan Logan, Orvis, Nautica, and more, as well as restaurants. All 11 buildings in this new complex have been designed in an Early American country style that harmonizes with the look of Peddler's Village, right across the road.

FLEA MARKET

Rice's Sale and Country Market (✉ Green Hill Rd., Solebury, near Peddler's Village, ☎ 215/297–5993) is a mostly open-air market with bargains on canned goods, clothing, linens, shoes, back-issue magazines, and plants; there are a few antiques, too. It opens Tuesday (year-round) and Saturday (March–December) around 6:30 AM and closes at 1:30 PM. Call for additional holiday openings.

Carversville

8 *4 mi northeast of Lahaska.*

One pleasure of traveling in Bucks County is driving on lovely back roads and discovering tiny old mill villages such as Carversville. If you're traveling east from Lahaska, make a left turn onto Aquetong Road and into one of the most beautiful areas of the state. At the **Carversville General Store** (✉ Carversville and Aquetong Rds., ☎ 215/297–5353), locals gather for gossip and take-out coffee and pick up picnic supplies.

Dining

$$–$$$ ✕ **Carversville Inn.** Its out-of-the-way location has made this circa-1813
★ inn one of the area's best-kept secrets. Chef Will Mathias's regional American cuisine with a Southern flair is now a local favorite. The menu changes seasonally, but you can always count on innovative sauces such as roast red-pepper horseradish on grilled filet mignon or rosemary demiglacé on rack of lamb. ✉ *Carversville and Aquetong Rds.,* ☎ *215/297–0900. AE, MC, V. Closed Mon.*

Lumberville

9 *3 mi east of Carversville.*

In tiny Lumberville you can picnic along the Delaware Canal or on Bull's Island, accessible by the footbridge across the Delaware River. Open since 1770, the **Lumberville Store** is the focus of village life— the place to mail letters, buy groceries (and picnic supplies), and rent a bicycle (☞ Outdoor Activities and Sports, *below*). Across the street stands the Black Bass Hotel, a famous Colonial-period inn (☞ Dining and Lodging, *below*) that was once the country retreat of President Grover Cleveland. To get here from Carversville, continue to Fleecy Dale or Old Carversville roads (ignore the ROAD CLOSED sign—it's been there for years.) Both of these backcountry roads lead to River Road (Route 32) and Lumberville.

Dining and Lodging

$ ✕▥ **Black Bass Hotel.** This inn has been a favorite stopover along the Delaware River for more than 240 years. Although it sits snug within a region that witnessed many events of the American Revolution, don't look for any GEORGE WASHINGTON SLEPT HERE plaques: the hotel and its clientele were loyalists to the British Crown, and, coincidentally, its current owner, Herb Ward, is as Anglophile as they come. He's even adorned the inn with a fabulous collection of British royal memorabilia. A wayside inn (and it is truly wayside, since the hotel's facade sits directly on Route 32), the Black Bass also has an excellent restaurant ($$–$$$) and an outdoor deck overlooking the river—just the place for a picture-perfect summer dinner. ✉ Rte. 32, ☎ 215/297–5770, ℻ 215/297–0262. 9 rooms, 2 with bath. AE, DC, MC, V.

Outdoor Activities and Sports

A recommended 6-mi route for hikers and bikers starts in Lumberville. Cross the pedestrian bridge to Bull Island State Park; go south on the New Jersey side along the Delaware and Raritan Canal to Stockton. Cross the river again to Center Bridge, Pennsylvania, and head back up the Delaware Canal towpath to Lumberville.

Lumberville Store Bicycle Rental Co. (✉ River Rd., ☎ 215/297–5388) rents mountain bikes with wide tires from mid-April through November; daily rental is $25. The staff can direct you to scenic bike routes.

Point Pleasant

2 mi north of Lumberville.

This town's location on the Delaware River makes it a focus for recreational activities. It's a lovely area to explore, and two of the county's covered bridges are a few miles northwest of town. Two fine parks, **Tohickon Valley County Park** (Point Pleasant) and **Ralph Stover State Park** (Pipersville), are joined along Tohickon Creek near town.

More than 100,000 people a year—from toddlers to grandparents—negotiate the Delaware on inner tubes or in canoes from **Bucks County River Country Canoe and Tube** (✉ Byron Rd. at River Rd., ☎ 215/297–5000). The cost is around $15 per person, and the company also rents rafts and kayaks during its April through October season. A bus transports people upriver to begin three- or four-hour tube or raft rides down to the base. No food, cans, or bottles are permitted on the tube rides. Wear sneakers you don't mind getting wet and lots of sunscreen; life jackets are available at no charge. Reservations are required.

En Route Between the villages of Point Pleasant and Erwinna run some of the most Edenic stretches of the **Delaware Canal towpath,** parallel to River Road. This is the section of Bucks County that is reminiscent of the Cotswolds of England, with bridge-keeper lodges, corkscrew bends in the road, and vistas so picturesque they seem to drip off the canvas.

Erwinna

❿ *7 mi north of Point Pleasant.*

The bucolic river town of Erwinna is a fine place to unwind. There are three covered bridges nearby, and you can visit a park and a local winery. Nearby Tinicum was once home to Dorothy Parker and S. J. Perelman.

One of the most active in the county parks system, 126-acre **Tinicum Park** (✉ River Rd., ☎ 215/757–0571) has hiking, picnicking, fishing and more. On weekend afternoons from May through September (or by appointment), you can also tour the **Erwin-Stover House** (☎ 215/489–5133), an 1800 Federal house with 1840 and 1860 additions.

Sand Castle Winery opens it doors for tastings and tours of its vineyard and underground wine cellar. Ask about longer 2½-hour VIP tours, too. ⊠ *755 River Rd., Rte. 32,* ☎ *610/294–9181.* 🎫 *$3–$15 for tours.* ☉ *Weekdays 9–6, Sat. 10–6, Sun. 11–6.*

Dining and Lodging

$$–$$$ ✕🏠 **Evermay on-the-Delaware.** The Barrymores used to play croquet
★   on the lawn in front of this cream-color clapboard house, a fine Victorian mansion along the Delaware. Today, Evermay is as popular for its restaurant ($$$$; open Friday–Sunday for one dinner seating) as for its stylish hostelry; reservations a month in advance are essential. William Finnegan serves an impressive prix-fixe six-course dinner. His contemporary American menu offers a choice of two entrées, such as grilled sea bass on noodles with spaghetti squash and rack of lamb on wilted baby spinach, and includes champagne, hors d'oeuvres, and a cheese course. Upstairs (try to book a room with a river view) and in the nearby cottage and carriage house, guest rooms are filled with antiques and fresh flowers. A breakfast of fresh fruit compote, croissants, cereal, juice, and coffee is served in the garden room. Could anything be nicer than taking predinner sherry or afternoon tea in the stately parlor warmed by its twin fireplaces? ⊠ *River and Headquarters Rds., 18920,* ☎ *610/294–9100. 18 rooms. Restaurant. MC, V. CP.*

$–$$ ✕🏠 **Golden Pheasant Inn.** One of the prettiest places along the Delaware
★   Canal, this 1857 Bucks County landmark has been restored as a rustic yet elegant French auberge by Michel and Barbara Faure, a husband-and-wife team of chef and hostess. In the solarium of the restaurant ($$–$$$), diners eat beneath potted plants—and the stars—in a renovated greenhouse. Other diners prefer the tavern room, with its working fireplace, gleaming copper cooking vessels, and pierced tin chandeliers. An ex-chef at Paris's Ritz Hotel, Michel Faure deliciously melds the culinary traditions of the New and Old Worlds: Medallions of boned duck with a sauce of apricot brandy and salmon in a lobster-and-champagne sauce are favored choices. Upstairs are six guest rooms, all with four-poster beds and river or canal views; these are often booked months in advance. Note that some rooms front River Road, at times a heavily trafficked thoroughfare. ⊠ *River Rd., 18920,* ☎ *610/294–9595. 6 rooms. Restaurant. AE, D, DC, MC, V. CP.*

Upper Black Eddy

6 mi north of Erwinna.

This is another Bucks County river town that's a fine place in which to relax or explore the countryside. You can drive across the river here to Milford and explore the Jersey side of the Delaware. A few miles south of Milford are the antiques shops and restaurants of pretty Frenchtown; then you can recross to Uhlerstown and drive back north to Upper Black Eddy.

If you're here in fall, you can try a **Haunted Hayride,** a spook-filled evening ride through 256 acres of sinister woods. ⊠ *Bucks County River Country,* ☎ *215/297–5000.* 🎫 *$15.* ☉ *Oct.; call for days and times.*

Lodging

$–$$$ 🏠 **Bridgeton House on the Delaware.** Wide, screened porches and a terrace provide close-up views of the Delaware River and the bridge to Milford, New Jersey. Guest rooms are decorated with wall and ceiling folk murals. The informal sitting room has white wood walls and a glass wall overlooking the river. A two-course gourmet country breakfast is served, as are afternoon tea and sherry. Request a river view: Although other rooms face the road directly outside the front entrance, riverfront rooms have French doors to private screened porches. In the modern penthouse the marble fireplace and huge windows are delightful. ⊠ *River Rd., 18972,* ☏ *610/982–5856,* 𝖥𝖠𝖷 *610/982–5080. 8 rooms, 3 suites. MC, V. BP.*

Kintnersville

⓫ *5 mi northwest of Upper Black Eddy.*

Well-situated near the pleasures of the river and the towpath, the hamlet of Kintnersville is also just a few minutes' drive from 5,000-acre Nockamixon State Park (☞ Parks *in* Bucks County A to Z, *below*), a popular spot for boating, swimming, biking, and hiking. You can explore the scenic back roads and farm country of northern Bucks County, too.

Dining and Lodging

$–$$ ✕ **Great American Grill.** Bright primary colors, recorded music from the '50s and '60s, and tables stocked with paper and crayons (more than 200 creations by diners hang on the walls) set a casual tone at this cheerful eatery. The menu lists burgers, sandwiches, and ribs, as well as more sophisticated fare such as grilled sirloin marinated in beer and pasta with jumbo shrimp and vegetables with a lemon-garlic-dill sauce. ⊠ *Rtes. 32 and 611,* ☏ *610/847–2023. AE, D, DC, MC, V. Closed Mon. and Tues. Labor Day–Memorial Day.*

$$–$$$ 🏠 **Lightfarm Bed & Breakfast.** A visit to this 92-acre working farm with a creek and a pond yields bucolic charm and quiet. On the premises are sheep, pot-bellied pigs, chickens, and a peacock—great to occupy children over five, who are welcome here. Rooms in the 1811 stone farmhouse are furnished with period antiques, homemade quilts, and four-poster or canopy beds; some have fireplaces. A full Pennsylvania Dutch breakfast, with fresh fruit and entrées such as double-crust sausage pie, salmon pie, or apple pancakes, is included. ⊠ *2042 Berger Rd., 18930,* ☏ *610/847–3276,* 𝖥𝖠𝖷 *610/847–2926. 3 rooms, 1 suite. Hot tub. AE, D, MC, V. BP.*

$$ 🏠 **Bucksville House Bed & Breakfast.** This country-style inn was a stagecoach stop for over a century and later served a different mission as a speakeasy during Prohibition. The original 1795 building has fireplaces in some guest rooms, and plenty of antique quilts, baskets, and country Colonial furniture add warmth. On the inn's 4½ acres are a large pond and an herb and perennial garden. In summer the full breakfast—dishes might include three-cheese puffy omelets or fresh fruit parfait—is served on a modern octagonal deck; at other times you eat in an enclosed gazebo. ⊠ *4501 Durham Rd., 18930,* ☏ 𝖥𝖠𝖷 *610/847– 8948. 5 rooms. Library. AE, D, MC, V. BP.*

BUCKS COUNTY A TO Z

Arriving and Departing

By Bus
Greyhound Lines (☏ 800/231–2222) has four buses a day to Doylestown from Philadelphia. The trip takes 75–90 minutes and costs $8.50 one-way, $15.50 round-trip.

By Car
From Philadelphia the most direct route to Bucks County is I–95 north, which takes you near sights in the southern part of the county. I–95 crosses Route 32, which runs along the Delaware River past

Washington Crossing Historic Park and on to New Hope. New Hope is about 40 mi northeast of Philadelphia.

By Train

SEPTA (☎ 215/580–7800) provides frequent service from Philadelphia's Market Street East, Suburban, and 30th Street stations to Doylestown on the R5 line. The trip takes up to 85 minutes, depending on the number of local stops.

Getting Around

Bucks County is a large area—40 mi long and up to 20 mi wide—and is almost impossible to tour without a car. Main roads are River Road (Route 32), U.S. 202, and Rte. 611. One great pleasure of a visit here can be exploring country back roads.

Contacts and Resources

B&B Reservation Services

Bed & Breakfast Inns of Bucks and Hunterdon Counties (✉ Box 215, New Hope 18938, ☎ 800/794–5254, www.bucksinns) is an association of 15 inns, 11 of which are in Bucks County. **Bucks County Bed & Breakfast Association of Pennsylvania** (✉ Box 154, New Hope 18938, ☎ 800/982–1235, www.visitbucks.com) represents 32 area inns.

Emergencies

Ambulance, fire, police (☎ 911). There is an emergency room at **Doylestown Hospital** (✉ 595 W. State St., Doylestown, ☎ 215/345–2200).

Fishing

Anglers are drawn to the Delaware River and Lake Nockamixon for smallmouth bass, trout, catfish, and carp. The most popular event is the annual shad run (from early April to early June), which has spawned a festival in Lambertville, New Jersey, the last weekend in April. The required fishing license can be purchased at any area sporting goods shop. A three-day tourist license costs $15, and a seven-day license is $30; a trout stamp costs an extra $5.50. For a license and tips on where to fish, try the **Nockamixon Sports Shop** (✉ 808 Doylestown Pike, Quakertown, ☎ 215/538–9553). **Dave's Sporting Goods** (✉ 1127 N. Easton Rd./Rte. 611, north of Doylestown, ☎ 215/766–8000) can provide a license and fishing information.

Guided Tours

Bucks County Carriages (☎ 215/862–3582) offers 20-minute horse-drawn carriage tours. Horses are "parked" at the Logan Inn in New Hope, near the bakery in Peddler's Village, and at the Lambertville station in Lambertville, New Jersey. There are daytime and evening rides depending on the season and departure location. A ride to a catered picnic and customized tours are available by reservation.

Coryell's Ferry Ride and Historic Narrative (☎ 215/862–2050), which runs April through October, is a half-hour sightseeing ride on the Delaware River in a 65-ft, 49-passenger stern-wheeler.

From June through November, **Ghost Tours of New Hope** (☎ 215/957–9988) leads a one-hour lantern-led walk that explores the haunting tales of the area.

Marlene Miller of Executive Events Inc. (☎ 215/766–2211) has customized group tours and tour groups for individual travelers in 28-passenger minivans. Some trip themes include covered bridges, historic mansions, arts, wineries, antiques, and shopping.

Hot-Air Balloon Ride

Wings of Gold (☎ 215/244–9323) offers 30- and 60-minute hot-air balloon flights over Bucks County. Flights leave from Newtown, Richboro, or Lahaska, and are scheduled within two hours of sunrise or sunset, when the winds are best. Cost is $80–$165 per person.

Parks

Many parks throughout the county have canoes for rent, trails for biking and hiking, and camping facilities. Call the county park (☎ 215/757–0571) office for further information. The largest and best equipped area park is 5,000-acre **Nockamixon State Park** (⊠ Rte. 563, Quakertown, ☎ 215/529–7300), which has a 1,450-acre lake, boating and boat rentals, a swimming pool, a bike path, hiking trails, ice-skating and sledding in winter, and picnic areas.

The **Delaware Canal State Park** (⊠ 11 Lodi Hill Rd., Upper Black Eddy, ☎ 610/982–5560) follows the path of the Delaware Canal for 60 mi and is a National Historic Landmark. If you're interested in nature walks and guided tours, call the **Friends of the Delaware Canal** (☎ 215/862–2021) for their seasonal calendar of events.

Visitor Information

Bucks County Conference and Visitors Bureau (⊠ 152 Swamp Rd., Doylestown 18901, ☎ 215/345–4552 or 800/836–2825) is on the Fonthill property. It's open weekdays 9–5.

Central Bucks Chamber of Commerce (⊠ First Union Bank Bldg., 115 W. Court St., Doylestown 18901, ☎ 215/348–3913) has brochures with walking tours and other information. It's open weekdays 8:30–4:30.

New Hope Information Center (⊠ 1 W. Mechanic St., at Main St., New Hope 18938, ☎ 215/862–5880 for an automated menu of information; 215/862–5030 for a travel counselor) is a convenient place to stop or to contact in advance for area information. The center also has a free lodging referral service. It's open daily, usually 10–4, but hours vary seasonally.

10 LANCASTER COUNTY, HERSHEY, AND GETTYSBURG

In Lancaster County, especially among the Amish, an entirely different culture comes alive for you. Farmers drive horses in the fields, and drivers slow down for buggies on country roads. You can eat hearty Pennsylvania Dutch cooking and shop at farmers and antiques markets, quilt shops, and outlet stores. Beyond Lancaster County are the battlefield and museums at Gettysburg and the amusement park and chocolate-themed pleasures of Hershey.

NEATLY PAINTED FARMSTEADS dot the countryside of Lancaster County, nearly 65 mi west of Philadelphia. Wooden fences outline pastures, and the land looks like a huge quilt of neat rectangles. On country roads horse-drawn buggies jockey with horn-tooting cars for position. This is Pennsylvania's Amish Country, a place where time seems to stand still.

Updated by
Anne
Dubuisson
Anderson

Here, the plain and fancy live side by side. You can glimpse what rural life was like 100 years ago because whole communities of the "Plain" people—as the Old Order Amish are called—shun telephones, electricity, and the entire world of American gadgetry. Clinging to a centuries-old way of life, the Amish, one of the most conservative of the Pennsylvania Dutch sects, shun the amenities of modern civilization, using kerosene or gas lamps instead of electric lighting, horse-drawn buggies instead of automobiles. Ironically, in turning their backs on the modern world, the Amish have attracted its attention.

Today the county's main roads are lined with souvenir shops and sometimes crowded with busloads of tourists. The area's proximity to Philadelphia and Harrisburg has brought development as non-Amish farmers sell land. In fact, in 1999 the National Trust for Historic Preservation put Lancaster County on its annual list of the nation's 11 most endangered historic places because of rapid suburbanization. But beyond the commercialism and development, the general stores, one-room schoolhouses, country lanes, and tidy farms remain. You'll find instructive places to learn about the Amish way of life, pretzel factories to tour, quilts to buy, and a host of railroad museums to explore.

THE CULTURE OF THE PENNSYLVANIA DUTCH

The country's largest and oldest settlement of Plain people—70,000 people in more than 41 Amish, Mennonite, and Brethren sects—make Lancaster County their home. Collectively, they're known as the Pennsylvania Dutch. Despite their name, they aren't Dutch at all, but descendants of German and Swiss immigrants who came to the Lancaster area to escape religious persecution. Because of a corruption of the word *Deutsch,* meaning German, they became known as the "Dutch."

The Mennonite movement, named after its leader, Dutch Catholic priest Menno Simons, began in Switzerland in the early 16th century, the time of the Reformation. This radical religious group advocated nonviolence, separation of church and state, adult baptism, and individual freedom in choosing a religion. In 1710 eight families led by Mennonite bishop Hans Herr accepted William Penn's invitation to settle in Lancaster County.

In 1693 Swiss Mennonite bishop Jacob Amman, whose stricter interpretation of church tenets had attracted a following, broke off from the movement and formed his own group to adhere more to the founding beliefs and practices. This group became known as the Amish. Like the Mennonites, the Amish came to live in Lancaster County.

Today 137,000 Amish people live in North America, in 20 states and one Canadian province. Lancaster County has the second-largest community in the country, with 17,000 Old Order Amish (Holmes County, Ohio, is first). That the number of Amish has doubled in the last two decades suggests that theirs is still a viable lifestyle.

The eight Amish, 24 Mennonite, and nine Brethren groups differ in their interpretations of the Bible, their use of technology, the value they place on education, their use of English, and their degrees of interaction with outsiders. Brethren and Mennonite groups use modern conveniences more than Old Order Mennonites and Amish sects do, particularly the Old Order Amish, who shun modern technology.

The Amish religion and way of life stress separation from the world, caring for others of the faith, and self-sufficiency. What may appear as unusual behavior results from religious convictions based on biblical interpretation. The Amish, who reject compulsory school attendance and military registration, do not accept social security benefits or purchase life or property insurance.

Old Order Amish send their children to one-room schoolhouses with eight grades to a room. They avoid larger public schools to prevent the exposure of their children to the influence of "outsiders." Though Amish students study many of the traditional subjects, they learn less about science and technology than their worldly counterparts. The Supreme Court has ruled that Amish children need not attend school beyond the eighth grade, after which students learn agriculture, building trades, and domestic skills at home.

Farmers work with teams of mules to plow, plant, and harvest their crops. The average farm is small, about 55 acres, but good farming practices make the land extremely productive. Tobacco is one of the crops. When the tobacco leaves mature in September, whole families take to the fields to cut stalks, after which they hang them in rows from floor to ceiling in tobacco sheds.

Lancaster County's most visible sect, the Amish can be recognized by their clothing, which is similar to that worn by their ancestors. Dress and grooming symbolize each person's role in Amish society. Men must begin to grow a beard upon marriage, and they wear several different styles of hats to distinguish their age, status, and their religious district. Amish women wear full-length dresses, capes, and aprons. Those who are baptized wear white organdy caps and don't cut their hair.

Although some changes have been thrust upon them by the government, the Amish do change and update some rules themselves. Some have telephones in their barns or on the edge of their property, for emergency use only; many will accept a ride in an automobile or take public transportation. The Amish live a lively, rich life of discipline and caring. They seek to be at peace with themselves, their neighbors, their surroundings, and their God. For a further look into the world of the Amish, *see* "Portrait of an Amish Family" *in* Chapter 11.

HISTORIC LANCASTER, HERSHEY, AND GETTYSBURG

The Amish are not the only reason to explore Lancaster County. Lancaster, which the English named after Lancashire, is an intriguing place. This appealingly residential city of row houses is one of the nation's oldest inland cities, dating from 1710. Historic sites in the area include Wheatland, the home of James Buchanan. Around Lancaster you can visit the Landis Valley Museum, devoted to rural life before 1900. Ephrata Cloister provides a look at a religious communal society of the 1700s. And Main Street in Lititz, founded in 1756, is an architectural treat for strollers.

Western Lancaster County, which includes the towns of Marietta, Mount Joy, and Columbia, is a quieter part of the county, where you can bicycle down winding lanes, sample local wines and authentic Mennonite cooking, and explore uncrowded villages. Its history is rooted in the Colonial period. The residents are of Scottish and German descent, and architecture varies from log cabins to Victorian homes.

If you've brought your children as far as Lancaster, you may want to continue northwest to Hershey, the "Chocolate Town" founded in 1903 by Milton S. Hershey. Here the number-one attraction is Hersheypark, a theme park with kiddie and thrill rides, theaters, and live shows. Or you may wish to journey southwest to the battlefields and museums of Gettysburg, also within driving distance. Here—as in many other area destinations—you can journey back in time.

Pleasures and Pastimes

History and Culture
A visit to Lancaster County and the surrounding area captures a lot of history in a relatively small space. In towns such as Bird-in-Hand and Intercourse, you can see the Amish living their traditional lifestyle. Museums and activities help interpret complex social and religious history; a drive along country roads off the beaten path will also give you a feeling for this way of life. The city of Lancaster has Revolutionary War sites and President James Buchanan's home, Wheatland. Even if you're not a history buff, a trip to Gettysburg, site of the pivotal 1863 Civil War battle, can be a moving experience.

Dining
Like the German cuisine that influenced it, Pennsylvania Dutch cooking is hearty and uses ingredients from local farms. To sample regional fare, eat at one of the bustling restaurants where diners sit with perhaps a dozen other people and the food is passed around in bowls family style. Meals are plentiful and basic, including fried chicken, ham, roast beef, dried corn, buttered noodles, mashed potatoes, chowchow (pickle relish), bread, pepper cabbage, and more. Entrées are accompanied by traditional "sweets and sours," vegetable dishes made with a vinegar-and-sugar dressing. This is the way the Amish, who hate to throw things out, preserve leftover vegetables.

Be sure to indulge your sweet tooth with shoofly pie (made with molasses and brown sugar), *snitz* (dried apple) pie, and other kinds of pies, even for breakfast. Bake shops proudly point out that this region invented the hole in the doughnut by cutting out the center of *fastnacht* cakes; in fact, the English word *dunk* comes from the Pennsylvania Dutch *dunke*.

Lancaster County has numerous smorgasbords and reasonably priced family restaurants, along with a number of Continental and French restaurants in contemporary settings and historic inns. Unless otherwise noted, liquor is served. For price-category information, *see* Dining *in* Smart Travel Tips A to Z.

Lodging
Lancaster County lodgings are much like the people themselves—plain or fancy. You can rough it in one of the many campgrounds in the area, stay at a historic inn, or indulge yourself at a full-frills resort. A good selection of moderately priced motels caters to families. Though hotels welcome guests year-round, rates are highest in summer and lower at other times. Some inns and bed-and-breakfasts may have minimum stays in high season.

Many working Amish and non-Amish farms throughout Lancaster County welcome visitors to stay for a few days to observe and even participate in farm life. Operated as bed-and-breakfast establishments with a twist, the farms invite you to help milk the cows and feed the chickens and afterward share a hearty breakfast with the farmer and his family or help with other farm chores. Reservations must be made weeks in advance as most farms are heavily booked in summer. Some are listed with the towns in this chapter; the Pennsylvania Dutch Convention & Visitors Bureau (☞ Lancaster Country A to Z, *below*) has a listing of all area B&Bs and farms that welcome guests. For price-category information, *see* Lodging *in* Smart Travel Tips A to Z.

Shopping

Shoppers in Lancaster County will find everything from farmers markets to several hundred outlet stores. The county's main arteries, U.S. 30 and Route 340, are lined with gift shops and outlets. Some outlets are factory stores, with top-quality goods at big discounts. Others call themselves outlets but don't have good bargains. It's best to know the actual retail prices of items before leaving home; don't be misled by so-called sales.

On Sunday antiques hunters frequent the huge antiques malls along Route 272 between Adamstown and Denver. As many as 5,000 dealers may turn up on Extravaganza Days, held in late spring, summer, and early fall. You can spend hours browsing among old books and prints and looking at Victorian clothing, pewter, silver, pottery, and lots of furniture. Or you can stop in a store along a country road to shop for the crafts and handmade quilts for which the area is famous. Galleries, boutiques, roadside stands, and farmers markets abound, with a temptingly wide variety of merchandise.

Exploring Lancaster County

The city of Lancaster is close to the heart of Pennsylvania Dutch Country. East of it lie towns such as Intercourse and Bird-in-Hand, with markets, outlet shops, and sights that interpret Amish life. Also nearby is Strasburg, with its railroad museums. Less than half an hour north of Lancaster, the historic towns of Ephrata and Lititz are near farmers markets and antiques malls. The quiet western part of Lancaster County has the Susquehanna River towns of Columbia and Marietta, as well as country towns to the north. If you're on an extended tour of south-central Pennsylvania, you can also explore Gettysburg and Hershey, which are both west of the county.

Great Itineraries

Most people come to Lancaster County to get a glimpse of the Amish and their lifestyle. The territory covered is not that large, and you can see many area sights in a week, though you could spend twice that time. If you have only a couple of days, you'll probably want to concentrate on key Amish towns and Lancaster. With a few more days you can explore the area north of Lancaster or visit Strasburg. If you have up to a week, you can see the western part of the county and continue on to Hershey or Gettysburg.

Numbers in the text correspond to numbers in the margin and on the Lancaster County map.

IF YOU HAVE 2 DAYS

Begin your tour of Amish Country in **Intercourse** ② and visit People's Place, a cultural interpretation center with good introductory films and an exhibit for children. If you'd rather see the area by Amish buggy, follow Route 340 west to **Bird-in-Hand** ③ and take a tour with Aaron & Jessica's Buggy Rides. Also in this area are such sights as the Amish Farm and House. Farmers markets and shops will easily fill the day before you head to 🏨 **Lancaster** ① for the night. On Day 2 explore this historic city. The Heritage Center Museum shows the work of Lancaster County artists and craftspeople, past and present. The Historic Lancaster Walking Tour, given at midday, is a 90-minute stroll through the heart of town. On Tuesday or Friday be sure to visit the Central

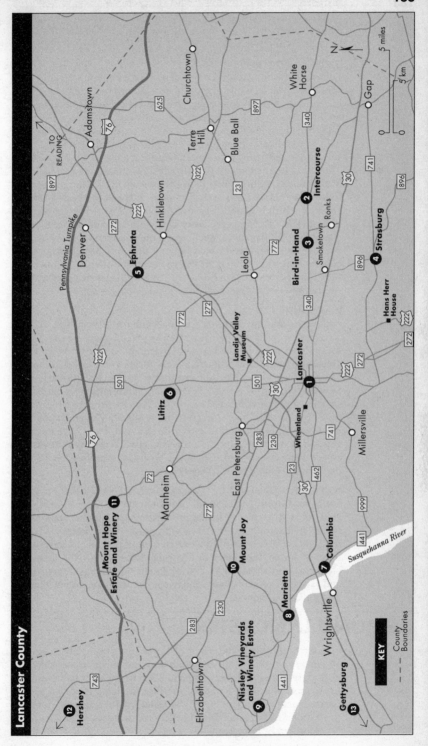

Lancaster County

Market, with its open-air stalls brimming with produce and baked goods. Antique lovers will want to see Historic Rock Ford Plantation, with its antiques and folk art.

IF YOU HAVE 4 DAYS

Follow the two-day itinerary above; on Day 3, continue to explore the **Lancaster** ① area. While in the city visit Wheatland, the home of former president James Buchanan, and the Hans Herr House. Take an hour or two to explore the country roads east of the city. Drive the side roads between Routes 23 and 340 to see Amish farms (the ones with windmills and green blinds) along the way. You can stop at roadside stands and farms with signs advertising quilts and fresh produce. Then head up the Oregon Pike (Route 272) to visit the Landis Valley Museum, an outdoor museum of Pennsylvania German rural life and folk culture before 1900, and drive on to ☒ **Ephrata** ⑤ and ☒ **Lititz** ⑥, either of which is good for an overnight. On Day 4 you can visit the Ephrata Cloister, tour a pretzel or chocolate museum in Lititz, or, depending on the day of the week, spend the day shopping for antiques. Another choice for Day 4 is to spend your time in ☒ **Strasburg** ④, which has the Railroad Museum of Pennsylvania and the don't-miss Strasburg Rail Road ride. Also here is the Amish Village, including a blacksmith shop, one-room schoolhouse, and smokehouse.

IF YOU HAVE 7 DAYS

Follow the four-day itinerary for the beginning of your trip. On Day 5 head west to the sleepy towns of Marietta, Columbia, and Mount Joy; any of these is fine for your overnight. The river town of ☒ **Columbia** ⑦ has the excellent National Watch and Clock Museum, as well as Wright's Ferry Mansion, the former residence of English Quaker Susanna Wright. The restored town of ☒ **Marietta** ⑧ is perfect for strolling and browsing. You can tour a historic brewery in ☒ **Mount Joy** ⑩ or take the wine-tasting tour at the **Nissley Vineyards and Winery Estate** ⑨, near Bainbridge. On Days 6 and 7 you have a choice, depending on your interests. You can visit ☒ **Hershey** ⑫, with its amusement park, zoo, and Chocolate World, or tour the Civil War battlefields and museums of ☒ **Gettysburg** ⑬.

WHEN TO TOUR LANCASTER COUNTY, HERSHEY, AND GETTYSBURG

Lancaster County can be hectic, especially on summer weekends and in October, when the fall foliage attracts crowds. Farmers markets and family-style restaurants overflow with people. The trick is to visit the top sights and then get off the beaten path. If possible, plan your trip for early spring, September, or Christmas season, when the area is less crowded. You should note that although many restaurants, shops, and farmers markets close Sunday for the Sabbath, commercial attractions remain open.

AROUND LANCASTER

Lancaster, in roughly the center of the county, has plenty to see and also makes a good base for exploring the surrounding countryside. East of the city, between Routes 340 and 23 in towns with names such as Intercourse, Blue Ball, Paradise, and Bird-in-Hand, live most of Lancaster County's Amish community. Strasburg, to the southeast, has sights for train buffs. No more than 12 mi north of Lancaster, Ephrata and Lititz are lovely, historic towns.

When you are visiting among the Amish, remember to respect their values. They believe that photographs and videos with recognizable reproductions of them violate the biblical commandment against making graven images. You will be asked to refrain from photographing or making videos of the Amish, and you should comply.

Lancaster

❶ *75 mi west of Philadelphia.*

Near the heart of Pennsylvania Dutch Country, Lancaster is a colorful small city that combines the Colonial past with the Pennsylvania Dutch present. During the French and Indian War and the American Revolution, its craftsmen turned out fine guns, building the city's reputation as the arsenal of the Colonies. And on September 27, 1777, Lancaster became the national capital for a day, as Congress fled the British in Philadelphia. Today markets and museums preserve the area's history. East of town on U.S. 30 are some of the area's more commercial attractions, such as miniature golf, and fast-food eateries.

The **Historic Lancaster Walking Tour,** a 90-minute stroll through the heart of this old city, is conducted by costumed guides who impart anecdotes about 50 points of architectural and historical interest covering six square blocks. Tours depart from the visitor center downtown. ⊠ *S. Queen and Vine Sts. near Penn Sq.,* ☎ *717/392–1776.* ⌖ *$5.* ☉ *Tours April.–Oct., Tues. and Fri.–Sat. at 10 and 1, Sun.– Mon. and Wed.–Thurs. at 1; Nov.–Mar., by reservation only.*

★ **Central Market,** which began with open-air stalls in 1742, is where locals shop for fresh fruit and vegetables, meats (try the Lebanon bologna), flowers, and baked goods such as sticky buns and shoofly pie. The current Romanesque building, in the heart of town, was constructed in 1889 and is one of the oldest covered markets in the country. It's a good place to pick up food for a picnic. ⊠ *Penn Sq.,* ☎ *717/291–4723.* ☉ *Tues. and Fri. 6–4, Sat. 6–2.*

The **Demuth Foundation** includes the restored 18th-century home, studio, and garden of Charles Demuth (1883–1935), one of America's first modernist artists. A watercolorist, Demuth found inspiration in the geometric shapes of machines and modern technology. A few of his works are usually on display. The complex includes a museum shop and the oldest operating tobacco shop (1770) in the country. ⊠ *120 E. King St.,* ☎ *717/299–9940.* ⌖ *Donation requested.* ☉ *Feb.–Dec., Tues.–Sat. 10–4, Sun. 1–4.*

The Old City Hall, reborn as the **Heritage Center Museum,** showcases the work of Lancaster County artisans and craftspeople—clocks, furniture, homemade toys, Fraktur (documents in a style of calligraphy with folk art decorations), and Pennsylvania long rifles. Some exhibits are on display permanently, while others rotate. ⊠ *King and Queen Sts. on Penn Sq.,* ☎ *717/299–6440.* ⌖ *Donation requested.* ☉ *May–Dec., Tues.–Sat. 10–5.*

Historic Rock Ford Plantation is the restored home of General Edward Hand, Revolutionary War commander, George Washington's adjutant, and member of the Continental Congress. Eighteenth-century antiques and folk art are displayed in a 1794 Georgian-style mansion. The **Kauffman Museum,** in the restored 18th-century barn, holds the Zoe and Henry Kauffman collection of pewter, brass, copper, tin, firearms, and furniture. ⊠ *Lancaster County Park, 881 Rock Ford Rd.,* ☎ *717/392–7223.* ⌖ *$4.50.* ☉ *Apr.–Oct., Tues.–Fri. 10–4, Sun. noon–4. The Kauffman Museum can be visited by appointment only.*

★ **Wheatland** was the home of the only president from Pennsylvania, James Buchanan, who served from 1857–1861. The restored 1828 Federal mansion and outbuildings display the 15th president's furniture just as it was during his lifetime. A one-hour tour includes a profile of the only bachelor to occupy the White House. ⊠ *1120 Marietta Ave., Rte. 23, 1½ mi west of Lancaster,* ☎ *717/392–8721.* 🎟 *$5.50.* ☉ *Apr.–mid-Dec., daily 10–4.*

★ The **Hans Herr House,** the oldest in Lancaster County, is considered the best example of medieval-style German architecture in North America. The subject of several paintings by Andrew Wyeth, the house was the Colonial home of the Herr family, to whom the Wyeths are related. Today the house is owned by the Lancaster Mennonite Historical Society, which educates the public about the Mennonite religion through exhibits in its visitor center. The 45-minute tours cover the grounds and the 1719 sandstone house, a former Mennonite meeting place. ⊠ *1849 Hans Herr Dr., 5 mi south of Lancaster off U.S. 222,* ☎ *717/464–4438.* 🎟 *$3.50.* ☉ *Apr.–Nov., Mon.–Sat. 9–4.*

The **Landis Valley Museum** is an outdoor museum of Pennsylvania German rural life and folk culture before 1900. Owned by brothers Henry and George Landis, the farm and village are now operated by the Pennsylvania Historical and Museum Commission. You can visit more than 15 historical buildings, from a farmstead to a country store. There are demonstrations of skills such as spinning and weaving, pottery making, and tinsmithing, the products of which are for sale in the Weathervane Shop. ⊠ *2451 Kissel Hill Rd., off Oregon Pike, Rte. 272,* ☎ *717/ 569–0401.* 🎟 *$7.* ☉ *Mar.–Dec., Mon.–Sat. 9–5, Sun. noon–5.*

☾ The 44 acres of games and rides at **Dutch Wonderland** amusement park are suited for families with younger children. Most rides are tame. Diving shows, an animated bear show, and concerts supplement the rides. ⊠ *2249 U.S. 30, east of Lancaster,* ☎ *717/291–1888.* 🎟 *$20.95 for unlimited rides.* ☉ *Memorial Day–Labor Day, daily 10–6 or later; Labor Day–Oct. and Easter–Memorial Day, Sat. 10–6, Sun. 11–6.*

Dining and Lodging

$$ ✕ **The Log Cabin.** Consistency is the appeal here: several generations
★ have made this their special-occasion place for classic fare such as veal Milanese (dipped in bread crumbs and Parmesan and fried) and steaks served with local produce. The steaks, as well as lamb chops and seafood, are prepared on a charcoal grill in this 1928 expanded log cabin on a wooded hillside. The atmosphere in the 10 candelit dining rooms is elegant, and an impressive collection of 18th-and 19th-century American paintings enhances the setting. ⊠ *11 Lehoy Forest Dr., off Rte. 272, 6 mi northeast of Lancaster, Leola,* ☎ *717/626–1181. AE, MC, V. No lunch.*

$$ ✕ **Market Fare.** American fare, including steaks, seafood, and veal, is served in a cozy dining room with upholstered armchairs and 19th-century paintings, drawings, and photographs. Homemade soups and breads highlight the diverse menu. A children's menu and a lighter menu are also available. The café upstairs offers a light breakfast, quick lunch, and takeout. ⊠ *Market and Grant Sts., across from Central Market,* ☎ *717/299–7090. AE, D, DC, MC, V.*

$–$$ ✕ **Center City Grill.** Casual but elegant, this bar and restaurant has a convenient downtown location for those exploring the city center. The varied international menu has choices from Thai chicken in peanut-and-ginger sauce to gourmet pizzas and quiche Lorraine. Most nights there is dancing to DJ-spun tunes, and you can listen to live jazz on Sunday evening. A children's menu is available. ⊠ *10 S. Prince St.,* ☎ *717/299–3456. AE, D, DC, MC, V.*

$–$$ ✕ **J-M's Bistro and Pub.** A new restaurant on the edge of town is a favorite among locals for its relaxed, convivial setting. Wood and brass touches echo the style of a French bistro. You can choose among a wide variety of well-prepared foods, from salads and gourmet pizzas to superb prime rib and rack of lamb. ⊠ *300 W. James St.,* ☏ *717/392–5656. AE, D, MC, V.* ☾ *No lunch.*

$ ✕ **Lancaster Dispensing Co.** Fajitas, salads, sandwiches, and nachos are served until midnight in this stylish, boisterous, Victorian pub. The selection of imported beers is extensive. You can hear live music on weekends. ⊠ *33–35 N. Market St.,* ☏ *717/299–4602. AE, D, MC, V.*

$ ✕ **The Pressroom.** The menus look like newspapers, and headline banners hang over the bar in this casual bistro in an old warehouse. The open kitchen has an exposed baking hearth. On the menu are sandwiches (named after newspaper cartoon characters), salads, pizza, and pasta dishes. In summer you can eat in the park outside. ⊠ *26–28 W. King St.,* ☏ *717/399–5400. AE, MC, V.*

$$–$$$ ▥ **Holiday Inn Lancaster Host Resort and Conference Center.** This sprawling family resort has a striking marble lobby and comfortable, contemporary rooms with cherry-wood furnishings. The golf course and grounds are beautifully landscaped. A camp program for children ages 1–12 is offered daily during the summer and on weekends throughout the year. ⊠ *2300 Lincoln Hwy. E (U.S. 30), 17602,* ☏ *717/299–5500 or 800/233–0121. 330 rooms. 2 restaurants, piano bar, indoor-outdoor pool, 27-hole golf course, miniature golf, 12 tennis courts, children's programs. AE, DC, MC, V.*

$$–$$$ ▥ **King's Cottage.** An elegant 1913 Spanish Mission Revival mansion
★ on the National Register of Historic Places has been transformed into a B&B. The blend of decorative and architectural elements encompasses Chippendale-style dining room furniture and an art deco fireplace and stained-glass windows. A library and an outdoor goldfish pond are additional pleasures. The price includes full breakfast and afternoon tea; a small kitchen is available to guests. ⊠ *1049 E. King St., 17602,* ☏ *717/397–1017 or 800/747–8717,* ℻ *717/397–3447. 8 rooms, 1 cottage. Library. D, MC, V. BP.*

$$–$$$ ▥ **Willow Valley Family Resort and Conference Center.** This mom-and-pop operation has blossomed into a large, stylish family resort. Attractive rooms surround the striking skylighted atrium lobby; the ones overlooking the atrium are the most attractive and the most expensive. Since the resort is Mennonite owned, no liquor is permitted on the premises. ⊠ *2416 Willow St. Pike, 17602,* ☏ *717/464–2711 or 800/444–1714,* ℻ *717/464–4784. 353 rooms. 2 restaurants, outdoor pool, 2 indoor pools, hot tub, sauna, steam room, 9-hole golf course, 2 tennis courts, exercise room, recreation room. AE, D, DC, MC, V.*

$$ ▥ **Best Western Eden Resort Inn.** Attractive grounds and spacious
★ rooms with cherry-wood Colonial furnishings make a stay here pleasant. The inn has a stunning tropical indoor pool and whirlpool under a retractable roof; request a poolside room. The chef at Arthur's is noted for seafood and pasta dishes; casual fun food is presented in Garfield's. ⊠ *222 Eden Rd., U.S. 30 and Rte. 272, 17601,* ☏ *717/569–6444 or 800/528–1234,* ℻ *717/569–4208. 275 rooms, 40 suites. 2 restaurants, indoor pool, outdoor pool, sauna, tennis court, exercise room. AE, D, DC, MC, V. CP.*

$$ ▥ **Lancaster Hilton Garden Inn.** An elegant, contemporary hotel popular with business travelers offers oversize rooms, many with cathedral ceilings and large desks. There's free coffee in the rooms. The hotel is in a corporate center on the edge of town. ⊠ *101 Granite Run Dr., intersection of Rtes. 72 and 283, 17601,* ☏ *717/560–0880. 155 rooms. Restaurant, indoor pool, exercise room, meeting rooms. AE, D, DC, MC, V.*

Nightlife and the Arts

The 1,600-seat **American Music Theatre** (⊠ 2425 Lincoln Highway E, ☏ 717/397–7700 or 800/648–4102) presents full-scale productions, such as "Country Jukebox," designed to celebrate American music. There are afternoon and evening shows.

The draws at the 400-seat **Dutch Apple Dinner Theater** (⊠ 510 Centerville Rd., at U.S. 30, ☎ 717/898–1900) are a candlelight buffet plus Broadway musicals and comedies such as *Camelot* and *Fiddler on the Roof.* Call for reservations for matinees and dinner shows.

A National Landmark, the 19th-century **Fulton Opera House** (⊠ 12 N. Prince St., ☎ 717/397–7425) is home to the Fulton Theater Company, the Actors Company of Pennsylvania, the Lancaster Symphony Orchestra, and the Lancaster Opera.

Outdoor Activities and Sports

The **Holiday Inn Lancaster Host Resort and Conference Center** (⊠ 2300 Lincoln Hwy. E, ☎ 717/299–5500) has 27 holes of regulation golf. Greens fees are $53 for 18 holes and include the use of a cart. Rental clubs are available.

Shopping

CRAFTS

Although craftspeople in the Lancaster County area produce fine handiwork, folk art, quilts, and needlework, much of the best work is sold to galleries nationwide and never shows up in local shops. Still, there are some good places you can check.

Artisan's Porch (⊠ 2467A Lititz Pike/Rte. 501, ☎ 717/519–0199) carries jewelry, pottery, porcelain, woven handbags, and other high-quality crafts by many contemporary Pennsylvanian artists. The store is closed Monday and Tuesday.

The **Olde Mill House Shoppes** (⊠ 105 Strasburg Pike, ☎ 717/299–0678), one of Lancaster's oldest country stores, stocks a fine choice of pottery, folk art, country and Shaker furniture, and primitive ceiling and table lighting.

Pandora's Antiques (⊠ 2014 Old Philadelphia Pike, just east of U.S. 30, ☎ 717/299–5305) sells antique quilts and textiles made in Lancaster County. Call ahead.

Among the few places that carry fine local crafts is the **Weathervane Shop** (⊠ 2451 Kissel Hill Rd., ☎ 717/569–9312), at the Landis Valley Museum (☞ *above*), where craftspeople sell the wares they make on-site—tin, pottery, leather, braided rugs, weaving, and cane chairs.

OUTLETS

U.S. 30 is lined with outlets of varying quality; be sure to check the retail prices of whatever you want before you leave home. With more than 120 stores, from Lenox to London Fog and the huge Reading China & Glass, the **Rockvale Square Factory Outlet Village** (⊠ U.S. 30 and Rte. 896, ☎ 717/293–9595) is the largest outlet center in Lancaster. The **Tanger Outlet at Millstream** (⊠ 311 Outlet Dr., Rte. 30 E, ☎ 717/ 392–7202) is a collection of 53 designer outlets, including Ann Taylor and Brooks Brothers. The **Dutch Gems and Jewelry Outlet** (⊠ 2208 Lincoln Hwy. E, ☎ 717/396–0810) sells unusual gems and jewelry, especially gemstone jewelry and handmade rings, pendants, earrings, and bracelets.

Intercourse

❷ *10 mi east of Lancaster.*

Intercourse is a center of Amish life. Many places that will help you better understand this community can be found between here and

Bird-in-Hand (☞ *below*). The town is at the intersection, or intercourse, of two roads (today's Routes 340 and 772), which is how it got its name in Colonial times.

★ ℭ The **People's Place,** a "people-to-people interpretation center," provides an excellent introduction to the Amish, Mennonite, and Hutterite communities. A 30-minute multiscreen slide show titled *Who Are the Amish?* has close-ups of Amish life and perceptive narration. 20Q (short for 20 Questions), an interactive family museum, highlights the differences between Amish and Mennonite societies. Children can try on bonnets and play in the "feeling box." Don't miss the collection of wood carvings by Aaron Zook. There's a bookstore, too. ⊠ *3513 Old Philadelphia Pike/Rte. 340,* ☏ *717/768–7171 or 800/390–8436.* ⌦ *$4.* ☉ *Memorial Day–Labor Day, Mon.–Sat. 9:30–8; Labor Day– Memorial Day, Mon.–Sat. 9:30–5.*

Dining and Lodging

$ ✕ **Kling House.** The Kling family home has been converted into a pleasant, casual restaurant that serves American cuisine throughout the day. The turkey Reuben and sausage platter are favorites, as are the *knepp* (ham) entrées, which come with a complimentary appetizer of red-pepper jam and cream cheese with crackers. The soups are homemade, and desserts are luscious. A children's menu is available. ⊠ *Kitchen Kettle Village, Rtes. 340 and 772,* ☏ *717/768–8261. D, MC, V. Closed Sun. No dinner Mon.–Wed.*

$ ✕ **Stoltzfus Farm Restaurant.** Homemade Pennsylvania Dutch foods are served family style in a small country farmhouse, with most ingredients grown on the farm. Most dishes are so tasty (especially the ham loaf with vinegar and brown sugar) you'll want the recipes—and the owners will happily supply you with them. ⊠ *Rte. 772E, ½ mi east of Rte. 340,* ☏ *717/768–8156. Closed Sun. and Dec.–Mar.; call for limited hours in Apr. and Nov.*

$ ⚠ **Spring Gulch Resort Campground.** Glorious farmland and forest are the setting for the campsites (pleasantly shaded) and a limited number of more expensive rental cottages (two-night minimum stay is $169). A full schedule of weekend activities includes country dances and chicken barbecues. ⊠ *Rte. 897 between Rtes. 340 and 322, New Holland 17557,* ☏ *717/354–3100 or 800/255–5744. 500 sites, 4 cottages. 2 pools, lake, spa, miniature golf, tennis courts, exercise room, volleyball, fishing, recreation room.*

Shopping

Amishland Prints (⊠ 3504 Old Philadelphia Pike, ☏ 717/768–7273) sells prints depicting the Amish in rural daily life as well as landscapes by artist and folklorist Xtian Newswanger.

Kitchen Kettle Village (⊠ Rte. 340, ☏ 717/768–8261 or 800/732–3538) consists of 32 shops showcasing local crafts, including decoy carving; furniture making; leather tooling; relish-, jam-, and jelly-making; and tin punching. The Kling House (☞ Dining and Lodging, *above*) is here, too, and Lapp Family Farms sells great ice cream. The shops are closed Sunday.

The **Old Country Store** (⊠ 3510 Old Philadelphia Pike, ☏ 717/768– 7101) carries items from more than 450 local craftspeople, including quilts and discounted fabrics. A small Quilt Museum displays antique Amish and Mennonite quilts.

The **Old Road Furniture Company** (⊠ 3457 Old Philadelphia Pike, ☏ 717/768–7171 or 800/760–7171) has lovely furniture handcrafted by Amish craftspeople, including harvest and farm tables, chairs, chests, and desks. The store is closed Sunday.

Bird-in-Hand

❸ *3 mi west of Intercourse.*

This village, like many others, took its name from the sign on an early inn and tavern. Today it is a center for the Pennsylvania Dutch farming community.

★ ☺ **Aaron & Jessica's Buggy Rides** provides tours of the countryside in an authentic Amish carriage. ⊠ *Rte. 340 between Bird-in-Hand and Intercourse at Plain & Fancy Farm,* ☏ *717/768–8828.* ⌨ *$10.* ☉ *Mon.– Sat., 8 AM–dusk.*

On **Abe's Buggy Rides** Abe chats about the Amish during a 2-mi spin down country roads in an Amish family carriage. ⊠ *2596 Old Philadelphia Pike,* ☏ *717/392–1794.* ⌨ *$10.* ☉ *Mon.–Sat. 9 AM–dusk.*

The **Amish Experience** is a multimedia theatrical presentation about the history of the Amish, using 3-D sets, multiple screens, and special effects. In *Jacob's Choice,* the teenage main character struggles between traditional ways and the temptations of the present. ⊠ *Rte. 340 between Bird-in-Hand and Intercourse at Plain & Fancy Farm,* ☏ *717/768–8400.* ⌨ *$6.50.* ☉ *Apr.–June, Mon.–Sat. 8:30–5, Sun. 10–6; July–Oct., Mon.– Sat. 8:30–8, Sun. 9:30–6; Nov.–Mar., daily 10–5; shows on the hour.*

The **Amish Country Homestead,** a re-creation of a nine-room Old Order Amish house, is the fictional home of the characters in the Amish Experience film *Jacob's Choice* (☞ *above*). You can learn about the clothing of the Amish and how they live without electricity. ⊠ *Rte. 340 between Bird-in-Hand and Intercourse at Plain & Fancy Farm,* ☏ *717/768–3600.* ⌨ *$5.* ☉ *July–Oct., Mon.–Sat. 9:45–6:45; Apr.– June and Nov., Mon.–Sat. 9:45–4:45; Dec.–Mar., weekends 10–4:45.*

The **Amish Farm and House** has 40-minute tours through a 10-room circa-1805 house furnished in the Old Order Amish style. A map guides you to the farmstead's animals, waterwheel, and barns. ⊠ *2395 Lincoln Hwy. E, Smoketown,* ☏ *717/394–6185.* ⌨ *$5.95.* ☉ *Apr.– May and Sept.–Oct., daily 8:30–5; Nov.–Mar., daily 8:30–4; June–Aug., daily 8:30–6.*

The **Folk Craft Center, Museum, Shops, and B&B,** housed in 18th- and 19th-century buildings, has displays of pottery, household implements, toys, glassware, quilts, and early Pennsylvania Dutch memorabilia. An antique loom is on exhibit in a log cabin built in 1762. Woodworking, weaving, and print-shop demonstrations show early techniques. In spring and summer the ornamental and herb gardens come alive with color. The bed-and-breakfast, an 1845 farmhouse, has four suites. ⊠ *441 Mt. Sidney Rd., ½ mi west of town, north of Rte. 340, Witmer,* ☏ *717/397–3609.* ⌨ *$5.* ☉ *Apr.–Nov., Mon.–Sat. 9–5, Sun. 11–4.*

Dining and Lodging

$ ✕ **Amish Barn Restaurant.** Pennsylvania Dutch cuisine is served family style, which means generous helpings of meat and produce, breads, and pies. Apple dumplings and shoofly pie are specialties. You can also choose from an à la carte menu. No liquor is served. ⊠ *3029 Old Philadelphia Pike/Rte. 340, between Bird-in-Hand and Intercourse,* ☏ *717/768–8886. AE, D, MC, V.*

$ ✕ **Bird-in-Hand Family Restaurant.** This family-owned diner-style
★ restaurant has a good reputation for hearty Pennsylvania Dutch home cooking. The menu is à la carte, but there's a lunch buffet weekdays. It's an excellent place to sample local specialties such as apple dumplings and chicken potpie. No liquor is served. ⊠ *2760 Old Philadelphia Pike/Rte. 340,* ☏ *717/768–8266. MC, V. Closed Sun.*

$ ✕ **Good 'N Plenty.** Don't bother to ask for a menu here: The servers
★   just bring out heaps of Pennsylvania Dutch food. You share a table with
about a dozen other customers and are treated to hearty regional fare,
including traditional sweets and sours. More than 650 can be served
at this bustling family-style restaurant, nicely set within a remodeled
Amish farmhouse. ⊠ *Rte. 896, ½ mi north of U.S. 30,* ☎ *717/394–
7111. MC, V. Closed Sun. and Jan.*

$ ✕ **Miller's Smorgasbord.** Miller's presents a lavish spread with a good
★   selection of Pennsylvania Dutch foods. The breakfast buffet (served daily
June–October and on weekends November–May) is sensational, with
omelets, pancakes, and eggs cooked to order, fresh fruits, pastries, bacon,
sausage, potatoes, and much more. This is one of the few area restaurants open Sunday. ⊠ *2811 Lincoln Hwy. E/U.S. 30, Ronks,* ☎ *717/
687–6621. AE, D, MC, V.*

$ ✕ **Plain & Fancy Farm.** This family-style restaurant serves heaping
helpings of stick-to-your-ribs Pennsylvania Dutch food. Also on the
grounds are specialty shops and other attractions. ⊠ *Rte. 340 between
Bird-in-Hand and Intercourse,* ☎ *717/768–4400. AE, MC, V.*

$$ 🛏 **Bird-in-Hand Family Inn.** Plain, clean, comfortable rooms and a
friendly staff are the highlights of this family-run motel. There's com-
plimentary coffee in the rooms. ⊠ *2740 Old Philadelphia Pike/Rte.
340, 17505,* ☎ *717/768–8271 or 800/537–2535,* 🇫🇦🇽 *717/768–1768.
100 rooms. Restaurant, indoor pool, outdoor pool, tennis court, recre-
ation room, playground. AE, D, DC, MC, V.*

$–$$ 🛏 **Village Inn of Bird-in-Hand.** The Victorian flavor of this three-story
country inn, built in 1734 to serve travelers along the Old Philadel-
phia Pike, is tempered by the modern comforts of cable TV and phones.
Continental breakfast, an evening snack, and a two-hour tour of the
area are complimentary. Guests have pool and tennis privileges at the
nearby Bird-in-Hand Family Inn (☞ *above*). ⊠ *2695 Old Philadelphia
Pike/Rte. 340, 17505,* ☎ *717/293–8369 or 800/914–2473. 5 rooms,
6 suites. AE, D, MC, V. CP.*

$ 🏕 **Historic Mill Bridge Village and Campresort.** This campground is
attached to a restored 18th-century village. Guests have free admission to village and buggy rides. There's a general store on the grounds.
⊠ *S. Ronks Rd., ½ mi south of U.S. 30, Ronks 17579,* ☎ *717/687–
8181 or 800/645–2744. 101 sites. Snack bar, fishing.*

Shopping

Bird-in-Hand Farmers Market (⊠ Rte. 340, ☎ 717/393–9674) is an
indoor market with produce stands, baked goods, gift shops, outlets,
and a snack counter. It's open Wednesday through Saturday from July
through October; Wednesday, Friday, and Saturday April–June; and
Friday and Saturday December–March.

Strasburg

④ *5 mi south of Bird-in-Hand.*

Although settled by French Huguenots, the village of Strasburg is
today a community of Pennsylvania Dutch. It's best known as the railroad center of eastern Pennsylvania; railroad buffs can easily spend a
day here. You can also visit the Amish Village, which has buildings typical of the area.

🌀 The **Strasburg Rail Road** offers a scenic 45-minute round-trip excursion through Amish farm country from Strasburg to Paradise on a rolling
antique chartered in 1832 to carry milk, mail, and coal. Called America's oldest short line, the Strasburg run has wooden coaches pulled
by an iron steam locomotive. You can lunch in the dining car or buy
a box lunch in the restaurant at the station and have a picnic at Groff's

Grove along the line. ⊠ *Rte. 741,* ☎ *717/687–7522.* ⊇ *$8.25 round-trip.* ☉ *Apr.–June and Sept., daily 11–4; July–Aug., daily 10–7; Oct.–Mar., weekends noon–3; closed 1st 2 wks in Jan. Trains depart every 30–60 min depending on season; call for schedule.*

★ ☾   The **Railroad Museum of Pennsylvania,** across the road from the Strasburg Rail Road, holds 75 pieces of train history, including 13 colossal engines built between 1888 and 1930; 12 railroad cars, among them a Pullman sleeper; sleighs; and railroad memorabilia documenting the history of Pennsylvania railroading. More than 50 of the pieces of equipment are kept indoors in the Rolling Stock Hall. ⊠ *Rte. 741,* ☎ *717/687–8628.* ⊇ *$6.* ☉ *May–Oct., Mon.–Sat. 9–5, Sun. noon–5; Nov.–Apr., Tues.–Sat. 9–5, Sun. noon–5.*

★ ☾   The **National Toy Train Museum,** the showplace of the Train Collectors Association, displays antique and 20th-century model trains. The museum has five huge operating layouts, with toy trains from the 1800s to the present, plus nostalgia films and hundreds of locomotives and cars in display cases. Take the kids to see the special hands-on layouts every Friday from June through August. ⊠ *Paradise La. just north of Rte. 741,* ☎ *717/687–8976.* ⊇ *$3.* ☉ *May–Oct. and Christmas wk, daily 10–5; Apr. and Nov.–mid-Dec., weekends 10–5.*

☾   **Choo-Choo Barn, Traintown, USA,** is a family hobby that got out of hand: What started in 1945 as a single train chugging around the Groff family Christmas tree is now a 1,700-square-ft display of Lancaster County in miniature, with 16 trains and 140 figures and vehicles in O-gauge. Every five minutes a house catches on fire, and fire engines turn on their hoses to extinguish the blaze. Flag bearers march in a Memorial Day parade, and animals perform in a three-ring circus. Periodically the overhead lights dim, and it becomes night, when streetlights glow and locomotive headlights pierce the darkness. ⊠ *Rte. 741,* ☎ *717/687–7911.* ⊇ *$3.* ☉ *Apr.–Dec., daily 10–5.*

The **Amish Village** offers guided tours through an authentically furnished Amish house. Afterward you can wander around the grounds of the village, which includes a one-room schoolhouse, a blacksmith shop, and an operating smokehouse built for the Amish Village by Amish craftsmen. ⊠ *Rte. 896 between U.S. 30 and Rte. 741,* ☎ *717/687–8511.* ⊇ *$5.75.* ☉ *Mar.–mid-May and Sept.–Oct., daily 9–5; mid-May–Aug., daily 9–6; Nov.–Feb., house tours weekends 9–4.*

Dining and Lodging

$$ ✕ **Iron Horse Inn.** This rustic pub and candlelighted restaurant is housed in the original 1780s Hotel Strasburg. Best bets are the catch of the day, the homemade breads, and, for dessert, the great warm apple pie. The wine list is extensive. There's live entertainment on weekends. ⊠ *135 E. Main St.,* ☎ *717/687–6362. AE, D, DC, MC, V. Closed Mon. Dec.–May.*

$–$$ ✕ **Washington House Restaurant.** One of the restaurants at the Historic Strasburg Inn (☞ *below*) offers fine candlelight dining in two Colonial-style dining rooms. The American menu lists steaks, jumbo lump crab cakes, and wild game. The lunch buffet is bountiful. ⊠ *Rte. 896, Historic Dr.,* ☎ *717/687–9211. AE, D, DC, MC, V.*

$–$$$ ⊡ **Historic Strasburg Inn.** The five buildings of this Colonial-style inn are set on 58 peaceful acres overlooking farmland. The rooms, simply and comfortably furnished, have rocking chairs. A Continental-plus breakfast, served in the Washington House Restaurant, is included. ⊠ *Rte. 896, Historic Dr., 17579,* ☎ *717/687–7691 or 800/872–0201,* FAX *717/687–6098. 101 rooms. 2 restaurants, pool, exercise room, volleyball. AE, D, DC, MC, V. BP.*

$–$$ ⊞ **Fulton Steamboat Inn.** At Lancaster County's busiest intersection, across from rows of outlet stores, are a small lake, waterfalls, the piped-in sounds of a river, and a hotel that looks just like a steamboat. Named after Lancaster native Robert Fulton, who built the first successful passenger steamer in 1807, the tri-level hotel aims to please all land-locked boaters. The uppermost deck has whirlpool baths and private outdoor decks; the no-smoking middle level has staterooms with two queen-size beds; and the bottom level has cabins with nautical nuances and bunk beds. Rooms have turn-of-the-century-style furnishings, microwaves, and mini-refrigerators. Package plans include meals and admission to area attractions. ⊠ *Rtes. 30 and 896, Box 333, 17579,* ☎ *717/299–9999 or 800/922–2229 outside PA,* ℻ *717/299–9992. 96 rooms. Restaurant, indoor pool, exercise room. AE, MC, V.*

$–$$ ⊞ **Hershey Farm Restaurant and Motor Inn.** This motel just south of Bird-in-Hand overlooks flower and vegetable gardens, a picture-perfect pond, and a farm. Ask for one of the large rooms in the newer building. The handy restaurant offers a buffet and reasonably priced à la carte meals. There are walking trails on the grounds. ⊠ *Route 896, Ronks 17572,* ☎ *717/687–8635 or 800/827–8635,* ℻ *717/687–8638. 57 rooms, 2 suites. Restaurant, no-smoking rooms, pool, playground. AE, D, MC, V. BP.*

$–$$ ⊞ **Limestone Inn Bed and Breakfast.** Richard and Denise Waller are the gracious hosts in their 1786 Georgian home, listed on the National Register of Historic Places. A formal living room, a library, and a sitting room with a fireplace serve as common areas; you may also relax outside by the fish pool in the small garden. The bedrooms are decorated in traditional Colonial colors with Amish quilts and four-poster beds. The B&B is in the center of the village, within walking distance of many Strasburg attractions. ⊠ *33 E. Main St., 17579,* ☎ *717/687– 8392 or 800/278–8392,* ℻ *717/687–8366. 6 rooms, 5 with private bath. Library. No credit cards. BP.*

$–$$ ⊞ **Strasburg Village Inn.** This historic circa-1788 house, conveniently
★ located in the heart of town, has rooms elegantly appointed in the Williamsburg style. Most have a canopy or four-poster bed; three have a whirlpool bath. A sitting/reading room is on the second floor; an old-fashioned porch overlooks Main Street. Full breakfast in the adjacent ice-cream parlor is included. ⊠ *1 W. Main St., 17579,* ☎ *717/687– 0900 or 800/541–1055. 6 rooms, 6 suites. AE, D, MC, V. BP.*

$ ⊞ **Mill Stream Country Inn and Restaurant.** Long a popular choice, this freshly renovated motel overlooks a picturesque stream. Request a room in the rear to get the prettiest view. Breakfast is available in the restaurant, but no alcohol is served. Guests have exercise privileges at Willow Valley Family Resort (☞ Lancaster, *above*), a sister property. ⊠ *Rte. 896, 17576,* ☎ *717/299–0931,* ℻ *717/295–9326. 52 rooms, 3 suites. Restaurant, pool.. AE, D, MC, V. BP.*

Ephrata

❺ *22 mi north of Strasburg, 12 mi northeast of Lancaster.*

Ephrata has a well-known farmers market and Ephrata Cloister, the legacy of an early religious community. North of town, antiques markets draw huge crowds.

Ephrata Cloister preserves the remains of a religious communal society founded in 1728, when dissident brethren split from a group that had arrived four years earlier. The monastic Protestants of Ephrata lived an ascetic life of work, study, and prayer. They ate one meal a day of grains, fruits, and vegetables and encouraged celibacy (the last sister died in 1813). The society was best known for its a cappella singing and its Fraktur, as well as for its publishing center and the medieval German architecture of the buildings. Guides lead 45-minute tours of three restored buildings, after which you can browse through the stable, print shop, and craft shop. ⊠ *Rtes. 272 and 322,* ☏ *717/733–6600.* ▭ *$5.* ⊙ *Mon.–Sat. 9–5, Sun. noon–5.*

★ The **Green Dragon Farmers Market and Auction** is a traditional agricultural market with a country carnival atmosphere. Each Friday livestock and agricultural commodities are auctioned in the morning. Local Amish and Mennonite farmers tend many of the 400 indoor and outdoor stalls selling meats, fruits, vegetables, fresh-baked pies, and dry goods. One of the state's largest farmers markets (occupying 30 acres), it also has a flea market and an evening auction of small animals. Try the sticky buns at Rissler's Bakery and the sausage sandwiches at Newswanger's. ⊠ *955 N. State St., off Rte. 272,* ☏ *717/738–1117.* ⊙ *Fri. 9 AM–10 PM.*

Dining and Lodging

$$ ✕ **The Restaurant at Doneckers.** Classic and country French cuisine is served downstairs amid Colonial antiques and upstairs overlooking a country garden. The kitchen is known for its chateaubriand for two, sautéed Dover sole with strawberry sauce, steak au poivre, the daily chef's veal special, and salmon. The service is fine, the wine cellar extensive. From 2:30 to 4 light fare is served. ⊠ *333 N. State St.,* ☏ *717/738–9501. AE, D, DC, MC, V. Closed Wed., Sun.*

$$ ✕ **Stoudt's Black Angus.** Prime rib cut from certified Angus beef is the
★ specialty of this Victorian-style restaurant, adjacent to the Black Angus Antiques Mall. Also notable are its raw oyster bar and German dishes such as Wiener (veal) and *Schwabian* (pork) schnitzel. Stoudt's beer, brewed right next door, is on tap. On weekends from August through October, a Bavarian Beer Fest with German bands, a pig roast, and ethnic food takes over Brewery Hall. There are brewery tours Saturday at 3 and Sunday at 1. The restaurant is 6 mi northeast of Ephrata. ⊠ *Rte. 272, Adamstown,* ☏ *717/484–4385. AE, DC, MC, V. No lunch Mon.–Thurs.*

$$–$$$$ ▦ **The Inns at Doneckers.** Four properties dating from the 1770s to 1920s have been tastefully furnished with French country antiques and decorated by hand stenciling. Rooms are light and airy; suites have fireplaces and whirlpool baths. You can shop for crafts (☞ Shopping, *below*) and clothing here, too, and a restaurant (☞ *above*) is also part of the development. ⊠ *318–324 N. State St., 17522,* ☏ *717/738–9502. 27 rooms, 13 suites. Restaurant, shops. AE, D, DC, MC, V. CP.*

$–$$$ ▦ **Smithton Inn.** This B&B, a historic former stagecoach inn built in
★ 1763, has been lovingly and authentically restored with hand-tooled furniture, woodwork, and architectural details true to the period. The rooms have fireplaces and canopy beds; the third-floor suite has a skylight, cathedral ceiling, and Franklin stove fireplace. Nice touches abound: oversize pillows, nightshirts, and flowers. Feather beds are available upon request when you book a room. Outside are a lily pond, a fountain, English lawn furniture, and a huge dahlia garden. Full breakfast is included, as is complimentary coffee and tea. ⊠ *900 W. Main St., at Academy Dr., 17522,* ☏ *717/733–6094. 7 rooms, 1 suite. AE, MC, V. BP.*

Shopping

ANTIQUES
Large antiques malls line Route 272 north of Ephrata between Adamstown and Denver and offer plenty of temptations.

Heritage I and II Antique Centers (⊠ Heritage I, Rte. 272, 1 mi north of Pennsylvania Turnpike Exit 21, ☏ 717/484–4646; ⊠ Heritage II,

Rte. 272, 2 mi south of Pennsylvania Turnpike Exit 21, ☎ 717/336–0888), two of the area's many antiques cooperatives, have more than 200 dealers set up in over 25,000 square ft of indoor space. Both are open daily from 9 to 5.

The huge **Renninger's Antique and Collector's Market** (⊠ Rte. 272, ½ mi north of Pennsylvania Turnpike Exit 21, Adamstown, ☎ 717/336–2177) draws thousands of collectors and dealers on Sunday from 7:30 to 5. Nearly 400 indoor stalls, open year-round, overflow with every conceivable type of antique, while the outdoor flea market adds to the selection on good-weather days.

Shupp's Grove (⊠ Just off Rte. 897, south of Adamstown, ☎ 717/484–4115), the oldest of the Adamstown antiques markets, has acres of dealers in an outdoor tree-shaded grove. Tables are piled with antiques, art, and collectibles. The market is open weekends from April through October, 7–5.

At **Stoudt's Black Angus Antiques Mall** (⊠ Rte. 272, Adamstown, ☎ 717/484–4385) more than 500 dealers display old books and prints, estate jewelry, linens, china and glassware, coins, and plenty of furniture, inside and outside. There's also a restaurant (☞ Dining and Lodging, *above*). The mall is open Sunday from 7:30 to 5.

CRAFTS

The **Artworks at Doneckers** (⊠ 100 N. State St., ☎ 717/738–9503 or 800/209–2787) houses over 30 galleries showing the works of local painters, sculptors, potters, and stencil makers. It's closed Wednesday.

The Mennonite Central Committee operates **Ten Thousand Villages and Nav Jiwan International Tea Room** (⊠ Rte. 272 just north of Ephrata Cloister, ☎ 717/721–8400). Part of a job-creation program designed to aid developing countries, the store stocks more than 3,000 items—including jewelry, Indian brass, onyx, needlework, baskets, toys, hand-woven rugs, and clothing—from more than 30 countries. Sales in January and July offer some terrific bargains. Each week for lunch the Nav Jiwan (Hindi for "new life") Tea Room serves the cuisine of a different country; the restaurant also has a Friday night dinner buffet. The store is closed Sunday.

Lititz

❻ *10 mi southwest of Ephrata.*

Lititz was founded in 1756 by Moravians who settled in Pennsylvania to do missionary work among the Native Americans. Its tree-shaded main street, lined with 18th-century cottages and shops selling antiques, crafts, clothing, and gifts, is a fine place for a walk. Around the main square are the Moravian communal residences, a church dating from 1787, and a hospital that treated the wounded during the Revolutionary War. You can pick up a Historical Foundation walking tour brochure at the **General Sutter Inn** (☞ Lodging, *below*) or at the **Johannes Mueller House** (⊠ 137–139 Main St., ☎ 717/626–7958).

At the **Julius Sturgis Pretzel House,** the nation's oldest pretzel bakery, pretzels are twisted by hand and baked in brick ovens the same way Julius Sturgis did it in 1861. At the end of the 20-minute guided tour, you can try your hand at the almost extinct art of pretzel twisting. ⊠ *219 E. Main St., ☎ 717/626–4354. ☎ $2. ☉ Mon.–Sat. 9–5.*

The first thing visitors notice in Lititz is the smell of chocolate emanating from the **Wilbur Chocolate Company's Candy Americana Museum and Factory Candy Outlet,** which has a small museum of candy-related memorabilia and a very large retail store. ⊠ *48 N. Broad St.,* ☎ *717/626–3249.* ⊡ *Free.* ☉ *Mon.–Sat. 10–5.*

Lodging

$$ ⊞ **Swiss Woods.** Innkeepers Werner and Debrah Mosimann designed
★   this chalet while they were still living in Werner's native Switzerland. They planted it on 30 acres, creating an open and airy, European-style bed-and-breakfast with light pine furnishings and contemporary country decor. Nestled on the edge of the woods overlooking Speedwell Forge Lake, the chalet is surrounded by extensive flower gardens. Each room has its own patio or balcony. ⊠ *500 Blantz Rd., 17543,* ☎ *717/627–3358 or 800/594–8018,* ℻ *717/627–3483. 6 rooms, 1 suite. Hiking, boating, fishing. AE, D, MC, V. BP.*

$–$$ ⊞ **General Sutter Inn.** Built in 1764, the oldest continuously run inn
★   in Pennsylvania was named after the man who founded Sacramento in 1839, 10 years before the discovery of gold on his California property started the gold rush; Sutter retired in Lititz. This Victoriana lover's delight has furnishings that range from Pennsylvania folk art to Louis XIV sofas and marble-top tables. The inn stands at the crossroads of town, within easy walking distance of the buildings of the historic district. The tavern is a good place to mingle with locals, and its brick patio is inviting in summer. ⊠ *14 E. Main St., corner of Rtes. 501 and 772, 17543,* ☎ *717/626–2115,* ℻ *717/626–0992. 16 rooms, 3 suites. Restaurant, bar, coffee shop. AE, D, MC, V.*

WESTERN LANCASTER COUNTY

You can avoid the crowds and commercialism of parts of eastern Lancaster County by staying in the peaceful backwater towns along or near the Susquehanna River, including Columbia, Marietta, and Mount Joy. There's plenty of scenery and Colonial history to explore, and you can sample good Mennonite food here.

Columbia

❼   *10 mi west of Lancaster.*

It's a quiet town now, but Columbia and other river communities were very important in the days when rivers were one of the easiest methods of transportation. Eighteenth-century Quaker missionary John Wright worked in this area, and two of his sons set up a ferry that became an important transportation point for settlers moving west. Today museums and the tranquil countryside are diversions.

★   A visit to the newly expanded **National Watch and Clock Museum** provides an entertaining trip through the history and future of timekeeping. The Time Tunnel takes you from exhibits of water clocks through a turn-of-the-century watch and clock shop and a 20th-century watch factory. More than 10,000 timepieces and time-related items are on view, including early sundials; a 19th-century Tiffany globe clock; a German Black Forest organ clock with 94 pipes; moon-phase wristwatches; and the showstopper, the Engle Clock, an 1877 timepiece intended to resemble the famous astronomical cathedral clock of Strasbourg, France. ⊠ *514 Poplar St.,* ☎ *717/684–8261.* ⊡ *$6.* ☉ *Tues.–Sat. 10–5, Sun. noon–4.*

The **Market House and Dungeon,** built in 1869, is one of the oldest continuously operating farmers markets in the state. You can buy handcrafted jewelry, baked goods, meat, fruits, and vegetables from local farms. The basement of the market used to be a dungeon; you can still see the ground-level windows through which prisoners were shoved down a chute into the darkness. ⊠ *308 Locust St., off Rte. 441,* ☎ *717/684–2468.* ☉ *Farmers market: Fri. 7–4, Sat. 7–noon. Dungeon by appointment only; contact* ⊠ *Susquehanna Heritage Visitors Center, 3rd and Linden Sts.,* ☎ *717/684–5249.*

Wright's Ferry Mansion was the residence of English Quaker Susanna Wright, a silkworm breeder whose family helped open Colonial Pennsylvania west of the Susquehanna. The 1738 stone house showcases period furniture in the Philadelphia William & Mary and Queen Anne styles and a great collection of English needlework, ceramics, and glass, all predating 1750. ⊠ *38 S. 2nd St.,* ☎ *717/684–4325.* ⌨ *$5.* ☉ *May–Oct., Tues.–Wed. and Fri.–Sat. 10–3.*

En Route　For a view of the Susquehanna River as it snakes through the valley, follow the hiking trail from the parking area at **Chickies Rock County Park** (⊠ Rte. 441 between Columbia and Marietta) to Chickies Rock, an outcropping high above the water. Bring a picnic lunch.

Dining and Lodging

$$　✕ **Prudhomme's Lost Cajun Kitchen.** Transplanted southerners and other Cajun food fans come from as far away as Philadelphia and Baltimore to dine at the only restaurant for miles where you can taste crawfish étouffée, fried alligator, and other specialties. They are prepared as hot as you like them by David Prudhomme, whose famous Uncle Paul perfected these flavors. Blackened pork chops, pastas, and other dishes are options for the less adventurous diner. ⊠ *Rte. 462 and Cherry St.,* ☎ *717/684–1706. AE, D, MC, V. No dinner Sun. No lunch Mon.*

$–$$　🏠 **The Columbian.** In this Victorian mansion in the heart of the village, a tiered staircase leads to rooms filled with antiques. Several rooms have fireplaces. The rate includes an ample country breakfast, often prepared with herbs from the garden. ⊠ *360 Chestnut St., 17512,* ☎ *717/684–5869 or 800/422–5869. 6 rooms, 2 suites. Playground. MC, V. BP.*

Marietta

❽ *8 mi northwest of Columbia.*

Almost 50% of the buildings in Marietta are listed on the National Historic Register; the architecture ranges from log cabins to more recent Federal and Victorian homes. This restored river town, now seeing new life as an artists' community, is perfect for a stroll past the well-preserved facades of art galleries and antiques shops.

❾ At the 52-acre **Nissley Vineyards and Winery Estate,** you can review the grape-growing process on a self-guided tour. This scenic winery, which produces award-winning vintage wines, also has tastings, and bottles are for sale. You can picnic on the grounds. ⊠ *140 Vintage Dr., northwest of Marietta near Bainbridge, 1½ mi off Rte. 441,* ☎ *717/426–3514.* ⌨ *Free.* ☉ *Mon.–Sat. 10–5, Sun. 1–4.*

Lodging

$　🏠 **Olde Fogie Farm.** You can milk the goats and bottle-feed the calves on this organic farm. The old frame home has an Amish cookstove; the property has a petting farm, a creek, a pond, a playhouse, and a stable for pony rides. ⊠ *106 Stackstown Rd., 17547,* ☎ *717/426–3992. 2 rooms, 1 with bath; 2 efficiency apartments. No credit cards. BP.*

Shopping

George's Woodcrafts (⊠ 9 Reichs Church Rd., ☎ 717/426–1004 or 800/799–1685) sells handcrafted furniture in walnut, oak, and cherry for every room in the house. You can watch items being made and then put in an order. The store is closed Sunday.

Mount Joy

⑩ *5 mi northeast of Marietta.*

This small town holds a historic brewery and some good restaurants. Dating from before the Civil War, **Bube's Brewery** (☞ Dining and Lodging, *below*) is the only brewery in the United States that has remained intact since the mid-19th century. A guided tour takes you 43 ft below the street into the brewery's vaults and passages, which were built in a cave; these passages also served as part of the Underground Railroad. It's a pleasant way to learn about beer making in Victorian times. ⊠ *102 N. Market St.,* ☎ *717/653–2056.* ☜ *$3.50.* ☉ *Tours Memorial Day–Labor Day, daily 10–5.*

Dining and Lodging

$–$$ ✕ **Bube's Brewery.** The only intact pre-Prohibition brewery in the country contains three unique restaurants. The Bottling Works, in the original bottling plant of the brewery, serves steaks, light dinners, salads, burgers, and subs. Alois's offers prix fixe six-course international dinners (reservations required; closed Monday) in a Victorian hotel attached to the brewery. The Catacombs serves traditional steak and seafood dishes in the brewery's aging cellars below street level. A feast master presides over a medieval-style dinner (reservations required) every Sunday night. Wine and ale flow, musicians entertain, and diners participate in the festivities. In addition, Bube's has an outdoor beer garden in summer. ⊠ *102 N. Market St.,* ☎ *717/653–2056. AE, D, MC, V. No lunch Sun.*

$–$$ ✕ **Groff's Farm.** Abe and Betty Groff's 1756 farmhouse restaurant has
★   received national attention for its hearty Mennonite fare. Candlelight, fresh flowers, and original Groff Farm country fabrics and wall coverings contribute to the homey ambience. House specialties include chicken Stoltzfus, farm relishes, and cracker pudding. Dinner begins with chocolate cake. Lunch is à la carte, dinner à la carte or family style but served at your own table. ⊠ *650 Pinkerton Rd.,* ☎ *717/653–2048. Reservations essential. AE, D, DC, MC, V. Closed Sun.–Mon.*

$ ▥ **Rocky Acre Farm.** Here you can sleep in a 200-year-old stone farmhouse that was once a stop on the Underground Railroad. This is a dairy farm with calves to feed, cows to milk, and dogs, kittens, roosters, and sheep—in the meadow, of course—to enjoy. There's fishing and boating in the creek. A full hot breakfast is served daily. ⊠ *1020 Pinkerton Rd., 17552,* ☎ *717/653–4449. 8 rooms, 2 efficiency units. Boating, fishing. No credit cards. BP.*

Manheim

7 mi northeast of Mount Joy.

Baron Henry William Stiegel founded the small town of Manheim and manufactured Stiegel flint glassware here in the 18th century. Today a major draw is a winery a few miles north of town.

⑪ The **Mount Hope Estate and Winery** is an elegant 19th-century mansion with a vineyard on the grounds. Originally built in 1800 in the Federal style, the house was Victorianized and enlarged to its current 32 rooms in 1895. Turrets, hand-painted 18-ft ceilings, Egyptian marble fireplaces, gold-leaf wallpaper, and crystal gas chandeliers are just some of the decorative elements. Tours, led by costumed guides, are followed by a formal wine tasting of Mount Hope Wines in the billiards room. Afterward you can take a stroll through the estate greenhouse and gardens. ⊠ *5 mi north of Manheim on Rte. 72, ½ mi from Exit 20 of the Pennsylvania Turnpike,* ☎ *717/665–7021, ext. 125.* ☜ *$5.* ☉ *Tours May–June, weekends; July–Sept., daily; by reservation only.*

Lodging

$ 🏠 **Jonde Lane Farm.** Breakfast with your Mennonite host family is served every day but Sunday at this 100-acre working dairy and poultry farm. Ponies, chickens, and cats are conspicuous. The four guest rooms include a family room that can sleep seven people. You can fish on the property. ✉ *1103 Auction Rd., 17545,* ☎ *717/665–4231. 4 rooms, 2 with bath. Fishing. MC, V. Closed Thanksgiving–Easter. BP.*

Nightlife and the Arts

The seasonal **Pennsylvania Renaissance Faire,** on the grounds of the Mount Hope Estate and Winery (☞ *above*), transforms the winery into a 16th-century English village with human chess matches, jousting and fencing tournaments, knighthood ceremonies, street performances, craft demonstrations, jesters, and Shakespearean plays performed on 11 outdoor stages. ✉ *5 mi north of Manheim on Rte. 72, ½ mi from Exit 20 of Pennsylvania Turnpike,* ☎ *717/665–7021.* 🎟 *$17.95.* ☉ *Aug.–Labor Day, weekends 10–6:30; early Sept.–mid-Oct., weekends 10:30–6.*

HERSHEY AND GETTYSBURG

It's easy to combine a trip to Lancaster County with two popular sights not more than an hour's drive from Lancaster. Hershey, to the northwest, has an amusement park and some chocolate-themed attractions. Gettysburg, to the southwest, is the county seat of Adams County and the site of Gettysburg National Military Park and museums that examine the significance of the Civil War battle.

Hershey

⑫ *30 mi northwest of Lancaster.*

Hershey is Chocolate Town, a community built around a chocolate factory and now home to a theme park, the Hershey Museum, and other diversions for children and adults. Founded in 1903 by confectioner Milton S. Hershey, a Mennonite descendant, it celebrates chocolate without guilt, from streetlights shaped like foil-wrapped kisses to avenues named Chocolate and Cocoa. Hershey is also known as a fine golf center. You can call ☎ 800/437–7439 for brochures and room reservations.

☼ At **Hersheypark** they take seriously the saying "You are what you eat." Where else can you find walking Hershey Bars and dancing Reese's Peanut Butter Cups? On 100 landscaped acres are 50 rides, games of chance, five theaters, and ZooAmerica (☞ *below*), with animals from North America. Begun in 1907 as a playground for chocolate factory employees, Hersheypark has been called America's cleanest and greenest theme park. Among its historic rides are the Comet, a 1946-vintage wooden roller coaster, and a carousel built in 1919 with 66 hand-carved wooden horses. ✉ *Hersheypark Dr., Rte. 743 and U.S. 422,* ☎ *717/534–3090.* 🎟 *$30.95 includes ZooAmerica.* ☉ *Memorial Day–Labor Day, daily 10–10 (some earlier closings); May and Sept., weekends only, call for hrs.*

☼ **ZooAmerica,** on the grounds of Hersheypark (☞ *above*), is an 11-acre wildlife park with more than 250 animals from throughout North America in re-creations of their natural habitats. ✉ *Rte. 743 and U.S. 422,* ☎ *717/534–3860.* 🎟 *$5.75 (or included in Hersheypark admission price).* ☉ *Mid-June–Aug., daily 10–8; Sept.–mid-June, daily 10–5.*

★ ☼ At **Hershey's Chocolate World,** a 10-minute automated ride takes you through the steps of producing chocolate (the crowds are now too large for actual factory tours). It also serves as the town's official visitor center. Chocolate aficionados get to see the entire process from picking the cocoa beans to making candy bars in Hershey's candy kitchens. Afterward you may taste-test your favorite Hershey confection and buy gifts in a spacious conservatory filled with tropical plants. ⊠ *Park Blvd.*, ☎ *717/534–4900.* ⚏ *Free.* ☉ *Fall–spring, Mon.–Sat. 9–5; summer, daily 9–8.*

★ The **Hershey Museum** preserves the story of Milton S. Hershey, who founded the town bearing his name and just about everything in it. The main exhibition, *Built on Chocolate*, displays Hershey artifacts and memorabilia. Displays of chocolate bar wrappers and cocoa tins show their evolution through the years, while black-and-white photos of the town from the '30s, '40s, and '50s are hung side by side with color photos of the same sites today. *Adam Danner's World* documents the daily lives of Pennsylvania Germans, and the Native American Collection has art and artifacts from Hershey's personal collection. A children's area provides a hands-on experience. ⊠ *170 W. Hersheypark Dr.*, ☎ *717/534–3439.* ⚏ *$4.25.* ☉ *Memorial Day–Labor Day, daily 10–6; Labor Day–Memorial Day, daily 10–5.*

Hershey Gardens began with a single 3½-acre plot of 8,000 rose bushes and has grown to include 10 theme gardens on 23 landscaped acres, with 1,200 varieties of roses and 22,000 tulips. The gardens come to life in spring as thousands of bulbs burst into bloom. Flowering displays last until fall, when late roses open. ⊠ *Hotel Rd. near Hotel Hershey*, ☎ *717/534–3493.* ⚏ *$4.25.* ☉ *May–Oct., daily 9–5.*

Chocolatetown Square is a 1-acre park downtown where free concerts are held in summer. ⊠ *Intersection of Cocoa and E. Chocolate Aves., near wooden gazebo,* ☎ *717/534–3411 for upcoming events.*

OFF THE
BEATEN PATH

INDIAN ECHO CAVERNS – One of the largest caves in the northeastern United States has a 45-minute guided walking tour of its underground wonderland. Bring a sweater; no strollers are allowed. The children will enjoy panning for gold at Gem Hill Junction; there are horse-drawn carriage rides and a petting zoo, a gift shop, and a picnic area. The caverns are about 3 mi west of Hershey. ⊠ *Off U.S. 322, Hummelstown,* ☎ *717/566–8131.* ⚏ *$8.* ☉ *Memorial Day–Labor Day, daily 9–6; Labor Day–Memorial Day, daily 10–4.*

Dining and Lodging

$ ✕ **Hershey Pantry.** This lace-curtained, family-friendly restaurant serves generous portions of simple food made with fresh ingredients. The menu includes pastas, sandwiches, salads, and homemade desserts; the hearty breakfasts are notable. ⊠ *801 E. Chocolate Ave.,* ☎ *717/ 533–7505. No credit cards. Closed Sun.*

$$$$ ✕▥ **Hotel Hershey.** The grande dame of Hershey, this gracious Mediter-
★ ranean villa-style hotel is a quiet, sophisticated resort with plenty of options for recreation, starting with the golf course that surrounds the hotel. Inspired by the fine European hotels Milton S. Hershey encountered in his travels, it was part of his building program to lift his town out of the Great Depression. Elegant touches abound, from the mosaic-tile lobby to rooms with iron beds, maple armoires, paintings from local artists, and tile baths. Lawn bowling and nature trails are added amenities. Dining options are the Fountain Café, the casual Clubhouse Café, and the formal Circular Dining Room, which overlooks the gardens, fountains, and reflecting pools. Some packages include meals. ⊠ *Hotel Rd.,* ☎ *717/533–2171 or 800/533–3131. 241 rooms. 3 restaurants, indoor-outdoor pool, sauna, 9-hole golf course, 3 tennis courts, exercise room. AE, D, DC, MC, V.*

$$–$$$ ⊡ **Hershey Lodge & Convention Center.** This bustling, expansive modern resort caters to both families and business travelers and has two casual restaurants suitable for children, plus a somewhat more formal room for adult dining. The hotel hosts groups of up to 1,300 in its Chocolate Ballroom, and it can be hectic during conventions. Ask for a room in the newly renovated Guest Tower. ⊠ *W. Chocolate Ave. and University Dr., 17033,* ☎ *717/533–3311 or 800/533–3131. 457 rooms. 3 restaurants, indoor pool, outdoor pool, miniature golf, 2 tennis courts, exercise room, recreation room, convention center. AE, D, DC, MC, V.*

Outdoor Activities and Sports

The **Country Club of Hershey** (⊠ 1000 E. Derry Rd., ☎ 717/533–2464) maintains two private 18-hole courses, which are available to guests of the Hotel Hershey. Greens fees are around $100. The **Hotel Hershey** (⊠ Hotel Rd., ☎ 717/533–2171) offers nine holes on the hotel grounds. Greens fees are $12. A public 18 holes known as the **South Course** (⊠ 600 W. Derry Rd., ☎ 717/534–3450) is short but demanding. Greens fees are $44–$52. **Spring Creek Golf** (⊠ 450 E. Chocolate Ave., ☎ 717/ 533–2847), a nine-hole course, was originally built by Milton Hershey for youngsters to hone their strokes. Greens fees are $11.

Shopping

Ziegler's Antiques Mall (⊠ Intersection Rtes. 322 and 743, ☎ 717/533–7990) has 75 dealers and an assortment of antiques and collectibles. It is housed in Hershey's largest parabolic barn, which formerly belonged to the Milton Hershey School. The mall is open Thursday–Monday 10–5:30.

Ziegler's in the Country (⊠ Rte. 743, ☎ 717/533–1662) is on a restored 1850s homestead, with several buildings from that era. An air-conditioned barn has space for 92 dealers and an herb and spice shop (open on weekends). You can shop Thursday–Monday 9–5.

Gettysburg

⓭ *53 mi west of Lancaster on U.S. 30.*

"The world will little note, nor long remember, what we say here, but it can never forget what they did here." These words from Abraham Lincoln's famous address were delivered in Gettysburg to mark the dedication of its national cemetery in November 1863. Four months earlier, from July 1 to 3, 51,000 Americans were killed, wounded, or counted as missing in the bloodiest battle of the Civil War. The events that took place in Gettysburg during those few days marked the turning point in the war. Although the struggle raged on for almost two more years, the Confederate forces never recovered from their losses. At the national military park and 20 museums in Gettysburg, you can recapture the power of those momentous days. If you have limited time, the military park is the key site to visit. Choose other sites based on your interests; the town has everything from wax museums to historic houses.

The **Gettysburg Travel Council,** in the former Western Maryland Railroad Passenger Depot, has free brochures and maps of area attractions. Be sure to pick up a self-guided walking tour map of the town's Historic District, centered in and around Baltimore Street. You'll find a number of museums along the route, as well as markers that point out homes and sites significant to the history of the town and to the battle. ⊠ *35 Carlisle St.,* ☎ *717/334–6274.* ☉ *Daily 8:30–5.*

The **Gettysburg Tour Center** is the departure point for two-hour narrated tours of the battlefield. Open-air double-decker buses depart every

15–45 minutes. ⊠ *778 Baltimore St.,* ☎ *717/334–6296.* 🎫 *$13.95.*
⊙ *Jan.–June and Sept.–Dec., daily 9–5; July–Aug., daily 9–9.*

★ At what is now **Gettysburg National Military Park,** General Robert E.
Lee and his Confederate troops encountered the Union forces of General George Meade. The 5,700 acres are now adorned with more than
1,000 markers and monuments honoring the casualties of the battle.
More than 30 mi of marked roads lead through the park, highlighting key battle sites. It's best to begin your exploration at the visitor
center (☞ *below*). ⊠ *97 Taneytown Rd.,* ☎ *717/334–1124.* 🎫 *Free.*
⊙ *Park roads 6 AM–10 PM.*

The Gettysburg National Military Park **Visitor Center** offers a free map
with an 18-mi driving tour through the battlefield, as well as an orientation program, Civil War exhibits, and current schedules of ranger-
conducted programs and talks. The park service also provides free
walking-tour maps, which have short 1-mi loops that include the sites
of some of the battle's most pivotal engagements; 3½- and 9-mi trails
are also marked.

To best understand the battle, begin by viewing the **Electric Map,**
which uses colored lights to illustrate deployments and clashes during
the three days of fighting. Sit on the south side for the best view. Private, licensed guides may also be hired at the center. ⊠ *97 Taneytown
Rd.,* ☎ *717/334–1124.* 🎫 *Free; Electric Map $2.50.* ⊙ *Daily 8–5, but
call for later summer hrs; map shows every 45 min.*

The **Cyclorama Center** contains a 19th-century in-the-round painting
that puts you in the center of Pickett's Charge, the South's ill-fated frontal
assault during the last day of the battle. ⊠ *Taneytown Rd., adjacent
to the visitor center,* ☎ *717/334–1124.* 🎫 *$2.50.* ⊙ *Showings daily,
every 30 min, 9–4:30.*

★ The **Gettysburg National Cemetery,** dedicated by President Abraham
Lincoln in his Gettysburg Address, is now the final resting place of more
than 7,000 honorably discharged servicemen and their dependents. ⊠
Off Baltimore Pike, across the street from the visitor center. 🎫 *Free.*
⊙ *Daily dawn–dusk.*

The **National Civil War Wax Museum** presents the story of the Civil
War era and the Battle of Gettysburg through 200 life-size figures in
30 scenes, including a reenactment of the Battle of Gettysburg and an
animated Abraham Lincoln delivering his Gettysburg Address. ⊠ *297
Steinwehr Ave.,* ☎ *717/334–6245.* 🎫 *$4.50.* ⊙ *Mar.–Dec., daily 9–
7; Jan.–Feb., weekends 9–5.*

The **Hall of Presidents and First Ladies** re-creates in wax the nation's
chief executives from Washington to Clinton, as well as their wives (with
reproductions of their inaugural gowns). The museum also contains a
room displaying paintings by President Dwight D. Eisenhower. ⊠ *789
Baltimore St.,* ☎ *717/334–5717.* 🎫 *$5.75.* ⊙ *June–Aug., daily 9–9;
Mar.–May and Sept.–Nov., daily 9–5.*

Soldier's National Museum depicts 10 major battles of the Civil War
in miniature dioramas and a life-size encampment scene from the night
of July 2, 1863. ⊠ *777 Baltimore St.,* ☎ *717/334–4890.* 🎫 *$5.75.* ⊙
June–Aug., daily 9–9; Mar.–May and Sept.–Nov., daily 9–5.

The **Lincoln Train Museum** aims to recapture Lincoln's journey from
Washington to Gettysburg in November 1863 to dedicate the national
cemetery. A 12-minute ride simulates the sights, sounds, and most of
all the feel of traveling on a period railcar. The museum also houses
the Alexander Model Train and Military Rail Collection. ⊠ *425 Stein-*

wehr Ave., ☎ *717/334–5678.* ☞ *$5.75.* ☉ *May–June, daily 9–9, July–Aug., daily 9 AM–10 PM; Sept.–Nov., daily 9–5.*

The **Lincoln Room Museum** houses the bedroom where President Lincoln finished writing the Gettysburg Address; the furnishings are copies. Through a tape featuring a re-creation of Lincoln speaking his thoughts, doubts, and dreams on November 18, 1963, you can learn the story behind his words and understand what motivated them. ⊠ *12 Lincoln Sq.,* ☎ *717/334–8188.* ☞ *$3.50.* ☉ *Summer, daily 9–7:30; reduced hrs off-season.*

General Lee's headquarters, which at press time was scheduled to reopen in April 2000 after renovations, is one of the few historic houses in Gettysburg open to the public. Here, on July 1, 1863, Lee planned his strategy for the now-famous battle. The old stone building houses a fine collection of Civil War relics. ⊠ *Rte. 30W, 8 blocks west of Lincoln Sq.,* ☎ *717/334–3141.* ☞ *$3.* ☉ *Mar.–Nov., daily 9–9.*

The recently restored **Schriver House** was the home of George and Henrietta Schriver and their two children. After George joined the Union troops and his family fled to safety, the home was taken over by Confederate sharpshooters, two of whom were killed in its garret during the battle. The tour provides insight into the lives of Gettysburg's citizens, who endured fighting on their city's busiest streets. ⊠ *309 Baltimore St.,* ☎ *717/ 337–2800.* ☞ *$5.* ☉ *Mon.-Sat. 10–5, Sun. noon–5.*

★ The **Eisenhower National Historic Site** offers a glimpse into the life and times of General and later President Dwight D. Eisenhower. This bucolic farm was his peaceful retreat from 1951 until his death in 1969. Besides the brick-and-stone farmhouse, preserved in 1950s style, there are a number of outbuildings. The farm adjoins the battlefield and is administered by the park service, which has daily ticketed tours only on a first-come, first-served basis from the visitor center. ⊠ *Off Millerstown Rd.,* ☎ *717/334–1124.* ☞ *$5.25; tickets at Gettysburg National Military Park Visitor Center (☞ above).* ☉ *Mar.– Nov., daily 9–4.*

Dining and Lodging

$–$$ ✕ **Blue Parrot Bistro.** This cavernous, bustling bar and restaurant is within walking distance of many hotels and attractions. The Blue Parrot serves up creatively prepared light entrées including salads and portobello and smoked Gouda quesadillas as well as heavier fare such as meat loaf stuffed with andouille sausage. ⊠ *35 Chambersburg St.,* ☎ *717/337–3739. MC, V. Closed Sun., Mon.*

$$–$$$ ✕▦ **Historic Farnsworth House Restaurant & Inn.** The restaurant ($$) ★ at this B&B serves up Civil War–era dishes such as game pie, peanut soup, pumpkin fritters, and spoon bread in an 1810 building that still shows bullet holes from the battle. The tranquil outdoor garden has sculptures and fountains. Each guest room is lushly and individually decorated with such Victoriana as period sewing machines, Victrolas, and antique clothing. The inn also conducts ghost tours of Gettysburg (open to guests and the public for $6) that begin with dramatizations and stories in the basement's ghoulish Mourning Theater. Also on the grounds are an art and book gallery and Civil War memorabilia shop. A full breakfast is included. ⊠ *401 Baltimore St.,* ☎ *717/334–8838. 9 rooms. Restaurant. AE, D, MC, V. BP.*

$$ ✕▦ **Historic Dobbin House Tavern.** This unique old tavern in the Historic District was built in 1776, making it the oldest building in town. Fine Continental cuisine and 18th-century specialties are served in restored rooms with hand-carved woodwork, fireplaces, and antiques. The Alexander Dobbin Restaurant has six rooms in which you can dine by candlelight seated in wing chairs in the parlor or at a table in the

dining room. Lighter fare is served in the Springhouse Tavern. The adjacent Gettystown Inn has rooms with antiques and four-poster beds. Rates include full breakfast and tea and coffee in the parlor of the 1860s home. ⌧ *89 Steinwehr Ave., 17325,* ☎ *717/334–2100. 5 rooms, 1 suite. Restaurant. AE, MC, V. BP.*

$$
★ **Best Western Gettysburg Hotel 1797.** The hotel is a pre–Civil War structure in the heart of the downtown historic district, but the interior was completely rebuilt in 1991. Rooms are furnished in traditional style, and suites have fireplaces and whirlpool baths. Ask about the cannonball from the battle that is still embedded in the brick wall across the street. Coffee and tea are complimentary. ⌧ *1 Lincoln Sq., 17325,* ☎ *717/337–2000,* 𝖥𝖠𝖷 *717/337–2075. 60 rooms, 23 suites. Restaurant, pool. AE, D, DC, MC, V.*

$$ **James Gettys Hotel.** Although it flourished as a hotel in the 1920s, this four-story 1787 building just off the town square was later converted into apartments and a youth hostel. In its newest incarnation, it thrives again as an affordably priced, attractively furnished suite-only hotel. Each suite has a sitting room with a kitchenette including a refrigerator, microwave oven, and small dining table. A Continental breakfast is included and is left in each suite the night before. ⌧ *27 Chambersburg St., 17325,* ☎ *717/337–1334,* 𝖥𝖠𝖷 *717/334–2103. 11 suites. Kitchenettes. AE, D, MC, V. CP.*

$–$$ **Baladerry Inn.** This restored 1812 home on the edge of the battlefield served as a field hospital during the Battle of Gettysburg. The inn, set on extensive landscaped grounds, consists of the main house and a carriage house. The rooms are filled with antiques, and those on the ground floor of the carriage house have their own patios. The full breakfast is complimentary, as are coffee and tea. ⌧ *40 Hospital Rd., 17325,* ☎ *717/337–1342. 8 rooms. Tennis court. AE, D, MC, V. BP.*

$ **Artillery Ridge Campground.** You can pitch a tent or park an RV a mile south of the military park visitor center. There's a pond for fishing. ⌧ *610 Taneytown Rd., 17325,* ☎ *717/334–1288. 45 tent sites, 105 camper or RV sites. Pool, horseback riding, fishing, bicycles. D, MC, V.*

Shopping
Old Gettysburg Village (⌧ 777 Baltimore St., ☎ 717/334–8666), a collection of shops in the center of the tourist district, has an art gallery showing paintings of the battle by Dale Gallon, the town's artist-in-residence.

The Horse Soldier (⌧ 777 Baltimore St., within Old Gettysburg Village shopping center, ☎ 717/334–0347) provides a shopping experience that's more like visiting a museum. Carrying one of the country's largest collections of military antiques—everything from bullets to discharge papers—the shop even offers its customers help in researching their ancestors' war records prior to 1910. The store is closed Wednesday.

LANCASTER COUNTY A TO Z

Arriving and Departing

By Bus
Greyhound Lines (☎ 800/231–2222) has three runs daily between Philadelphia and Lancaster's R&S Bus Terminal (⌧ 22 W. Clay St.). The ride takes about 2½ hours.

By Car
From Philadelphia take the Schuylkill Expressway (I–76) west to the Pennsylvania Turnpike. Lancaster County sights are accessible from Exits 20, 21, and 22. For a slower, more scenic route (at least until it

hits the commercial outskirts of Lancaster), follow U.S. 30 west from Philadelphia. Be prepared for stop and go traffic the first 10 mi or so. It's about 65 mi to the Pennsylvania Dutch Country.

By Train

Amtrak (☎ 215/824–1600 or 800/872–7245) has regular service from Philadelphia's 30th Street Station to the Lancaster Amtrak station (✉ 53 McGovern Ave.). Trips take 80 minutes.

Getting Around

By Car

A car is the easiest way to explore the spread-out sights in the area; it also lets you get off the main roads and into the countryside. Lancaster County's main arteries are U.S. 30 (also known as the Lincoln Highway and Lancaster Pike) and Route 340 (sometimes called the Old Philadelphia Pike). Some pleasant back roads can be found between Routes 23 and 340. Vintage Road is a country road running north over U.S. 30 and then along Route 772 west to Intercourse. You get a look at some of the farms in the area and also see Amish schoolhouses, stores, and the Amish themselves. Remember that you must slow down for horse-drawn buggies when you're driving on country roads.

Contacts and Resources

B&B Reservation Agencies

Lancaster County Bed-and-Breakfast Inns Association (✉ 2835 Willow Street Pike, Willow Street 17548, ☎ 717/464–5588 or 800/848–2994) is a group of 16 B&Bs in the area. For other agencies, *see* B&B Reservation Services *in* Chapter 4.

Emergencies

Ambulance, fire, police (☎ 911).

Guided Tours

Amish Farmlands (✉ Rte. 340 at Plain & Fancy Farm, between Bird-in-Hand and Intercourse, ☎ 717/768–3600 or 800/441–3505) has large bus or minivan tours. Most popular is the two-hour Amish farmlands trip, with stops at an Amish farmhouse, a wine tasting, and shopping for crafts. On Tuesday tours to Hershey are available.

Brunswick Tours (✉ National Wax Museum, U.S. 30E, Lancaster, ☎ 717/397–7541 or 800/979–8687) provides private guides who will tour with you in your car. It also has a self-guided auto audiotape tour with 28 stops that begins at the Pennsylvania Dutch Convention & Visitors Bureau and takes three or four hours.

Glick Aviation (✉ 311 Airport Dr., off Rte. 340, Smoketown, ☎ 717/394–6476), at Smoketown Airport, offers 18-minute flights in a four-seater plane (pilot plus three), with a splendid aerial view of rolling farmlands.

The **Mennonite Information Center** (✉ 2209 Millstream Rd., Lancaster, ☎ 717/299–0954) has local Mennonite guides who will join you in your car. These knowledgeable guides will lead you to country roads, produce stands, and Amish crafts shops and also acquaint you with their religion.

Hospitals

Lancaster has three emergency rooms: **Community Hospital of Lancaster** (✉ 1100 E. Orange St., ☎ 717/239–4000); **Lancaster General Hospital** (✉ 555 N. Duke St., ☎ 717/290–5511); and **St. Joseph's Hospital**

(✉ 250 College Ave., ☎ 717/291–8111). For nonemergency referrals call the **Lancaster City & County Medical Society** (☎ 717/393–9588).

Pharmacies

Strasburg Pharmacy (✉ 326 Hartman Bridge Rd./Rte. 896, 2 mi south of U.S. 30, Strasburg, ☎ 717/687–6058) is open weekdays 9–9, Saturday 9–5. **Weis Pharmacy** (✉ 1603 Lincoln Hwy. E, Lancaster, ☎ 717/394–9826) is open weekdays 9–9, Saturday 9–6.

Visitor Information

The **Pennsylvania Dutch Convention & Visitors Bureau** (✉ 501 Greenfield Rd., Lancaster 17601, ☎ 717/299–8901 or 800/735–2629) has brochures and maps, direct phone connections to local hotels, and the 14-minute multi-image slide presentation ($1 charge) *There Is a Season,* which serves as a good introduction to the area. It's open daily 8:30–5, 8–6 in summer.

The **Mennonite Information Center** (✉ 2209 Millstream Rd., Lancaster 17602-1494, ☎ 717/299–0954 or 800/858–8320) serves mainly to "interpret the faith and practice of the Mennonites and Amish to all who inquire." It has information on local inns and Mennonite guest homes as well as a 20-minute video about the Amish and Mennonite people. On display is a reproduction of the Hebrew Tabernacle ($5 charge). It's open Monday–Saturday 8–5.

The **Susquehanna Heritage Tourist Information Center** (✉ 445 Linden St., Box 510, Columbia 17512, ☎ 717/684–5249) has information about visiting the Susquehanna River town of Columbia.

11 PORTRAITS OF PHILADELPHIA AND THE PENNSYLVANIA DUTCH COUNTRY

Portrait of an Amish Family

What to Read & Watch Before You Go

PORTRAIT OF AN AMISH FAMILY

YOU'LL SPOT JOSEPH Stoltzfus working his fields with a team of horses as you drive the back roads of Lancaster County. You will certainly encounter his somber black buggy on one of the traffic-choked highways. Perhaps you will exchange a few words with his wife, Becky, in her plain dark dress and white cap, if you stop by their farmhouse to buy fresh eggs or to inspect the home-made quilts she has for sale. You might see their younger children playing in the yard of a one-room schoolhouse. And on certain Sundays you may pass the farmhouse where the Stoltzfus family and other Amish people gather to worship.

Stoltzfus is the most common of a dozen Amish family names; Jacob and Becky and their seven children are fictitious but typical of the more than 17,000 Amish (pronounced *Ah*-mish) in this area. Their roots and religious traditions reach back to 16th-century Europe. Every detail of their lives, from their clothing to the way they operate their farms, is an expression of their faith in God and their separateness from "the world"; every detail is dictated by the *Ordnung,* the rules of their church.

Becky Stoltzfus, like Amish women of any age, wears a one-piece dress in a dark color. The sleeves are long and straight, and her full skirt is hemmed modestly halfway between knees and ankles. The high, collarless neck is fastened shut in front with straight pins; buttons and safety pins are forbidden, although the Ordnung of some church districts allows hooks and eyes. She wears black stockings rolled below the knee and black low-heeled oxfords. At home in warm weather Becky and her family go barefoot.

Soon after her daughters were born, Becky made sure they wore the white organdy prayer cap. When Katie turned 12, she changed to a black cap for the Sunday preaching; after she marries she will wear the white cap all the time. Subtle differences in the head covering tell the Amish a great deal about one another. The width of the front part, the length of the ties, the style of the seams, and the way the pleats are ironed

indicate where the woman lives and how conservative or liberal her church district is.

Becky has never cut or curled her hair, nor has she let it hang loose. She pins it in a plain knot at the back of her neck. She parts little Hannah's hair in the middle, plaits it, and fastens the two little braids in the back. When Becky is away from home, she wears a black bonnet with a deep scoop brim over her prayer cap.

The clothes Jacob wears are also carefully dictated by the Ordnung of his church district. For Sunday preaching he wears a *Mutze,* a long black frock coat with split tails and hook-and-eye closings but no collar or lapels. His vest is also fastened with hooks and eyes. Jacob's broadfall or "barn-door" trousers have no zipper, just a wide front flap that buttons along the sides; they have no creases and no belt—homemade suspenders hold them up. There are buttons on his shirt, the number specified by the Ordnung. Colored shirts are permitted, but stripes and prints are out. Neckties are forbidden.

When he's not dressed up, Jacob hangs up his Mutze and puts on a *Wamus,* a black sack coat with either a high, round neck or V-neck but neither lapels nor outside pockets. Sometimes the Wamus has hooks and eyes, but more liberal church districts allow buttons.

In winter Jacob and his sons wear broad-brim black felt hats; in summer they switch to straw. Ben and Ezra, Jacob's younger boys, have been wearing hats with 3-inch brims since they were little. Sam, the oldest son, wears a hat with a crease around the top of the crown, a sign (along with his sprouting beard) that he is newly married. The hat is a status symbol among the Amish. The grandfather's hat is higher in the crown than the father's, and its brim is 4 inches wide. The width of an Amish man's hat brim also signifies his degree of conservatism: the broader the brim, the more conservative the wearer.

Jacob's long beard is as much the mark of an Amish man as a broad-brim hat. He shaves only his upper lip, since mustaches are against the rules. He cuts his hair straight around, well below the ears. Ben and Ezra have theirs parted in the middle, with bangs across the forehead. Cutting it short—up to the earlobe—is a form of rebellion.

THE STYLE OF THE AMISH BUGGY is as carefully prescribed as the style of the hat. The Stoltzfus family owns a black carriage with a gray top and big wooden wheels. The battery-powered side lamps, reflectors, and bright orange triangles have been added as required by Pennsylvania state law. The iron-tire wheels are precisely set, toed in slightly, farther apart at the top than at the bottom. A gear assembly at the pivot of the front axle adds stability. The brakes are operated by hand, an iron block pressed hard against the rear tire. This kind of brake is prescribed by the Ordnung; different groups permit different kinds of brakes. The Ordnung tells the buggy owner whether or not he may have roll-up side curtains or sliding glass doors, and if he is allowed a dashboard, a whipsocket, and other variations. Incidentally, the Amish can—and do—ride in cars owned by non-Amish people and travel on trains, buses, and even airplanes and taxis. But they are not allowed to *own* a car.

No electric wires lead from the power lines along the road into the neat, well-kept buildings of the Stoltzfus farm, a difference that distinguishes Amish farms from those of their non-Amish neighbors. The farms are small, no more than 50 or 60 acres, which is all that can be handled by a farmer limited to horse power.

The Stoltzfus house is spacious and uncluttered. There is no wall-to-wall carpeting to vacuum; instead, plain and unpatterned linoleum covers the floor. There are no curtains to wash or draperies to clean; although some church districts allow plain curtains on the lower half of the windows, this district permits only dark-green roller shades. There are no slipcovers or upholstery because upholstered furniture is not allowed.

Becky has a large kitchen where the family eats around a big wooden table. Afterward Becky and Katie and Hannah clean up the kitchen, wash the dishes, and put away leftover food in the gasoline-operated refrigerator. A one-cylinder engine in the cellar chugs noisily, powering the water pump, but many Amish families still rely on windmills or water power. A creek that runs through a farm also supplies water. Although labor-saving devices are generally forbidden, Becky does have a washing machine that runs by gasoline. Her stove burns kerosene; she would prefer bottled gas, but that is forbidden by the Ordnung of her district. She uses a treadle sewing machine and sews by the bright and steady light of a gasoline lamp.

About once a year it is the Stoltzfuses' turn to host the every-other-Sunday preaching service. As many as 175 people may attend: There are 90 members in the district, and double that number when unbaptized children are counted. The removable partitions built into the downstairs walls are folded back and furniture moved aside. The district's backless oak benches are brought in and set up in rows.

Jacob and Becky Stoltzfus are fluent in English, but the language they speak among themselves is Pennsylvania Dutch, a German dialect related to the dialects spoken in the part of Germany from which their Amish ancestors came. It is primarily a spoken language and spelling varies with the writer. "Dutch" actually means *Deutsch*, or German, and some scholars call the dialect Pennsylvania German. Many Pennsylvanians of German descent speak the dialect, but among the Amish it is the mother tongue, the first language an Amish child learns to speak and another mark of separation from the world.

When Hannah, Becky's youngest child, starts school, she will learn to speak and read and write in the language of "the world." Jacob and Becky want their children to know English because their survival depends on good business relationships with English-speaking people.

About the same time Hannah Stoltzfus starts to learn English, she will also be taught High German, the language of religion. The family Bible is written in High German, and she and her brothers and sisters must learn to read it. By the time they are baptized, in their late teens, they will be able to understand most of the Sunday sermon and to join in the prayers and hymns. Most Amish can't carry on a conversation in High German and have no need to do so unless they are ordained church officials who must preach sermons and pray. But everyone needs to be able to read and to listen.

THE OUTSIDER MAY NOT NOTICE the inconspicuous building on a back road where Ben and Ezra and Annie Stoltzfus attend school, along with eight grades of children in one room. They are taught by a young Amish woman with only an eighth-grade education. Amish children are not sent to public school, and Amish schools continue only as far as the eighth grade. That's time enough to learn the basics of reading, writing, and arithmetic.

Schools are built to serve children within a 2-mi radius so that no one has far to walk. Some children go to old one-room schoolhouses once owned by the public school district. When districts consolidated, the Amish bought the obsolete schools and remodeled them—not modernizing them but ripping out the electric wiring. Since none was available near the Stoltzfus farm, the Amish fathers in that area built a plain cinder-block structure with big windows to take advantage of natural light.

Stepping into an Amish schoolhouse is like entering a time machine and emerging 80 or more years in the past. At 8:30 the teacher pulls the rope to ring the old-fashioned bell on the roof. Then the children line up and file through the big front door into the cloakroom. They hang their hats and jackets on pegs, line up their lunch boxes, and go quietly to their carefully refinished old-fashioned desks.

The school day begins with the roll call. During peak periods of farm work, the Amish close down the schools for a few days; they stop earlier in the spring than the public schools. They make up for the time by taking only a short Christmas break and celebrating none of the national holidays.

Next, the teacher reads to the pupils from the German Bible, then everyone recites the Lord's Prayer in German. Except for the lessons in reading German Scriptures and prayers, the teacher speaks exclusively English in the classroom.

Beside the teacher's desk is a "recitation bench." There are more than 30 students in the eight grades, and each class of three or four or five comes forward by turns to recite its lessons. There is no competition to come up with the answer first, and they all respond in a singsong chorus.

Because it is essential to the work of a farmer, arithmetic is considered very important. Picking readers (books) for the pupils was not easy. The parents want the subject matter to be farm children, not city life; they want the stories to teach a moral lesson; fairy tales, myths, and fantasies are taboo.

During the 15-minute morning recess, Ezra and Ben and the other boys play baseball. One of the rules of the Amish schoolyard is that children are never allowed to stand around by themselves; everyone must be included in the group. Annie and the older girls play blindman's bluff; the younger ones, joined by their teacher, race around in a game of tag.

The Amish want their children to learn to work together as a group, not to compete as individuals. Preserving tradition is a goal; reasoning abstractly is not. Asking too many questions is not acceptable. Discipline is strict; the only voices heard in the schoolroom are those of the teacher and the pupils who are reciting. The Amish expect pupils to master the material unquestioningly: Memorization replaces reasoning in a culture dominated by oral tradition. Thoroughness is valued more than rapid learning. Teachers believe that intellectual talents are a gift from God and that children should be encouraged to use the gift by helping others in the school.

BEFORE THE DAY IS OVER, there is time for singing. Singing is a vital part of the Amish tradition, important in their religious life and in their social life as well. There are no songs with harmonization for the Amish; unaccompanied unison singing is the universal rule. The Amish have their own style of singing, in which the leader (*Vorsanger*) sings the first word and everybody else joins in for the rest of the line.

For years public school authorities were in conflict with the Amish. Truancy laws were enforced, and Amish fathers were often arrested and jailed for refusing to send older children to school. But in 1972 the United States Supreme Court ruled that the Amish are exempt from state compulsory education laws that require a child to attend beyond the eighth grade; they found that such laws violate Constitutional rights to freedom of religion.

Today the Amish accept the idea of sending their children to school for eight years to learn what they need to survive in the 20th-century rural economy. But what Amish children really need to know in order to survive in the Amish culture they learn from their parents and from other adults in the community. Most of the practical knowledge of farmers and housewives is acquired not in books but in a family apprenticeship.

The marriage of Jacob and Becky Stoltzfus is a very practical affair. The Amish are quite realistic about their expectations. They do not marry for love or romance but out of mutual respect and the need for a partner in the kind of life they expect to live. The farmer needs a wife, and they both need children. Marriage is essential to the Amish community; divorce is unknown; separation is rare. Marriage is the climax of the rite of passage that begins with baptism, the signal of the arrival of adulthood and sober responsibility.

From the time they reach the age of *Rum Schpringe* (running around—about 16 for boys, a bit younger for girls) and for the next half-dozen years until each marries, Joe Stoltzfus and his sister Katie do much of their socializing at Sunday-night singings, usually held at the farm where the preaching service took place in the morning. Singings are functions of the church district, which helps keep dating and eventually marriage within the group.

Although outsiders believe that the social life of an Amish teenager begins with a singing and ends with a buggy ride home at a respectably early hour, Amish dating is actually much livelier. Among the more liberal groups, the old-fashioned singings can turn quickly into rowdy, foot-stomping hoedowns. A few bring out harmonicas, guitars, and other forbidden instruments; older boys haul in cases of beer. Few outsiders attend these events.

On the "off Sunday," when there is no preaching service, young unmarried people go courting—but always in secret. Before they marry, they are never seen together in public as a couple except as they leave a singing or a barn dance.

Bundling, the practice of courting in bed fully clothed, is usually attributed to the Amish. No one is quite sure whether the Amish do or don't, but the consensus is that the girl's parents, rather than the Ordnung, have the final say.

THERE IS A SAYING that if a boy can persuade his girl to take off her prayer cap, she'll have sex with him. Evidently that doesn't happen often because the rate of premarital pregnancies among the Amish is quite low. Premarital sex is forbidden, birth control is taboo, and sex education is nonexistent.

When Jacob's son Sam married Sarah Beiler, their wedding was held after the harvest in November. December is the second most popular month for weddings, and there are traditionally only two possible days in the week for the ceremony: Tuesday and Thursday. Sarah chose Thursday. Now they're living on the Stoltzfus farm.

The average age at marriage of Amish couples has been rising because of the problems of accumulating enough money to establish a household and to acquire land. Many Amish parents retire while they are still relatively young, especially if they have a son who needs a farm. Sam and Sarah have moved into the "grandfather's house," a section of Jacob's farmhouse built to accommodate a second generation. In a few years, when Sam assumes full responsibility for the farm and has children, he and Sarah will move into the larger part of the house, and Jacob and Becky will move into the grandfather's house.

TO UNDERSTAND THE AMISH as something more than a quaint anachronism, turn back the calendar to 16th-century Europe. The Roman Catholic Church wielded tremendous influence, and many blamed the church for society's ills. When Martin Luther launched the Protestant Reformation in 1517, he had many opponents in addition to the Roman Catholic Church. One was Ulrich Zwingli, a radical Swiss Protestant, who also opposed Conrad Grebel. Grebel's followers wanted to establish free congregations of believers baptized as adults who made a confession of faith and committed themselves freely to a Christian life. Backing Zwingli, the Great Council of Zurich announced that babies must be baptized within eight days after their birth, or the parents would be exiled.

This marked the beginning of Anabaptism, which means "rebaptized." Regarded as radically left wing, the Anabaptist movement posed a threat to the Roman Catholic and Protestant establishments. Anabaptist leaders were imprisoned, beaten, and killed; by the end of the 16th century nearly all the Anabaptists of Switzerland and Germany had been put to death.

But the movement spread through Central and Western Europe. Menno Simons, a former Roman Catholic priest, became one of those persecuted for Anabaptist preaching. His followers were called Mennonites. And although they were hounded by Catholics and other Protestants, dissension began to grow among the Mennonites themselves. A principal source of disagreement was the interpretation of the *Meidung,* the practice of shunning church members who had broken a rule. Shunning was based on St. Paul's advice to the Corinthians to avoid keeping company and eating with sinners. The Mennonites interpreted this to mean the member was to be subjected to Meidung only at communion. But Jacob Amman, a young Mennonite bishop, insisted that the Meidung meant that the rule-breaker must be shunned totally, even by his family.

The controversy grew, and in 1697 the stubborn and fiery Jacob Amman broke from the Mennonites. His followers, known as the Amish, became known for their unwillingness to change. Although the difference in clothing detail was not a primary issue, it did become symbolic of the split. The Amish became known as the *Haftlers* (Hook-and-eyers), while the more worldly Mennonites were called the *Knopflers* (Buttoners).

Meanwhile, King Charles II of England granted a large province in the American colonies to William Penn. A devout Quaker, Penn believed he could offer refuge, freedom, and equality to the persecuted. Penn arrived in 1682, and the following year Francis Daniel Pastorius of the Frankfort Land Company brought the first group of Mennonites to Pennsylvania. The first Amish immigrants left Switzerland and the Palatinate of Germany in 1727, settling near Hamburg north of Reading.

By the start of the Revolutionary War, about half of the 225,000 Pennsylvania colonists were German, but only a small minority were Amish and Mennonite. The English scorned the Germans and tried to anglicize them. But the Amish and Mennonites were determined to hold on to their religion.

The Amish of Pennsylvania were all of one conservative mind until 1850, when a schism divided the Amish into two main factions. The more progressive group built meeting houses, which earned them the label "Church Amish," to distinguish them from the stricter "House Amish," who continued to worship in their homes. Since then innumerable splits have been caused by various interpretations of the Meidung or by different details of the Ordnung.

Every society changes to some extent, and in every society there are a few people who cannot adjust. The Amish are no exception. Many leave; there is generally a shortage of young men in the Amish community because most of the dissidents who leave are male. But some exert pressure for changes in the Ordnung that result in splits. Today there are 8 Amish, 24 Mennonite, and 9 Brethren groups in the Lancaster area.

The ultimate control exerted by the Amish to keep the members in strict adherence to the Ordnung is the Meidung. No one will speak to the person, eat with him, conduct business with him, or have anything to do with him while he is under the ban. It can last for a lifetime, unless the sinner mends his ways, begs for forgiveness, and is readmitted to fellowship by a unanimous vote of the congregation.

Visitors are sometimes surprised to learn that "Pennsylvania Dutch" and "Amish" are not synonymous. Many of the early settlers of Pennsylvania came from Germany at Penn's invitation; many were farmers, most were Protestant, and they spoke the same dialect. Despite these similarities, the Amish refer to all non-Amish as "English." These English include the Pennsylvania Dutch who permit hex signs on their farms (the Amish do not) and whose ancestors decorated useful items such as furniture with colorful designs. The work of Amish craftsmen is competent but plain.

The Amish are generally friendly and hospitable people. Tape recorders and cameras are not welcome, but a visitor who is sincerely interested in the Amish people and does not act like an interrogator can quietly learn something about their unique way of life.

—Carolyn Meyer

WHAT TO READ & WATCH BEFORE YOU GO

Fiction

"Writing fiction set in Philadelphia is tough," says novelist Steve Lopez. "There is nothing you can make up that is any more unbelievable than what actually happens here." Nonetheless, Lopez succeeded with *Third and Indiana*, a hard-edged story set in Philadelphia's "badlands;" *The Sunday Macaroni Club*; and *Land of Giants*. *God's Pocket*, by Pete Dexter; *South Street*, by David Bradley; and *Payback*, by Philip Harper, also capture the grittier side of the City of Brotherly Love.

Michael Shaara's Pulitzer Prize–winning *The Killer Angels* is a gripping account of the battle at Gettysburg.

History and Background

Philadelphia: A 300-Year History, with essays edited by Russell F. Weigley, is the best overall text. Catherine Drinker Bowen's *Miracle at Philadelphia* tells the story of the Constitution.

For biographies of seven Philadelphians, read *Philadelphia: Patricians and Philistines, 1900 to 1950*, by John Lukacs. *Puritan Boston and Quaker Philadelphia* by the late E. Digby Baltzell, is a scholarly work that compares the two cities. *Christopher Morley's Philadelphia* is edited by Ken Kalfus. Robert Lawson's *Ben and Me*, a classic children's story, gives a mouse's view of Ben Franklin's life.

Buzz Bissinger's *A Prayer for the City* assesses the struggles and achievements of Mayor Ed Rendell during the 1990s. *South Philadelphia*, by Philadelphia *Inquirer* reporter Murray Dubin, is both a memoir and an oral history that describes a well-known neighborhood. Harry D. Boonin's illustrated *The Jewish Quarter of Philadelphia: A History and Guide 1881–1930* traces the story of the area around South Street. Philip Stevick's *Imagining Philadelphia* looks at how visitors to Philadelphia since 1800 have perceived the city.

Sightseeing and Touring

The Foundation for Architecture's *Philadelphia Architecture: A Guide to the City* contains maps, photos, biographies of noted Philadelphia architects, and descriptions of almost 400 sites. *Historic Houses of Philadelphia*, by Roger W. Moss, includes stunning color photos and historical notes about 50 of the area's museum homes. Francis Morrone's 1999 *Architectural Guidebook to Philadelphia* is illustrated with photographs. *Cultural Connections, Museums and Libraries of Philadelphia and the Delaware Valley*, by Morris J. Vogel, has photos and text on sites throughout the region. *Frank Furness: The Complete Works*, by George E. Thomas, Jeffrey A. Cohen, and Michael J. Lewis, assesses one of Philadelphia's most original architects. *Eastern State Penitentiary: Crucible of Good Intentions*, by Norman Johnston, discusses the influence of the city's massive prison.

Guides to Philadelphia's spectacular collection of outdoor art include: *Sculpture of a City*, by the Fairmount Park Art Association, with text and photos; *Philadelphia's Outdoor Art: A Walking Tour*, by Roslyn F. Brenner, describing more than 50 works of art along Benjamin Franklin Parkway; and the comprehensive *Public Art in Philadelphia*, by Penny Balkin Bach. Garden lovers will want to study *Gardens of Philadelphia and the Delaware Valley*, by William M. Klein Jr., which has photographs. *Rediscovering the Wissahickon*, by Sarah West, gives mapped geology and history walks for this lovely area of Fairmount Park.

Other selections are *Country Walks and Bikeways in the Philadelphia Region*, by Alan Fisher; *Philadelphia and Its Countryside*, by Ruth Hoover Seitz, which has photographs; and *The Mid-Atlantic's Best Bed & Breakfasts*, by Fodor's Travel Publications. *Pennsylvania*, a Compass America Guide by Douglas Root, has color photographs and historical and cultural information.

Videos

Rocky, with Sylvester Stallone (1976), and its four sequels describe the adventures of an underdog Philadelphia boxer. *Philadelphia* (1993) stars Tom Hanks as a lawyer who is dismissed from his job because he is battling AIDS. In *Witness* (1985) Philadelphia police detective Harrison Ford has to live undercover with the Amish. The four-hour movie *Gettysburg*, based on Michael Shaara's novel *The Killer Angels*, captures the intensity of the Civil War battle.

INDEX

NOTES

NOTES

NOTES

NOTES

Fodor's

Looking for a different kind of vacation?

Fodor's makes it easy with a full line of specialty guidebooks to suit a variety of interests—from adventure to romance to language help.

Fodor's. For the world of ways you travel.